WOODWORKING PROJECTS
FOR YOUR SHOP

POPULAR WOODWORKING BOOKS
CINCINNATI, OHIO
www.popularwoodworking.com

Table of Contents

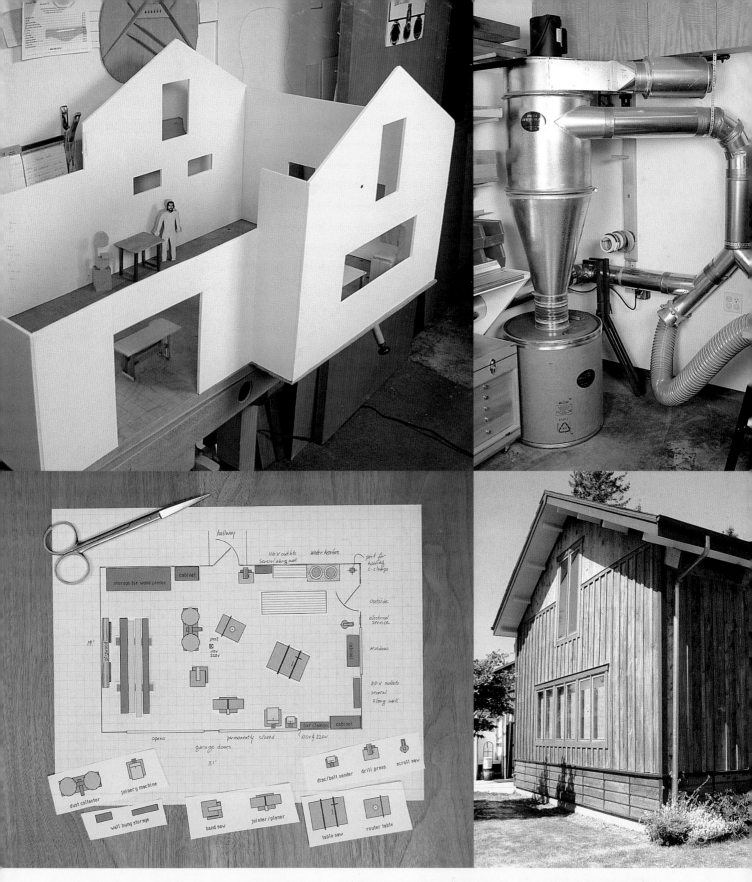

How to Design and Build Your Ideal Woodshop, revised edition

page 255

Introduction

Whether you want more workspace or just a more efficient setup, you'll find everything you need for the perfect woodshop in this book. Danny Proulx gives you 12 problem-solving projects that are guaranteed to give your woodshop new life by maximizing space and increasing shop efficiency. Each design ensures that the blades, jigs and attachments for all of your tools are within arm's reach.

From master cabinet-maker Jim Stack you get 15 stylish, yet practical designs for tool boxes and chests. Perfect for hand tools and power tools alike, these projects range from elegant rolling cabinets to utilitarian tote boxes. There's something for everyone here, no matter what your skill level.

And from Bill Stankus, you'll learn how to make the most of the space you have. Whether your woodshop is in a garage, basement, outbuilding or even a closet, he'll show you how to bring your ideal woodshop to life.

All the guidance you need to turn your current shop into the woodshop of your dreams is in this book. Get started now!

DANNY PROULX

BUILDING WOODSHOP WORKSTATIONS

POPULAR WOODWORKING BOOKS

CINCINNATI, OHIO
www.popularwoodworking.com

table of contents

ROUTER TABLE CABINET

SHOP-MADE 12" DISC SANDER

MOBILE TABLE SAW CENTER

MULTIFUNCTION POWER TOOL CABINET

PROJECTS

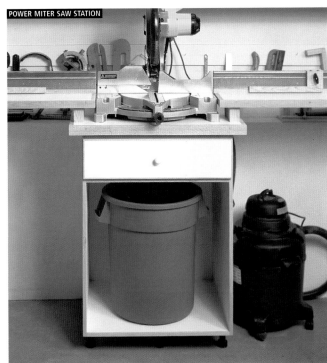

POWER MITER SAW STATION

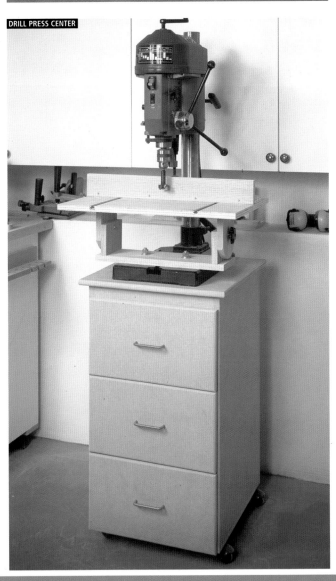

DRILL PRESS CENTER

introduction

Maximizing space, creating multifunctional tool stations and increasing shop efficiency are the goals of this book. These three criteria will impact the design of each project.

Woodworkers are bombarded with ads from tool manufacturers. Each year we see dozens of new power tools, many of which are benchtop units. Oscillating sanders, planers, joiners, scroll saws, power miter saws and so on, are must-haves for a woodworker's shop. However, most home workshops suffer from one common problem — a lack of space. You'll often find the garage or basement filled with tools, leaving very little free space to work.

Power tool stations can be multifunctional because you don't need a great number of tools for most projects. Building multiuse tool stations has become popular because they serve a number of operations in the woodshop. This book will show different tool stations that can serve a number of power tools.

The other serious issue confronting the home woodworker is the requirement to share space. A woodworking shop in a garage is typical of that situation. A number of tools, like the router table, for example, can be static stations because they can be used against a wall. Tools that must be used with clearance on all sides, however, such as a table saw, have to be movable. To meet the needs of a shared space, a number of these projects will be movable.

The power miter saw station is a major player in the space efficiency design issue throughout this book. It is a center tower with "wings" to support long boards at the saw station. The wings are constructed at a height that will allow the multifunction power tool cabinets to be rolled underneath for storage. A number of the other portable tool stations will be designed to fit under the miter saw station.

The first chapter deals with base and wall cabinets, because storage is a key element when creating an efficient shop. The next chapter details a workbench that not only is functional, but also recovers valuable floor space under the bench. Space recovery and maximizing every square inch of a workshop is the goal, and projects like the Power Tool Storage Station and the Saw Outfeed Table and Storage Cabinet meet that objective. The Mobile Table Saw Center and the Router Table Cabinet address the work efficiency needs of two important shop power tools.

I hope you build a number of these projects and they help increase the joy you get by working in your woodshop. As someone often repeated to me when I was young, "The trick is to work smarter, not harder."

Base- and Wall-Mounted Workshop Cabinets

Good-quality storage cabinets with doors are just as important as any power tool workstation in your shop. They store all types of tools and hardware, organize your materials and prolong the life of your tools. The base cabinets also serve as a support medium for countertops. That's a pretty good deal for a few dollars' worth of sheet material and a handful of screws.

The cabinets detailed in this chapter are frameless-style cabinetry. Unlike the traditional-styled cabinet, they don't have a wooden face frame installed.

The base cabinets are different from wall cabinets because they don't have a top board, but they do require a top rail to provide countertop overhang clearance. Both are built following the same simple principles.

The selection of sheet materials used to build your shop cabinets is a personal choice. Almost any material can be used as long as it's ⁵⁄₈" or thicker, and of reasonable quality. I've chosen

white melamine-coated particleboard (PB) for a number of reasons.

First, the PB is coated, making it easy to clean. Secondly, the doors can be made from the same material without the need to apply a finish and the edges can be finished with iron-on tape. Finally, the white cabinets reflect almost all the light that strikes them, helping to illuminate the shop.

The cabinets will be sturdy and long-lasting if you properly join the particleboard with the correct fasteners, and the edges will be chip free if you use the correct saw blade.

These cabinets can be fitted with drawers, pullouts in the base units and adjustable shelves. They are constructed using bottom-mounted drawer glides, adjustable legs and hidden hinges. The end result will be a high-quality cabinet at a reasonable cost.

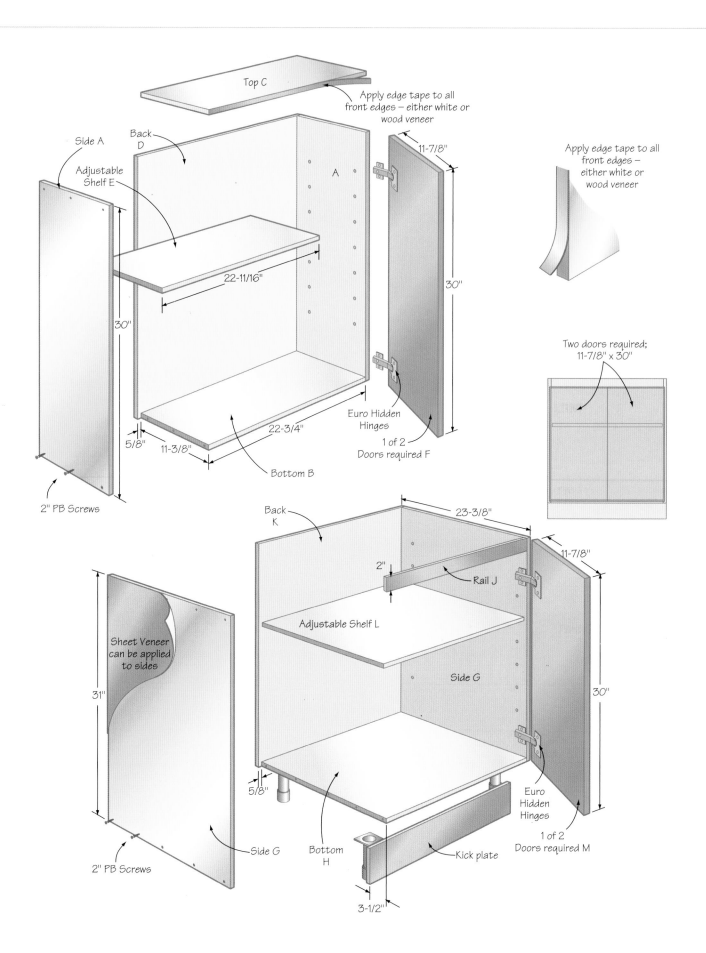

Top C

Apply edge tape to all
front edges – either white or
wood veneer

Side A

Back
D

Adjustable
Shelf E

A

11-7/8"

Apply edge tape to all
front edges –
either white or
wood veneer

22-11/16"

30"

30"

30"

Two doors required;
11-7/8" x 30"

5/8"

11-3/8"

22-3/4"

Bottom B

Euro Hidden
Hinges

1 of 2
Doors required F

2" PB Screws

Back
K

23-3/8"

11-7/8"

2"

Rail J

Sheet Veneer
can be applied
to sides

Adjustable Shelf L

31"

Side G

30"

5/8"

Side G

Bottom
H

Euro
Hidden
Hinges

1 of 2
Doors required M

2" PB Screws

Kick plate

3-1/2"

materials list ▪ INCHES

REFERENCE	QUANTITY	PART	STOCK	THICKNESS	WIDTH	LENGTH	COMMENTS
24"-WIDE WALL CABINET							
A	2	sides	melamine PB	5/8	11 3/8	30	
B	1	bottom	melamine PB	5/8	11 3/8	22 3/4	
C	1	top	melamine PB	5/8	11 3/8	22 3/4	
D	1	back	melamine PB	5/8	24	30	
E	2	shelves	melamine PB	5/8	11 3/8	22 11/16	
F	2	doors	melamine PB	5/8	11 7/8	30	
24"-WIDE BASE CABINET							
G	2	sides	melamine PB	5/8	23 3/8	31	
H	1	bottom	melamine PB	5/8	23 3/8	22 3/4	
J	1	top rail	melamine PB	5/8	2	22 3/4	
K	1	back	melamine PB	5/8	24	31	
L	1	shelf	melamine PB	5/8	23 3/8	22 11/16	
M	2	doors	melamine PB	5/8	11 7/8	30	

HARDWARE

Edge tape
Shelf pins
2" PB screws
Hidden hinges
5/8" PB screws
3" Screws
1" Screws
Right-angle brackets
Adjustable cabinet legs
Plinth clip
Drawer glides
Drawer handles
Door handles

materials list ▪ MILLIMETERS

REFERENCE	QUANTITY	PART	STOCK	THICKNESS	WIDTH	LENGTH	COMMENTS
610MM-WIDE WALL CABINET							
A	2	sides	melamine PB	16	289	762	
B	1	bottom	melamine PB	16	289	578	
C	1	top	melamine PB	16	289	578	
D	1	back	melamine PB	16	610	762	
E	2	shelves	melamine PB	16	289	577	
F	2	doors	melamine PB	16	301	762	
610MM-WIDE BASE CABINET							
G	2	sides	melamine PB	16	594	787	
H	1	bottom	melamine PB	16	594	578	
J	1	top rail	melamine PB	16	51	578	
K	1	back	melamine PB	16	610	787	
L	1	shelf	melamine PB	16	594	577	
M	2	doors	melamine PB	16	301	762	

HARDWARE

Edge tape
Shelf pins
51mm PB screws
Hidden hinges
16mm PB screws
76mm Screws
25mm Screws
Right-angle brackets
Adjustable cabinet legs
Plinth clip
Drawer glides
Drawer handles
Door handles

Shop Tip

Both wall and base cabinet materials lists are based on using 5/8"-thick melamine particleboard.

Wall cabinets are usually 12"-deep by 30"-high. Base cabinets are 24"-deep by 35 1/4"-high. Adding a 3/4"-thick top to the base cabinet means the top surface will be 36" from the floor. If you want a different height, alter the height of the back and side boards.

BUILDING A 24" WALL CABINET

Calculating Cabinet Door Sizes

The size of cabinet doors that will be mounted on hidden hinges (100°-opening, full-overlay hinges) can be easily calculated. First, measure the inside dimension of the cabinet to be fitted with doors.

A 24"-wide cabinet, built using the materials list shown for this project, has an inside dimension of $22\frac{3}{4}$" (24"-wide cabinet minus two $\frac{5}{8}$" side thicknesses). Add 1" to this measurement and that's the required door width. In this example, the door width would be $23\frac{3}{4}$", which is a little too wide. Door widths should be less than 18" wide if possible.

I can install two doors that are $11\frac{7}{8}$" wide in place of the $23\frac{3}{4}$" door. The width for each of the two doors is found by adding 1" to the inside cabinet dimension, then dividing by 2.

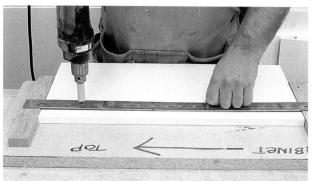

STEP 1 ■ The exposed edges of all cabinet parts must be covered. I use a heat-activated edge tape and apply it with an old household iron. Run a small roller along the tape surface before the glue cools and dries to properly seat the tape. Excess edge tape can be trimmed with a sharp chisel or double-edged trimmer that is available at woodworking stores.

STEP 2 ■ Holes for the adjustable shelves are drilled in the cabinet sides before assembly. I use a simple jig made with a flat steel bar and wooden blocks mounted to a small sheet of plywood. The drill bit's travel is limited by a piece of dowel on the drill bit. My shelf pins are 5mm ($\frac{3}{16}$") in diameter. Holes in the steel bar on my jig are 5mm in diameter and spaced $1\frac{1}{4}$" apart. Drill as many holes as you require. The spacing isn't critical but be sure you know the diameter of your shelf-pin holes before drilling.

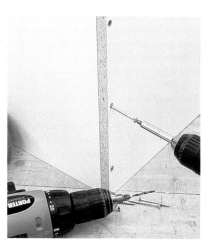

STEP 3 ■ Attach the two side boards A to the bottom B and top C using 2" PB screws. Drill a pilot hole for each screw and align the bottom and top boards with the top and bottom edges of the sides.

STEP 4 ■ The full-thickness back D should be as wide and as high as the cabinet. It is attached using 2" PB screws in drilled holes spaced about 6" apart.

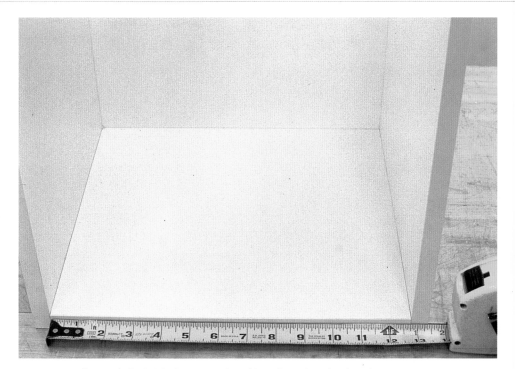

Cabinet Sizes

The dimensions for a cabinet of any width from 10" to 36" can easily be calculated. Begin your calculations by deciding the final cabinet width. If a 33"-wide wall cabinet is needed, I subtract the two ⅝" side thicknesses from the total width needed to find my bottom and top board dimensions. Thus, they would have to be 31¾" wide by the standard 11⅜" deep. The backboard size equals the total width and height of the cabinet, or 33" wide by 30" high.

Determine the door sizes as previously detailed, install hinges and the cabinet is complete. Follow the construction steps for all cabinets, no matter how wide.

STEP 5 ■ As discussed, the inside dimension of a cabinet determines the door size when using full-overlay hidden hinges. Adding 1" to the interior width and dividing by 2 means I will need two 11⅞"-wide doors F. Upper frameless cabinet doors normally cover the edges of the top and bottom board, and are the same height as the cabinet.

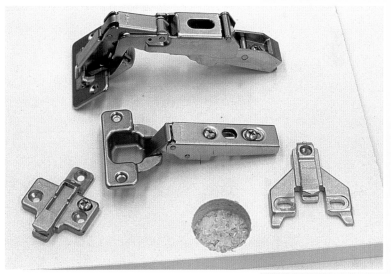

STEP 6 ■ Apply heat-activated edge tape to all four edges of each door. Using a flat-bottomed hinge-boring bit in a drill press, drill two 35mm-diameter holes into each door to accept the hidden-hinge assemblies. The holes are normally located 4" from each end and ⅛" from the door's edge.

STEP 7 ■ The standard hidden hinge is a full-overlay 100°–120°-opening hinge. The term full-overlay refers to the door position when attached with this hinge. It will overlay or cover the side end edge by almost ⅝". The mounting plate attaches to the cabinet side. The standard hinge is shown in the middle, and the mounting plate that is commonly used is shown on the left.

The top hinge is a 170°-opening model, and the mounting plate on the right is used to attach the hinge to a face frame.

Basic Construction Principles of Frameless Cabinetry

Frameless cabinetry is strong and sturdy when properly constructed, however, you should use quality materials such as cabinet-grade melamine particleboard. To be designated cabinet-grade, the board must have a high-quality core material and a melamine layer. Inexpensive board isn't a low-pressure laminate type and often has a melamine layer that's painted or glued.

The cabinet parts are joined with special fasteners, like the ones used in this project, such as the particleboard screw. Drill pilot holes for all screws to achieve the maximum hold.

Melamine particleboard is available in different thicknesses. The $^5/_8$" and $^3/_4$" sizes are the most common, so use whichever size is readily available in your area. I will be using $^5/_8$"-thick material, but if you decide to use $^3/_4$", or that's all there is available in your area, follow the same process as previously described to determine cut sizes. The steps are the same no matter which thickness is used. The cabinet width, minus the side thicknesses in total, equals the bottom and top board width, and so on.

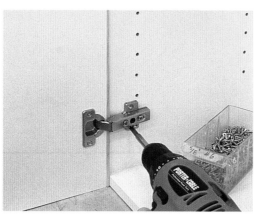

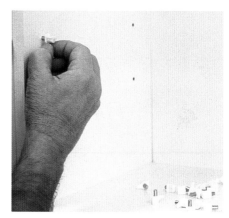

STEP 8 ▪ Use $^5/_8$" particleboard screws to secure both hinges to the door. Align the hinge body with a square to ensure it's parallel to the door edge.

STEP 9 ▪ Attach the hinge plate on the hinge body and align the door (in its normally open position) against the cabinet. Place a $^1/_8$"-thick spacer between the door edge and the cabinet edge. Next, drive $^5/_8$" PB screws through the holes in the hinge plate to secure the door.

This is a simple and accurate alignment procedure for mounting doors with hidden hinges without measuring or using jigs. The procedure will work only with 100° to 120° full-overlay hidden hinges. If you want to install the wider 170°-opening hinges, follow the procedures for using a 100° to 120° hinge. Once the hinge plate is secured, remove the standard hinge and install the wide-opening model on the door. The mounting plate is correctly located for all hinges but must be installed using the standard-opening model.

STEP 10 ▪ Mount the cabinets to the wall using 3"-long screws driven into wall studs. If you have a series of cabinets, secure the front edges to each other with 1" screws. Complete the installation by installing the shelves E on shelf pins in the drilled holes.

BUILDING A 24" BASE CABINET

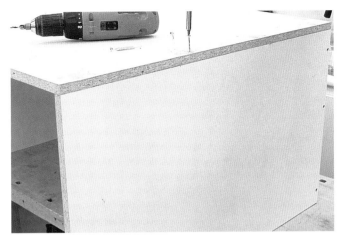

STEP 11 ■ Apply tape to all exposed panel edges as detailed in previous steps. If you plan on having adjustable shelves in your base cabinet, drill the holes at this point. Attach the cabinet sides G to the bottom board H using 2" PB screws.

STEP 12 ■ A base cabinet does not require a top board because the cabinet will be covered with a counter or other work surface. Attach the backboard K making sure the bottom and sides are aligned flush to the outside edges. Drill pilot holes and attach the backboard with 2" PB screws 6" to 8" apart.

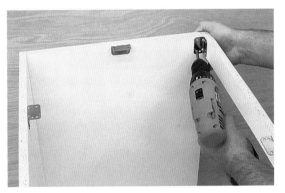

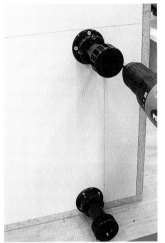

STEP 13 ■ A 2"-high upper rail J must be installed on a frameless base cabinet. This will provide overhang clearance for the countertop and doors. The 30"-high doors are 1" below the top edge of this rail. Use one 2" PB screw per end. Drive the screw into a pilot hole that's located as close to the center of the rail as possible.

STEP 14 ■ Install right-angle brackets to strengthen the upper rail. One bracket per end using ⅝" screws will support the rail. The other brackets installed on the base will be used to secure the countertop. The number of brackets required will vary with cabinet size; however, one every 12" apart will be adequate to secure the counter.

STEP 15 ■ I use adjustable cabinet legs on most of my base cabinets. I don't have to build a base frame, and the legs are adjustable for easier cabinet installation. The legs are plastic, so water and other liquids that sometimes spill in the shop do not affect them. Cabinet legs are secured with ⅝" screws and are set 3" back from the front edge of the cabinet.

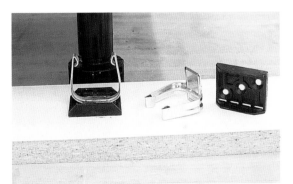

STEP 16 ■ Kick plates aren't necessary with shop cabinets, but if you want to use them, they can be attached with a plinth clip. This piece of hardware is designed to secure kick plates to cabinet legs with spring clips.

Finally, complete the base by installing cabinet doors M. They are 30" high and are located 1" below the top edge of the cabinet rail. The space above both doors is used to provide clearance for a countertop. Follow the same procedures as detailed for building the wall cabinet.

BUILDING DRAWERS

STEP 17 ▪ Tip an upper cabinet on its back and you have a drawer box. The same construction procedures are used for both units. Drawer boxes don't need adjustable shelf holes or doors, but they are identical to upper cabinets in every other way.

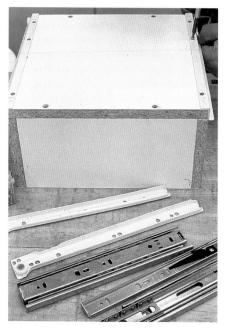

STEP 18 ▪ Drawer boxes can be mounted with many glide systems. I use ³⁄₄-extension glides (a 22" drawer box pulls out about 15") and full-extension glides (the 22" drawer box comes all the way out). The full-extension (FX) glides mount on the drawer box side, and the ³⁄₄-type glides mount on the drawer bottom and side. Both styles require a ¹⁄₂" clearance on each side of the box between the cabinet sides. The clearance dimensions required with most glide systems are critical, so accurate cutting of parts is important. The FX glides (chrome model in picture) are used when full access to the drawer box is needed, but they are about three times more expensive than the standard ³⁄₄-extension models.

STEP 19 ▪ Follow the manufacturer's instructions when installing drawer glides. Most of the drawer hardware on the market can be installed by drawing a guideline inside the cabinet using a carpenter's square. The square's tongue is held tight to the cabinet's face so the guideline will be at a perfect right angle to the side board's front edge.

Frameless cabinets do not have rails, so it can be tricky calculating drawer box sizes with a multiple bank of drawers. A good rule is to leave 1" of space below and above each drawer box. That means there will be a 2" space between drawer boxes because each one requires that 1" clearance above and below.

Each drawer box height can be found by dividing the number of boxes needed into the final space available. I will need three boxes approximately 7¹⁄₂" high (22³⁄₈" divided by 3). Or, I can have any combination of three box heights that equal 22³⁄₈" high. You may want two large bottom drawers at 9" each and a small top-drawer box that's 4³⁄₈" high. Any combination of sizes is fine as long as the 1" clearance above and below the drawer box is respected.

The base cabinets stand on plastic legs and will accept a dozen different countertop or work-surface styles. You can use plywood with a coat of paint or a fancier laminate-covered top. Countertops or work surfaces for the base cabinets can be built in many ways. The design depends on your needs. I'll build different work surfaces throughout the book and you can select the style that's best for you.

You aren't limited to melamine particleboard when building these cabinets. Sheet goods such as medium-density fiberboard (MDF), plywood or plain particleboard are all fine. Low-cost sheet material can be protected with a good coat of paint.

STEP 20 ■ The drawer face is similar to a door because all four edges must be covered with tape. The width of each drawer face is 1" greater than the inside dimension of the cabinet; the same calculation is used to find door widths. The height of drawer faces is determined by the position of the free space above each drawer box.

Here is an easy way to accurately locate drawer faces on the drawer box. First, determine which handles or pulls will be used and drill the mounting holes in the drawer face only. Install the drawer boxes. Position the drawer face on the cabinet and drive a screw through the handle holes into the drawer box. The face is located and secured properly, so you can pull out the drawer and install screws from the interior of the drawer box into the back of the drawer face. Now remove the screws from the front of the drawer face and finish drilling the handle holes. Finally, install the handles.

The Practical Workbench

I'm sure there are one hundred ways to build a workbench, and all of them are correct if they meet your needs. Here's a workbench that fills all my requirements and one that will hopefully be useful in your workshop.

A bench doesn't have to be pretty. A good hardwood that's straight and flat, with a few blemishes, is just fine. After all, we're going to be pounding, clamping, dragging and abusing the top in the years to come. The bench should be strong and heavy enough to withstand a bit of pushing and pulling when we are working wood.

I used ash for my bench and tried to keep the best faces for my top surface. Even though I selected the wood carefully, I did have a few little checks and knots to fill. This wood wasn't a select grade, so I didn't expect perfection. Carefully sort through the lesser grades of lumber and pick the best pieces for your bench. It may not win a beauty contest, but the price will be a lot less than select-grade lumber.

A bench needs one or two good vises and, since a bench has a great deal of space below, a storage cabinet for frequently used tools. This bench has five drawers for tools and a shelf for tucking those tools aside when you are working on a project, keeping them within easy reach.

I installed two Veritas vises on my bench. The twin-screw model is a well-machined and very useful tool. The single-screw model mounted on the right side of the bench is perfect for my work. Both vises are available at Lee Valley Tools. The bench can be mounted on wheels, the vise styles and positions can be changed and the size can be altered for your shop. It's well worth your time and money to build a good workbench because it will be an important part of your shop for many years.

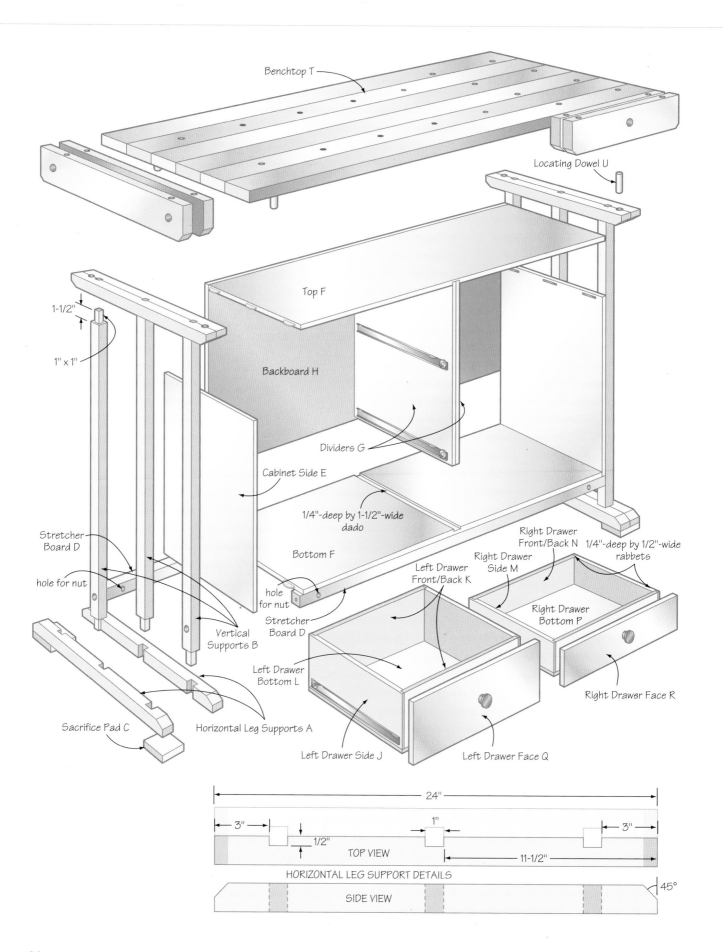

Benchtop T

Locating Dowel U

1-1/2"

1" x 1"

Top F

Backboard H

Dividers G

Cabinet Side E

1/4"-deep by 1-1/2"-wide dado

Right Drawer Front/Back N

1/4"-deep by 1/2"-wide rabbets

Right Drawer Side M

Stretcher Board D

hole for nut

hole for nut

Bottom F

Stretcher Board D

Left Drawer Front/Back K

Right Drawer Bottom P

Vertical Supports B

Left Drawer Bottom L

Right Drawer Face R

Sacrifice Pad C

Horizontal Leg Supports A

Left Drawer Side J

Left Drawer Face Q

24"

3"

1"

3"

1/2"

TOP VIEW

11-1/2"

HORIZONTAL LEG SUPPORT DETAILS

45°

SIDE VIEW

REFERENCE	QUANTITY	PART	STOCK	THICKNESS	WIDTH	LENGTH
A	8	horizontal supports	solid hardwood	1½	1½	24
B	6	vertical supports	solid hardwood	1½	1½	33½
C	4	sacrifice pads	solid hardwood	1	3	3
D	2	stretcher boards	solid hardwood	1½	2½	44
E	2	cabinet sides	veneer plywood	¾	16¾	20
F	2	bottom & top boards	veneer plywood	¾	16¾	42½
G	2	dividers	veneer plywood	¾	16¾	19
H	1	backboard	veneer plywood	¾	20	44

TWO LEFT-SIDE DRAWER BOXES

REFERENCE	QUANTITY	PART	STOCK	THICKNESS	WIDTH	LENGTH
J	4	sides	birch plywood	½	6¾	16
K	4	fronts & backs	birch plywood	½	6¾	19
L	2	bottoms	birch plywood	½	16	19½

THREE RIGHT-SIDE DRAWER BOXES

REFERENCE	QUANTITY	PART	STOCK	THICKNESS	WIDTH	LENGTH
M	6	sides	birch plywood	½	3⅝	16
N	6	fronts & backs	birch plywood	½	3⅝	19
P	3	bottoms	birch plywood	½	16	19½

DRAWER FACES

REFERENCE	QUANTITY	PART	STOCK	THICKNESS	WIDTH	LENGTH
Q	2	faces	veneer plywood	¾	9¾	21½
R	2	faces	veneer plywood	¾	6¾	21½
S	1	faces	veneer plywood	¾	6	21½

BENCHTOP

REFERENCE	QUANTITY	PART	STOCK	THICKNESS	WIDTH	LENGTH
T	1	benchtop	solid hardwood	1½	30	72
U	4	locating dowels	solid hardwood			
		(1" diameter by 2½" long)				

HARDWARE

5 Sets of 18"-long, ¾-extension glides (use full-extension glides if desired)

Drawer handles or knobs

PB screws

Bolts, nuts and washers as detailed

Plate joinery biscuits (#20)

Glue

4" x ⅜"-Diameter bolts with washers and nuts

Wood edge tape

1½" PB screws

1" Brad nails

½" Screws

1" Screws

OPTIONAL

1 Front vise (Veritas Tools by Lee Valley Tools #70G08.02)

1 Twin-screw vise (Veritas Tools by Lee Valley Tools #05G12.22)

4 Bench dogs (Veritas Tools by Lee Valley Tools #05G04.04)

REFERENCE	QUANTITY	PART	STOCK	THICKNESS	WIDTH	LENGTH
A	8	horizontal supports	solid hardwood	38	38	610
B	6	vertical supports	solid hardwood	38	38	851
C	4	sacrifice pads	solid hardwood	25	76	76
D	2	stretcher boards	solid hardwood	38	64	1118
E	2	cabinet sides	veneer plywood	19	425	508
F	2	bottom & top boards	veneer plywood	19	425	1080
G	2	dividers	veneer plywood	19	425	483
H	1	backboard	veneer plywood	1938	20	44

TWO LEFT-SIDE DRAWER BOXES

REFERENCE	QUANTITY	PART	STOCK	THICKNESS	WIDTH	LENGTH
J	4	sides	birch plywood	13	171	406
K	4	fronts & backs	birch plywood	13	171	483
L	2	bottoms	birch plywood	13	406	496

THREE RIGHT-SIDE DRAWER BOXES

REFERENCE	QUANTITY	PART	STOCK	THICKNESS	WIDTH	LENGTH
M	6	sides	birch plywood	13	92	406
N	6	fronts & backs	birch plywood	13	92	483
P	3	bottoms	birch plywood	13	406	496

DRAWER FACES

REFERENCE	QUANTITY	PART	STOCK	THICKNESS	WIDTH	LENGTH
Q	2	faces	veneer plywood	19	248	546
R	2	faces	veneer plywood	19	171	546
S	1	faces	veneer plywood	19	152	546

BENCHTOP

REFERENCE	QUANTITY	PART	STOCK	THICKNESS	WIDTH	LENGTH
T	1	benchtop	solid hardwood	38	762	1829
U	4	locating dowels	solid hardwood			
		(1" diameter by 2½" long)				

HARDWARE

5 Sets of 457mm-long, ¾-extension glides (use full-extension glides if desired)

Drawer handles or knobs

PB screws

Bolts, nuts and washers as detailed

Plate joinery biscuits (#20)

Glue

102mm × 10mm-Diameter bolts with washers and nuts

Wood edge tape

38mm PB screws

25mm Brad nails

13mm Screws

25mm Screws

OPTIONAL

1 Front vise (Veritas Tools by Lee Valley Tools #70G08.02)

1 Twin-screw vise (Veritas Tools by Lee Valley Tools #05G12.22)

4 Bench dogs (Veritas Tools by Lee Valley Tools #05G04.04)

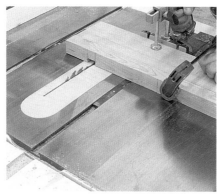

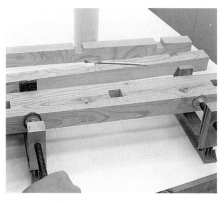

STEP 1 ■ Rip and crosscut the eight horizontal supports A at 1½"-square by 24"-long, and the six vertical supports B at 1½"-square by 33½"-long. A good crosscut blade on a table saw will be required to cut the 1½"-thick material. A sliding table on your table saw, a radial-arm saw or power miter box can be used to crosscut the parts.

STEP 2 ■ The eight horizontal supports A each require three dadoes that are 1"-wide by ½"-deep. Two of the dadoes are located 3" from each end, and the third is located directly in the center. Dadoes can be cut on a table saw. If possible, gang four pieces together at one time and mark the pairs; this will ensure that sets are matched for joining.

STEP 3 ■ Glue two horizontal supports A together, forming a board with three 1"-square through-mortises. The eight supports will make four horizontal support members. Use dowels, biscuits or simply edge-glue the pieces to each other.

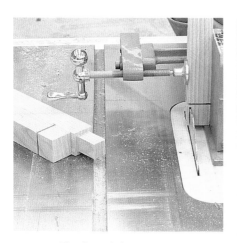

STEP 5 ■ Cut a 45° corner on the end of all four horizontal supports A. Use a ¼" roundover bit in your router to ease all the corners on the vertical supports B, and the top edges of the bottom two horizontal supports A. Don't round over the bottom of the lower horizontal supports that touch the floor or the two top horizontal supports.

STEP 4 ■ The six vertical supports B require a 1"-square by 1½"-long tenon centered on each end. These tenons can be cut on a table saw with a miter slide or, if you have one, a tenoning jig.

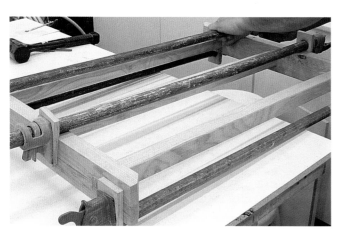

STEP 6 ■ Build both leg assemblies using glue and clamps. The tenons should fit snugly into the mortises. Set aside both leg units until the adhesive cures.

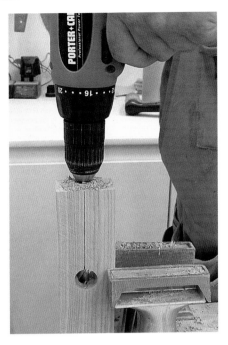

STEP 8 ■ Cut the two stretcher boards D to the size indicated in the materials list. Drill a 1"-diameter through-hole, centered 4" from each end on both stretchers. Then drill the ends of both boards using a $^3/_8$"-diameter bit. The holes are located on the center of each end and are drilled 4" deep to meet the 1"-diameter through-holes.

STEP 7 ■ To save wear and tear on the lower horizontal supports, install sacrifice pads. These are 3"-square by 1"-thick and are attached with screws only. When the pads wear because the bench is moved a great deal or become damaged by moisture or liquids on the floor, simply replace the pads.

STEP 9 ■ Drill a $^1/_2$"-deep by 1"-diameter hole 4" above the bottom of each vertical support B. Center the hole on the four vertical uprights, making sure your measurements are from the bottom of the vertical supports and not the lower edge of the horizontal supports. Next, drill a $^3/_8$"-diameter through-hole in the center of each 1"-diameter hole for the assembly bolts. Attach both leg assemblies together using the two stretchers. Use 4"-long by $^3/_8$"-diameter bolts and washers to secure the base. The 1" hole on the outside of each vertical support will allow you to recess the bolt head, and the 1"-diameter through-hole in the stretcher board D will be used to attach the nuts to the bolts.

STEP 10 ■ Cut the drawer carcass parts as detailed in the materials list. I am using $^3/_4$"-thick oak veneer plywood to contrast the solid ash.

Apply wood edge tape to all front and top edges of the side boards E. The backboard H requires edge tape on the top and both side edges, as do the front edges of boards F.

Use a router to cut a $^1/_4$"-deep by $1^1/_2$"-wide dado in the center inside face of both top and bottom boards for the dividers.

STEP 11 ■ I used three #20 biscuits and glue to attach the carcass sides E to the bottom and top boards F. Dowels or screws and glue can also be used.

THE PRACTICAL WORKBENCH   **25**

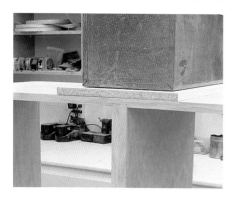

STEP 12 ▪ Apply glue to both dadoes and place the dividers G into those dadoes. Use a heavy weight on top of the carcass until the adhesive sets and the dividers are fixed solidly n place.

I'm using two dividers for strength because I don't want the dividers to flex, which may interfere with the drawer runners if a lot of weight is added to the top board of the carcass. It's possibly overbuilt at this point, but I'd rather have more support than needed instead of just enough.

STEP 13 ▪ The backboard H is attached with #20 biscuits and glue. Clamp it in place until the adhesive sets up.

STEP 14 ▪ Put the drawer carcass in the bench frame. Rest the bottom board on both stretchers, aligning the backboard with the outside face of the back stretcher. Use 1½" PB screws to secure the carcass to the bench frame. Do not use glue, so it can be removed if the bench must be moved.

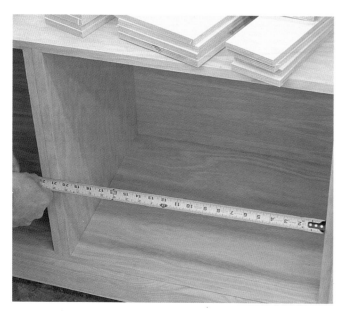

STEP 15 ▪ I'm installing drawers on both sides of the carcass. One side will have three drawers and the other side two.

Calculating drawer sizes means subtracting 1" from the interior carcass width for most drawer glides. However, it's well worth purchasing your glides at this point to verify the installation instructions.

In a frameless-style cabinet, such as this one, drawer height is found by following a few simple rules. Each drawer box should have 1" clearance above and below. That required space means there will be a 2" space between drawer boxes. The interior space is 18½" high, meaning on a two-drawer bank we must subtract 4" from that height (1" above and below each drawer box for purposes of calculating drawer height), and divide the result by two. The drawer height for the two-drawer bank will be 18½" minus 4" divided by 2, or 7¼" high.

The same calculations apply to the three-drawer bank. The drawer boxes will be 18½" minus 6" divided by 3, or approximately 4⅛" high, to provide the correct clearance.

Cut all the drawer parts to size as detailed in the materials list. These boxes will be constructed using ½" baltic birch plywood.

STEP 16 ▪ Each drawer box side J and M will need a rabbet cut ½" wide by ¼" deep on each inside face at both ends. The back and front boards will fit into these rabbets. Use a router table or table saw to make the cuts.

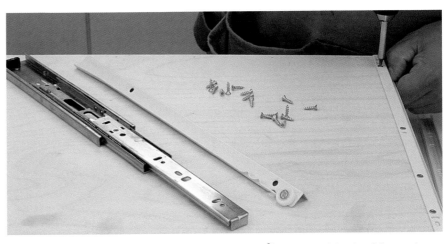

STEP 17 ▪ Join the drawer box sides to the back and front boards using glue and 1" brad nails. The nails will hold the joint until the glue dries. Glue and nail the bottom boards to the drawer box frames.

STEP 18 ▪ Attach drawer runners to each box. I am using ¾-extension glides, but full-extension glides (silver in the photo) can also be used if you require full access to the drawer. The full-extension models are two to three times more expensive than the ¾-extension type, but worth the extra cost if you need to fully access the drawer box.

Attach the runners using ½" screws and follow the manufacturer's instructions.

STEP 19 ▪ Mount the cabinet runners using a level line as a guide, or with a drawer glide-mounting jig.

Install one glide at the bottom of each cabinet section, and one 8" above the bottom board in the two-drawer cabinet. The three-drawer section has one set of runners at the bottom, one at 7" above the bottom board, and the top runner set 14" above the bottom.

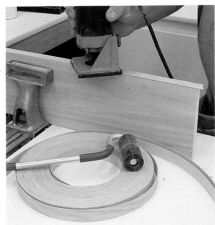

STEP 20 ▪ The drawer faces Q, R and S are made using ¾"-thick veneer plywood. All four edges of each drawer face have wood veneer tape applied.

STEP 21 ▪ Here's an easy way to accurately locate drawer faces. First, drill the handle hole (or holes) in the drawer face, not through the drawer box at this point. Position the drawer face against the cabinet with the drawer box in place. Once located, drive a wood screw through the handle hole and into the drawer box until the face is secure. Next, open the drawer and drive 1" screws through the back of the drawer box front board, into the drawer face. Finally, remove the screws from the handle holes, drill holes completely through the box and install the handles or knobs.

STEP 22 ▪ My benchtop T is constructed using six 5½"-wide boards that are 1½" thick. The boards are left longer than 72" and will be trimmed to size once the top is sanded. Thick boards can be joined with a double-biscuit technique that's shown in the photo.

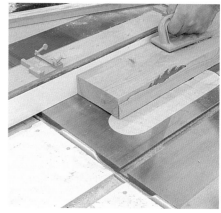

STEP 23 ■ To prepare rough boards for joining, flatten one face on a jointer.

STEP 24 ■ Next, press the flat face against the jointer fence and mill one edge at 90° to the prepared face.

STEP 25 ■ Cut the remaining rough edge parallel to the jointed edge, and at 90° to the prepared face, on a table saw. Hold the jointed edge of the board tight to the saw fence and the prepared face flat on the saw table.

STEP 26 ■ Use a planer to dress the rough face parallel to the prepared face. The board is now ready to be joined to other boards.

STEP 27 ■ Join the boards with clamps on the top and bottom face as shown. This over-and-under technique will help to ensure that your top will set up flat. Tighten the clamps until you see just a little of the glue squeeze out. Clamps set too tight will squeeze out a lot of glue, starving the joint and possibly making it fail.

STEP 28 ■ Complete the top by scraping off the excess glue and sanding smooth. Trim to the required 30"-wide by 72"-long size. Turn the top facedown on the floor. Set the leg and carcass assembly upside down on the bottom face of the top so it's equally spaced side to side and front to back. Drill small pilot holes through the upper horizontal support and into the top. One hole at the end of each support is required.

STEP 29 ■ Drill 1"-diameter holes, 1" deep, in the bottom face of the top using the small drill holes from the previous step as a guide. Cut and install four 2½"-long by 1"-diameter dowels in the holes using glue.

Drill 1"-diameter holes completely through the upper horizontal supports using the pilot holes as a guide. Once the adhesive sets, put the top on the base assembly with the dowels set into the four holes. You may need to widen the diameter of the horizontal support holes with sandpaper to install the top.

I drilled ¾"-diameter holes in my benchtop to accommodate round bench dogs. Both vise jaws also had ¾"-diameter holes drilled for the round dogs. These bench dogs can be used with either vise to clamp flat boards that need to be sanded or planed.

The size of this bench, the number of drawers in the storage carcass, the height and the accessory equipment can all be modified to suit your requirements. My bench is 36" high, but that may not be suitable for everyone. If this plan isn't right for you, change the dimensions.

Hardwood is an excellent choice for any workbench. A bench will be around for many years, and may be passed to future generations of woodworkers, so use the best quality hardwood you can afford.

I finished my bench with three coats of oil-based polyurethane that is commonly used on hardwood floors. I gave the top a good coat of hard paste wax to further protect the surface from liquids and adhesive spills.

This is a great project. I hope you'll enjoy your new workbench as much as I enjoy mine.

STEP 30 ■ My front vise is a single-screw model made by Veritas Tools, available from Lee Valley Tools. I followed the installation instructions and added two 1½"-thick wood jaws.

STEP 31 ■ The end vise I used is also made by Veritas and is a twin-screw model. When using large end vises on this bench, be sure the moving mechanics of the vise clear the bench supports. I used 7¼"-high wood jaws, centering the screws 3" up from the bottom edge of the boards, so both screws would clear the upper horizontal supports.

Power Miter Saw Station

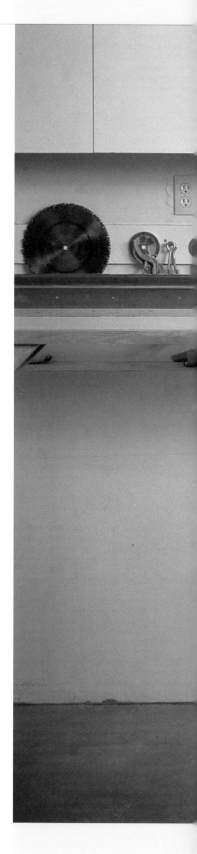

I wanted to meet a number of requirements when I designed my ultimate power miter saw station.

First, the station tower had to be wide enough so I could tuck a large garbage pail inside. It also had to have easy access so I could clear and throw away scraps of wood. I sometimes get lazy and forget to remove the small scraps of wood after cutting. These pieces can contact the blade on the next cut and shoot out of the saw like a wild bullet. I have seen too many close calls using this saw, so this design feature was high on my list.

I also wanted the station fences or "wings" on my station to be high enough so I could use the floor space; I will be storing rolling workstations under the saw fences. My table height is 42" off the ground and the fences are about 2½" higher.

The station tower has a drawer to store wrenches, instruction books and any other saw accessories. I usually spend time searching the shop for these items,

so I promised myself they would have a place in the station.

I was tired of using poorly designed stop blocks that could be used only for material cuts starting at 6" or more. Why couldn't a zero stop be made? I think that need was met with my stop-block system.

Finally, the "wings" had to be strong because they would be 4' to 8' long without a center support. I used hardwood and steel to edge the sheet material and make the stop-block system. The fences are extremely strong and will not deflect under heavy loads.

I used melamine particleboard (PB) for my sheet material and hardwood trim to absorb the bumps and hits during heavy use. I decided to install adjustable plastic cabinet legs so I could level the fences.

This power miter saw station is perfect for my work. It has met all my needs and is a pleasure to use. I'm sure it will be a useful addition to your shop, as well.

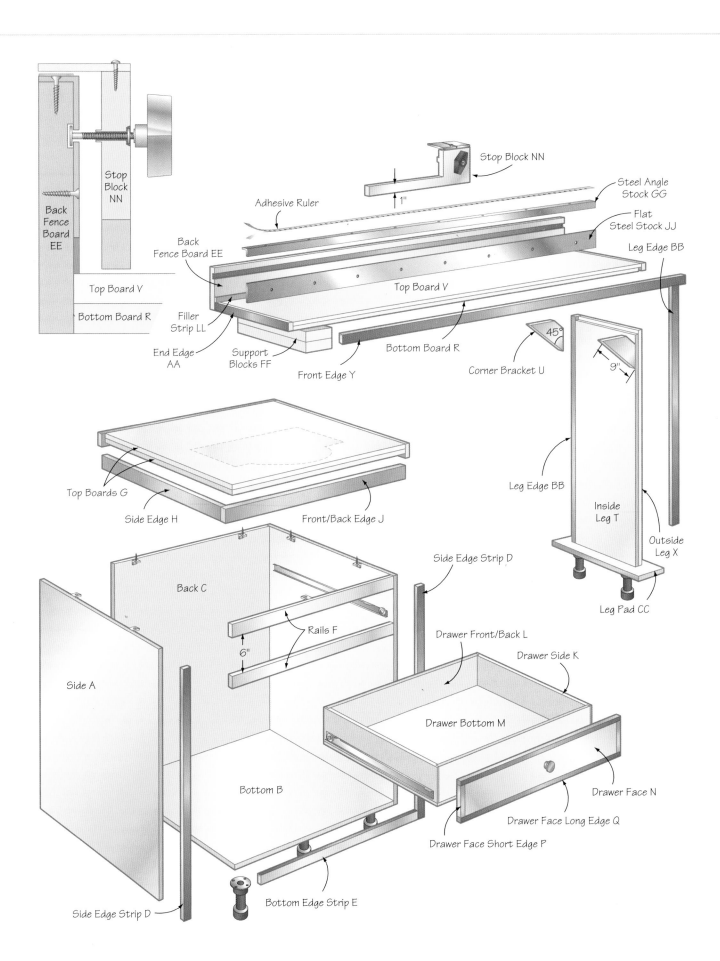

Stop Block NN

Back Fence Board EE

Stop Block NN

Top Board V

Bottom Board R

Adhesive Ruler

Stop Block NN

1"

Steel Angle Stock GG

Flat Steel Stock JJ

Leg Edge BB

Back Fence Board EE

Top Board V

Filler Strip LL

End Edge AA

Support Blocks FF

Front Edge Y

Bottom Board R

Corner Bracket U

45°

9"

Leg Edge BB

Inside Leg T

Outside Leg X

Leg Pad CC

Top Boards G

Side Edge H

Front/Back Edge J

Back C

Rails F

6"

Side Edge Strip D

Drawer Front/Back L

Drawer Side K

Side A

Drawer Bottom M

Drawer Face N

Bottom B

Drawer Face Long Edge Q

Drawer Face Short Edge P

Side Edge Strip D

Bottom Edge Strip E

REFERENCE	QUANTITY	PART	STOCK	THICKNESS	WIDTH	LENGTH	COMMENTS
TOWER							
A	2	sides	melamine PB	$5/8$	24	36	
B	1	bottom	melamine PB	$5/8$	26	24	
C	1	back	melamine PB	$5/8$	26	$35^3/8$	
D	2	side edge strips	solid hardwood	$1/4$	$5/8$	36	
E	1	bottom edge strip	solid hardwood	$1/4$	$5/8$	26	
F	2	rails	solid hardwood	$1/4$	$1^1/2$	26	
G	2	top boards	melamine PB	$5/8$	$25^1/4$	$30^1/2$	
H	2	side edges	solid hardwood	$1/4$	$1^1/2$	$25^1/4$	
J	2	front & back edges	solid hardwood	$1/4$	$1^1/2$	32	
K	2	drawer sides	melamine PB	$5/8$	$4^3/8$	22	
L	2	drawer front & back	melamine PB	$5/8$	$4^3/8$	$23^3/4$	
M	1	drawer bottom	melamine PB	$5/8$	22	25	
N	1	drawer face	melamine PB	$5/8$	$6^1/2$	$26^1/2$	
P	2	drawer face edges	solid hardwood	$1/4$	$5/8$	$6^1/2$	
Q	2	drawer face edges	solid hardwood	$1/4$	$5/8$	27	
FENCE WINGS							
R	1	bottom board	melamine PB	$5/8$	7	$71^3/8$	
S	1	bottom board	melamine PB	$5/8$	7	$47^3/8$	
T	2	inside legs	melamine PB	$5/8$	7	$38^7/8$	
U	4	corner brackets	solid hardwood	$3/4$	$3^1/2$	9	
V	1	top board	melamine PB	$5/8$	7	72	
W	1	top board	melamine PB	$5/8$	7	48	
X	2	outside legs	melamine PB	$5/8$	7	$39^1/2$	
Y	1	front edge	solid hardwood	$3/4$	$1^1/4$	$73^1/2$	
Z	1	front edge	solid hardwood	$3/4$	$1^1/4$	$49^1/2$	
AA	4	end edges	solid hardwood	$3/4$	$1^1/4$	7	
BB	4	leg edges	solid hardwood	$3/4$	$1^1/4$	$38^7/8$	
CC	2	leg pads	solid hardwood	$3/4$	$3^1/2$	$8^1/2$	
DD	1	back fence board	solid hardwood	$3/4$	$5^1/4$	$49^1/2$	
EE	1	back fence board	solid hardwood	$3/4$	$5^1/4$	$73^1/2$	
FF	2	support blocks	solid hardwood	$1^1/2$	$2^{11}/16$	6	
GG	1	angle stock	steel	$1/8$	1×1	72	
HH	1	angle stock	steel	$1/8$	1×1	48	
JJ	1	flat stock	steel	$1/8$	2	72	
KK	1	flat stock	steel	$1/8$	2	48	
LL	1	filler strip	solid hardwood	$1/8$	$3/4$	72	
MM	1	filler strip	solid hardwood	$1/8$	$3/4$	48	
NN	2	stop blocks	solid hardwood	$3/4$	$3^7/8$	14	

HARDWARE

10 Adjustable plastic cabinet legs

1 – 22" Drawer glide set

7 Metal right-angle brackets

2 Metal self-sticking measuring tapes

1 – $5/16$"-Diameter closet bolt set

2 Stop-block handles

1 Drawer handle

2 – 2" x 3" Plastic or Plexiglass

Metal washers

White iron-on edge tape

Screw cover caps

Screws as detailed

Glue

Wood plugs

2" PB screws

Biscuits or confirmat screws

$5/8$" Screws

Brad nails

Wood putty

1" Screws

3" Screws

Pan head screws and washers

REFERENCE	QUANTITY	PART	STOCK	THICKNESS	WIDTH	LENGTH	COMMENTS
TOWER							
A	2	sides	melamine PB	16	610	914	
B	1	bottom	melamine PB	16	660	610	
C	1	back	melamine PB	16	660	899	
D	2	side edge strips	solid hardwood	6	16	914	
E	1	bottom edge strip	solid hardwood	6	16	660	
F	2	rails	solid hardwood	6	38	660	
G	2	top boards	melamine PB	16	641	775	
H	2	side edges	solid hardwood	6	38	641	
J	2	front & back edges	solid hardwood	6	38	813	
K	2	drawer sides	melamine PB	16	112	559	
L	2	drawer front & back	melamine PB	16	112	603	
M	1	drawer bottom	melamine PB	16	559	635	
N	1	drawer face	melamine PB	16	165	673	
P	2	drawer face edges	solid hardwood	6	16	165	
Q	2	drawer face edges	solid hardwood	6	16	686	
FENCE WINGS							
R	1	bottom board	melamine PB	16	178	1813	
S	1	bottom board	melamine PB	16	178	1204	
T	2	inside legs	melamine PB	16	178	987	
U	4	corner brackets	solid hardwood	19	89	229	
V	1	top board	melamine PB	16	178	1829	
W	1	top board	melamine PB	16	178	1219	
X	2	outside legs	melamine PB	16	178	1004	
Y	1	front edge	solid hardwood	19	31	1867	
Z	1	front edge	solid hardwood	19	31	1258	
AA	4	end edges	solid hardwood	19	31	178	
BB	4	leg edges	solid hardwood	19	31	987	
CC	2	leg pads	solid hardwood	19	89	216	
DD	1	back fence board	solid hardwood	19	133	1258	
EE	1	back fence board	solid hardwood	19	133	1867	
FF	2	support blocks	solid hardwood	38	69	152	
GG	1	angle stock	steel	3	25 x 25	1829	
HH	1	angle stock	steel	3	25 x 25	1219	
JJ	1	flat stock	steel	3	51	1829	
KK	1	flat stock	steel	3	51	1219	
LL	1	filler strip	solid hardwood	3	19	1829	
MM	1	filler strip	solid hardwood	3	19	1219	
NN	2	stop blocks	solid hardwood	19	98	356	

HARDWARE

10 Adjustable plastic cabinet legs

1 – 559mm Drawer glide set

7 Metal right-angle brackets

2 Metal self-sticking measuring tapes

1 – 8mm-Diameter closet bolt set

2 Stop-block handles

1 Drawer handle

2 – 51mm x 76mm Plastic or Plexiglass

Metal washers

White iron-on edge tape

Screw cover caps

Screws as detailed

Glue

Wood plugs

51mm PB screws

Biscuits or confirmat screws

16mm Screws

Brad nails

Wood putty

25mm Screws

76mm Screws

Pan head screws and washers

BUILDING THE POWER MITER SAW STATION

STEP 1 ▪ Cut the two sides A and bottom board B as detailed in the materials list. The joinery can be PB screws (on the right in the photo), biscuits (center) or confirmat screws (left). The confirmat screws are European-designed fasteners that are used to assemble melamine PB cabinetry. They are high-quality fasteners, but they do require a special step drill and accurate placement. The drill bits are expensive and brittle. The PB screws are designed to join this material, and the heads can be hidden with plastic cover caps.

I am using 2" PB screws placed 6" apart along the joint. Small white caps or white adhesive covers are available at woodworking and home stores.

STEP 2 ▪ The inset backboard C is joined to the sides and bottom board with 2" PB screws. The back face of the backboard is flush with the back edges of the side and bottom boards.

STEP 4 ▪ The cabinet edges could suffer a few knocks and bumps, so I installed hardwood edge strips D and E on the bottom and two side panels. Use glue and brad nails to secure the strips of wood. Fill the nail holes with wood putty and sand the strips smooth.

STEP 3 ▪ I'm installing six adjustable plastic legs on my tower cabinet. The front legs are set back 3" and secured with four ⅝" screws. Position the flanges of the front and rear outside legs under the edges of the side boards. The load will be transferred directly to the sides, through the legs and onto the floor.

You can build and install a 4"-high base frame made with solid lumber or sheet material if there isn't a danger of liquid spills or water leaks on your shop floor. If water is an issue, or your shop floor isn't level, adjustable cabinet legs are the perfect solution.

Shop Tip

You can avoid splitting panels by keeping screws 1" away from any board end when joining sheet goods. Always drill a pilot hole for the screws to ensure maximum hold.

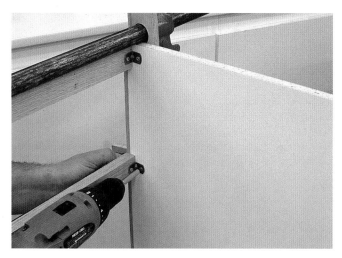

STEP 5 ■ Install the two hardwood rails F, one at the top of the cabinet and the other below it, leaving a 6" space between the rails for a drawer. Secure the rails with right-angle brackets and ⅝" screws, or use pocket holes if you have a jig. Apply a little glue on the front edges to secure the rails to the side wood strips. Clamp until the adhesive cures.

STEP 6 ■ Install seven right-angle brackets using ⅝" screws. One is located in the middle of the top rail and two on each of the back and side boards. These brackets will be used to secure the cabinet top.

STEP 8 ■ Attach the banded top to the cabinet using 1" screws through the right-angle brackets previously installed. The top overhangs the back by ¾" and by 2⅜" on each side.

STEP 7 ■ The cabinet top G is 32" wide by 26¾" deep overall. It is made with two layers of ⅝"-thick melamine PB, and joined with 1" screws from the underside. A ¾"-thick by 1½"-wide hardwood band, H and J, is applied to all four edges. Use glue and 2" screws in a ⅜" counterbored hole and fill the holes with wood plugs. You can also use biscuits (plate joinery) if you prefer that method.

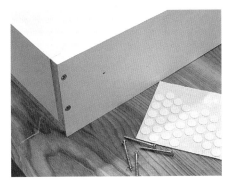

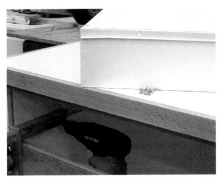

STEP 9 ■ Drawer boxes are commonly 1" less in height and width when using most ¾-extension drawer glide sets. This rule is also applied to most full-extension drawer glide sets. However, read the installation instructions with your hardware before cutting the drawer box parts.

Cut the drawer box parts K through M and apply iron-on edge tape to the upper edges of the side, back and front boards. The side edges of the bottom board also require edge tape.

STEP 10 ■ Join the sides to the back and front boards using 2" PB screws. The bottom board is also installed using 2" screws about 8" apart. Cut the bottom board square and it will ensure that your drawer box is square. The box should be 5" high by 25" wide by 22" deep. The screw heads can be covered with plastic caps or white stick-on covers. Refer to chapter one for more details.

STEP 11 ■ Mount the drawer glide runners on the cabinet sides, attach the two drawer runners to the box using ⅝" screws and test fit your drawer. The cabinet runners can be installed using a straight line made with a carpenter's square, or a drawer glide-mounting jig.

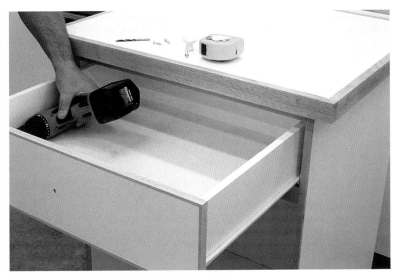

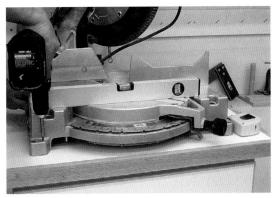

STEP 12 ■ The finished size of the drawer face is 7" high by 27" wide. I made my drawer face with ⅝"-thick melamine PB and ¼"-thick by ⅝"-wide hardwood strips on all four edges. The strips were installed with glue and brad nails. To ensure perfect drawer-face alignment, drill the handle or knob holes in the drawer face only. Put the drawer box in the cabinet, hold the drawer face in its correct position, and drive screws through the holes securing it to the drawer box. Then carefully open the drawer and secure the face by driving 1" screws through the drawer box front board into the back of the drawer face. Remove the screw (or screws) in the handle holes and drill through the drawer box. Finally, install the handle to complete the installation.

STEP 13 ■ Place the tower section where it will be used in your shop and level the cabinet front to back and side to side. Center the miter saw on the top and secure it with screws or bolts. It's difficult to generalize on methods to secure your saw because so many models are available. However, once you have it installed trace an outline on the top with a permanent marker. If the saw has to be removed from the station, it can easily be returned to the same position using the trace lines.

BUILDING THE FENCE PLATFORMS

STEP 14 ■ The right-side fence platform on my station will be 6' long, and the left side will be 4' long. Both will be built with 7"-wide melamine PB and edged with ¾" hardwood that's 1¼" wide so it will cover the double-thickness melamine PB pieces. The lengths of these fence platforms are determined by the amount of space you have available and the type of cutting you do in your shop. Change the lengths of the horizontal boards to suit your shop.

Cut the inside legs T and bottom boards R and S to size. Attach the horizontal bottom shelves to the inside leg top ends using 2" PB screws. Cut the four brackets U and attach two at each corner using 2" screws.

STEP 15 ■ Cut the two top boards V and W, as well as the two outside legs X, to size. Attach the boards as shown in the drawing, using 1" screws from the underside of the bottom top board and back side of the inside leg board. The photo shows proper placement of the boards with the fence assembly's top board resting upside down on the workbench. Two screws, 8" apart and placed in 1" from the edges, will create a solid melamine "sandwich." Hide the screw heads on the legs with plastic caps or stickers.

STEP 16 ■ All the exposed edges, with the exception of the two back edges on the horizontal platforms, are banded with ¾"-thick by 1¼"-wide hardwood. Use glue and screws, in counterbored holes, to attach the hardwood to the front and ends of both platforms, as well as the back and front edges of the legs. Fill the screw head holes with wood plugs.

STEP 17 ■ The size of the leg pad CC will depend on the style of leg you install. My legs require a wide base so I attached a 3½"-wide pad with screws and glue. The legs are secured with four ⅝" screws.

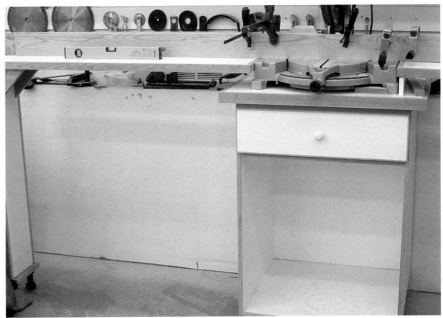

STEP 19 ■ Clamp a long straightedge across the saw bed. Level each fence platform by blocking the end that rests on the tower tabletop and adjusting the legs at the ends. The fence platforms must be flush with the saw platform. Set the face of the platform fences $\frac{1}{8}$" behind the saw fence because we will be installing $\frac{1}{8}$"-thick steel on the fence.

STEP 18 ■ The back fence boards must be cut and grooved before being attached. The groove is $\frac{1}{2}$" wide by $\frac{1}{8}$" deep and is located $\frac{3}{4}$" down from the top edge of each fence board. Attach the fence boards DD and EE with glue and 2" screws. The boards are installed with the groove at the top and facing inward toward the platform. The bottom of each fence board is flush with the bottom face of the lower melamine fence platform boards R and S.

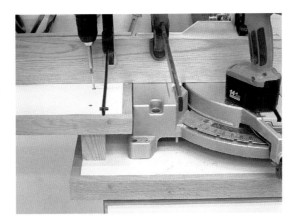

STEP 20 ■ Cut two support blocks FF (the block thickness I needed to match my saw's platform was $2\frac{11}{16}$") and attach them to the tower tabletop with screws driven from the underside of that top. Use 3" screws to secure the platforms to each block, making certain the fence platforms are level with the saw's platform.

Shop Tip

Construct or buy a wall bracket if you are concerned about bumping the platforms with heavy lumber. The platforms are solid and stable, but you may want extra support, so attach a bracket between the legs and a wall. The miter station tower can also be anchored to the wall for extra stability, however, the tower and fence platforms are rigid and will remain aligned under normal usage.

STEP 21 ■ The next step is to build a stop-block system. First, drill and attach $\frac{1}{8}$"-thick steel angle stock parts GG and HH on the top of each platform fence board. Steel angle and flat stock is available at most hardware and home stores. The steel angle stock is $\frac{7}{8}$" wide on the inside face and will rest $\frac{1}{8}$" lower than the top of the fence groove. Be sure to countersink the screw heads so the adhesive steel ruler will lay flat on top of the angle stock.

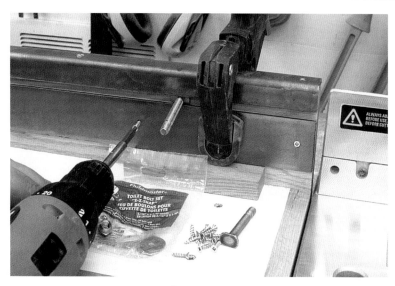

STEP 22 ■ Drill and countersink the ⅛"-thick by 2"-wide steel flat stock pieces JJ and KK. The holes should be about 6" apart and countersunk so the screw heads are below the stock's surface. Attach the flat steel to the back fence boards using ⅝" screws.

The bolts that will be used for the stop assemblies are a toilet or closet bolt set; they are ⁵⁄₁₆"-diameter bolts with large, flat oval heads. Clamp the flat steel below the angle stock with a bolt in the groove. The bolts should move freely, but you shouldn't be able to pull them out.

STEP 23 ■ Once the steel pieces have been installed and the bolts are moving freely along the length of each track, cut and install filler strips LL and MM. These strips will make the fence flush from top to bottom. Use glue and brad nails to secure the strips.

STEP 24 ■ Install self-sticking measuring tapes on top of each angle iron. You'll need left-to-right and right-to-left reading tapes. The zero mark on each ruler should align with the end of each angle iron closest to the miter saw.

STEP 25 ■ Cut stop-block boards NN as shown in the materials list. They will be trimmed to size on the miter station. Set the table saw fence for a ⅝"-thick cut with the blade 1" high. Run both boards through the saw, on edge. Reset the blade 2½" high and run both boards through the saw once again after flipping them. The result will be a ⅛"-thick by ¼"-wide tenon on the back face of each board. The tenon will slide in the space between both pieces of steel and stabilize the stop block.

STEP 26 ■ Cut the stop-block boards on a band saw or with a jigsaw, as shown. The first 3" of the board should be full height and the remainder 1" high. Remember that you'll need a right and left stop-block assembly, so pay close attention to how the cut lines are laid out on each board.

I decided to use steel for these long fence platforms because I didn't want any deflection, and the result was impressive. Both fence systems are stable and rigid.

The fence platforms are high enough so I can store other workstations underneath, which is a real bonus in any shop. I used melamine PB for the field and oak hardwood for the edges; however, any sheet material and wood banding can be used. The smooth surface of the melamine makes it easy to slide the boards being cut, but materials such as medium-density fiberboard will serve the same purpose.

The dimensions of the tower can be changed if you find the height unsuitable. My tower interior width was designed to hold a large plastic pail for scraps, but it can be narrower if you don't need a scrap pail. My platform is wide because my 12" miter saw has a large bed. Smaller saws are common, so design your tower top to hold the saw you own. I don't think there are much wider miter saws on the market, but it's well worth taking the time to measure your saw before building the tower.

You can include many other features in your design. For example, a rack could be attached to the outside face of the side boards to hold saw blades. Or the drawer could be divided with partitions for various tools and documents that are needed for your saw. I also considered adding another cabinet beside the tower with adjustable shelves for storing small cutoffs that can be used for other projects.

If you don't have access to adjustable legs, or prefer a solid base, you can construct one with 2x4 material or plywood. The steel, closet bolts and knobs are common hardware items and should be readily available at your local hardware store.

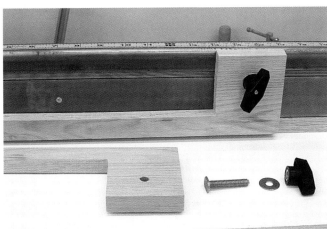

STEP 27 ■ Drill a $\frac{3}{8}$"-diameter hole through the middle of each tenon on both stop blocks. The holes should be centered on the width of the full-height portion of each block. Use a closet bolt and washer with a suitable knob to attach each block. I found the knobs at my local hardware store with a thread pattern that matched the closet bolt set. Most woodworking stores also carry these knobs in many styles.

Shop Tip

You can use aluminum stock, but steel is about one-half the cost and is much stronger. The same fence system can also be built using an aluminum T-track set into a groove in the back fence board. I've opted for steel in this case because it strengthens the fence platforms.

STEP 28 ■ The stop-block position is determined by a clear plastic indicator screwed to the top of each stop block. Clear plastic or Plexiglass is available at craft and plastic supply stores.

Cut two pieces each 2" wide by 3" long. Scribe a fine line in the plastic with an awl or other sharp tool. Use a permanent marker to fill the scratch with ink. Attach the indicator to the stop block with pan head screws and washers in oval-shaped holes that will allow side-to-side adjustment. Align the mark on the plastic indicator to zero on the tape measure and trim the tongue on the stop block with your miter saw. That's your zero measurement for each block, and if you need to fine-tune the adjustment, loosen the screws and move the plastic indicator.

Multifunction Power Tool Cabinet

A power tool stand is a great addition to any workshop; however, if you have limited space, need to move the tools out of the way for your car or don't use certain tools on a regular basis, a dedicated power tool station is not much use. I think you'll find this tool cabinet answers all those needs.

This versatile tool cabinet has a removable platform that locks securely into place in less than a minute. It can be used with dozens of power tools that are secured to individual mounting boards. The cabinet has four locking wheels, an open shelf for accessories, and a drawer to store all the documentation and extra parts that come with your tools.

The cabinet is built with tough, inexpensive ⅝" melamine particleboard (PB) and hardwood edging so it will last for years. It can be tucked away in a corner or stored under the miter saw station wings described in chapter three.

The top and tool platforms are constructed using ¾"-thick medium-density fiberboard (MDF), which is another inexpensive sheet material. The drawer is ⅝" melamine PB and mounted on ¾-extension, bottom-mount drawer glides. The cabinet also has enough room to store a second power tool on its mounting platform, in the bottom section.

This has been one of the most valuable cabinets I've built for my shop. Moving the power tools to my work area, with all the accessories on board where I can quickly locate them, is a real benefit, and I'm enjoying my work even more. I was so pleased with this mobile tool cabinet that I built two and may build another in the near future. I hope you'll find it just as useful and build one or two for your shop.

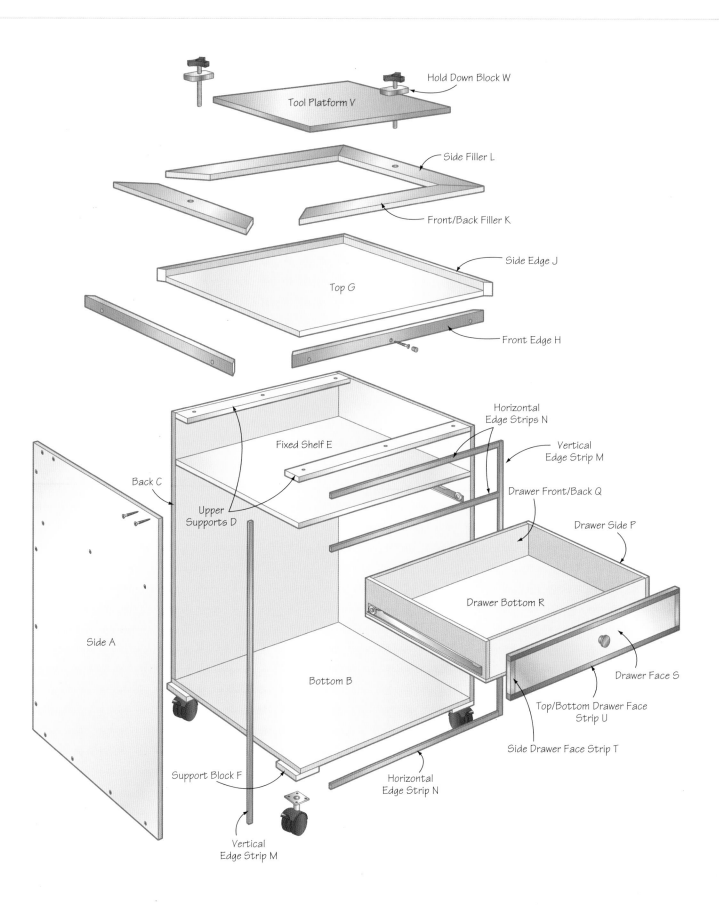

Hold Down Block W

Tool Platform V

Side Filler L

Front/Back Filler K

Side Edge J

Top G

Front Edge H

Horizontal
Edge Strips N

Fixed Shelf E

Vertical
Edge Strip M

Back C

Drawer Front/Back Q

Drawer Side P

Upper
Supports D

Side A

Drawer Bottom R

Bottom B

Drawer Face S

Top/Bottom Drawer Face
Strip U

Side Drawer Face Strip T

Support Block F

Horizontal
Edge Strip N

Vertical
Edge Strip M

REFERENCE	QUANTITY	PART	STOCK	THICKNESS	WIDTH	LENGTH	COMMENTS
A	2	sides	melamine PB	⁵/₈	20	32	
B	1	bottom	melamine PB	⁵/₈	20	26	
C	1	back	melamine PB	⁵/₈	26	31³/₈	
D	2	upper supports	melamine PB	⁵/₈	4	26	
E	1	fixed shelf	melamine PB	⁵/₈	19³/₈	26	
F	4	support blocks	hardwood	³/₄	3¹/₂	3¹/₂	
G	1	top	melamine PB	⁵/₈	21	30	
H	2	front & back edges	hardwood	³/₄	1³/₈	31¹/₂	angle-cut
J	2	side edges	hardwood	³/₄	1³/₈	22¹/₂	angle-cut
K	2	front & back top fillers	MDF	³/₄	2¹/₄	30	angle-cut
L	2	side fillers	MDF	³/₄	2¹/₄	21	angle-cut
M	2	vertical edge strips	hardwood	¹/₄	⁵/₈	32	
N	3	horizontal edge strips	hardwood	¹/₄	⁵/₈	26	
P	2	drawer sides	melamine PB	⁵/₈	4³/₈	18	
Q	2	drawer front & back	melamine PB	⁵/₈	4³/₈	23³/₄	
R	1	drawer bottom	melamine PB	⁵/₈	18	25	
S	1	drawer face	melamine PB	⁵/₈	6¹/₂	26¹/₂	
T	2	side drawer face strips	hardwood	¹/₄	⁵/₈	6¹/₂	
U	2	top/bottom drawer face strips	hardwood	¹/₄	⁵/₈	27	
V	3	tool platforms	MDF	³/₄	16¹/₂	25¹/₂	
W	2	hold-down blocks	hardwood	³/₄	1¹/₂	3	

HARDWARE

4 Locking wheel casters

1 – 18" Drawer glide set

2 Knobs, ¹/₄"-diameter thread

2 Hanger bolts, 2¹/₂"-long x ¹/₄"-diameter thread

2 – ¹/₄" Metal washers

White iron-on edge tape

Screw cover caps

Screws as detailed

Glue

Wood plugs

2" Screws

Biscuits

Dowels

1¹/₄" Screws

1" Screws

Brad nails

Wood putty

⁵/₈" Screws

REFERENCE	QUANTITY	PART	STOCK	THICKNESS	WIDTH	LENGTH	COMMENTS
A	2	sides	melamine PB	16	508	813	
B	1	bottom	melamine PB	16	508	660	
C	1	back	melamine PB	16	660	797	
D	2	upper supports	melamine PB	16	102	660	
E	1	fixed shelf	melamine PB	16	493	660	
F	4	support blocks	hardwood	19	89	89	
G	1	top	melamine PB	16	533	762	
H	2	front & back edges	hardwood	19	35	800	angle-cut
J	2	side edges	hardwood	19	35	572	angle-cut
K	2	front & back top fillers	MDF	19	57	762	angle-cut
L	2	side fillers	MDF	19	57	533	angle-cut
M	2	vertical edge strips	hardwood	6	16	813	
N	3	horizontal edge strips	hardwood	6	16	660	
P	2	drawer sides	melamine PB	16	112	457	
Q	2	drawer front & back	melamine PB	16	112	603	
R	1	drawer bottom	melamine PB	16	457	635	
S	1	drawer face	melamine PB	16	165	673	
T	2	side drawer face strips	hardwood	6	16	165	
U	2	top/bottom drawer face strips	hardwood	6	16	686	
V	3	tool platforms	MDF	19	419	648	
W	2	hold-down blocks	hardwood	19	38	76	

HARDWARE

4 Locking wheel casters

1 – 457mm Drawer glide set

2 Knobs, 6mm-diameter thread

2 Hanger bolts, 64mm-long x 6mm-diameter thread

2 – 6mm Metal washers

White iron-on edge tape

Screw cover caps

Screws as detailed

Glue

Wood plugs

51mm Screws

Biscuits

Dowels

32mm Screws

25mm Screws

Brad nails

Wood putty

16mm Screws

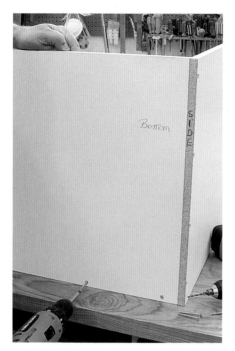

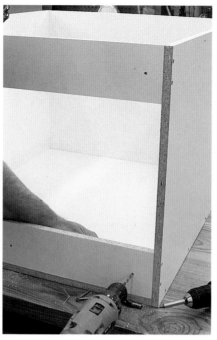

STEP 1 ■ Cut the sides A, bottom B and back C to the sizes listed in the materials list using ⅝" melamine PB. Attach the sides to the bottom board using 2" PB screws in pilot holes spaced 6" apart. The inset backboard is also attached with screws through the side and bottom boards.

The joinery can be done with PB screws, biscuits or dowels and glue. The screw heads can be covered with plastic or self-adhesive cover caps.

STEP 2 ■ The two upper supports D are added so the cabinet sides remain parallel at the top. They will also be used to secure the top board. Cut the two supports to length, installing the front board flush with the edges of the side panels. Secure the boards with 2" PB screws, placed 1" in from each edge to avoid splitting the boards. Drill through-holes for the screws, which will be used to secure the top.

STEP 3 ■ The middle fixed shelf E is installed 6" below the bottom surface of the upper supports. Holding a shelf accurately in place is difficult, so I've cut two 24⅛"-high temporary spacers to properly locate the shelf. Use a square to mark the screw position in the center of the fixed shelf's edge on the side and back panels. Drive 2" screws, in pilot holes, through the panels to secure the shelf. Cover the screw heads with caps.

STEP 4 ■ Attach four caster support blocks F on the corners of the cabinet. Position the blocks so the outside edges are flush with the outside edges of the cabinet. Use 2" screws on the outside edges through the blocks and into the back or side boards. The inner edges are secured with 1¼" screws into the bottom board.

Shop Tip

Many woodworkers have a sliding table for crosscutting panels; however, it isn't safe to use the fence and another guide device when crosscutting because there's a possibility that the board will bind in the blade and be thrown backwards. Instead you can use the measuring feature on your saw fence by adding a stop block. The panel being cut on a sliding table will leave the block before it completes

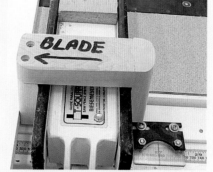

the cut, making the operation safe. Remember to add 1" (with a 1"-thick block) to the fence distance to account for the stop-block thickness.

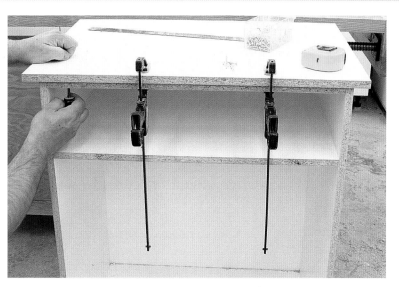

STEP 5 ▪ Mount four locking casters on the blocks using 1¼" screws or lag bolts.

STEP 6 ▪ Attach the cabinet top G with an overhang of ½" on the front and back. The sides will have an overhang of 1⅜". Use 1" screws through the upper supports D to secure the top board.

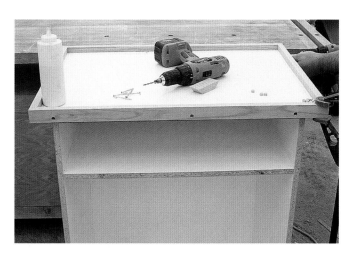

STEP 7 ▪ The top board G is banded with ¾"-thick by 1⅜"-high hardwood. The hardwood edge is flush with the bottom face of the top board and ¾" above the top's surface. Cut the corners of the hardwood banding at 45° and secure them with biscuits and glue or, as I'm using, screws and glue. Fill the counterbored holes with wood plugs and sand smooth.

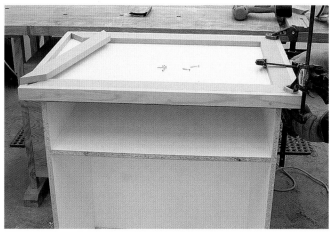

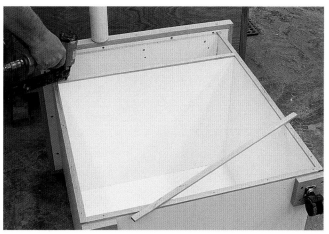

STEP 8 ▪ The tabletop fillers K and L are ¾" MDF. One sheet of 4x8 MDF has enough material for six tool platforms as well as the 2¼"-wide filler boards. The corners are joined at 45°, and the fillers are held in place with 1¼" screws from the underside of the tabletop.

STEP 9 ▪ Lay the cabinet on its back and trim the edges with ¼"-thick by ⅝"-wide hardwood strips M and N. Attach the strips with glue and brad nails. Fill the nail holes with wood putty and sand smooth.

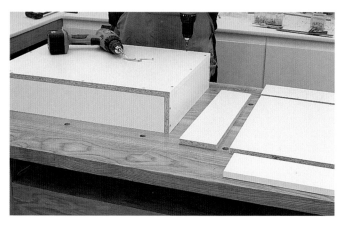

STEP 10 ▪ The next step is to build an accessory drawer under the fixed shelf. The drawer box is 5" high by 18" deep and 1" narrower than the inside cabinet width, or 25". It will be installed with bottom-mounted $^3/_4$-extension drawer glides. The drawer box is constructed using $^5/_8$"-thick melamine PB.

Cut the drawer sides P, front and back Q and drawer bottom R. Use iron-on edge tape to cover the top edges of the sides, back and front boards, as well as the side edges of the bottom board.

STEP 11 ▪ Attach the drawer box sides to the back and front boards using 2" PB screws in pilot holes. Attach the bottom using 2" PB screws.

STEP 13 ▪ The drawer face S is 2" wider and 2" higher than the drawer box, or 27" wide by 7" high. The drawer face is trimmed with $^1/_4$"-thick by $^5/_8$"-wide hardwood strips. To arrive at the final height, cut the melamine PB center $^1/_2$" less in width and height.

Attach the edge strips T and U with glue and brad nails. Fill the holes with wood putty and sand the edges smooth.

STEP 12 ▪ Install the drawer glide hardware following the manufacturer's instructions. The cabinet runners are installed with the bottom track 6" below the fixed storage shelf E. Use a carpenter's square to draw a screw-hole reference line or a drawer glide-mounting jig to install the runners with $^5/_8$" screws.

STEP 14 ▪ Attach the face to the drawer box using 1" screws through the back side of the drawer box front board. I drill the handle hole (or holes) in my drawer face and drive a screw through that hole to temporarily secure the face board in the proper position. Then I gently open the drawer and install the 1" screws through the back. Once the face is secure, I remove the screw from the handle hole and drill completely through the drawer box to install a knob or handle.

STEP 15 ■ The tool platforms V are ³/₄"-thick MDF. I cut three platforms for each of my two mobile tool stations. However, you can make as many as you need to mount your power tools. A platform without a tool can be used as a mobile worktable when needed.

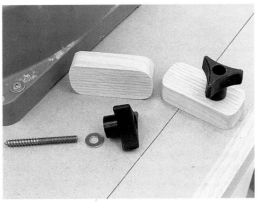

STEP 16 ■ The tool platforms are held in place with a simple lock assembly. Screw a 2¹/₂"-long by ¹/₄"-diameter hanger bolt into the side fillers, 1" back from the inside edge. Cut and round over the corners of a ³/₄"-thick by 3"-long piece of hardwood. Drill a ⁵/₁₆"-diameter hole in this hold-down block W, 1" from an end, and slip it over the hanger bolt. Place a metal washer on the bolt and attach a ¹/₄"-diameter threaded knob. One block on each side will secure the tool platform when the knobs are tightened.

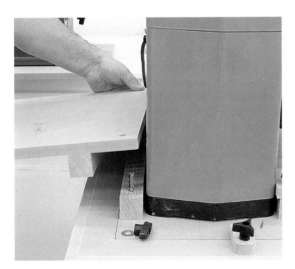

STEP 17 ■ Benchtop power tools, like the planer shown in this photograph, require infeed and outfeed tables. If they were fixed in place, the tool would be larger than the platform's footprint, making storage difficult. You can easily build removable platforms using hanger bolts, spacer cleats and knobs. In this example my feed tables are longer than the factory-supplied models and will provide more support for the material being machined.

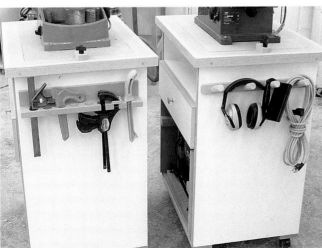

STEP 18 ■ Dozens of different tool holders can be attached to the sides of your mobile power tool cabinets. Extension cords, safety equipment and other accessories required when working with different benchtop power tools can be installed.

Most of the benchtop power tools in my shop will fit on the 16¹/₂"-deep by 25¹/₂"-wide platforms; however, the cabinet size should meet your needs. Build it to the dimensions shown in this chapter or change the width, height or depth as needed. If you do alter the platform size, be sure it will fit in the lower section of the cabinet to take advantage of all the storage space.

I used melamine particleboard and medium-density fiberboard, but any sheet material you feel comfortable with will work just as well. I like these materials because they are inexpensive and, in the case of melamine PB, already finished with a tough coating. Both materials can be securely joined using PB screws.

These power tool stations are mobile but can be made stationary by replacing the wheels with a fixed base. They'll work just as well against a wall if you have the space available. I opted for mobile units because they can be tucked away under the wings of my power miter saw station, built in chapter three.

Power Tool Storage Station

The multifunction power tool cabinets I built in chapter four are great. So great, in fact, that I've mounted a number of my benchtop tools on the interchangeable table inserts. However, I discovered that I needed more storage space for these tools on platforms.

I didn't want a cabinet that took up a lot of valuable space in my shop, so I designed this tall storage station. It uses less than 3' square of shop floor to store a number of power tools. This storage station is the perfect companion to the tool cabinet in chapter four.

The station is built with ⅝"-thick melamine particleboard (PB) and has holes drilled 2" apart for plastic-covered steel shelf pins. The pins can be placed in any of the vertical holes, allowing you to design your own storage arrangement.

You don't have to remove the benchtop tools from their drop-in platforms; they slide right into the storage station on the steel pins. Each platform rests on six shelf pins, so they are well supported.

The tool station can be made with less than two sheets of material, which means it's not expensive to build. The tools mounted to the platforms drop into the multifunction cabinet and you're ready to work. Fast access to tools, compact storage and a reasonable construction cost make this storage station well worth building. It can also be used with shelf boards for other shop tools, even if you don't build the multifunction cabinet in chapter four. Simply cut shelf boards to fit and locate the pins to suit your storage requirements.

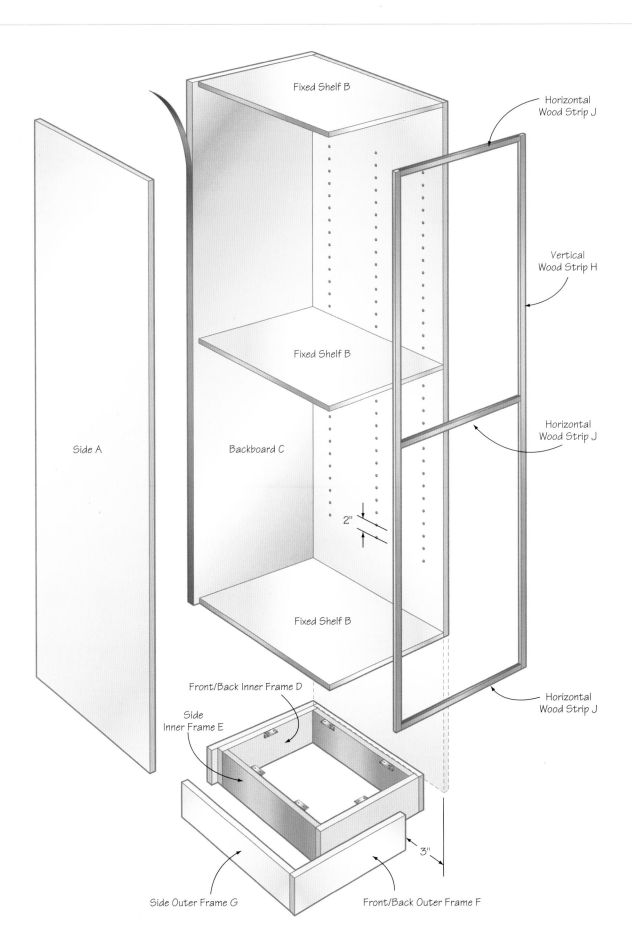

Fixed Shelf B

Horizontal
Wood Strip J

Fixed Shelf B

Vertical
Wood Strip H

Side A

Backboard C

Horizontal
Wood Strip J

2"

Fixed Shelf B

Front/Back Inner Frame D

Side
Inner Frame E

Horizontal
Wood Strip J

3"

Side Outer Frame G

Front/Back Outer Frame F

materials list ▪ INCHES

REFERENCE	QUANTITY	PART	STOCK	THICKNESS	WIDTH	LENGTH	COMMENTS
A	2	sides	melamine PB	5/8	25 1/2	84	
B	3	fixed shelves	melamine PB	5/8	16 9/16	25 1/2	
C	1	backboard	melamine PB	5/8	17 13/16	84	
D	2	front & back inner frame	melamine PB	5/8	3	16 9/16	
E	2	side inner frame	melamine PB	5/8	3	20	
F	2	front & back outer frame	melamine PB	5/8	3	17 13/16	
G	2	sides outer frame	melamine PB	5/8	3	21 1/4	
H	2	vertical wood strips	solid wood	1/4	5/8	84	
J	3	horizontal wood strips	solid wood	1/4	5/8	16 9/16	

HARDWARE

6 Metal right-angle brackets

Steel shelf pins as required

2" PB screws

Brad nails

Glue

White screw head cover caps

Iron-on edge tape

1" PB screws

5/8" Screws

Wood putty

materials list ▪ MILLIMETERS

REFERENCE	QUANTITY	PART	STOCK	THICKNESS	WIDTH	LENGTH	COMMENTS
A	2	sides	melamine PB	16	648	2134	
B	3	fixed shelves	melamine PB	16	420	648	
C	1	backboard	melamine PB	16	453	2134	
D	2	front & back inner frame	melamine PB	16	76	420	
E	2	sides inner frame	melamine PB	16	76	508	
F	2	front & back outer frame	melamine PB	16	76	453	
G	2	sides outer frame	melamine PB	16	76	539	
H	2	vertical wood strips	solid hardwood	6	16	2134	
J	3	horizontal wood strips	solid hardwood	6	16	420	

HARDWARE

6 Metal right-angle brackets

Steel shelf pins as required

51mm PB screws

Brad nails

Glue

White screw head cover caps

Iron-on edge tape

25mm PB screws

16mm Screws

Wood putty

STEP 1 ■ Cut the two sides A and drill holes for the steel shelf pins. The hole diameter should match the shelf pin you decide to use. There are three vertical rows of holes in each side; one is in the center of the panel and the other two are located 1½" in from the front and back edges. Space the holes 2" apart and begin drilling the columns 12" from the top and bottom.

I am using a shop jig made of ⅝"-thick melamine and a wood dowel as a drill depth limiter. The dowel stop is set 1⅛" above the drill end for a ½"-deep hole in the cabinet sides.

STEP 2 ■ The three fixed shelves B are located at the bottom, top and middle of each side panel. Use 2" PB screws in pilot holes to attach the two sides to the shelves. The screw heads can be covered with white cover caps, or you could use biscuits and glue if you don't want fasteners showing. The position of the middle shelf isn't critical as long as it's near the midpoint of the cabinet for side panel support.

STEP 3 ■ Cover both long edges of the backboard C with melamine iron-on edge tape. Attach the back to the cabinet carcass using 2" PB screws spaced about 8" apart. The carcass will be square if the backboard is cut square. You can ensure a proper fit by aligning one corner of the back with the carcass and securing it with a screw. Next, attach each of the following three corners in order, aligning and fastening each with a screw, then install the remaining screws between the corners.

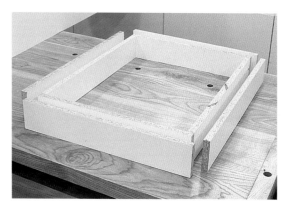

STEP 4 ■ The base frame is built with ⅝"-thick melamine PB. I normally build solid base platforms using two thicknesses of material. The 3"-high pieces of PB are often the waste or cutoffs after the carcass parts are cut, so doubling the base frame thickness is inexpensive insurance.

The inside frame is 16⁹⁄₁₆" wide by 21¼" deep, and the outside frame is 17¹³⁄₁₆" wide by 22½" deep because the frame is set 3" back from the front edge of the cabinet. The base frame will support the cabinet sides and transfer the load to the floor. Apply white edge tape to the outside edges of the back and front boards as these cut ends will be visible.

STEP 5 ■ Build the inner frame using 2" PB screws. The outer frame parts are secured to the inner frame with 1" PB screws through the back faces of the inner frame.

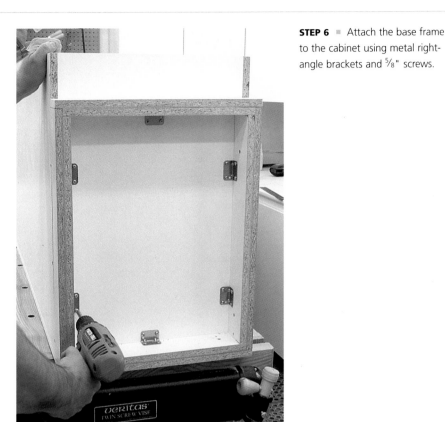

STEP 6 ▪ Attach the base frame to the cabinet using metal right-angle brackets and ⅝" screws.

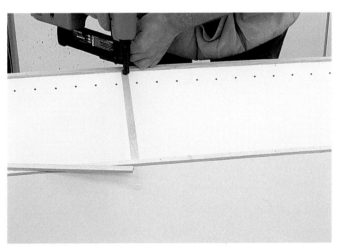

STEP 7 ▪ Glue and nail the wood strips H and J to the front edges of the cabinet sides and fixed shelves. Fill the nail holes with wood putty and sand smooth.

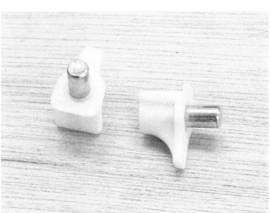

STEP 8 ▪ Use steel or plastic-covered steel shelf pins to properly support the tool platforms.

construction **NOTES**

This project is simple to build and has become a valuable space saver in my shop. I've used melamine PB, but the storage cabinet can be built with any sheet material, such as MDF or plywood.

Plastic adjustable cabinet legs can be used in place of the solid base frame. The legs are often installed when moisture is an issue in the shop. If your shop floor is uneven, plastic adjustable legs may be the obvious choice for your base.

As discussed, the position of the middle shelf isn't critical; however, take note of the benchtop tools you plan to store and secure the shelf close to the middle to maximize tool storage. Three of your benchtop tools on platforms may fit below the fixed shelf if it is positioned at a certain height. Measure the spaces required for your tools and position the shelf accordingly to maximize storage.

If dust is a serious problem in your shop, you might consider installing a door on the cabinet. The door width equals the cabinet's interior width plus 1" when using hidden hinges. The door height is the same as the cabinet side board's height. Using those calculations, you'll need a door that's 17⁹⁄₁₆" wide by 84" high. Drill 35mm-diameter holes, ⅛" from the edge of the door, and install the hinges as detailed in chapter one. Standard-opening hinges, in the 100° to 120° range, cannot be used because the door edge opens into the cabinet's interior space. Use the wide 170° hinges for this application to permit easy installation and removal of the tool platforms.

Mobile Table Saw Center

The first and most important issue you should deal with before starting construction on this Mobile Table Saw Center is the determination of the final table saw height. My saw table is 34" above the floor, which may not be suitable for everyone. The total height is the sum of the wheels, cabinet and benchtop saw heights.

Support your saw at different heights to find one that suits you, then, to determine the cabinet dimensions, subtract the height of the saw and wheels from the total height you've chosen.

Building a mobile table saw center for your benchtop table saw will improve the ease and accuracy of your work. It's well accepted that a good fence and sliding table or crosscut sled are valuable add-ons to any saw. Drawers for storage, a good dust collection system, quick access to accessories as well as the mobility feature combine to make using the saw fun and easy.

This cabinet top should accommodate any benchtop saw, but it's worth measuring yours before you start building the center. The cabinet length addresses a couple of issues. First, it allows you to store tools such as push sticks, hearing protection, miter slides and other often-used accessories in a place where they can be seen and easily accessed. Second, the top supports extended fence tables and protects the guide rail extensions. Finally, the cabinet is long enough for a dust chamber, two large drawers and a storage section with adjustable shelves.

My center will be used in a shop that needs access to a good saw once or twice a month. When the saw isn't needed, simply roll it against a wall or tuck it into an unused corner. If you have a small shop, use a table saw for your woodwork only on an occasional basis or share your garage shop with the family car, this project is for you.

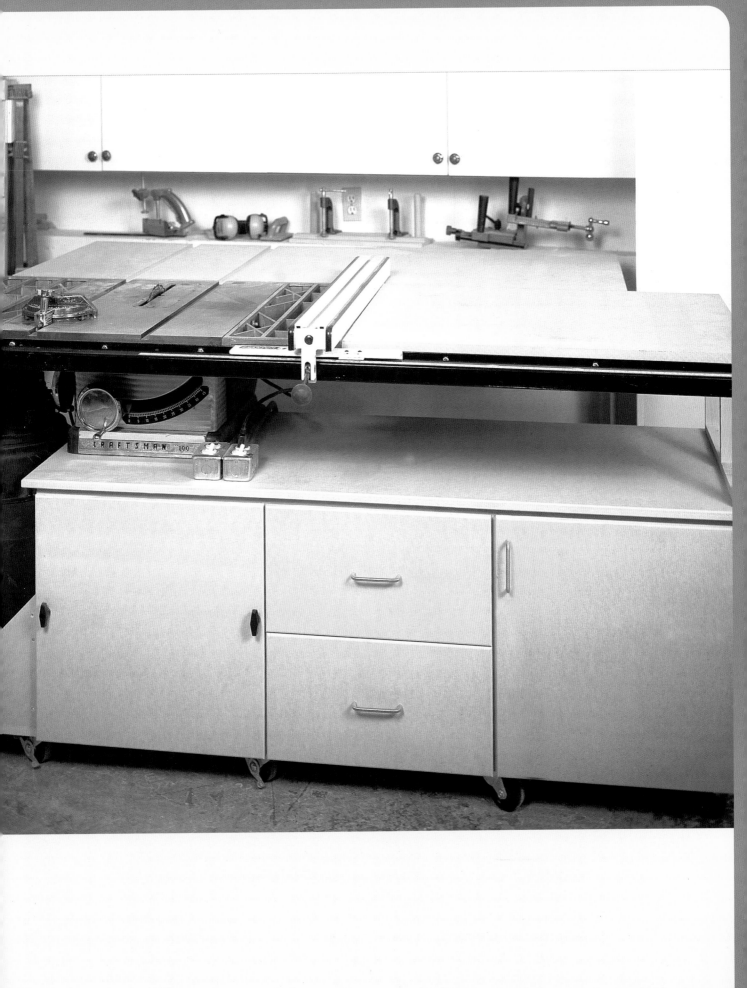

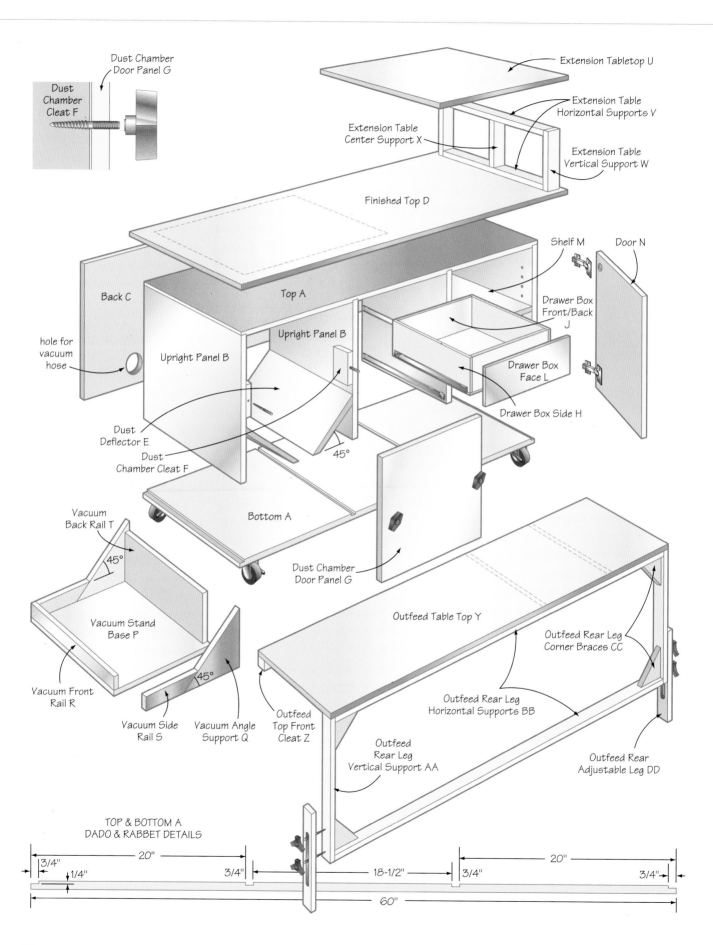

Dust Chamber
Door Panel G

Dust Chamber Cleat F

Dust
Chamber
Cleat F

Extension Tabletop U

Extension Table
Horizontal Supports V

Extension Table
Center Support X

Extension Table
Vertical Support W

Finished Top D

Back C

hole for
vacuum
hose

Top A

Upright Panel B

Upright Panel B

Dust
Deflector E

Dust
Chamber Cleat F

45°

Shelf M

Door N

Drawer Box
Front/Back
J

Drawer Box
Face L

Drawer Box Side H

Bottom A

Vacuum
Back Rail T

45°

Vacuum Stand
Base P

Dust Chamber
Door Panel G

Outfeed Table Top Y

Outfeed Rear Leg
Corner Braces CC

Outfeed Rear Leg
Horizontal Supports BB

Vacuum Front
Rail R

45°

Vacuum Side
Rail S

Vacuum Angle
Support Q

Outfeed
Top Front
Cleat Z

Outfeed
Rear Leg
Vertical Support AA

Outfeed Rear
Adjustable Leg DD

TOP & BOTTOM A
DADO & RABBET DETAILS

3/4"

20"

1/4"

3/4"

18-1/2"

3/4"

20"

3/4"

60"

REFERENCE	QUANTITY	PART	STOCK	THICKNESS	WIDTH	LENGTH	COMMENTS
A	2	top & bottom	MDF	$3/4$	$22^1/2$	60	
B	4	upright panels	MDF	$3/4$	$22^1/2$	16	
C	1	back	MDF	$3/4$	17	60	
D	1	finished top	MDF	$3/4$	25	62	
E	2	dust deflectors	MDF	$3/4$	10	$22^1/2$	angle-cut
F	2	dust chamber cleats	MDF	$3/4$	2	4	
G	1	dust chamber door panel	MDF	$3/4$	20	$16^1/2$	
H	4	drawer box sides	MDF	$3/4$	$5^1/4$	22	
J	4	drawer box fronts & backs	MDF	$3/4$	$5^1/4$	16	
K	2	drawer box bottoms	MDF	$3/4$	$17^1/2$	22	
L	2	drawer box faces	MDF	$3/4$	$8^3/16$	19	
M	1	shelf	MDF	$3/4$	$19^3/16$	$22^3/8$	
N	1	door	MDF	$3/4$	20	$16^1/2$	
P	1	vacuum stand base	MDF	$3/4$	18	$23^1/4$	
Q	2	vacuum angle supports	MDF	$3/4$	$11^1/4$	$11^1/4$	cut at 45°
R	1	vacuum front rail	MDF	$3/4$	3	$23^1/4$	
S	2	vacuum side rails	MDF	$3/4$	3	$8^3/4$	angle-cut
T	1	vacuum back rail	MDF	$3/4$	10	$21^3/4$	
U	1	extension tabletop	MDF	$3/4$	27	33	
V	2	ext. horizontal supports	hardwood	$3/4$	$1^1/2$	24	
W	2	ext. vertical supports	hardwood	$3/4$	$1^1/2$	12	
X	1	ext. center support	hardwood	$3/4$	$1^1/2$	$10^1/2$	
Y	1	outfeed tabletop	MDF	$3/4$	27	64	
Z	1	outfeed top front cleat	hardwood	$3/4$	$1^1/4$	64	
AA	2	rear leg vertical supports	hardwood	$3/4$	$1^1/2$	28	
BB	2	rear leg horizontal supports	hardwood	$3/4$	$1^1/2$	$62^1/2$	
CC	4	rear leg corner braces	hardwood	$3/4$	$5^1/4$	$5^1/4$	angle-cut
DD	2	rear adjustable legs	hardwood	$3/4$	$1^1/2$	16	

HARDWARE

8 Locking wheel casters

2 - 22" Drawer glide sets

Adjustable shelf pins as detailed

2 - 107° Hidden hinges

8 Knobs

8 Hanger bolts, 2"-long x $1/4$"-diameter thread

Door and drawer handles as detailed

Electrical switch, plug and junction boxes

Screws as detailed

Glue

2" PB screws

Biscuits

$1^1/4$" Screws

Brad nails

$5/8$" Screws

$1^1/2$" Screws

$1^1/2$"-Long by $1/4$"-diameter carriage bolts with washers & nuts

T-square fence system

2" Wood screws

REFERENCE	QUANTITY	PART	STOCK	THICKNESS	WIDTH	LENGTH	COMMENTS
A	2	top & bottom	MDF	19	572	1524	
B	4	upright panels	MDF	19	572	406	
C	1	back	MDF	19	432	1524	
D	1	finished top	MDF	19	635	1575	
E	2	dust deflectors	MDF	19	254	572	angle-cut
F	2	dust chamber cleats	MDF	19	51	102	
G	1	dust chamber door panel	MDF	19	508	419	
H	4	drawer box sides	MDF	19	133	559	
J	4	drawer box fronts & backs	MDF	19	133	406	
K	2	drawer box bottoms	MDF	19	445	559	
L	2	drawer box faces	MDF	19	208	483	
M	1	shelf	MDF	19	488	569	
N	1	door	MDF	19	508	419	
P	1	vacuum stand base	MDF	19	457	590	
Q	2	vacuum angle supports	MDF	19	285	285	cut at 45°
R	1	vacuum front rail	MDF	19	76	590	
S	2	vacuum side rails	MDF	19	76	222	angle-cut
T	1	vacuum back rail	MDF	19	254	552	
U	1	extension tabletop	MDF	19	686	838	
V	2	ext. horizontal supports	hardwood	19	38	610	
W	2	ext. vertical supports	hardwood	19	38	305	
X	1	ext. center supports	hardwood	19	38	267	
Y	1	outfeed tabletop	MDF	19	686	1626	
Z	1	outfeed top front cleat	hardwood	19	32	1626	
AA	2	rear leg vertical supports	hardwood	19	38	711	
BB	2	rear leg horizontal supports	hardwood	19	38	1588	
CC	4	rear leg corner braces	hardwood	19	133	133	angle-cut
DD	2	rear adjustable legs	hardwood	19	38	406	

HARDWARE

8 Locking wheel casters

2 - 559mm Drawer glide sets

Adjustable shelf pins as detailed

2 - 107° Hidden hinges

8 Knobs

8 Hanger bolts, 51mm-long x 6mm-diameter thread

Door and drawer handles as detailed

Electrical switch, plug and junction boxes

Screws as detailed

Glue

51mm PB screws

Biscuits

32mm Screws

Brad nails

16mm Screws

38mm Screws

38mm-Long by 6mm-diameter carriage bolts with washers & nuts

T-square fence system

51mm Wood screws

STEP 1 ■ Cut the top and bottom boards A to the size indicated in the materials list. Each panel requires two ¾"-wide dadoes and two ¾"-wide rabbets. All of the cuts are ¼" deep. Refer to the illustration for positioning.

STEP 2 ■ The four upright panels B are attached to the top and bottom boards in the dadoes and rabbets. Use glue and four 2" PB screws per end, in pilot holes, to secure the panels.

STEP 3 ■ The back C is attached to the carcass using biscuits and glue. If you don't have a biscuit joiner, screws and glue will work just as well.

STEP 4 ■ The finished top D is a ¾"-thick piece of MDF with the upper and lower edges rounded over. Use a ¼"-radius roundover bit in your router to ease these edges. The front and both sides overhang the cabinet carcass by 1". Use glue and 1¼" screws, from the underside, to attach the top board. Four screws per section will be enough to secure the top.

STEP 5 ■ The left-end compartment will be used as a dust collection chamber. Install the two deflectors E by first cutting the edges at 45° and securing them to the cabinet bottom board and panels using glue and brad nails.

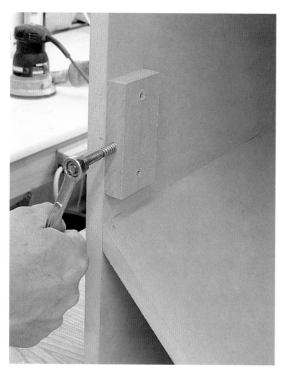

STEP 6 ▪ Two support cleats F are attached to the dust chamber side panels with glue and 1¼" screws. They are aligned flush with the front edges of the vertical panels. Drill pilot holes in the center edge of each cleat to accept the wood screw end of ¼"-diameter hanger bolts. Leave about 1" of the ¼"-diameter machine thread in front of the cleat's edge so a handle can be threaded onto the shaft.

STEP 7 ▪ Cut the dust chamber door panel G to the size indicated in the materials list and round over its front face edge with a ¼"-radius router bit. Hold the door so its bottom edge is flush with the bottom face of the bottom board and press it into the hanger bolts to mark their location. The door overlays each vertical partition by ⅜". Drill ⅜"-diameter holes in the panel and attach it to the cabinet with ¼" threaded knobs on the hanger bolts. The hanger bolts and knobs are available at many wood-working and home improvement stores.

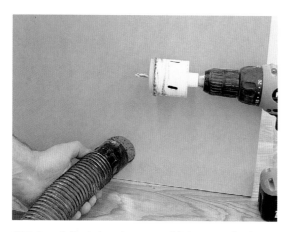

STEP 8 ▪ Drill a hole as low as possible between the dust chamber deflectors through the backboard of the cabinet. This hole will be used to attach a vacuum hose. My vacuum, along with many others on the market, comes with a 2¼"-outside-diameter hose. This is a common hose size, but you should check the size of your hose before drilling the hole. The hole diameter can be as large as 4", with an appropriate fitting, if you plan on using a large dust collection system.

STEP 9 ▪ The center section is 18½" wide and will contain two drawers. My drawer boxes are 17½" wide. They are 22"-deep by 6"-high, made with ¾"-thick MDF.

Cut all the drawer parts H, J and K and assemble by attaching the sides H to the back and front boards J using glue and 2" PB screws. Keep the screws at least 1" away from any edge to avoid splitting the MDF.

Once the sides are secured to the back and front boards, install the bottom using glue and screws. If the bottom board has been cut square, your drawer box will be square.

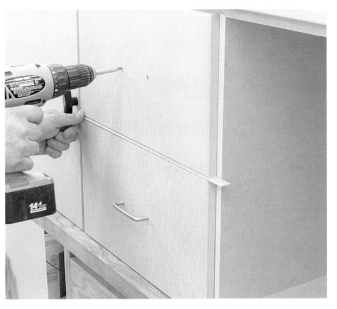

STEP 10 ▪ Install the drawer glides on the drawer boxes and inside the cabinet. Use ³⁄₄- or full-extension glides, installing them following the manufacturer's instructions. One set of glides is mounted at the bottom of the cabinet, and the other set is attached 8" above the bottom board.

STEP 11 ▪ The drawer faces L are secured to the drawer boxes using 1¹⁄₄" screws through the back face of each front drawer board. I made the total height of the two drawer faces the same as the dust chamber door. Leave a ¹⁄₈" gap between the faces so each one will measure 8³⁄₁₆" high. The drawer faces will overlay each vertical partition edge by ¹⁄₄" so the faces are 19" wide.

Use a ¹⁄₄" roundover router bit to ease the front face edges of each door panel, then install the handles of your choice.

STEP 12 ▪ You can add an adjustable shelf to the right-side compartment if required. For drilling the shelf-pin holes, you can make a jig with a 3"-wide by 15¹⁄₂"-high piece of ³⁄₄"-thick sheet material scrap. Drill a series of holes in the jig, spacing them about 1¹⁄₄" apart. Place a short piece of wood dowel on the drill bit, leaving about 1¹⁄₄" of drill bit exposed. Drill two columns of holes in each vertical partition in that section using the jig and drill stop. You'll get accurately aligned holes without drilling all the way through the cabinet sides.

STEP 13 ▪ Cut the shelf board M to size. Install adjustable shelf pins in the holes and put the shelf in place.

STEP 15 ■ The left side of this saw cabinet has a platform that will hold my vacuum cleaner. Check the dimensions of your vacuum cleaner to verify it will fit before cutting the parts.

I have cut and attached two support boards Q, cut in the shape of a triangle, to help secure the platform. Use glue and 2" screws to attach the angle supports to the stand base.

STEP 14 ■ The right-end cabinet door N is made of ³/₄" MDF with the front face edges rounded over using a ¹/₄"-radius router bit. It's 16¹/₂" high to align with the tops of the drawer faces, and is mounted using 107° full-overlay hidden hinges. Normally, door width is determined by adding 1" to the interior dimension of the cabinet. However, I'm sharing a partition with the drawer faces, so I've added ³/₄" to the interior width so my door will be 20" wide. Drill two 35mm holes, 4" from the top and bottom edges, with the holes ¹/₈" from the door edge. Install the hinges with mounting plates attached.

Hold the door in the open position, 90° to the face of the cabinet, and put a ¹/₈" spacer between the door and cabinet edge. Drive ⁵/₈" screws through the plates to secure the hinges to the cabinet sides. Check the door fit and adjust.

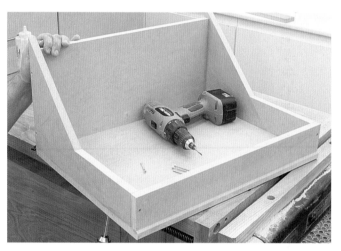

STEP 16 ■ The rails R, S and T are 3" high and attached to the base with screws and glue. The front and back rails are straight, while the side rails are angle-cut on one end at 45° to meet the angle supports.

STEP 17 ■ Attach the vacuum stand to the cabinet carcass, aligning it flush with the underside of the bottom board. Use 1¹/₂" screws through the back rail into the cabinet side boards to secure the platform.

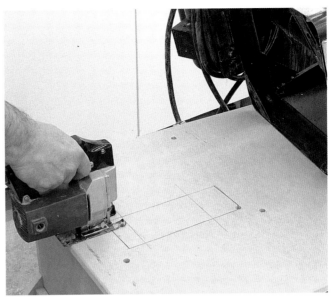

STEP 18 ■ I used 4"-high, heavy-duty locking wheels on my saw station. They are attached with 1½"-long by ¼"-diameter carriage bolts through the cabinet base board. The wheels are located directly under the center panels and as close to the right end as possible. The left-end casters are positioned halfway under the cabinet, and the other half of the caster flange supports the vacuum stand. Push the carriage bolts through the holes in the base board and secure the casters with washers and nuts.

STEP 19 ■ Locate your benchtop saw on top of the cabinet, above the dust chamber where it will be permanently attached. The table saw blade throws most of its dust ahead and directly below the blade. Mark the hold-down bolt locations as well as the leading edge position of the saw blade on the cabinet top. Cut a large hole in the tabletop through the two layers into the dust chamber. Most of the dust will be directed into the hole by the blade, and the vacuum cleaner will draw air through that hole to collect the dust. Test the dust collection and adjust the hole size if necessary.

STEP 20 ■ I wired my saw to a switch with a power-indicator light. Your saw may already have a switch, so this step won't be needed. However, if you do need one and are uncomfortable with electrical wiring, call a professional.

I also installed a switched plug to control my vacuum cleaner. Both electrical boxes are surface mounted to the cabinet top in front of the table saw.

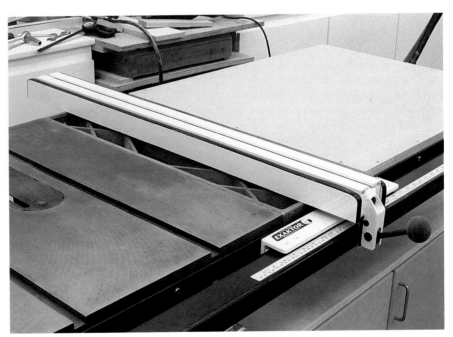

STEP 21 ■ The best upgrade for your table saw is a high-quality T-square fence system. Older saws often had poorly designed fences that were sometimes hard to keep in adjustment and required constant maintenance. The new fences are accurate, well built and easy to align. Many of the new T-square fence systems, like this model from Exaktor Woodworking Tools, come with a rear angle bar that provides support for an extended table.

STEP 22 ■ The extension table material is ¾"-thick MDF with a hardwood frame. The length of panel U will depend on the model of T-square fence you purchase and the remaining distance on your cabinet after a table saw has been installed.

STEP 23 ■ The outfeed table is also made with ¾"-thick MDF. The front edge that rests on the table saw support bracket has a hardwood spacer, cleat Z, to level the outfeed tabletop's surface to the bench saw top surface. I will be supporting the front edge of my outfeed table on the angle bar that was supplied with the T-square fence I installed. If you don't have the fence upgrade, attach metal angle stock or a hardwood cleat to the back of your saw.

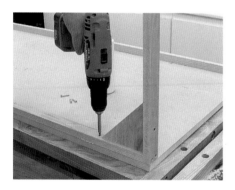

STEP 24 ■ The rear leg assembly (AA and BB) is made with ¾"-thick by 1½"-wide hardwood. Use 2" wood screws and glue to build the assembly. I wanted to keep the weight to a minimum, so I used this light-duty leg system. Most of the support will be provided at the front edge of this table because it's attached to the saw. When not in use, lower the saw blade and move your fence to the far right end of the saw, then rest the table on top and wheel the workstation to its storage area.

The frame is about three-quarters of the distance between the floor and underside of the outfeed table, or 28" in my case. Attach the leg frame to the underside of the outfeed table with glue and 1¼" screws.

STEP 25 ■ Cut two adjustable legs DD about 16" long and rout a ¼"-wide slot in the center of each one starting and stopping 2" from each end. Use ¼"-diameter hanger bolts and knobs to attach the adjustable legs to the leg frame. Position the hanger bolts so they can be adjusted 2" above and below the correct table height, assuming the workstation is resting on a level floor.

STEP 26 ■ Install two ¼"-diameter hanger bolts into the bottom edge of the front support cleat on the outfeed table. Align the table on the rear support of your saw and drill a ⅜"-diameter hole at each end to match the position of the hanger bolts. Attach the outfeed table to the saw by placing the hanger bolt shafts in the holes and securing them with the proper-size knobs.

STEP 27 ▪ Rout slots in the outfeed table in line with the table saw's miter slide slots.

You will need about four sheets of ¾"-thick MDF and one 10' length of 1x6 hardwood for the cabinet construction, plus the hardware as noted.

I used MDF, but any sheet material is suitable, so pick one that meets your budget and preference. Melamine particleboard would be a good choice or, if you prefer, any plywood with a smooth surface.

This is the perfect saw cabinet if your workshop is located in a garage. At the end of each woodworking session the entire station can be quickly pushed against a wall. The cabinet can be used as a static saw station by replacing the wheels with a simple base frame.

Final table saw height is the most important issue to deal with before starting construction. There are many types of benchtop saws and all of them are different heights and widths. The cabinet tabletop should be suitable for most saws, if not all, but it would be wise to verify the depth of your equipment before cutting the sheet material to size. Wheel assemblies also come in different heights, so purchase the style you want before starting the project.

STEP 28 ▪ If you plan on doing a lot of crosscutting on your saw workstation, consider buying one of the new sliding table systems. They increase the flexibility of the saw and let you cut wide panels easily and with increased safety. Some of the table systems, like this Exaktor EX26 table, have a release feature that will let you quickly install and remove the unit without disturbing any adjustments.

STEP 29 ▪ The extended side table is a great place to install a router. The workstation can then be used for sawing and router work because the T-square fence system is used for both operations.

BUILDING A TABLE SAW CROSSCUTTING SLED

materials list ▪ **INCHES**

QUANTITY	PART	STOCK	THICKNESS	WIDTH	LENGTH	COMMENTS
1	platform	plywood	$^3/_4$	30	36	
2	runners	hardwood	$^3/_8$	$^3/_4$	30	
2	fences	2x4 stock	$1^1/_2$	$3^1/_2$	36	
1	blade guard	2x4 stock	$1^1/_2$	$3^1/_2$	10	

HARDWARE

1" Screws

Glue

materials list ▪ **MILLIMETERS**

QUANTITY	PART	STOCK	THICKNESS	WIDTH	LENGTH	COMMENTS
1	platform	plywood	19	762	914	
2	runners	hardwood	10	19	762	
2	fences	2x4 stock	38	89	914	
1	blade guard	2x4 stock	38	89	254	

HARDWARE

25mm Screws

Glue

A crosscutting sled is one of the handiest and safest table saw accessories you'll ever own. It is simple to build and a real pleasure to use when cutting wide panels.

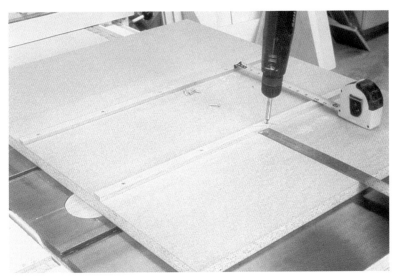

STEP 1 ▪ Cut the platform, making sure it's accurately sized and square. Cut the two hardwood runners and test fit them in the table saw miter grooves. A proper fit will allow the runners to run freely with minimal side play. Attach the runners to the platform with 1" screws and glue. Make sure they're accurately spaced to match the table saw grooves.

STEP 2 ▪ Using your saw fence and a framing square, install the back rail with screws and glue and align it at 90° to the fence.

STEP 3 ▪ Install the front rail using the same procedures.

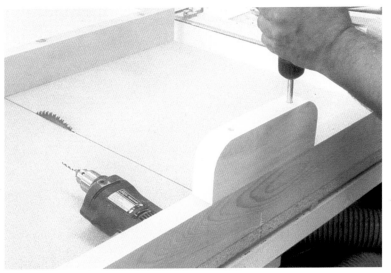

STEP 4 ▪ Attach the blade guard centered over the blade on the back rail. Round over each end of the guard board with a belt sander to eliminate the sharp corners.

Router Table Cabinet

I've seen a lot of router table systems, tried many and had a number of different designs in my shop over the years. However, I always found something lacking in the designs and often promised myself that I would build a router table cabinet to suit my needs one day. Well, that day has arrived, and I'm pleased with the results.

My list of design demands included an adjustable fence that had an opening range of at least 12". How many times have you wanted to run a groove in a wide board and couldn't because your router fence system opened only a couple of inches? My dream table had to have a miter slide track, be at least 35" high and have a large, solid-surface table to support boards properly. I was really tired of balancing large panels on small flimsy tables.

Accessory storage and proper dust collection rounded out my list of "wants" for the ideal router cabinet. I hesitate to say ultimate router station because there's always something miss-ing that I'll discover later, but this cabinet is close to perfect for my work and it didn't cost a fortune to build.

I used ¾"-thick MDF sheet material. It's a great board for this application because the MDF is heavy, which will keep the cabinet stable, and it's easy to machine. I've detailed two leg options, one for a movable cabinet and the other for a cabinet that will be permanently located. The knobs and aluminum tracks are available at all wood-working outlets and are reasonably priced.

Have fun building of this router cabinet. You'll have easy access to the router and good dust collection. I'm sure you'll appreciate the bit storage slide-outs and great storage drawers for all your router accessories.

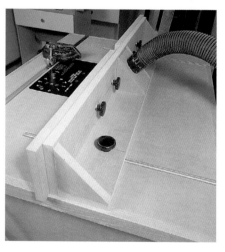

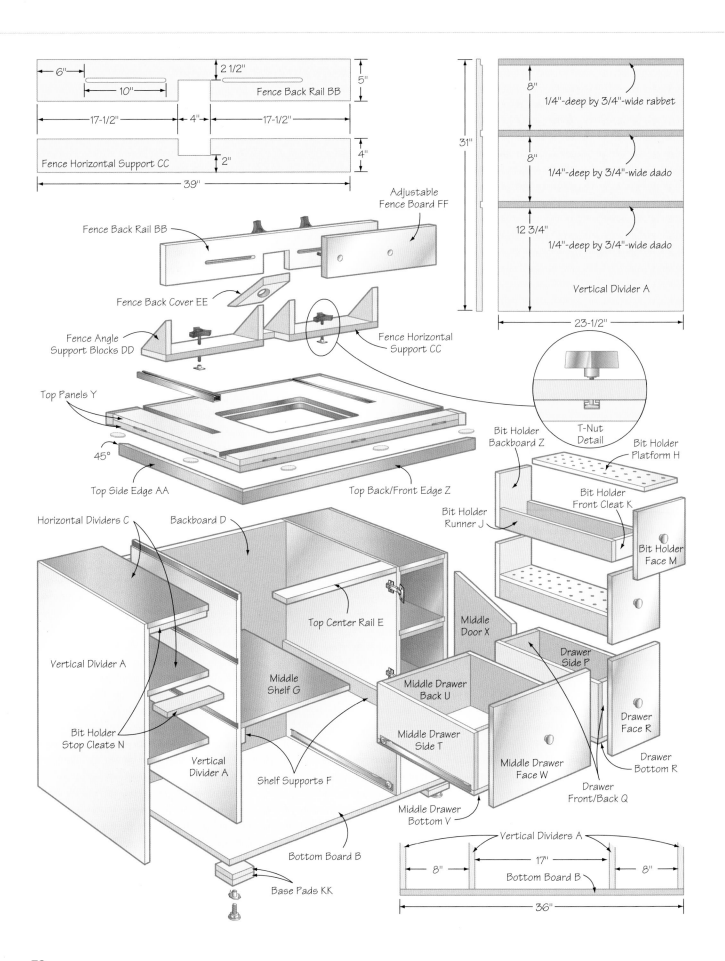

6"

10"

2 1/2"

5"

Fence Back Rail BB

17-1/2"

4"

17-1/2"

Fence Horizontal Support CC

2"

4"

39"

31"

8"

1/4"-deep by 3/4"-wide rabbet

8"

1/4"-deep by 3/4"-wide dado

12 3/4"

1/4"-deep by 3/4"-wide dado

Vertical Divider A

23-1/2"

Fence Back Rail BB

Adjustable
Fence Board FF

Fence Back Cover EE

Fence Angle
Support Blocks DD

Fence Horizontal
Support CC

T-Nut
Detail

Top Panels Y

45°

Top Side Edge AA

Top Back/Front Edge Z

Bit Holder
Backboard Z

Bit Holder
Platform H

Bit Holder
Front Cleat K

Bit Holder
Runner J

Bit Holder
Face M

Horizontal Dividers C

Backboard D

Top Center Rail E

Middle
Door X

Middle Drawer
Back U

Drawer
Side P

Vertical Divider A

Middle
Shelf G

Drawer
Face R

Bit Holder
Stop Cleats N

Vertical
Divider A

Middle Drawer
Side T

Shelf Supports F

Middle Drawer
Face W

Drawer
Bottom R

Drawer
Front/Back Q

Bottom Board B

Middle Drawer
Bottom V

Vertical Dividers A

Base Pads KK

8"

17"

8"

Bottom Board B

36"

materials list ▪ **INCHES**

REFERENCE	QUANTITY	PART	STOCK	THICKNESS	WIDTH	LENGTH	COMMENTS
A	4	vertical dividers	MDF	3/4	23 1/2	31	
B	1	bottom board	MDF	3/4	23 1/2	36	
C	6	horizontal dividers	MDF	3/4	8 1/2	23 1/2	
D	1	backboard	MDF	3/4	31 3/4	36	
E	1	top center rail	MDF	3/4	3	17	
F	2	shelf supports	MDF	3/4	3	23 1/2	
G	1	middle shelf	MDF	3/4	17	23 1/2	
H	4	bit holder platforms	MDF	3/4	7 15/16	22	
J	8	bit holder runners	MDF	3/4	2 1/2	22	
K	4	bit holder front cleats	MDF	3/4	2 1/2	6 7/16	
L	4	bit holder backboards	MDF	3/4	7 15/16	7 15/16	
M	4	bit holder front faces	MDF	3/4	9	8 1/2	
N	4	bit holder stop cleats	MDF	3/4	2	8	
P	4	drawer sides	MDF	3/4	9 1/4	22	
Q	4	drawer fronts & backs	MDF	3/4	9 1/4	5 1/2	
R	2	drawer bottoms	MDF	3/4	7	22	
S	2	drawer faces	MDF	3/4	9	13 7/8	
T	2	middle drawer sides	MDF	3/4	7 3/4	22	
U	2	drawer front & back	MDF	3/4	7 3/4	14 1/2	
V	1	drawer bottom	MDF	3/4	16	22	
W	1	middle drawer face	MDF	3/4	17 3/4	13 7/8	
X	1	middle door	MDF	3/4	17 3/4	17 1/4	
Y	2	top panels	MDF	3/4	37 3/4	27 3/4	
Z	2	top back & front edges	hardwood	3/4	1 1/2	39 1/4	
AA	2	top side edges	hardwood	3/4	1 1/2	29 1/4	
BB	1	fence back rail	MDF	3/4	5	39	
CC	1	fence horizontal support	MDF	3/4	4	39	
DD	4	fence angle support blocks	MDF	3/4	4	4	angle-cut
EE	1	fence back cover	MDF	3/4	4	5 1/4	angle-cut
FF	2	adjustable fence boards	MDF	3/4	5	19 1/2	

BASE OPTION #1

REFERENCE	QUANTITY	PART	STOCK	THICKNESS	WIDTH	LENGTH	COMMENTS
GG	2	sides	MDF	3/4	3	20	
HH	2	front & back boards	MDF	3/4	3	4 1/2	
JJ	1	top	MDF	3/4	6	20	
	2	heavy-duty wheels, 3 3/4" high					

BASE OPTION #2

REFERENCE	QUANTITY	PART	STOCK	THICKNESS	WIDTH	LENGTH	COMMENTS
KK	8	base pads	MDF	3/4	3	3	
	4	metal adjustable leveling feet					

HARDWARE

4 Drawer knobs or pulls

3 Sets of 22" drawer glides

2 - 107° Hidden hinges and plates

1 - 48"-Long aluminum miter slide track

1 - 48"-Long aluminum T-track

6 - 1" by 1/4"-Diameter threaded knobs

1 Power bar with switch

1 1/2" PB screws as detailed

5/8" PB screws as detailed

Glue

Pocket screws

Brad nails

2" Screws

T-nuts

REFERENCE	QUANTITY	PART	STOCK	THICKNESS	WIDTH	LENGTH	COMMENTS
A	4	vertical dividers	MDF	19	597	787	
B	1	bottom board	MDF	19	597	914	
C	6	horizontal dividers	MDF	19	216	597	
D	1	backboard	MDF	19	806	914	
E	1	top center rail	MDF	19	76	432	
F	2	shelf supports	MDF	19	76	597	
G	1	middle shelf	MDF	19	432	597	
H	4	bit holder platforms	MDF	19	202	559	
J	8	bit holder runners	MDF	19	64	559	
K	4	bit holder front cleats	MDF	19	64	163	
L	4	bit holder backboards	MDF	19	202	202	
M	4	bit holder front faces	MDF	19	229	216	
N	4	bit holder stop cleats	MDF	19	51	203	
P	4	drawer sides	MDF	19	235	559	
Q	4	drawer fronts & backs	MDF	19	235	140	
R	2	drawer bottoms	MDF	19	178	559	
S	2	drawer faces	MDF	19	229	352	
T	2	middle drawer sides	MDF	19	197	559	
U	2	drawer front & back	MDF	19	197	369	
V	1	drawer bottom	MDF	19	406	559	
W	1	middle drawer face	MDF	19	451	352	
X	1	middle door	MDF	19	451	438	
Y	2	top panels	MDF	19	959	705	
Z	2	top back & front edges	hardwood	19	38	997	
AA	2	top side edges	hardwood	19	38	743	
BB	1	fence back rail	MDF	19	127	991	
CC	1	fence horizontal support	MDF	19	102	991	
DD	4	fence angle support blocks	MDF	19	102	102	angle-cut
EE	1	fence back cover	MDF	19	102	133	angle-cut
FF	2	adjustable fence boards	MDF	19	127	496	

BASE OPTION #1

GG	2	sides	MDF	19	76	508	
HH	2	front & back boards	MDF	19	76	115	
JJ	1	top	MDF	19	152	508	
	2	heavy-duty wheels, 95mm high					

BASE OPTION #2

KK	8	base pads	MDF	19	76	76	
	4	metal adjustable leveling feet					

HARDWARE

4 Drawer knobs or pulls

3 Sets of 559mm drawer glides

2 - 107° Hidden hinges and plates

1 - 1219mm-Long aluminum miter slide track

1 - 1219mm-Long aluminum T-track

6 - 25mm by 6mm-Diameter threaded knobs

1 Power bar with switch

38mm PB screws as detailed

16mm PB screws as detailed

Glue

Pocket screws

Brad nails

51mm Screws

T-nuts

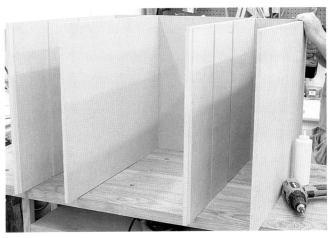

STEP 1 ■ Prepare the four vertical dividers A by cutting them to size and forming the dadoes and rabbets in each panel as shown. All the rabbets and dadoes are ¾" wide by ¼" deep.

STEP 2 ■ The bottom board B is secured to the dividers with glue and 1½" screws in pilot holes. Align the two sets of dividers, spaced 8" apart, with the dadoes and rabbets facing each other. The middle section should be 17" wide between panels. Keep the screws 1" away from any panel end and use four screws per divider, driven through the bottom board.

STEP 3 ■ Install the six horizontal dividers C in the dadoes and rabbets. Use glue and clamps to secure the sections.

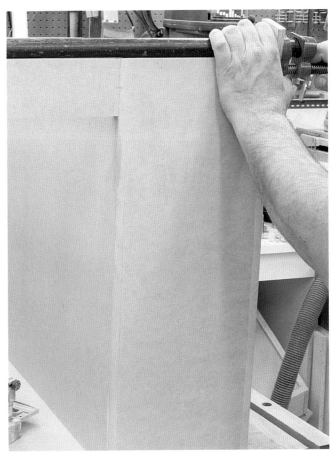

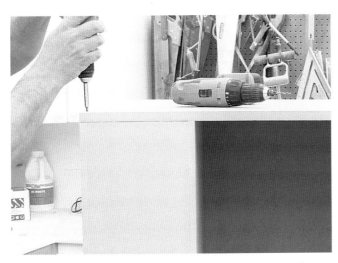

STEP 4 ■ Attach the backboard D to the cabinet using glue and 1½" screws. If you've carefully cut the back panel square, the cabinet will be properly aligned.

STEP 5 ■ The top center rail E is attached with one ¾"-thick edge facing forward. Secure it with biscuits, or pocket screws and glue if you don't have a biscuit joiner. This rail will be attached to the underside of the tabletop.

This cabinet is on its back with the top facing the camera.

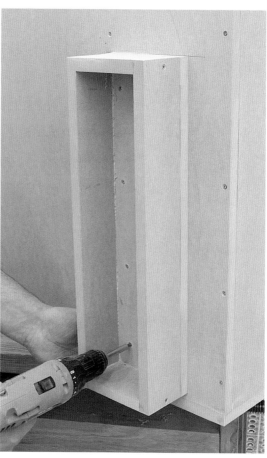

STEP 7 ▪ The other half of base option #1 is a box made with ³⁄₄" MDF using the parts GG, HH and JJ. It's attached to the bottom of the cabinet with 1¹⁄₄" screws and glue. If the cabinet has to be moved often, you can lift the fixed base end and push it along the floor on the wheels.

The height of my fixed base portion is 3³⁄₄" to match the wheel height. If you do use this setup, purchase the wheels first so the correct height can be verified. After installing both options, I've decided to use base #2 on my cabinet, as described in step 29.

STEP 6 ▪ If you plan to use base option #1, attach two heavy-duty locking wheel assemblies to one side of the cabinet.

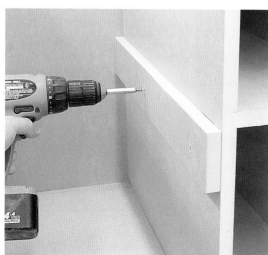

STEP 8 ▪ Install the two shelf supports F in the middle section. They are secured with glue and 1¹⁄₄" screws. Their top edges are 12³⁄₄" above the bottom board. Cut the middle shelf G to the size indicated in the materials list and secure it to the cleats with glue and brad nails.

STEP 9 ▪ The four bit holder slide-outs are made with ³⁄₄"-thick MDF. Each holder board has a series of holes for ¹⁄₄"- and ¹⁄₂"-diameter router bits. I spaced my holes 2" apart with the two outside rows 1¹⁄₂" in from each board's edge and the third row in the center.

The holder platforms H are attached to the runners J with glue and 1¹⁄₂" screws. The runners are flush with the outside long edges of the holder platforms. A front lower cleat K is also attached to the holder platform in the same way. The backboards L are attached to the rear of each assembly with glue and 1¹⁄₂" screws. Use a ¹⁄₄" roundover bit in your router to soften the front edges of the slide-out faces M. Once the face is aligned on the slide-out, attach each face with 1¹⁄₄" screws through the front lower cleat.

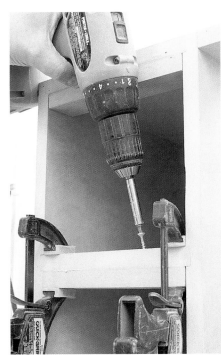

STEP 10 ■ Cut and attach the four stop cleats N with glue and 1¼"-long screws. These cleats will stop the slide-out when fully extended. When it's necessary to remove or install the slide-outs, simply tip them upward to move past the stop cleats.

STEP 11 ■ The two outside lower drawer boxes are 7" wide by 10" high by 22" deep and made with ¾"-thick MDF. Attach the drawer sides P to the back and front boards Q using glue and 1½" screws. The bottom boards R are also secured to the sides, front and bottom board edges with 1½" screws and glue to form the drawer boxes. Use 22" bottom-mount drawer glides, or full-extension glides if you prefer, to install the drawer boxes in the cabinet.

STEP 12 ■ The lower outside drawer box faces S have their front edges rounded over using a ¼" router bit. They are secured to the drawer boxes with 1¼" screws through the inside of the box. Install the faces so they are aligned with the slide-out fronts, leaving a ⅛" gap between each front.

STEP 13 ■ The lower middle drawer box is 8½" high by 16" wide by 22" deep. Build the box using ¾" MDF with parts T, U and V following the same steps as the outside lower drawer boxes. Mount this box using 22" drawer glides.

STEP 14 ■ Round over the front edges of drawer face W using a ¼" router bit. Attach it to the drawer box with 1¼" screws, being careful to leave equal spacing on both sides, with its top aligned to the two outside drawer faces.

STEP 15 ▪ Cut the door X to size and round over the front face edges. I used full-overlay 107° hinges with standard mounting plates. Drill 35mm holes, ⅛" from the door edge, to secure the hinges. Hold the door in its normally open position, with a ⅛"-thick spacer between the door and cabinet edge, and secure the mounting plates with ⅝" screws.

STEP 16 ▪ The top is made by gluing two ¾"-thick MDF panels together. Cut both panels Y a little oversize so they can be trimmed to a finished size when the adhesive has cured. The top is banded with 1½"-high by ¾"-thick hardwood and is secured in place with biscuits. Cut the edges Z and AA to size with 45° miters on each end to join the corners.

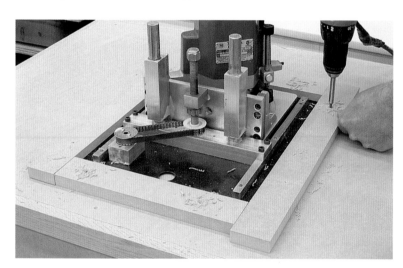

STEP 17 ▪ Turn the top upside down on the router cabinet. It should overhang the front edge by 1½" and the sides by 1⅝". I will be using a Rout-R-Lift plate made by JessEm Tool Company, but any plate can be installed using the following method. Place the router plate on the center of the table and 5" back from the front edge of the top. Fasten strips of wood around the plate with screws. These strips will be used as a template to guide your router.

STEP 18 ▪ The router base should have a bushing guide installed to run against the strips of wood. The size of the bushing should equal the depth of cut for the wing or slot cutter bit that will be used to form a groove on the top side of the table to inset the router plate flush with the top face. My wing bit cuts ½" deep, so I want the hole to be smaller than the strip edges by ½" on all sides. Cut the hole using the guide bushing and router bit.

STEP 19 ▪ Flip the top right side up and use the wing cutter to groove the top. The router plate should be flush with the tabletop's surface. I hand-formed the corners to match my router plate. It may also be necessary in your case to use a sharp knife and chisel to carve the corners. Fasten the top to the cabinet using 2" screws through the horizontal supports and middle top rail.

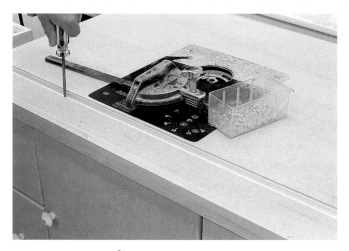

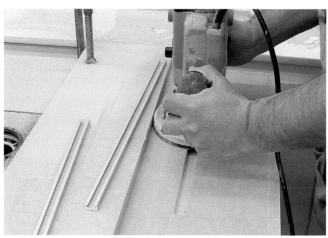

STEP 20 ■ I installed a ¾" miter slide track in my tabletop. Cut the groove for the slide track as close to the front edge of your router plate as possible. This track required a 1"-wide groove cut parallel to the router plate. I drilled the track and secured it to the top with ⅝" screws. The track is available through most woodworking supply stores.

STEP 21 ■ The T-track, which will be used to lock the adjustable fence, is also attached to the top in grooves. Rout the grooves on each side, parallel to the plate, and match the size of track you purchased, making sure they are flush with the tabletop surface. Once again, the tracks are secured with ⅝" screws.

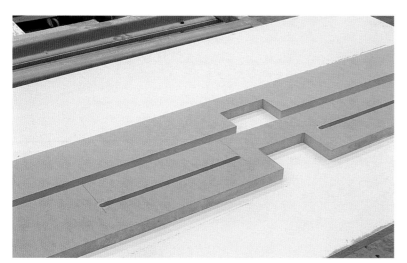

STEP 22 ■ All of the fence parts are made with ¾"-thick MDF. The fence back rail BB has two ⅜"-wide grooves routed into the center and through the board. The grooves start 6" from each end and stop 16" from each end. This rail also requires a 4"-wide by 2½"-high notch, centered on the length of the board. The horizontal support CC also has a notch that is 4" wide by 2" high in the center of the board. Both notches can be cut with a band saw or jigsaw.

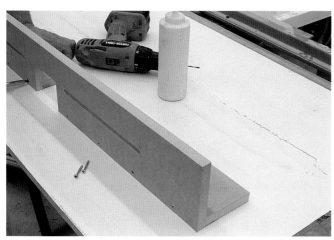

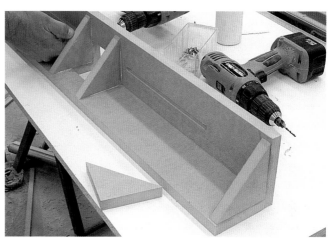

STEP 23 ■ Attach the fence back rail BB to the horizontal support CC with 1½" screws and glue at about 4" on center.

STEP 24 ■ The four right-angle fence supports DD are 4" x 4" blocks of ¾" MDF cut at 45°. Use glue and 1½" screws to attach the supports to the fence assembly. One support is installed at either end and the remaining two on each side of the cutout notch in the fence boards.

STEP 25 ■ The back cover EE for the fence cutout has a 45° miter on both ends. Apply glue to all edges and secure the cover with a few brad nails on the top and bottom edge.

STEP 26 ■ Drill a 2¼"-diameter hole in the center of the back cover. This will be used to friction-fit a vacuum hose.

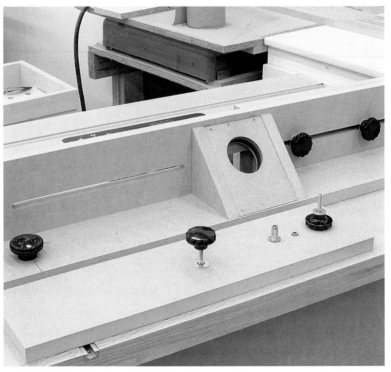

STEP 27 ■ Center the fence assembly on the router table and drill two ⅜"-diameter holes in the horizontal support over the center of each T-track. Use a T-nut and knob with a 1"-long by ¼"-diameter threaded shaft screwed into the nut. Tighten the knobs and verify that the fence locks securely.

STEP 28 ■ The adjustable fence boards FF have two T-nuts driven into the front faces. Counterbore the hole so the nuts are slightly below the fence face. Position the nuts so both fences can come together in the center and travel about 4" out from the center.

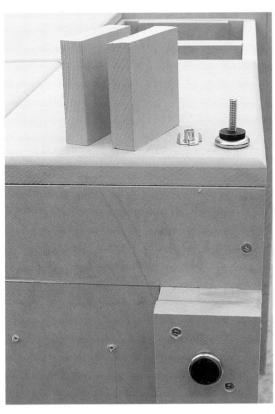

STEP 29 ■ I will be using base option #2, as illustrated. Two pads KK are glued together and attached to the bottom, 3" back from the front edge of the cabinet and on both back corners. Drill holes for ¼"-diameter T-nuts and install a threaded metal foot in the center of each block as shown.

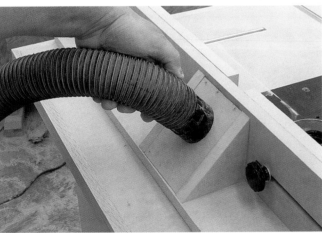

STEP 30 ■ My 2¼"-outside-diameter vacuum hose on my shop vacuum is a snug fit in the dust hole and provides good particle removal.

STEP 31 ■ I purchased and attached a construction-grade power bar, made by Belkin Components, called a Surge-Master HD. This device is designed to control electrical equipment such as saws, compressors and routers. The vacuum cleaner and router will be plugged into the power bar and controlled by a switch. I will also have spare plugs that are overload protected, which I can use in the shop for other electrical equipment.

You will need four sheets of ¾"-thick MDF to build this cabinet. I used about 13' of hardwood to edge the top, as well.

I used MDF, but any ¾" sheet material will be fine, and the same construction dimensions and procedures can be used. If you decide to use another material, look for a smooth surface so your router work will slide easily on the top.

Pay special attention to the final height of your cabinet. My cabinet, with the adjustable legs in base option #2, puts my top surface at about 35" above the floor. That's a comfortable height for me, but your requirements may be different. Adjust the vertical divider heights to meet your needs.

All of the aluminum track, knobs and related hardware are sold at most woodworking stores. Woodworkers tend to make jigs and shop-built tool accessories, so this line of hardware has become very popular.

I considered adding a dust collection port in the router compartment, but the dust doesn't seem to be that great a problem. My vacuum pulls most of the dust at the fence; however, routing a material that creates fine dust may cause a buildup in the compartment. If that's the case, drilling a dust port and making a Y-fitting so the vacuum could collect from the fence and router compartment would be an easy fix.

Drill Press Center

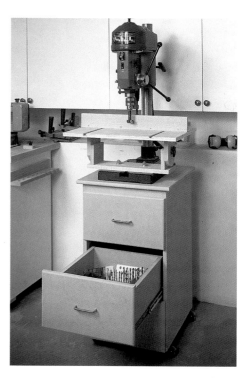

A drill press is a valuable asset in any woodworking shop. Drill presses are available as floor or bench models and have adjustable tables or heads. However, they all lack storage space and have tables that are difficult to adjust.

I built the storage cabinet portion of this project to be used with both floor and bench drill presses. The bench model can be bolted to the top, or the cabinet can be wheeled over the base on floor-model units. If you do own a floor-model press, measure the width and height of the base to be sure the cabinet can be rolled over the base. If the base is too large, change the cabinet dimensions to suit your drill press.

The full-extension top cabinet drawer can hold drill bits on an indexed board, while the remaining drawers can contain accessories, literature and other tools used with your drill press. If you need the drill press table on your floor-model unit lower than the cabinet height, simply roll it out of the way.

Bench-model presses can be mounted on the top, and the station, both cabinet and drill press, can be rolled to any area of your shop.

Many woodworkers will appreciate the wide adjustable table. It can be tipped for angular drilling to the front or rear of your drill press. The adjustable fence is an important option that is missing on most drill units. Woodworkers use drill press fences a great deal and often have to clamp a straight-edged board to the press table. This fence is adjustable, easily locked in place and quick to move where needed.

The drill press center is easy to build, inexpensive and well worth the time invested. It's a great workstation to use, and I'm sure you'll quickly appreciate its value.

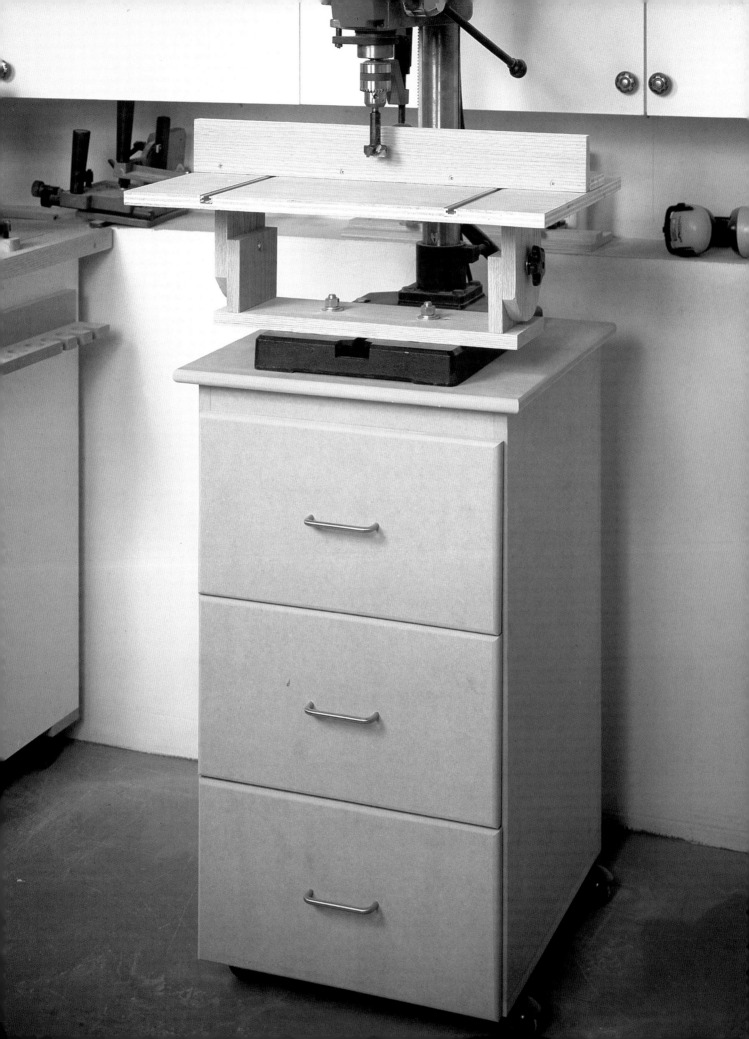

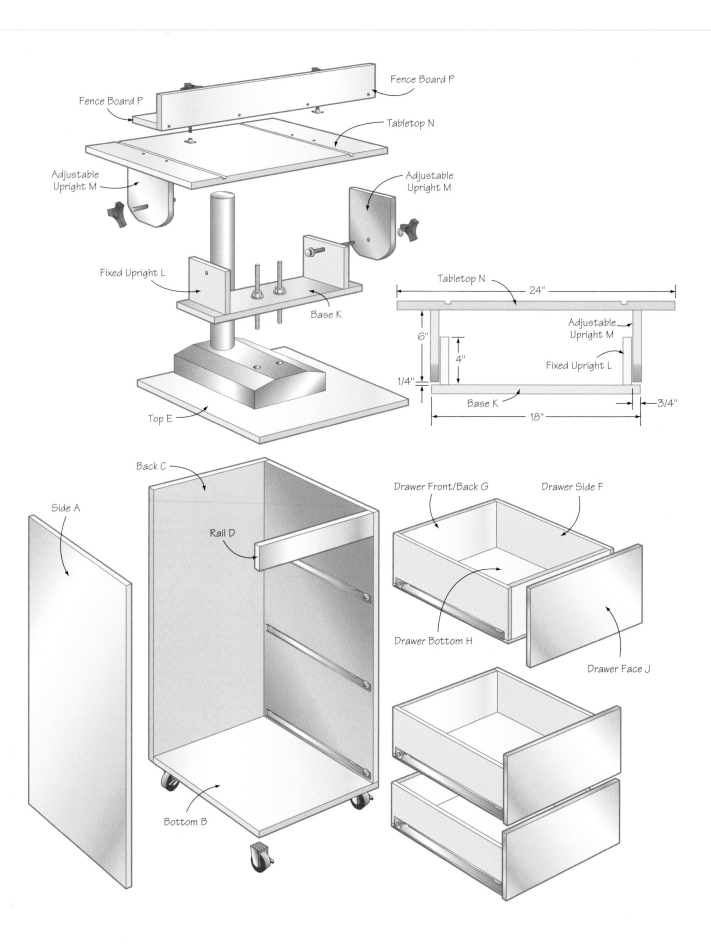

Fence Board P

Fence Board P

Tabletop N

Adjustable
Upright M

Adjustable
Upright M

Fixed Upright L

Base K

Tabletop N   24"

Adjustable
Upright M

6"

4"

Fixed Upright L

1/4"

Base K

3/4"

18"

Top E

Back C

Side A

Rail D

Drawer Front/Back G   Drawer Side F

Drawer Bottom H

Drawer Face J

Bottom B

materials list ■ **INCHES**

REFERENCE	QUANTITY	PART	STOCK	THICKNESS	WIDTH	LENGTH	COMMENTS
CABINET							
A	2	sides	MDF	$^3/_4$	19	30	
B	1	bottom	MDF	$^3/_4$	18	19	
C	1	back	MDF	$^3/_4$	18	$30^3/_4$	
D	1	rail	MDF	$^3/_4$	2	$16^3/_4$	
E	1	top	MDF	$^3/_4$	20	21	
F	6	drawer sides	MDF	$^3/_4$	$6^1/_4$	18	
G	6	drawer fronts & backs	MDF	$^3/_4$	$6^1/_4$	14	
H	3	drawer bottoms	MDF	$^3/_4$	$15^1/_2$	18	
J	3	drawer faces	MDF	$^3/_4$	$9^5/_8$	$17^1/_2$	
ADJUSTABLE DRILL TABLE							
K	1	base	hardwood	$^3/_4$	$5^1/_4$	18	
L	2	fixed uprights	hardwood	$^3/_4$	$5^1/_4$	4	
M	2	adjustable uprights	hardwood	$^3/_4$	$5^1/_4$	6	
N	1	tabletop	veneer ply	$^3/_4$	16	24	
P	2	fence boards	veneer ply	$^3/_4$	3	24	
Q	2	drill platforms	MDF	$^3/_4$	14	$16^3/_4$	

HARDWARE

Screws as detailed
Glue
3 Drawer handles
3 Sets of full-extension drawer glides
Right-angle brackets
Bolts and nuts as detailed
T-track
T-nuts
Knobs
$1^1/_2$" Screws
$^5/_8$" Screws
$1^1/_4$" Screws
4 Wheels
2" Screws
$^1/_4$" Carriage bolts with washer and knobs
$^1/_2$" Screws
$^1/_4$" x 20 Bolt and knob assembly with 1"-long shaft

---

materials list ■ **MILLIMETERS**

REFERENCE	QUANTITY	PART	STOCK	THICKNESS	WIDTH	LENGTH	COMMENTS
CABINET							
A	2	sides	MDF	19	483	762	
B	1	bottom	MDF	19	457	483	
C	1	back	MDF	19	457	781	
D	1	rail	MDF	19	51	425	
E	1	top	MDF	19	508	533	
F	6	drawer sides	MDF	19	158	457	
G	6	drawer fronts & backs	MDF	19	158	356	
H	3	drawer bottoms	MDF	19	394	457	
J	3	drawer faces	MDF	19	245	445	
ADJUSTABLE DRILL TABLE							
K	1	base	hardwood	19	133	457	
L	2	fixed uprights	hardwood	19	133	102	
M	2	adjustable uprights	hardwood	19	133	152	
N	1	tabletop	veneer ply	19	406	610	
P	2	fence boards	veneer ply	19	76	610	
Q	2	drill platforms	MDF	19	356	425	

HARDWARE

Screws as detailed
Glue
3 Drawer handles
3 Sets of full-extension drawer glides
Right-angle brackets
Bolts and nuts as detailed
T-track
T-nuts
Knobs
38mm Screws
16mm Screws
32mm Screws
4 Wheels
51mm Screws
6mm Carriage bolts with washer and knobs
13mm Screws
6mm x 20 Bolt and knob assembly with 25mm-long shaft

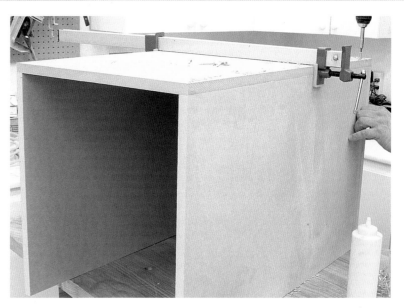

STEP 1 ▪ Cut the two sides A and bottom board B to size as detailed in the materials list. Attach the bottom to the sides using 1½" screws, spaced 6" apart, and glue. Note that both sides rest on the bottom board, and the screws are installed on the underside of the bottom, into the edges of the side boards. Remember to drill pilot holes for the screws.

STEP 2 ▪ The back C is attached to the cabinet sides and bottom board with 1½" screws and glue. A properly cut back will square the cabinet.

STEP 3 ▪ Cut and attach the top rail D using right-angle brackets and ⅝" screws. Apply glue to the rail ends and clamp securely when installing the brackets. The brackets are also installed on the sides, back and rail boards, and will be used to secure the cabinet top board.

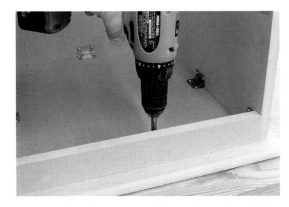

STEP 4 ▪ Round over the two sides and front edges of the top board E using a $\frac{3}{8}$" roundover bit in a router. Use $\frac{5}{8}$" screws in the right-angle brackets to secure the top. There should be a 1" overhang on both sides and a $1\frac{1}{4}$" overhang at the front edge. The top's back edge is aligned flush with the back face of the backboard.

STEP 5 ▪ The drawer boxes are 7" high by $15\frac{1}{2}$" wide by 18" deep. I made my drawer boxes using the same $\frac{3}{4}$"-thick MDF as was used to build the cabinet carcass.

Cut the drawer box parts F, G and H to size. Begin the assembly by attaching the sides to the back and front boards using $1\frac{1}{2}$" screws and glue. Two screws per joint, making sure the screws are kept 1" away from the tops and bottoms of the boards, will secure the joints.

STEP 6 ▪ The bottom boards are also attached to the side, back and front boards using $1\frac{1}{2}$" screws and glue.

STEP 7 ▪ I used 18" full-extension drawer glides to mount my drawer boxes. The bottom drawer is installed as close to the bottom board as possible. The remaining two drawer boxes are installed leaving a 2" space between them.

STEP 8 ▪ The drawer faces J are $9\frac{5}{8}$" high by $17\frac{1}{2}$" wide using $\frac{3}{4}$" MDF. The front edges are rounded over with a $\frac{3}{8}$" bit in a router. The bottom drawer face is aligned flush with the bottom edge of the cabinet base board and spaced $\frac{1}{8}$" apart. Secure the faces to the drawer boxes using $1\frac{1}{4}$" screws from inside the drawer box. Attach handles or knobs of your choice.

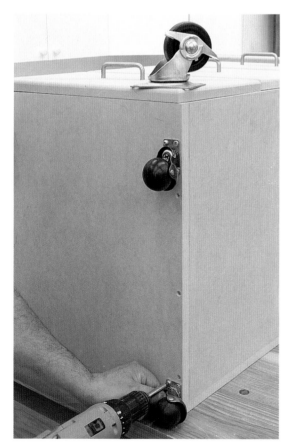

STEP 9 ▪ Install four wheels on the base, setting back the front set by 2". Use medium- or heavy-duty wheels, making sure they are high enough to straddle the drill press base if you own a floor model.

STEP 10 ▪ If you are using a benchtop drill press, mount it securely to the cabinet top with bolts or screws. If you own a floor-model press, you can skip this step.

STEP 11 ■ Using hardwood, cut the table base K and the two fixed uprights L to size. Secure both uprights to the base K with glue and 2" screws. The uprights are attached ¾" in from each end of the base K.

STEP 12 ■ Prepare the two adjustable uprights M by cutting them to the size indicated. Remove both lower corners on each board with a 45° cut that's 1½" from each end. Round over the corners with a belt sander, creating an arc on the bottom edge of each upright.

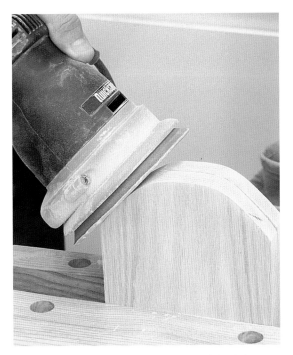

STEP 13 ■ Following the rough shaping with the belt sander, clamp the two uprights together and finish-sand so both have the same profile.

STEP 14 ■ Place the adjustable uprights M on the outside faces of each fixed upright L, aligning the edges of all boards. Use a ¼"-thick spacer under the adjustable uprights and drill a ¼"-diameter hole 3" down from their top edges through both boards. Center the hole on the width of each board and insert a ¼"-diameter carriage bolt, a large washer on the outside face and a knob to lock the uprights together.

STEP 15 ▪ Bolt the assembly to the table on your drill press. Each model will have different bolt hole patterns, so choose a method that suits your drill press table. Align the drill chuck center to the center of the table base board and tighten securely.

STEP 16 ▪ The tabletop N is a piece of $3/4$"-thick veneer plywood. Form two dadoes along the width of the board, 5" in from each edge. The T-track I'm using requires $3/8$"-deep dadoes, but your hardware may be different, so verify the track depth before cutting the dadoes. Cut the tracks to length and secure them in the dadoes using $1/2$" screws in countersunk holes at the bottom of the tracks.

STEP 17 ▪ Attach the top to the adjustable uprights using two 2" screws per upright. Align the top so it's equally spaced on both upright edges, side to side and back to front. Don't use glue in case the top has to be replaced in the future.

STEP 18 ▪ The fence is made with ¾"-thick veneer plywood. The horizontal and vertical members P are 3" high by 24" long. Attach the vertical board to the horizontal member with glue and four 2" screws. This simple but strong fence can be easily replaced if necessary.

STEP 19 ▪ Drill two ¼"-diameter holes in the horizontal fence board over the center of each T-track slot. To lock the fence, use a ¼" x 20 bolt and knob assembly with a 1"-long shaft screwed to T-nuts in the track.

STEP 20 ▪ I'm using one of the drawers, on full-extension drawer glides, to store and index my drill bits. Cut a piece of ¾" MDF to size for a drill platform Q. Drill the appropriate holes to store your bits and loosely sit the platform in the drawer box. New holes can be drilled as your bit inventory increases.

If you build the drill press center as detailed, you'll need about 1¼ sheets of MDF, a 2' x 2' piece of veneer-covered plywood and a 40"-long piece of 1x6 hardwood. The hardware is available at most woodworking stores.

Many configurations are possible for the cabinet, and the final dimensions will depend on the size of your drill press. The sizes shown in this project should be suitable for the majority of floor and benchtop drill presses.

Any ¾" sheet material can be used. I decided to use MDF because it's inexpensive, can be easily worked with standard woodworking tools, doesn't require edge finishing and is a stable material. However, particleboard or plywood can be substituted if one of them is a personal favorite of yours.

An additional knob and bolt can be added to double-lock each set of uprights. If you do a lot of heavy work on the drill press, you might want some added insurance that the table will remain level, so add another ¼" x 20 bolt and knob to each side. Remove the extra lock when adjustments to the table are needed. However, the one-knob-per-side setup securely locks the table, and it would take quite a bit of weight to move it.

You may want to drill a large round hole in the table to insert a sanding drum. The drum can be installed in the drill chuck and lowered through the hole. The large table and a drum will make a great power sanding accessory on your press. Dozens of drill press accessories are available, such as planers, plug cutters, hollow chisel mortise attachments and so on. The cabinet can be made with one drawer over a door with adjustable shelves or, as shown, three drawers on full-extension (FX) glides. The FX glides are the most expensive part of the project. To reduce costs, use an FX glide set on the drill bit drawer and bottom-mount glides on the remaining drawers.

Tool Sharpening and Maintenance Station

Sharpening equipment is a necessity in every woodworking shop. Dull tools are aggravating to work with and dangerous. Keeping chisels, turning tools, plane blades and carving tools in good condition is a fact of life in the woodshop.

Many woodworkers use water stones and waterwheel grinders. The stones have to be kept wet to work effectively, so that means a water bath. However, woodworking tools create dust, and when mixed with water, a brown sludge forms in the water bath. Those of you who use oil stones have the same problem with dust — a brown paste covering the stones and lapping plates. I'm sure I've spent more time cleaning the stones and water baths than on actual tool maintenance.

I decided to build a dedicated sharpening station for my 1" belt sander, wet and dry wheel grinder and water bath for my stones. But I vowed to solve the dust and water problems with this station. The flip-up cover is my answer for a dust-free center, and it works great!

This project may not look sleek and stylish, but it keeps my water baths and stones "paste free" and saves me a great deal of time previously wasted cleaning the equipment.

The power cords are routed through the top and plug into a power bar. Two large drawers provide all the space I need for sharpening accessories, extra blades for my tools and manuals related to my equipment. The section below the drawers is enclosed with doors for added dust-free storage. The station is mounted on locking wheels that allow me to bring it to any area in my shop.

If you want clean, almost dust-free sharpening equipment that's ready to use, then this project is for you. The cabinet won't win any beauty awards, but it's number one in the functional category.

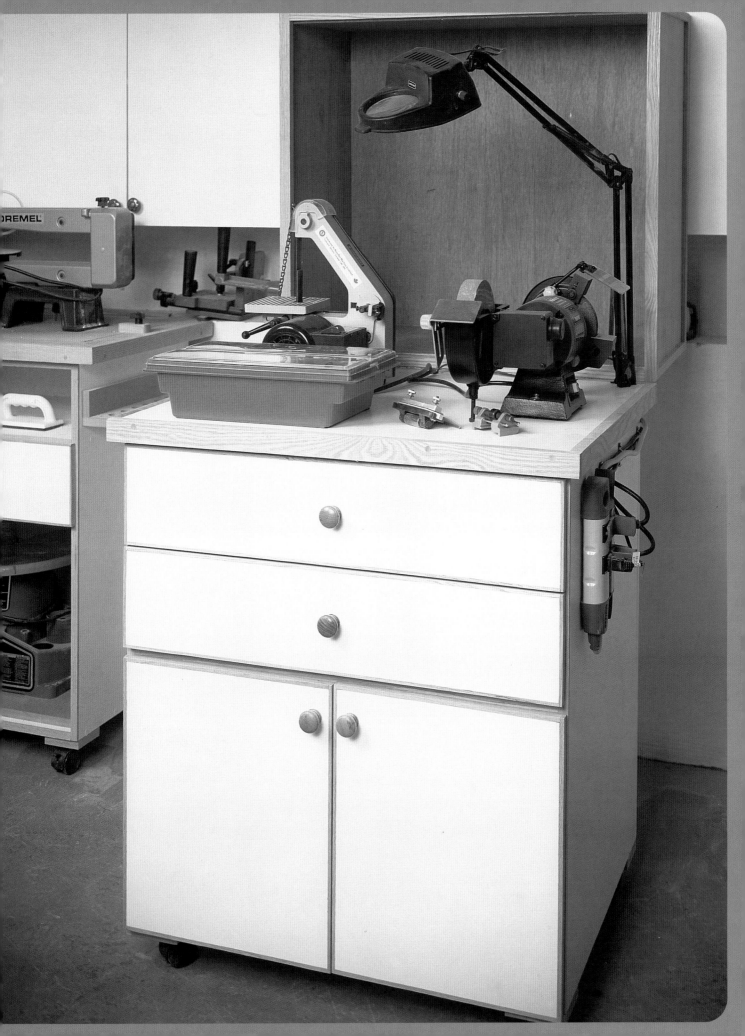

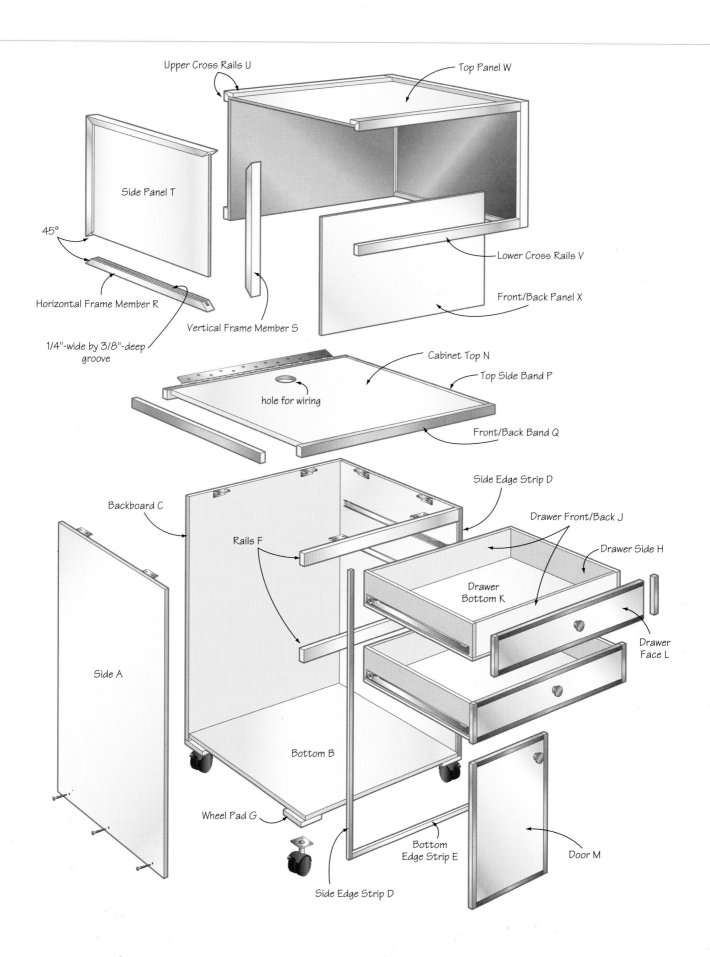

Upper Cross Rails U

Top Panel W

Side Panel T

45°

Horizontal Frame Member R

Vertical Frame Member S

1/4"-wide by 3/8"-deep groove

Lower Cross Rails V

Front/Back Panel X

Cabinet Top N

Top Side Band P

hole for wiring

Front/Back Band Q

Backboard C

Rails F

Side Edge Strip D

Drawer Front/Back J

Drawer Side H

Drawer Bottom K

Drawer Face L

Side A

Bottom B

Wheel Pad G

Side Edge Strip D

Bottom Edge Strip E

Door M

REFERENCE	QUANTITY	PART	STOCK	THICKNESS	WIDTH	LENGTH	COMMENTS
CABINET							
A	2	sides	melamine PB	$5/8$	$23^3/8$	32	
B	1	bottom	melamine PB	$5/8$	$23^3/8$	$28^3/4$	
C	1	backboard	melamine PB	$5/8$	30	32	
D	2	side edge strips	hardwood	$1/4$	$5/8$	32	
E	1	bottom edge strip	hardwood	$1/4$	$5/8$	$28^3/4$	
F	2	rails	hardwood	$3/4$	$1^1/2$	$28^3/4$	
G	4	wheel pads	hardwood	$3/4$	$3^1/2$	$3^1/2$	
H	4	drawer sides	melamine PB	$5/8$	$4^3/8$	22	
J	4	drawer fronts & backs	melamine PB	$5/8$	$4^3/8$	$26^1/2$	
K	2	drawer bottoms	melamine PB	$5/8$	22	$27^3/4$	
L	2	drawer faces	melamine PB	$5/8$	$6^1/2$	$29^3/4$	
M	2	doors	melamine PB	$5/8$	$14^7/8$	$17^1/2$	
N	1	cabinet top	melamine PB	$5/8$	$30^1/4$	$26^1/2$	
P	2	top side bands	hardwood	$3/4$	$1^1/2$	$26^1/2$	
Q	2	front & back bands	hardwood	$3/4$	$1^1/2$	$31^3/4$	
COVER							
R	4	horizontal frame members	hardwood	$3/4$	1	28	angle-cut
S	4	vertical frame members	hardwood	$3/4$	1	16	angle-cut
T	2	side panels	veneer ply	$1/4$	$15^1/4$	$27^1/4$	
U	4	upper cross rails	hardwood	$3/4$	$1^1/2$	$29^3/4$	angle-cut
V	2	lower cross rails	hardwood	$3/4$	$1^1/2$	$29^3/4$	
W	1	top panel	veneer ply	$1/4$	$30^3/8$	$26^3/8$	
X	2	front & back panels	veneer ply	$1/4$	$30^3/8$	$14^1/4$	

HARDWARE

8 Metal right-angle brackets

2″ PB screws as detailed

Brad nails as detailed

Glue

White screw head cover caps as detailed

4 Locking wheels

Iron-on edge tape

2 – 22″ Drawer glide sets

4 Knobs

4 – 107° Hidden hinges

1 – 28" Piano hinge

12" Length of small chain

1 Handle

1 Wire grommet

Metal angle brackets

Pocket screws

$1^1/4$" Screws

$5/8$" Screws

1" Screws

$1/2$" Screws

Biscuits

Wood plugs

Wire protector

materials list ▪ **MILLIMETERS**

REFERENCE	QUANTITY	PART	STOCK	THICKNESS	WIDTH	LENGTH	COMMENTS
CABINET							
A	2	sides	melamine PB	16	594	813	
B	1	bottom	melamine PB	16	594	730	
C	1	backboard	melamine PB	16	762	813	
D	2	side edge strips	hardwood	6	16	813	
E	1	bottom edge strip	hardwood	6	16	730	
F	2	rails	hardwood	19	38	730	
G	4	wheel pads	hardwood	19	89	89	
H	4	drawer sides	melamine PB	16	112	559	
J	4	drawer fronts & backs	melamine PB	16	112	673	
K	2	drawer bottoms	melamine PB	16	559	705	
L	2	drawer faces	melamine PB	16	165	756	
M	2	doors	melamine PB	16	378	445	
N	1	cabinet top	melamine PB	16	768	673	
P	2	top side bands	hardwood	19	38	673	
Q	2	front & back bands	hardwood	19	38	806	
COVER							
R	4	horizontal frame members	hardwood	19	25	711	angle-cut
S	4	vertical frame members	hardwood	19	25	406	angle-cut
T	2	side panels	veneer ply	6	387	692	
U	4	upper cross rails	hardwood	19	38	756	angle-cut
V	2	lower cross rails	hardwood	19	38	756	
W	1	top panel	veneer ply	6	772	670	
X	2	front & back panels	veneer ply	6	772	362	

HARDWARE

8 Metal right-angle brackets

51mm PB screws as detailed

Brad nails as detailed

Glue

White screw head cover caps as detailed

4 Locking wheels

Iron-on edge tape

2 – 559mm Drawer glide sets

4 Knobs

4 – 107° Hidden hinges

1 – 711mm Piano hinge

305mm Length of small chain

1 Handle

1 Wire grommet

Metal angle brackets

Pocket screws

32mm Screws

16mm Screws

25mm Screws

6mm Screws

Biscuits

Wood plugs

Wire protector

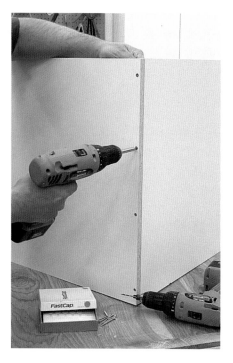

STEP 1 ▪ Join the sides A to the bottom board B by drilling 2" PB screws in pilot holes. Cover the screw heads with white stick-on caps or plastic covers.

STEP 2 ▪ Apply iron-on edge tape to both long vertical edges of backboard C. Attach the back to the sides and bottom board using 2"-long PB screws.

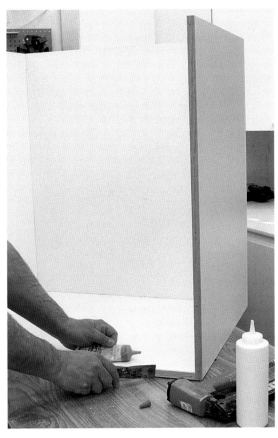

STEP 3 ▪ Glue and nail the solid-wood edge strips D and E to the front edges of the side and bottom boards. Fill the nail holes and sand smooth. I'm using oak hardwood for all my edge trim, but any solid wood can be used.

STEP 4 ▪ Cut and install the two wood rails F. Secure them to the cabinet with metal angle brackets, screws through the cabinet's side or, as I'm using, pocket screws. The top rail is flush with the top edges of the cabinet sides, and the middle rail is 13½" below the top edges. There should be a 12"-high opening between the two rails for the drawers.

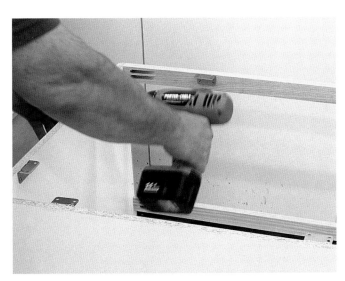

STEP 5 ▪ Install the eight right-angle brackets that will be used to secure the cabinet top board. The brackets are attached flush with the top edges of the side, backboard and upper rail. I installed two brackets on each panel and two on the rail.

STEP 6 ▪ The four wood wheel pads G can be installed using 1" screws through the bottom board into the pads. They should be installed under the edges of the back and side boards so the load on those panels will shift through the pads and wheels to the floor. Four screws per pad will hold them securely to the cabinet bottom. The locking wheels are attached with 1¼" screws. The wheels I used are 2½" high, and including the pads, the cabinet is 3¼" off the floor.

STEP 7 ■ The two drawer boxes are 5" high by 27³/₄" wide. Cut all drawer parts H, J and K to size. I used ⁵/₈"-thick melamine and secured the butt joints with 2" PB screws. Before assembling the boxes use iron-on edge tape to cover the top edges of the back, front and side boards, as well as the side edges of the bottom board. Attach the sides to the back and front boards using two screws per joint. Keep the screws at least 1" away from the edges of all boards to avoid splitting.

STEP 8 ■ The drawer box bottom board is attached to the bottom edges of the side, back and front boards with 2" PB screws.

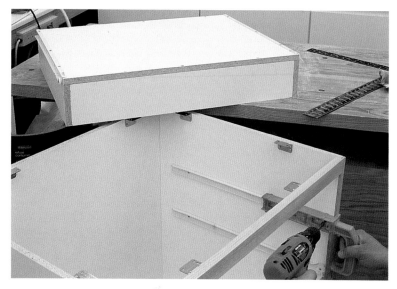

STEP 9 ■ Install the drawer boxes in the cabinet using 22" bottom-mount or, if you prefer, full-extension side-mount glides. The top glides are installed so the bottom of the top drawer box will be 5³/₄" below the lower edge of the top rail. Use ⁵/₈" screws and follow the installation instructions that come with your hardware.

STEP 10 ■ The drawer faces L are secured to the boxes with four 1" screws. Leave a ¹/₁₆" space between the upper and lower drawer face. I used ⁵/₈"-thick melamine PB trimmed with ¹/₄"-thick oak hardwood for my faces. You can use any material to make the drawer faces and doors as long as the finished sizes are the same as the dimensions detailed in the materials list. The drawer faces will overlap the top and middle rail by approximately ¹/₂".

STEP 12 ■ Drill two 35mm holes in each door, 3" on center from each end. The flat-bottomed hinge holes are drilled $\frac{1}{8}$" in from the door's edge.

STEP 11 ■ The door width is calculated by measuring the cabinet's inside width and adding 1". Since I want two doors on my cabinet, I will divide that number by two, (28$\frac{3}{4}$" plus 1" divided by 2), which means I'll need both doors to be 14$\frac{7}{8}$" wide. The doors are installed flush with the lower edge of the bottom board and overlay the middle rail by about $\frac{3}{8}$". I trimmed my door edges with oak, but as mentioned earlier, any material can be used as long as the overall dimensions of the doors are as stated in the materials list.

STEP 13 ■ Install two standard-opening hinges (between 100° and 120°) in each door and secure them with $\frac{1}{2}$"-long screws, making sure the hinges are 90° to the door's edge. Attach the hinge plates to the hinge body and hold the door against the cabinet in its normally open position with a $\frac{1}{8}$" spacer between the door and cabinet edge. Drive screws through the hinge-plate holes to secure the door. Remove the spacer and test the door alignment. Install handles or knobs on the drawers and doors.

STEP 14 ■ The cabinet top N is a sheet of $\frac{5}{8}$"-thick melamine PB with hardwood edge-banding. Attach the edge-banding P and Q with glue and biscuits or screws with wood plugs. Install the top with $\frac{5}{8}$" screws through the metal brackets previously installed. There should be a $\frac{7}{8}$" overhang on each side, a 1$\frac{1}{4}$" overhang on the front edge and a 2$\frac{1}{2}$" overhang at the back edge. The larger overhang on the back will be used to install a wire hole and grommet.

STEP 15 ■ Drill a wire hole in the back of the top, 1" from the rear edge. Use a wire protector (commonly found at stores that sell electronic supplies). The power cords can pass through the hole and be attached to a power bar.

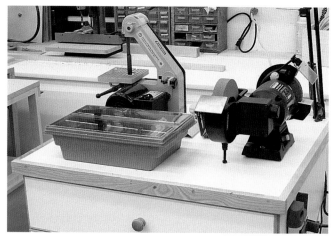

STEP 16 ▪ Install your sharpening tools on the cabinet top, keeping them 1" from any edge. I have a 1" belt sander, wet and dry wheel grinder, a water stone bath and a magnifying lamp. I also attached a power bar made by Stanley Tools on the cabinet side. Your equipment will be different from mine, but it should be installed at this time to determine the minimum inside height of the cover.

STEP 17 ▪ My cover is the full width and depth of the top, so I need 15" of inside clearance based on my equipment. The side frame will be made with hardwood that's 1" wide by ³/₄" thick. Both ends on frame members R and S are cut at 45° to create a mitered corner at each intersection. The side panels will be ¹/₄"-thick veneer plywood.

Cut a groove that's ¹/₄" wide on one 1" face of each horizontal and vertical ³/₈"-deep frame member. Miter the ends of each member so the long edge is the dimension stated in the materials list. The grooves are on the inside, short dimension of each mitered board. Assemble the two side frames with the panels T installed in the grooves. Use glue and brad nails, then clamp securely until the adhesive cures.

STEP 18 ▪ Prepare the four upper cross rails U by ripping a 45° miter along one edge of each board. The face of these rails should be 1¹/₂" wide after ripping the angle. Create a back-and-front upper cross rail assembly by gluing the boards together in pairs at the miter. You should have two assemblies that form a right angle. The boards can be glued and brad nailed or clamped. If you use brads, keep them ³/₈" back from the corner intersection so the edges can be rounded with a router bit.

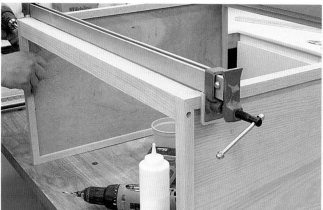

STEP 19 ▪ Join the two sides with the upper cross rails using glue and 2" screws in counterbored holes. These holes can be filled with wood plugs. One 2" screw and glue at each joint will securely hold the rails to the sides.

STEP 20 ▪ The two lower cross rails V are also secured with glue and one 2" screw at each end. Counterbore and fill the screw holes with wood plugs.

STEP 21 ■ Use a ¼" roundover bit to ease all the outside edges of the frame members. Do not round over the bottom edges of the cover, because it should sit tight and flat on the cabinet top.

STEP 22 ■ The top panel W and front and back panels X are attached to the inside of the cover with glue and ⅝" brad nails.

STEP 23 ■ Clamp the cover in place on the cabinet so its edges are flush with the outside edges of the top. Use a 28" piano hinge on the back side to secure the cover to the cabinet.

STEP 24 ■ Use a small chain about 12" long to limit the travel of the cover. Then install a handle on the front lower cross rail of the cover so it can be easily raised and lowered.

You need to deal with two important issues before beginning construction of this sharpening station. First, decide on a comfortable work-surface height and, if it is different from mine, change the height of the sides and backboard to suit your requirements.

Second, the type of equipment that will be mounted on this station will determine the size of the top and clearance requirements for the cover. The belt sander is normally the tallest piece of equipment and is the unit that determines the cover height.

I built my station using ⅝"-thick particleboard and oak hardwood for the trim; however, any sheet material will work just as well. If you do use another sheet material such as MDF or plywood, consider installing a melamine PB or high-pressure laminate top. A smooth surface that's easy to clean is a real bonus.

You may also want to put a self-adhesive foam or rubber gasket on the bottom edge of the cover to further protect the equipment from dust. The cover can be built in another style, with other materials, but a ⅝"-thick melamine PB prototype that I built was very heavy to lift. The frame and panel cover is light and easy to manage, which convinced me that it was the best design for this application.

Finally, change the drawer and door compartments if they don't meet your needs. Three or four small drawers may be more suitable, or for some of you, one drawer will be fine. This project should be designed and built to accommodate your sharpening requirements.

Mobile Workbench and Tool Cabinet

Does your woodworking shop share space with the family car? If you have a garage workshop, this project is perfect for you. The cabinet is mobile, has a large worktable and plenty of tool storage that can be secured with locks.

Many garage woodworkers spend half their time hauling out tools and setting up worktables. A mobile center reduces that lost time because all the tools are in one cabinet. The cabinet is also a worktable, so it can be wheeled to the center of your shop and you're ready to go with tools close at hand.

I used ³⁄₄" veneer plywood to build my cabinet, but the project can be built with plywood, MDF or any other ³⁄₄" sheet material that's reasonably priced. You'll need about three 4' x 8' sheets of material, locking wheels and drawer glide hardware, so calculate all the costs before you begin.

The storage space on the four pull-outs should hold all of the tools you fre-

quently use. The two large drawers can be used for smaller tools and documents. The mobile feature allows you to roll the cabinet to the side of your shop. Add a few locks as a safety feature, to stop curious youngsters from playing with potentially dangerous equipment.

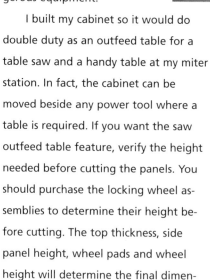

I built my cabinet so it would do double duty as an outfeed table for a table saw and a handy table at my miter station. In fact, the cabinet can be moved beside any power tool where a table is required. If you want the saw outfeed table feature, verify the height needed before cutting the panels. You should purchase the locking wheel assemblies to determine their height before cutting. The top thickness, side panel height, wheel pads and wheel height will determine the final dimensions of the cabinet.

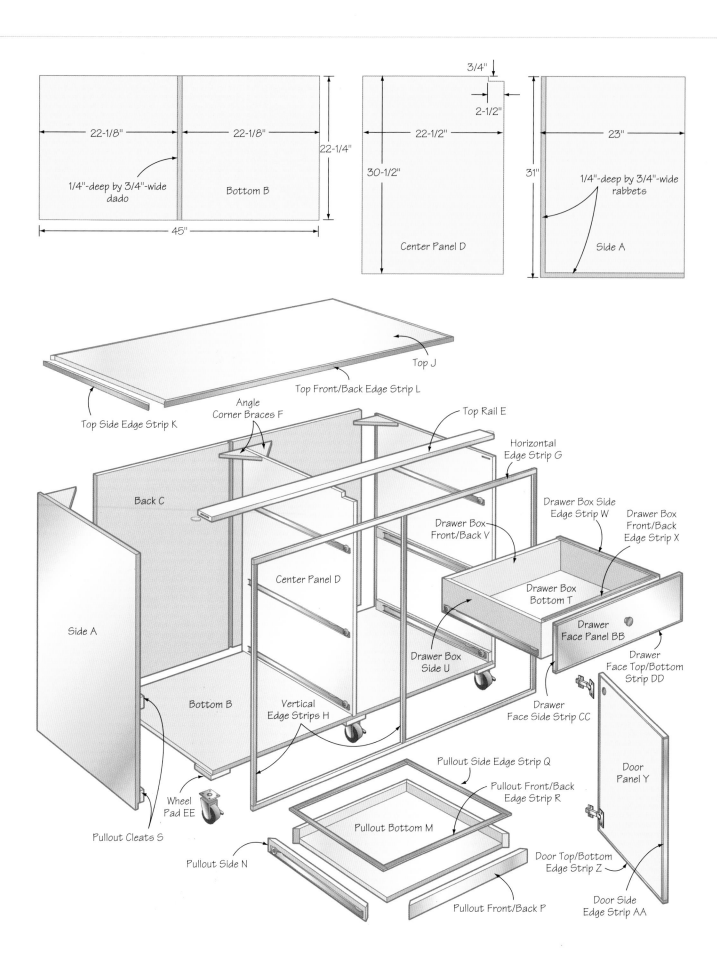

22-1/8"

22-1/8"

22-1/4"

1/4"-deep by 3/4"-wide dado

Bottom B

45"

3/4"

2-1/2"

22-1/2"

30-1/2"

Center Panel D

23"

31"

1/4"-deep by 3/4"-wide rabbets

Side A

Top J

Top Front/Back Edge Strip L

Top Side Edge Strip K

Angle Corner Braces F

Top Rail E

Horizontal Edge Strip G

Back C

Drawer Box Side Edge Strip W

Drawer Box Front/Back Edge Strip X

Center Panel D

Drawer Box Front/Back V

Drawer Box Bottom T

Side A

Drawer Box Side U

Drawer Face Panel BB

Drawer Face Top/Bottom Strip DD

Bottom B

Vertical Edge Strips H

Drawer Face Side Strip CC

Door Panel Y

Pullout Side Edge Strip Q

Pullout Front/Back Edge Strip R

Pullout Bottom M

Wheel Pad EE

Pullout Side N

Door Top/Bottom Edge Strip Z

Pullout Cleats S

Pullout Front/Back P

Door Side Edge Strip AA

materials list ▪ **INCHES**

REFERENCE	QUANTITY	PART	STOCK	THICKNESS	WIDTH	LENGTH	COMMENTS
A	2	sides	plywood	$3/4$	23	31	
B	1	bottom	plywood	$3/4$	$22^1/4$	45	
C	1	back	plywood	$3/4$	31	45	
D	1	center panel	plywood	$3/4$	$22^1/2$	$30^1/2$	
E	1	top rail	plywood	$3/4$	$2^1/2$	$44^1/2$	
F	4	angle corner braces	hardwood	$3/4$	3	3	angle-cut
G	2	horizontal edge strips	hardwood	$1/4$	$3/4$	46	
H	3	vertical edge strips	hardwood	$1/4$	$3/4$	$29^1/2$	
J	1	top	plywood	$3/4$	26	48	
K	2	top side edge strips	hardwood	$1/4$	$3/4$	26	
L	2	top front/back edge strips	hardwood	$1/4$	$3/4$	$48^1/2$	
M	4	pullout bottoms	plywood	$3/4$	$18^5/8$	$20^1/2$	
N	8	pullout sides	plywood	$3/4$	2	22	angle-cut
P	8	pullout fronts & backs	plywood	$3/4$	2	$20^1/8$	angle-cut
Q	8	pullout side edge strips	hardwood	$1/4$	$3/4$	22	
R	8	pullout front/back edge strips	hardwood	$1/4$	$3/4$	$18^5/8$	
S	4	pullout cleats	plywood	$3/4$	2	22	
T	2	drawer box bottoms	plywood	$3/4$	$19^3/8$	$20^1/2$	
U	4	drawer box sides	plywood	$3/4$	5	22	angle-cut
V	4	drawer box fronts/backs	plywood	$3/4$	5	$20^7/8$	angle-cut
W	4	drawer side edge strips	hardwood	$1/4$	$3/4$	22	
X	4	drawer front/back edge strips	hardwood	$1/4$	$3/4$	$19^3/8$	
Y	2	door panels	plywood	$3/4$	$22^1/8$	23	
Z	4	door top/bottom edge strips	hardwood	$1/4$	$3/4$	$22^5/8$	
AA	4	door side edge strips	hardwood	$1/4$	$3/4$	23	
BB	2	drawer face panels	plywood	$3/4$	$6^3/4$	$22^1/8$	
CC	4	drawer face side strips	hardwood	$1/4$	$3/4$	$6^3/4$	
DD	4	drawer face top/bottom strips	hardwood	$1/4$	$3/4$	$22^5/8$	
EE	6	wheel pads	hardwood	$3/4$	5	5	

HARDWARE

2" PB screws

Brad nails as detailed

Glue

6 Locking wheels

4 - 22" Drawer glide sets

2 - 22" Full-extension drawer glide sets

4 Knobs

4 - 107° Hidden hinges

24 - $1^1/2$"-Long x $5/16$"-diameter lag bolts

Finishing nails

#10 Biscuits or dowels

Wood putty

$1^1/4$" Screws

Iron-on edge tape

$5/8$" Screws

REFERENCE	QUANTITY	PART	STOCK	THICKNESS	WIDTH	LENGTH	COMMENTS
A	2	sides	plywood	19	584	787	
B	1	bottom	plywood	19	565	1143	
C	1	back	plywood	19	787	1143	
D	1	center panel	plywood	19	572	775	
E	1	top rail	plywood	19	64	1131	
F	4	angle corner braces	hardwood	19	76	76	angle-cut
G	2	horizontal edge strips	hardwood	6	19	1168	
H	3	vertical edge strips	hardwood	6	19	750	
J	1	top	plywood	19	660	1219	
K	2	top side edge strips	hardwood	6	19	660	
L	2	top front/back edge strips	hardwood	6	19	1232	
M	4	pullout bottoms	plywood	19	473	521	
N	8	pullout sides	plywood	19	51	559	angle-cut
P	8	pullout fronts & backs	plywood	19	51	511	angle-cut
Q	8	pullout side edge strips	hardwood	6	19	559	
R	8	pullout front/back edge strips	hardwood	6	19	473	
S	4	pullout cleats	plywood	19	51	559	
T	2	drawer box bottoms	plywood	19	493	521	
U	4	drawer box sides	plywood	19	127	559	angle-cut
V	4	drawer box fronts/backs	plywood	19	127	530	angle-cut
W	4	drawer side edge strips	hardwood	6	19	559	
X	4	drawer front/back edge strips	hardwood	6	19	493	
Y	2	door panels	plywood	19	562	584	
Z	4	door top/bottom edge strips	hardwood	6	19	575	
AA	4	door side edge strips	hardwood	6	19	584	
BB	2	drawer face panels	plywood	19	171	562	
CC	4	drawer face side strips	hardwood	6	19	171	
DD	4	drawer face top/bottom strips	hardwood	6	19	575	
EE	6	wheel pads	hardwood	19	127	127	

HARDWARE

51mm PB screws

Brad nails as detailed

Glue

6 Locking wheels

4 - 559mm Drawer glide sets

2 - 559mm Full-extension drawer glide sets

4 Knobs

4 - 107° Hidden hinges

24 - 38mm-Long x 8mm-diameter lag bolts

Finishing nails

#10 Biscuits or dowels

Wood putty

32mm Screws

Iron-on edge tape

16mm Screws

STEP 1 ⬚ Cut the two side panels A to the size shown in the materials list. Form a rabbet that's ¼" deep by ¾" wide on the inside bottom and back edge of each panel.

STEP 2 ⬚ Before preparing the bottom B and back C, refer to the construction notes at the end of this chapter regarding cutting the sheets for maximum yield. In the middle of each panel, rout a dado that's ¼" deep by ¾" wide. See the exploded illustration earlier in this chapter for positioning details.

STEP 3 ⬚ Attach the sides to the bottom and back panels, being careful to align the center dadoes. Use glue on all the joints and clamp tightly until secure. If you don't have long clamps for the case, use finishing nails to hold the joints until the glue sets.

STEP 4 ⬚ The center panel D needs a ¾"-deep by 2½"-long notch at the top front edge to receive the top rail E. Secure the panel with glue and clamps or finishing nails.

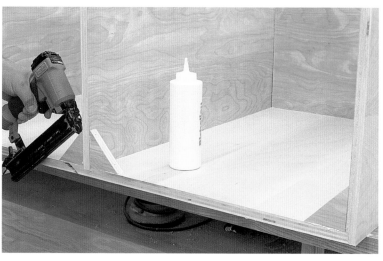

STEP 5 ■ The top rail E is secured to the center panel with glue and finishing nails. Carefully align the center panel so there is equal spacing in both sections of the cabinet. I secured both ends of the rail to the side panels using #10 biscuits; however, you can use dowels, pocket holes on the top side or screws and glue.

STEP 6 ■ The rear corners will have right-angle corner braces installed. These will be used to attach the top panel but will also add strength to the mobile case. Attach the four braces F with glue and brad nails.

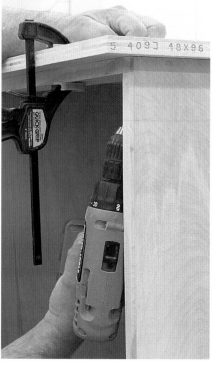

STEP 8 ■ The top panel J is attached with 1¼" screws through the front rail and four corner braces. Adjust the top so it extends 1¼" past each side and 1½" on the front of the cabinet. Cover the four edges of the top panel with hardwood edge strips K and L using glue and brad nails.

STEP 7 ■ The exposed front edges of the sides, rail and bottom panel are covered with ¼"-thick by ¾"-wide hardwood strips. Use glue and brad nails to attach the strips G and H. Fill the nail holes with wood putty.

Shop Tip

Don't glue the top in place, so it can be replaced after a few years of use. You might also decide to cover the top panel with a ¼" piece of hardboard that is tacked in place with a few screws. This inexpensive cover can be easily replaced if the top is damaged.

STEP 9 ■ The four pullouts are constructed using ³⁄₄" plywood veneer or other sheet material. The side, back and front boards are mitered at 45° on each corner. Cut the parts to the sizes detailed in the materials list and assemble each pullout using glue and brad nails. Notice that each pullout is 1³⁄₄" narrower than the cabinet space to allow for drawer glide clearance, and that a ³⁄₄"-thick spacing cleat is needed so the tray will clear the door.

STEP 10 ■ Trim the top edges of the pullout trays using ¹⁄₄"-thick by ³⁄₄"-wide hardwood strips Q and R. Attach the trim with glue and brad nails, then fill the nail holes with wood putty.

STEP 11 ■ Both cabinet sections require two spacing cleats S on the door hinge side. This will provide proper clearance for the pullouts. Attach the cleats with 1¹⁄₄" screws. Cover the exposed edges of the plywood with iron-on edge tape or hardwood strips. The cleats are positioned to meet the needs of your storage requirements.

STEP 12 ■ The four pullout trays are installed using Blum 22" bottom-mount drawer glide hardware. Fit the slides and test for proper operation.

STEP 13 ■ The two drawer boxes are constructed following the same steps as the pullout trays; however, the sides are 5" high and the width is increased by ¾" to 20⅞" because they don't have to clear door hinges. The box corners are mitered and assembled using glue and brad nails. The bottom board T is inset like the pullout tray bottoms. Trim the top edges with ¼"-thick hardwood strips W and X, or you can use iron-on edge tape.

STEP 14 ■ I mounted my drawers using Accuride 22" full-extension side-mounted drawer glides. Position the glide hardware so the bottom of each box is 6" below the underside of the top rail.

STEP 15 ■ The finished doors measure 22⅝" wide by 23½" high after the trim is attached to the panels. Cut the two panels Y and install the trim pieces Z and AA with glue and brad nails. Drill two 35mm holes, ⅛" away from the door edge, centered 4" from the top and bottom edge of each door. Install the hinges on the doors with the hinge plates attached. Align each door flush with the bottom edge of the cabinet in its normally open position. Put a ⅛"-thick strip of wood between the cabinet front edge and door. Drive ⅝" screws in the plate holes to secure the hinges to the cabinet sides. Remove the ⅛" spacing strip and test the operation of each door.

STEP 16 ■ Follow the same assembly steps when building the drawer fronts. The finished size of each front will be 7¼" high by 22⅝" wide. Use 1¼" screws to attach the drawer faces to the boxes. Use a ⅛"-thick spacer on top of the door to properly align the drawer faces.

STEP 17 ■ Use glue and two 1¼" screws to install the six wood wheel pads EE on the cabinet base. These pads should be placed at each corner and under the center vertical divider. The load on, and in, the cabinet will be transferred through the cabinet sides and center panel to the wheel pads and onto the wheels to the floor.

STEP 18 ■ Attach one heavy-duty swivel locking wheel on each pad. Use 1½"-long by 5/16"-diameter lag bolts in pilot holes to secure the wheels.

Cost is a concern when building this cabinet. Making the best use of the sheet materials is important, so plan your cutting diagrams carefully. You should crosscut along the width of the 4' x 8' sheet for large back, bottom and top panels. The top is a full 4', and the other two panels are almost as wide. Use a circular saw to crosscut each panel to a manageable size, then finish the cuts on your table saw.

You can, as I mentioned in the introduction, use any ¾" sheet material. Some reasonably priced plywood can be painted. MDF is inexpensive and a good material to paint, or you may want to use melamine PB. If your shop isn't too damp, any of the mentioned materials would be fine. If the shop is damp and water leaks are possible, you should use plywood.

Align the pullouts in the cabinet to suit your storage requirements. Don't use glue to secure them, so they can be moved should your needs change. The pullout trays work well on the bottom-mount drawer glides, but full-extension hardware can be used. The drawers can also be fitted with regular bottom-mount glides in place of the more expensive full-extension hardware to lessen the cost.

Install the hardwood wheel pads and use six heavy-duty locking wheels that swivel. Four wheels wouldn't support the load properly and may cause the bottom board to sag. The center wheels support a large part of the load and guarantee proper cabinet alignment for the pullouts and drawers.

Saw Outfeed Table and Storage Cabinet

For years my table saw outfeed table was part of a sheet of melamine particleboard (PB) supported by a pair of those inexpensive folding legs you can buy at a home store. The table wasn't very stable and could, and often did, move when I was cutting heavy sheet material on the saw. That safety issue alone made me look toward designing a better outfeed table.

Storage under the metal folding support legs was reduced because of their angle locking system. The legs weren't adjustable, so I was always leveling the table with small pieces of wood. It was a poor outfeed support system and something better, and safer, was needed.

This outfeed table and storage cabinet meets all of my needs. I built it using ³/₄"-thick MDF, so it's heavy and stable. It has an adjustable leg system, and the cabinet box provides a great deal of storage space. Adjustable shelves and doors allow me to customize the cabinet for my storage requirements.

The outfeed tabletop I need for my table saw is 3' wide by 6' long. Yours will most likely be different, so change the dimensions to suit your needs. The height will also be different for many of you, so adjust the vertical panel dimension. The cabinet top should be flush with your table saw top.

The cabinet height is a combination of top thickness, vertical panel length and adjustable leg height. If you plan on using an adjustable leg system, buy it before you start and note the height in the middle of the adjustment range. Then cut the side and center panels to the size required based on your table saw height.

The cabinet doesn't require doors if you plan on adding extra shelves to store short lengths of wood. You might want one section with doors for dust-free storage and the other without for small panel storage. There are many ways to configure the cabinet storage section based on your needs. No matter which storage setup you choose, you'll appreciate all the benefits of this solid outfeed table and storage center.

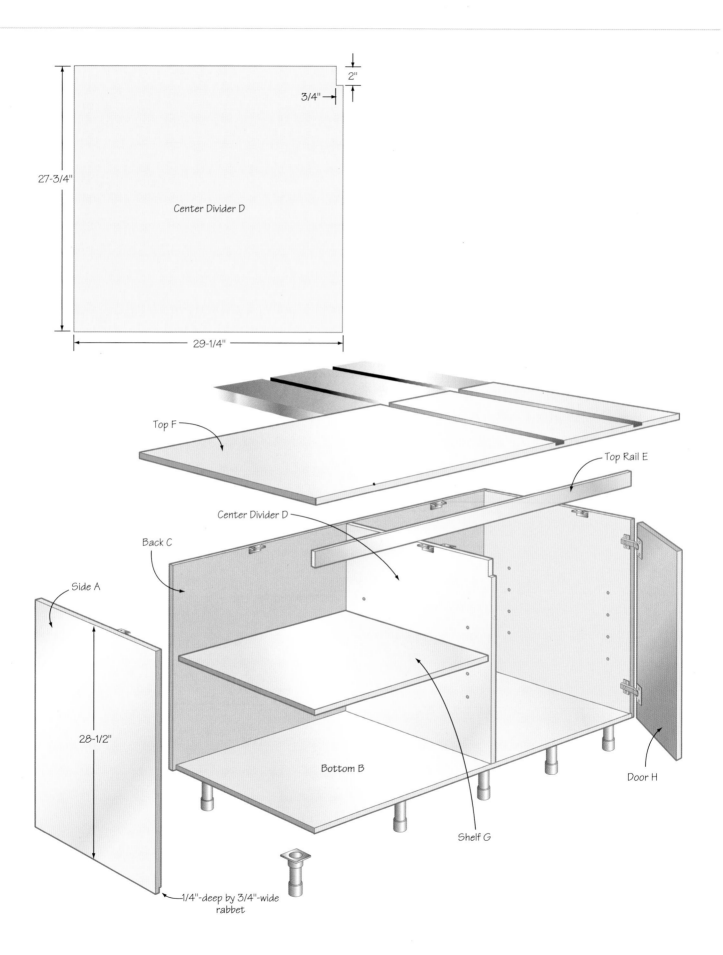

2"

3/4"

27-3/4"

Center Divider D

29-1/4"

Top F

Top Rail E

Center Divider D

Back C

Side A

28-1/2"

Bottom B

Shelf G

Door H

1/4"-deep by 3/4"-wide
rabbet

materials list ▪ **INCHES**

REFERENCE	QUANTITY	PART	STOCK	THICKNESS	WIDTH	LENGTH	COMMENTS
A	2	sides	MDF	3/4	29 1/4	28 1/2	
B	1	bottom	MDF	3/4	29 1/4	66 1/2	
C	1	back	MDF	3/4	28 1/2	67 1/2	
D	1	center divider	MDF	3/4	29 1/4	27 3/4	
E	1	top rail	MDF	3/4	2	66	
F	1	top	MDF	3/4	36	72	
G	2	shelves	MDF	3/4	32 9/16	29	
H	4	doors	MDF	3/4	16 5/8	27 1/2	

HARDWARE

2" PB screws as detailed

5/8" Screws as detailed

Glue

11 Right-angle brackets

10 Adjustable legs

8 Shelf pins

4 – 107° Full-overlay hinges

4 – 107° Half-overlay hinges

8 Standard hinge plates

4 Door handles

5/8" Screws

materials list ▪ **MILLIMETERS**

REFERENCE	QUANTITY	PART	STOCK	THICKNESS	WIDTH	LENGTH	COMMENTS
A	2	sides	MDF	19	743	724	
B	1	bottom	MDF	19	743	1689	
C	1	back	MDF	19	724	1715	
D	1	center divider	MDF	19	743	705	
E	1	top rail	MDF	19	51	1676	
F	1	top	MDF	19	914	1829	
G	2	shelves	MDF	19	827	737	
H	4	doors	MDF	19	422	699	

HARDWARE

51mm PB screws as detailed

16mm Screws as detailed

Glue

11 Right-angle brackets

10 Adjustable legs

8 Shelf pins

4 – 107° Full-overlay hinges

4 – 107° Half-overlay hinges

8 Standard hinge plates

4 Door handles

16mm Screws

STEP 2 ■ Both side panels require a rabbet that's ¼" deep by ¾" wide on their bottom inside edge. Next, cut the bottom board B to size and join the sides to the bottom board in the rabbets. The joints are secured with glue and four 2" screws on each panel. Remember to drill pilot holes for the screws.

STEP 1 ■ Cut cabinet sides A to the dimensions listed in the materials list. Drill adjustable shelf-pin holes in the inside face of each side panel. Mark the top of each panel so the first hole distance is referenced from the top edge. This important step will ensure that the center divider's shelf-pin holes will be in alignment with the side panel holes.

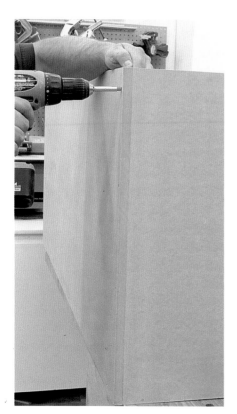

Shop Tip

Keep screws a minimum of 1" away from the end of MDF panels to avoid splitting the material.

STEP 4 ■ Drill a series of shelf-pin holes on each side of center divider D, being sure to mark and reference the first hole from the top edge of the panel. This will align the side and center divider shelf-pin holes.

Offset the columns of holes on each side of the panel by 1" to avoid drilling through the divider. On the top front edge of the panel, cut a notch that's ¾" deep by 2" high to receive the top rail. Secure the divider in the center of the cabinet, creating two sections that are 32⅝" wide. Use glue and screws through the back and bottom board to secure the divider.

STEP 3 ■ The back C fully overlays or covers the back edges of the sides and bottom board. Use glue and 2" screws, about 6" apart, to secure the back.

STEP 5 ▪ The top rail E is attached to the sides and in the notch of the center panel. The rail is only 2" wide, so screws driven in the end will usually split the MDF. I secured the rail with glue and right-angle brackets using ⁵⁄₈" screws. Both ends of the rail are aligned with the side's top and face edges. The rail will be secured to the underside of the cabinet top with more right-angle brackets and screws.

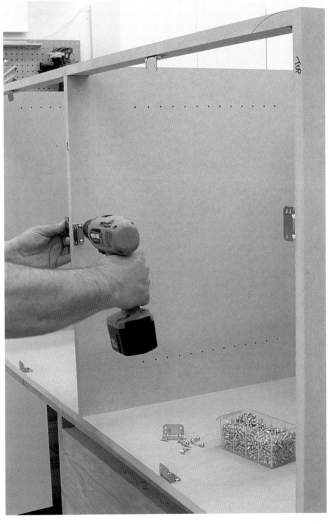

STEP 6 ▪ The base support for my table is its adjustable legs. You might opt for a solid base, made with ³⁄₄" MDF, but most shop floors are uneven and the adjustable leg is an ideal solution. These legs are available at most woodworking stores.

Attach 10 legs using the manufacturer's fastening recommendations. Two legs are placed under each cabinet side board and two under the center divider. The other four are attached in the middle of each section span.

A base or leg system placed directly under the cabinet's vertical panels will properly transfer the cabinet load to the floor. Set the legs 2" back from the front edge of the cabinet to provide space when someone is standing at the front of the cabinet.

STEP 7 ▪ Attach eight right-angle brackets in the center of each panel and on the center of each rail span in every section. These brackets, which will be used to secure the cabinet top, should be flush with the top edge of each panel.

STEP 8 ▪ The top board F is ³⁄₄"-thick MDF. Secure it to the cabinet using screws through the previously installed brackets.

The sides overhang the cabinet by 2¹⁄₄". The front overhang is 1", and the top extends past the back of the cabinet by 5". I've offset the front and back overhang so the cabinet won't interfere with my vacuum system behind the table saw. Adjust the top overhang to suit your shop setup.

STEP 9 ▪ Place the cabinet in its permanent location and level the top to the table saw top. Use a router and straightedge to cut two dadoes in the cabinet top that are in line with the miter slide tracks of the saw. Adjust the dado depth to match the track depth on the saw.

STEP 10 ▪ I installed two shelf boards G in my cabinet, but your storage needs may be different, so install as many as needed. The best shelf pin for this application has a full-metal shaft to support heavy loads. Install the pins in the drilled holes and test fit the shelves.

STEP 11 ■ The cabinet can be left as an open shelving unit or have doors installed. The doors are attached using 100° to 120° hidden hinges. Cut the four doors H, then drill two 35mm-diameter holes in each that are 4" on center from each end and ⅛" away from the door edge. Hinge holes are approximately ½" deep, but test fit the hinges to ensure they are seated correctly.

You can avoid using a combination of half- and full-overlay hinges by installing two center dividers. Follow the same installation steps for the second divider, being sure to leave equal spacing in both sections of the cabinet. You won't have to worry about offsetting shelf-pin hole columns with two dividers, and standard full-overlay hinges can be used on all the doors. Door width will change with the two-divider system, however. Measure the inside width of the cabinet, add 1" to that dimension and divide by 2; that's the required width of each door.

The cabinet interior is easily modified to suit your needs. Vertical dividers can be installed to create more than two sections, extra shelves can be added and doors can be installed on all or one section only. The cabinet can be easily customized for your shop.

If you plan on storing a lot of heavy items on the shelves, I suggest you use ¾"-thick plywood in place of the MDF. This two-section cabinet design requires wide shelves that can bend with heavy loads. If the shelves will be used to support heavy material or equipment, consider building the cabinet with three sections as a possible option.

As previously discussed, this cabinet design suits my table saw. Most saws are close in style and dimension, but you will have to make minor dimensional changes to suit your equipment. You might also consider mounting this cabinet on locking wheels if your table saw is mobile; however, you will need a level workshop floor for this option.

STEP 12 ■ The hinges on the two outside doors are full-overlay models, and the four on the inside doors are half-overlay. Install the hinges, with hinge plates attached, then mount the doors on the cabinets.

Hold the door in its normally open position, flush with the bottom edge of the base board. Place a ⅛"-thick strip of wood between the door edge and cabinet front edge. This spacing is needed to properly set the door-to-cabinet gap. Drive screws through the hinge-plate holes into the cabinet to secure the doors. Adjust the doors if necessary so there's a 1/16" gap in the center of each pair. Finally, install four handles of your choice.

Shop-Made 12" Disc Sander

This project is inexpensive and easy to build, providing you have an electric motor lying around your shop, or you plan on picking one up at the next neighborhood garage sale.

The cabinet, motor support and adjustable table system are built using ¾" MDF sheet material. A few pieces of hardware such as screws, hinges and a motor pulley are all that is needed to build this handy 12" disc sander.

I will be using the sander to round over small parts, sand flat edges and smooth band saw cuts. My wife wants this sander for her craftwork because it's a great tool for finish-sanding dozens of small parts. The disc runs quietly and quickly removes material with the proper paper grit.

The self-adhesive 12"-diameter sanding discs are available at woodworking stores. I use an 80-grit paper for general work and 150-grit paper for finer work. This disc sander is a safe tool, so woodworkers of all ages can use it. The platform is close to the disc and is an ideal support for your work, but it also serves as a safety guard should the disc loosen.

The woodworkers who have dropped into my shop while I was building this sander were impressed with the project, and a few more are being built. All my friends are hunting through old motors that they've been storing for years. Finally, a use for that electric motor you knew couldn't be thrown out!

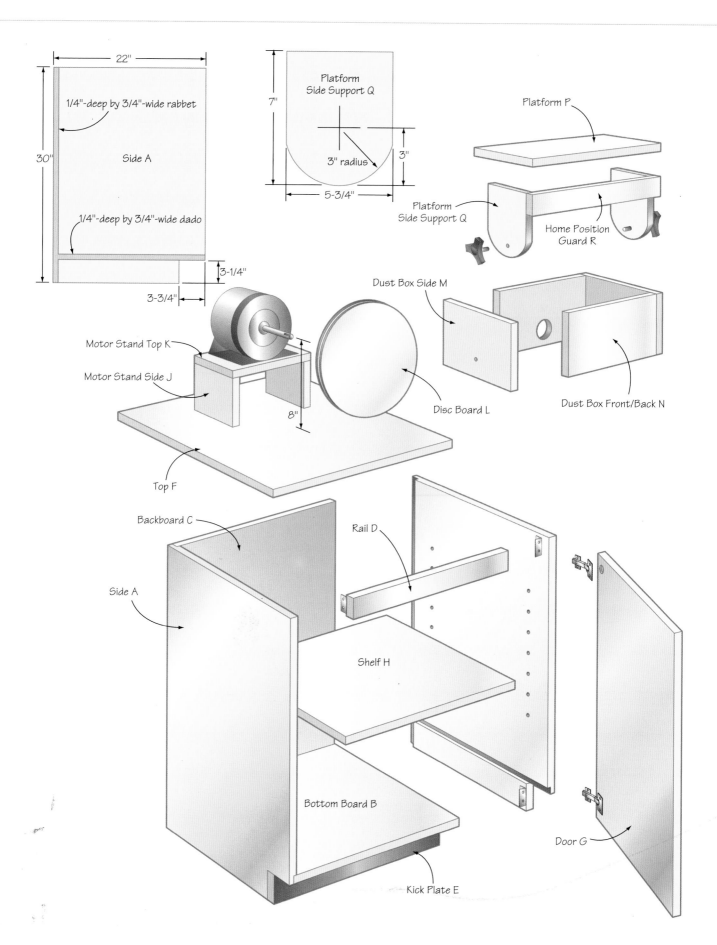

22"

1/4"-deep by 3/4"-wide rabbet

Side A

30"

1/4"-deep by 3/4"-wide dado

3-1/4"

3-3/4"

Platform
Side Support Q

7"

3" radius

3"

5-3/4"

Platform P

Platform
Side Support Q

Home Position
Guard R

Dust Box Side M

Motor Stand Top K

Motor Stand Side J

8"

Disc Board L

Dust Box Front/Back N

Top F

Backboard C

Rail D

Side A

Shelf H

Bottom Board B

Kick Plate E

Door G

materials list ▪ **INCHES**

REFERENCE	QUANTITY	PART	STOCK	THICKNESS	WIDTH	LENGTH	COMMENTS
A	2	sides	MDF	3/4	22	30	
B	1	bottom board	MDF	3/4	16	22	
C	1	backboard	MDF	3/4	16	26	
D	1	rail	MDF	3/4	2	15 1/2	
E	1	kick plate	MDF	3/4	3 1/4	17	
F	1	top	MDF	3/4	19	23 1/2	
G	1	door	MDF	3/4	16 1/2	26	
H	2	shelves	MDF	3/4	15 7/16	21	
J	2	motor stand sides	MDF	3/4	4 1/4	7	
K	1	motor stand top	MDF	3/4	10	7	
L	1	disc board	plywood	3/4	12 1/2	12 1/2	
M	2	dust box sides	MDF	3/4	8	6	
N	2	dust box front & back	MDF	3/4	13	6	
P	1	platform	MDF	3/4	8	18	
Q	2	platform side supports	MDF	3/4	5 3/4	7	
R	1	home position guard	MDF	3/4	3	16 1/16	

HARDWARE

1 1/2" Screws as detailed

Glue

8 Right-angle brackets

8 Shelf pins

2 – 107° Full-overlay hinges

1 Motor

1 Motor pulley

2 Knobs with 1/4" x 20" threaded shafts

2 T-nuts 1/4" x 20"

1 Door handle or knob

5/8" Screws

1 1/2" Screws

materials list ▪ **MILLIMETERS**

REFERENCE	QUANTITY	PART	STOCK	THICKNESS	WIDTH	LENGTH	COMMENTS
A	2	sides	MDF	19	559	762	
B	1	bottom board	MDF	19	406	559	
C	1	backboard	MDF	19	406	660	
D	1	rail	MDF	19	51	394	
E	1	kick plate	MDF	19	82	432	
F	1	top	MDF	19	483	597	
G	1	door	MDF	19	419	660	
H	2	shelves	MDF	19	392	533	
J	2	motor stand sides	MDF	19	108	178	
K	1	motor stand top	MDF	19	254	178	
L	1	disc board	plywood	19	318	318	
M	2	dust box sides	MDF	19	203	152	
N	2	dust box front & back	MDF	19	330	152	
P	1	platform	MDF	19	203	457	
Q	2	platform side supports	MDF	19	146	178	
R	1	home position guard	MDF	19	76	408	

HARDWARE

38mm Screws as detailed

Glue

8 Right-angle brackets

8 Shelf pins

2 – 107° Full-overlay hinges

1 Motor

1 Motor pulley

2 Knobs with 1/4" x 20" threaded shafts

2 T-nuts 6mm x 508mm

1 Door handle or knob

16mm Screws

38mm Screws

STEP 1 ■ Cut the sides A to size and drill two columns of holes for adjustable shelves on the inside face of each panel. Start the columns 4" from the top and end them about 4" from the bottom edges. Each column should be 2" in from the panel edge.

STEP 2 ■ Rout a $\frac{1}{4}$"-deep by $\frac{3}{4}$"-wide rabbet on the back inside face of each side panel A. They also need a $\frac{1}{4}$"-deep by $\frac{3}{4}$"-wide dado to accept the bottom board. The top edge of each dado should be 4" above the bottom edge of the side panel.

STEP 3 ■ The side panels also require a $3\frac{1}{4}$"-high by $3\frac{3}{4}$"-deep notch on their bottom front edge for the kick plate. Use a jigsaw, scroll saw or band saw to cut the notches.

STEP 4 ■ The bottom board B is attached to the side panels in the previously cut dadoes. Apply glue to the dadoes and clamp the sides to the bottom board until the adhesive sets.

STEP 6 ▪ The upper rail D can be attached with small biscuits, dowels or brackets and glue as I'm using. The top edge of the rail is flush with the top edges of the side panels.

STEP 5 ▪ The backboard C is installed in the two rabbets with glue. The assembly is clamped and 1½" screws are driven through the bottom board into the lower edge of the backboard. Once again, wait until the glue sets before removing the clamps.

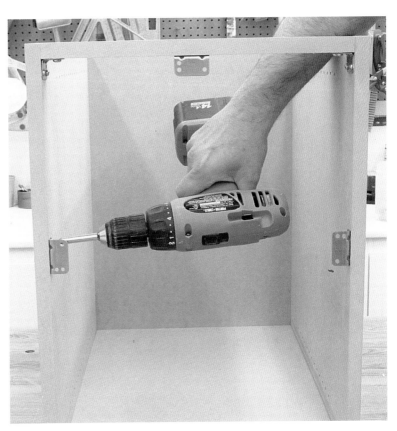

STEP 7 ▪ The kick plate E can also be secured with glue and right-angle brackets on the back side.

STEP 8 ▪ Install four right-angle brackets using ⅝" screws. The top of these brackets should be flush with the top edges of the sides, back and front rail. The brackets will be used to secure the cabinet top board.

STEP 9 ▪ Place the top board F on the cabinet with a 1" overhang on each side and a 1½" overhang on the front edge. The back edge is flush with the outside face of the backboard. Use ⅝" screws in the previously installed brackets to secure the top.

STEP 10 ▪ Install the hinges, with their hinge plates attached, on the door. Hold the door G in its normally open position, flush with the bottom edge of the base board B. Place a ⅛"-thick strip of wood between the door edge and cabinet front edge. This spacing is needed to properly set the door-to-cabinet gap. Drive screws through the hinge-plate holes into the cabinet to secure the door. Install a knob or handle of your choice, then cut and install the two shelf boards H.

STEP 11 ▪ Build a stand, as shown, to raise the center of the motor shaft 8" above the cabinet top. Leave about 10" in front of the stand. Your motor will probably be different from mine, so exact measurements are not given. The suggested dimensions should suit most electric motor sizes. See the construction notes at the end of this chapter for information on selecting a motor.

Use glue and 1½" screws through the underside of the top board to secure the motor stand. Attach the motor to the stand using whichever method is best suited to the motor you are using. My motor came equipped with a bracket, so I bolted the assembly through the stand top K.

STEP 12 ▪ For the disc board L, draw a 12⅛"-diameter circle on a ¾"-thick piece of plywood with a compass. Cut the circle as accurately as possible using a band saw, jigsaw or scroll saw. Measure the diameter of your pulley and draw a circle matching that size on the wood disc using the same center point.

Drill four holes through the pulley and attach it to the back face of the wood disc. Use screws that are long enough to anchor all the way into the thickness of the wood disc without puncturing the front face.

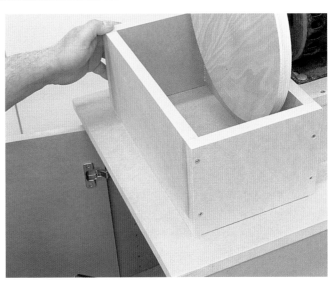

STEP 13 ◾ Install the disc and pulley assembly on the motor shaft, then lock it securely using the fastening system on your pulley. Wire the motor to a switch box and attach the box on the motor stand with screws.

Start the motor and true the disc using sandpaper. The disc should be sanded to 12" in diameter. Install 12"-diameter self-adhesive sandpaper to the front face of the wood disc.

STEP 14 ◾ Build a simple dust box with ³⁄₄"-thick MDF that's 14¹⁄₂"-wide by 8"-deep. The box should be 6" high and is assembled using glue and 1¹⁄₂" screws. Align the box on the cabinet top board with equal spacing on both sides. You will have to temporarily remove the disc to install the dust box. Secure the box to the cabinet with 1¹⁄₂" screws through the underside of the top.

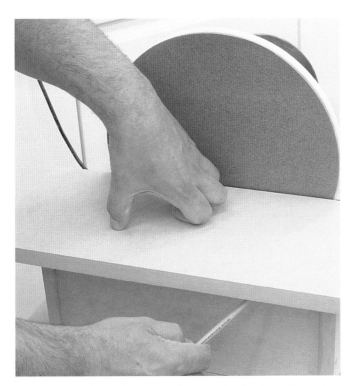

STEP 15 ◾ Cut the platform P and place it on the dust box with equal spacing on each side and ¹⁄₈" away from the sanding disc face. Trace the outline of the dust box on the underside of the platform.

STEP 16 ◾ Cut platform side supports Q, and draw a 3"-radius arc on the bottom edge of each board. Use a belt sander to form the arc on each support by sanding to the compass lines. Use glue and three 1¹⁄₂" screws to attach the side supports to the platform Q, keeping ¹⁄₃₂" away from the lines.

The home position guard R is secured to the sides of the platform supports with glue and screws. This guard will keep most of the dust in the box and help align the platform at its home position.

construction NOTES

The electric motor should be rated at ⅓ horsepower or more. These are common motors and should be available for a reasonable price at garage sales and flea markets.

The ⅓-horsepower motor I installed is powerful enough to handle my sanding requirements. However, you might be fortunate enough to find a good ½- or ¾-horsepower motor that will have the power to tackle any sanding job.

If you're not comfortable wiring the motor and switch unit, have someone who is familiar with electrical work complete this part of the project. Also, many motors have a reversible rotation feature so you might want to change the direction. My motor rotates counterclockwise as you face the disc, but it doesn't seem to matter which direction it rotates because the sander performs equally well in either rotation.

The cabinet can be built with any sheet material. I have one door and adjustable shelves for sandpaper storage, but drawers can be installed just as easily. The vacuum feature works well and does reduce the dust level that can be a serious concern with this tool. I think it's a worthwhile feature and suggest you have the vacuum on when using the sander.

STEP 17 ▪ Block the platform assembly so the top surface is aligned with the center of the sanding disc. Use a T-nut and knob with a threaded shaft on each side support to lock the platform in place. The home position guard will reference the platform at 90° to the sanding disc face, and the curved bottoms on the side supports will allow you to move the platform to any angle. The assembly can also be quickly tipped back to permit easy sandpaper removal and installation.

STEP 18 ▪ Tip the platform assembly back and remove the sanding disc. Drill a 2¼"-diameter hole in the backboard of the dust box. You can easily access the backboard through the rear of the motor stand. A standard 2¼"-diameter vacuum hose can now be attached to the dust box.

suppliers

Many suppliers have contributed products, material and technical support during the project-building phase of this book. I appreciate how helpful they've been and recommend these companies without hesitation.

ADAMS & KENNEDY – THE WOOD SOURCE
6178 Mitch Owen Road
P.O. Box 700
Manotick, Ontario K4M 1A6
613-822-6800
www.wood-source.com
Wood supply

DELTA MACHINERY
4825 Hwy. 45 North
P.O. Box 2468
Jackson, Tennessee 38302
800-223-7278 (in US)
800-463-3582 (in Canada)
www.deltawoodworking.com
Woodworking tools

EXAKTOR WOODWORKING TOOLS, INC.
4 Glenbourne Park
Markham, Ontario L6C1G9
800-387-9789
www.exaktortools.com
Accessories for the table saw

HOUSE OF TOOLS LTD.
100 Mayfield Common Northwest
Edmonton, Alberta T5P 4B3
800-661-3987
www.houseoftools.com
Woodworking tools and hardware

JESSEM TOOL COMPANY
124 Big Bay Point Road
Barrie, Ontario L4N 9B4
866-272-7492
www.jessem.com
Rout-R-Slide and Rout-R-Lift

LEE VALLEY TOOLS LTD.

USA:
P.O. Box 1780
Ogdensberg, New York 13669-6780
800-267-8735

Canada:
P.O. Box 6295, Station J
Ottawa, Ontario K2A 1T4
800-267-8761
www.leevalley.com
Fine woodworking tools and hardware

PORTER CABLE
4825 Highway 45 North
P.O. Box 2468
Jackson, Tennessee 38302-2468
800-487-8665
www.porter-cable.com
Woodworking tools

RICHELIEU HARDWARE
7900 West Henri-Bourassa
Ville St. Laurent, Quebec H4S 1V4
800-619-5446 (in US)
800-361-6000 (in Canada)
www.richelieu.com
Hardware supplies

ROCKLER WOODWORKING AND HARDWARE
4365 Willow Drive
Medina, Minnesota 55340
800-279-4441
www.rockler.com
Woodworking tools and hardware

TENRYU AMERICA, INC.
7964 Kentucky Drive, Suite 12
Florence, Kentucky 41042
800-951-7297
www.tenryu.com
Saw blades

TOOL TREND LTD.
140 Snow Boulevard
Concord, Ontario L4K 4C1
416-663-8665
Woodworking tools and hardware

VAUGHAN & BUSHNELL MANUFACTURING
11414 Maple Avenue
Hebron, Illinois 60034
815-648-2446
www.vaughanmfg.com
Hammers and other tools

WOLFCRAFT NORTH AMERICA
333 Swift Road
Addison, Illinois 60101-1448
630-773-4777
www.wolfcraft.com
Woodworking hardware and accessories

WOODCRAFT
P.O. Box 1686
Parkersburg, West Virginia 26102-1686
800-225-1153
www.woodcraft.com
Woodworking hardware and accessories

BUILDING THE PERFECT TOOL CHEST

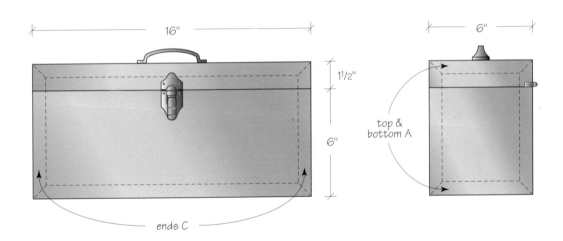

16"

1¹/₂"

6"

6"

top &
bottom A

ends C

BUILDING THE PERFECT TOOL CHEST

JIM STACK

POPULAR WOODWORKING BOOKS

CINCINNATI, OHIO

www.popularwoodworking.com

table of contents

I would like to say at the beginning: You will see photos in this book that demonstrate techniques of wood-working with power tools. The guards on the tools, especially the table saw, have been removed to clearly show the process. I do not advocate the use of power tools without all the proper guards and other safety items in place. Using power tools can be dangerous. Don't work while you are tired or in a hurry as that is how you get hurt. If a particular setup doesn't seem quite right to you — it probably isn't. Take the time to review the setup and make adjustments if necessary. I want you to have fun and be safe while you are woodworking.

Tool chests and boxes almost invariably reflect the style, talent and personality of the builder. Those of us who work with tools like to keep them organized and in good shape.

I offer several different ideas in this book to help you decide how you would like to store your tools. I

looked at a lot of books and magazine articles about building tool chests, and came away marveling at the creative ideas out there. I couldn't include all the ideas I wanted to; I just didn't have the space.

All the projects offered here are for you to adjust, resize and reconfigure to your own personal needs and tastes. I tried to include projects for novice to advanced woodworkers, and I think I succeeded. (If you can start right out by building Glen and Malcolm Huey's 21st-century tool cabinet, I applaud you wholeheartedly!)

I'm not a fan of long introductions, so let's build some tool chests.

This toolbox is perfect for holding all those everyday tools that you use around the house — a tack hammer, screwdrivers, tape ruler, extra screws and nails, etc.

The techniques used to make this box are simple and fun. As with all the projects in this book, you can change the dimensions to suit your particular needs. For example, it would be a simple matter to make this box twice as big.

I prefer to see the wood that I use to build my projects, so I used a clear finish on all but two of the projects in this book. Feel free to finish these projects as you like — with paint, stain or whatever suits your needs.

handy box

Detail of folding the miter joint

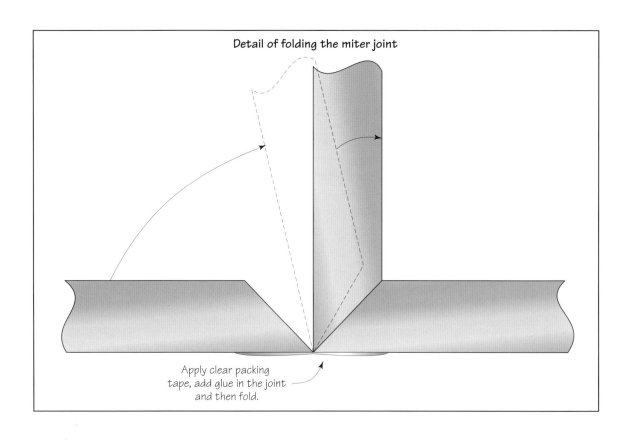

Apply clear packing
tape, add glue in the joint
and then fold.

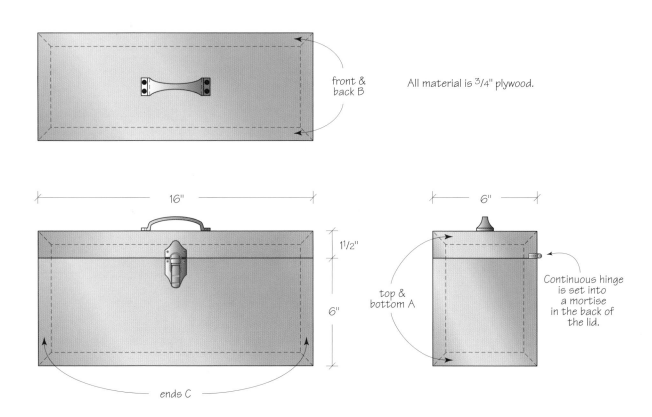

front &
back B

All material is 3/4" plywood.

16"

1¹/2"

6"

6"

top &
bottom A

Continuous hinge
is set into
a mortise
in the back of
the lid.

ends C

materials list

REFERENCE	QUANTITY	PART	STOCK	THICKNESS	WIDTH	LENGTH	COMMENTS
A	2	top & bottom	plywood	$^3/_4$	6	16	all edges have a 45° bevel
B	2	front & back	plywood	$^3/_4$	7$^1/_2$	16	all edges have a 45° bevel
C	2	ends	plywood	$^3/_4$	6	7$^1/_2$	all edges have a 45° bevel

hardware

- 1 continuous hinge $^3/_{16}$" × 1$^1/_2$" × 16"
- 1 drawbolt
- 1 screen door handle

MILLIMETERS

REFERENCE	QUANTITY	PART	STOCK	THICKNESS	WIDTH	LENGTH	COMMENTS
A	2	top & bottom	plywood	19	152	406	all edges have a 45° bevel
B	2	front & back	plywood	19	191	406	all edges have a 45° bevel
C	2	ends	plywood	19	152	191	all edges have a 45° bevel

hardware

- 1 continuous hinge 5mm × 38mm × 406mm
- 1 drawbolt
- 1 screen door handle

STEP-BY-STEP construction

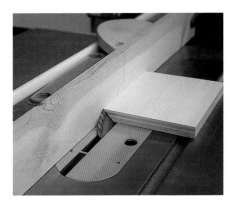

step 1 • Cut all the parts to size as shown in the materials list. Then tilt the table saw blade to 45° and attach a sacrificial fence to the saw's fence. Adjust this setup until you can cut a 45° bevel on the edge of the box parts. This setup allows you to cut bevels on parts that have already been cut to size, which is easier than trying to cut all the parts to size and bevel them at the same time.

step 2 • Double-check the 45° bevel to be sure that a perfect 90° corner is formed. This is critical for all the parts to join together squarely at glue-up time.

step 3 • Lay out the bottom A, the front and back B and the two ends C faceup as shown. Use clear packing tape to tape the joints, creating a hinge. Be sure that the sharp edges of the bevels come together as cleanly as possible when you apply the tape.

tip >> BEVEL CUTS ON PLYWOOD EDGES

Be careful when cutting and handling plywood after you've cut bevels on the edges. Plywood edges are fragile and can be easily chipped or nicked. Also, I've received some nasty cuts from these edges as they are sharp!

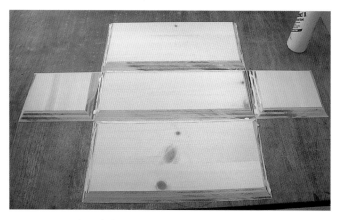

step 4 • Turn the whole assembly facedown, then apply glue to all the edges that will be coming together when it's folded up.

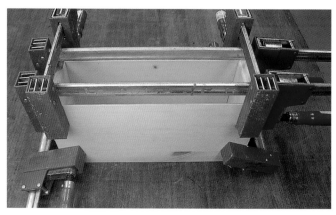

step 5 • You will need to use a few clamps to hold the side joints tightly. Don't use too much pressure, as that will distort the joint and cause it to open up at the sharp edges.

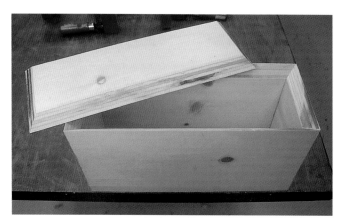

step 6 • When the glue has dried, remove the clamps, apply glue to the remaining beveled edges and attach the top.

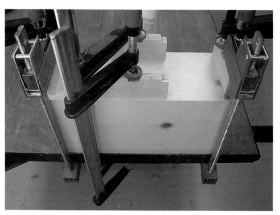

step 7 • Use blocks under the clamps to even out the pressure. At this point you might be wondering if you could tape the top to the assembly when all the parts are lying flat in step three, and I say, "Yes, you could!" (I didn't because I simply got ahead of myself.) If I made this again, I would tape all the parts and fold up all six sides at one time.

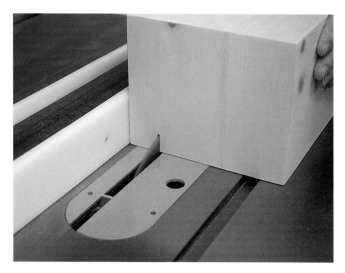

step 8 • When the glue has dried, gently scrape or sand away any glue squeeze-out. Cut the lid off the box, using the table saw.

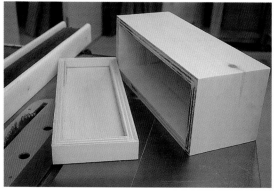

step 9 • The lid will fit perfectly on the box using this technique.

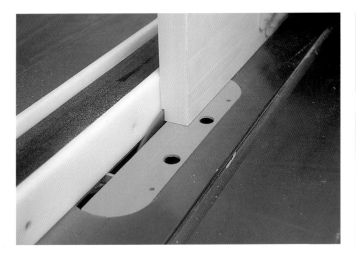

step 10 • Measure the thickness of the continuous hinge. Set the table saw fence to this measurement and make a through-cut.

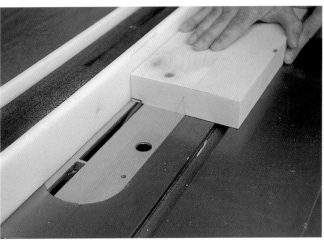

step 11 • Reset the fence to the width of the hinge leaf (this does not include the barrel of the hinge) and make the cleanup cut. This cut squares out the corner of the rabbet cut.

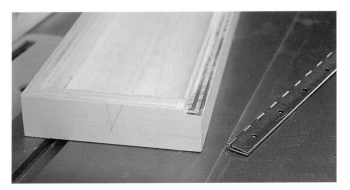

step 12 • This is the finished cut. If your saw blade is a little dull (as mine is), you will have some burn marks on your wood. This is OK, as the hinge will cover these marks. (I guess I should get my saw blade sharpened!)

step 13 • Install the hinge. If your cut is accurate, the hinge is lined up easily by holding the edge of the hinge leaf against the shoulder of the rabbet. By allowing the barrel of the hinge to extend beyond the edge of the box, the lid can be opened 180°.

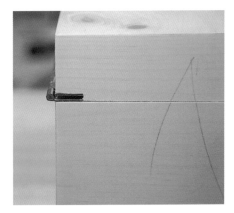

step 14 • This is a quick but neat and tidy way to install a hinge. You can now install the drawbolt and screen door handle.

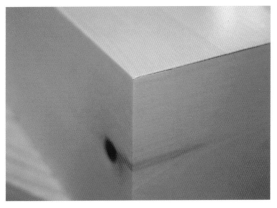

step 15 • When you've finished the box, the corners will have a nice, clean look. This is a strong joint. The gluing surface is large, and no splines or biscuits are needed.

small tool chest

One of the forklift drivers in our warehouse at F&W Publications was keeping an eye out for pallet wood for me. He found a 2" × 8" × 10' board of luan mahogany. When he showed it to me I was excited because it was colorful and had some nice grain patterns in it.

I used that board to build this toolbox. I made all the framework from the solid-wood board, and I used some scrap luan ¼" plywood for the panels.

This small toolbox will sit nicely on a bench but can be easily moved if the tools in it are needed elsewhere.

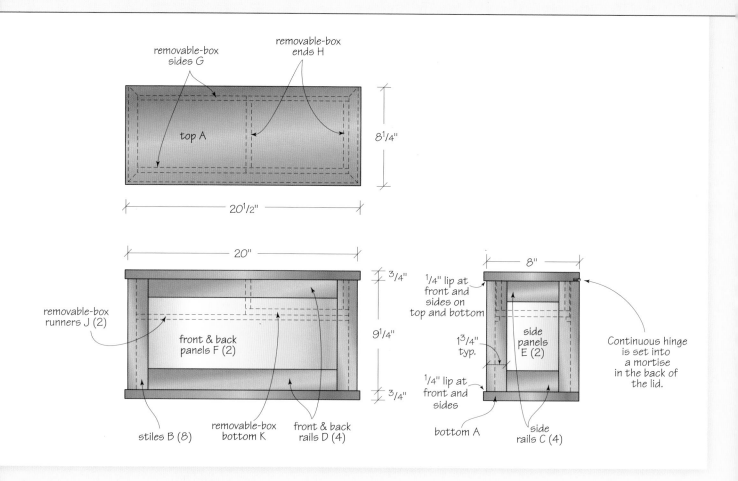

removable-box sides G

removable-box ends H

top A

8¹/₄"

20¹/₂"

20"

³/₄"

removable-box runners J (2)

front & back panels F (2)

9¹/₄"

³/₄"

stiles B (8)

removable-box bottom K

front & back rails D (4)

8"

¹/₄" lip at front and sides on top and bottom

side panels E (2)

Continuous hinge is set into a mortise in the back of the lid.

1³/₄" typ.

¹/₄" lip at front and sides

bottom A

side rails C (4)

materials list

INCHES

REFERENCE	QUANTITY	PART	STOCK	THICKNESS	WIDTH	LENGTH
A	2	top & bottom	hardwood	³/₄	8¹/₄	20¹/₂
B	8	stiles	hardwood	³/₄	1³/₄	9¹/₄
C	4	side rails	hardwood	³/₄	1³/₄	5¹/₂
D	4	front & back rails	hardwood	³/₄	1³/₄	17¹/₂
E	2	side panels	plywood	¹/₄	6³/₄	5¹/₂
F	2	front & back panels	plywood	¹/₄	6³/₄	17¹/₂
G	2	removable-box sides	hardwood	¹/₂	1¹/₂	8
H	2	removable-box ends	hardwood	¹/₂	1¹/₂	5³/₈
J	2	removable-box runners	hardwood	¹/₂	¹/₂	18¹/₂
K	1	removable-box bottom	plywood	¹/₄	6³/₈	8

MILLIMETERS

REFERENCE	QUANTITY	PART	STOCK	THICKNESS	WIDTH	LENGTH
A	2	top & bottom	hardwood	19	209	521
B	8	stiles	hardwood	19	44	235
C	4	side rails	hardwood	19	44	140
D	4	front & back rails	hardwood	19	44	445
E	2	side panels	plywood	6	171	140
F	2	front & back panels	plywood	6	171	445
G	2	removable-box sides	hardwood	13	38	203
H	2	removable-box ends	hardwood	13	38	137
J	2	removable-box runners	hardwood	13	13	470
K	1	removable-box bottom	plywood	6	162	203

hardware

- 1 continuous hinge ³/₁₆" × 1¹/₂" × 20"

hardware

- 1 continuous hinge 5mm × 38mm × 508mm

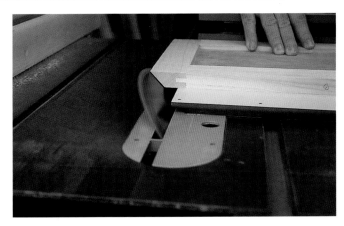

step 1 • Cut out the parts as listed in the materials list. Use parts B, C, D, E and F to build the front, back and side panels as shown in the sidebar "How to Assemble a Frame and Panel" in project seven. Then cut a 45° bevel on all the ends of the panels.

step 2 • Lay the panels faceup and end to end. Tape the joints with clear packing tape. If you like, press the tape flat with a steel or wooden roller.

step 3 • Flip the whole assembly face-down, apply glue to the bevel joints and fold it together.

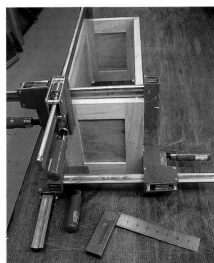

step 4 • Use clamps to hold the untaped corner joint until the glue dries. Be sure the assembly is square. Cut the rabbet in the top of the back panel (see project one, steps ten and eleven), attach the continuous hinge and install the top A. Attach the bottom A with screws and install the runners J for the removable box.

step 5 • Cut out the removable-box parts G, H and K and glue the front, back and sides together using butt joints.

step 6 • After the glue dries, glue the bottom K to the removable box assembly. Sand the whole project and finish. Glued butt joints are strong enough for this box because the bottom helps hold the whole assembly together.

When I was younger, I would sometimes go with my father when he made service calls. (He was a television repairman in the late 1950s and early 1960s.) I remember a case that he called his tube caddy. It was a suitcaselike chest that held vacuum tubes, soldering guns, a volt-ohm meter and some hand tools. I was fascinated with all the compartments that held the tubes. I would sit and go through the caddy while he worked.

This tool caddy is designed with that old tube caddy as the inspiration. The cabinet is made by folding oak veneer into the shape of the box and lid. The lid is mounted with duplex hinges, so it can be removed. This might be the handiest of all the chests in this book because of how easily the caddy can be carried using the suitcase handle.

tool caddy

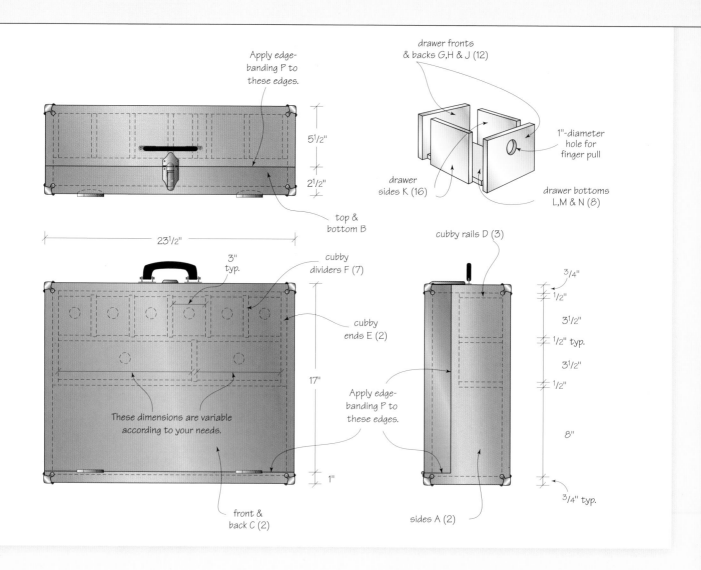

Apply edge-
banding P to
these edges.

5 1/2"

2 1/2"

top &
bottom B

23 1/2"

3"
typ.

cubby
dividers F (7)

cubby
ends E (2)

These dimensions are variable
according to your needs.

17"

Apply edge-
banding P to
these edges.

1"

front &
back C (2)

drawer fronts
& backs G,H & J (12)

1"-diameter
hole for
finger pull

drawer
sides K (16)

drawer bottoms
L,M & N (8)

cubby rails D (3)

3/4"
1/2"

3 1/2"

1/2" typ.

3 1/2"

1/2"

8"

3/4" typ.

sides A (2)

materials list

REFERENCE	QUANTITY	PART	STOCK	THICKNESS	WIDTH	LENGTH	COMMENTS
A	2	sides	oak plywood	3/4	8	18	45° bevel cut on all edges
B	2	top & bottom	oak plywood	3/4	8	23 1/2	45° bevel cut on all edges
C	2	front & back	oak plywood	3/4	18	23 1/2	45° bevel cut on all edges
D	3	cubby rails	plywood	1/2	4	21	
E	2	cubby ends	plywood	1/2	4	8 1/2	
F	6	cubby dividers	plywood	1/2	3 3/4 H	4 D	
G	12	drawer fronts & backs	poplar	3/8	3 1/2 H	3	
H	1	drawer front	poplar	3/8	3 1/2 H	12 1/2	
J	1	drawer front	poplar	3/8	3 1/2 H	8	
K	16	drawer sides	poplar	3/8	3 1/2 H	3 1/8	
L	6	drawer bottoms	poplar	3/8	3 1/8	2 1/4	
M	1	drawer bottom	poplar	3/8	3 1/8	11 3/4	
N	1	drawer bottom	poplar	3/8	3 1/8	7 1/4	
P		edge-banding	oak	1/16	3/4	16'	cut to sizes needed

hardware

- 8 corner protectors, chrome
- 2 duplex hinges 3/16" × 1 1/2" × 2 1/2"
- 1 suitcase handle, black
- 1 drawbolt, chrome

materials list

REFERENCE	QUANTITY	PART	STOCK	THICKNESS	WIDTH	LENGTH	COMMENTS
A	2	sides	oak plywood	19	203	457	45° bevel cut on all edges
B	2	top & bottom	oak plywood	19	203	597	45° bevel cut on all edges
C	2	front & back	oak plywood	19	457	597	45° bevel cut on all edges
D	3	cubby rails	plywood	13	102	533	
E	2	cubby ends	plywood	13	102	216	
F	6	cubby dividers	plywood	13	95 H	102 D	
G	12	drawer fronts & backs	poplar	10	89 H	76	
H	1	drawer front	poplar	10	89 H	318	
J	1	drawer front	poplar	10	89 H	203	
K	16	drawer sides	poplar	10	89 H	79	
L	6	drawer bottoms	poplar	10	79	57	
M	1	drawer bottom	poplar	10	79	298	
N	1	drawer bottom	poplar	10	79	184	
P		edge-banding	oak	2	19	5m	cut to sizes needed

hardware

- 8   corner protectors, chrome
- 2   duplex hinges 5mm × 38mm × 64mm
- 1   suitcase handle, black
- 1   drawbolt, chrome

construction

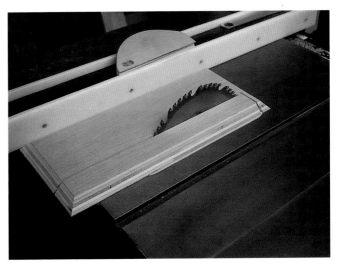

step 1 • Cut out all the caddy parts A, B and C as shown in the materials list. Cut the 45° bevel on all edges (see project one, step one). Lay out the door cutouts on the sides A and make the short cut. This is safely done on the table saw when using the miter gauge with a fence attached. Remember that one part will be face out and the other will be face in. This will create left and right sides.

step 2 • Make the long cut with the sides flat on the table saw. Raise the saw blade to its full height and cut almost to the crosscut saw kerf. Be aware of the blade undercut. Turn off the saw and wait for the blade to stop turning before removing the part. Remember that one cut will be made with the side part faceup and the other will be made with the part facedown in order to create left and right parts.

step 3 • Square the cutout with a handsaw. Clean up the little pieces of material remaining on the door part.

step 4 • Lay all the caddy parts faceup on a flat surface, align the bevels and tape the joints as shown. Turn the assembly over and fold it up dry. If all the parts have been cut squarely, the open joints should come together perfectly. Unfold, add glue to the bevel joints and fold the caddy together. Use clamps as needed to help hold the box square. These glued joints are quite strong.

step 5 • Cut the ¹⁄₁₆" hardwood strips P, fit them at the corners using miters and tape the miters so the whole edge-banding assembly can be glued on at one time.

step 6 • Apply an even coat of glue to the raw edges of the plywood. Be sure the glue covers the edges completely and that it isn't too thick. The glue will begin to get tacky at this point. I've discovered that this helps the edge-banding seat better and keeps it from shifting around.

step 7 • Be sure the miter joint lines up with the miter joints on the plywood. Hold the edge-banding in place with cauls and clamps.

step 8 • Use gluing cauls to even out the clamping pressure and to protect the edge-banding.

step 9 • After the edge-banding has been applied and sanded flush to the surface of the veneer, cut slots for the hinges using a biscuit joiner. Center the cut on the hinged joint of the lid and the box.

step 10 • Attach the duplex hinges (the hinge will come apart, allowing the lid to be removed from the box) to the lid and box. These hinges are slick and easy to use, as you can see.

step 11 • Cut the cubby rails D, ends E and dividers F to size. Cut the dado slots in the rails and glue the assembly together. Cut the drawer parts G through N to size. Glue the drawers together using butt joints (see project two, steps five and six), then sand and fit them to the cubby assembly. Drill 1"-diameter finger holes in the fronts of the drawers. Finish the caddy, install all of the hardware, load up the caddy and you're ready to go.

ten-drawer chest

Most woodworkers have several tools that are small, like screwdrivers, files, chisels, pliers, dividers and compasses. These can all be stored in shallow drawers, which is where this chest comes into the picture.

The design for the chest came from a couple of inspirations. One was a Craftsman-style bookcase plan. The chest is made of quarter-sawn white oak, and the sides and top are shaped like the bookcase. The other inspiration came from multidrawer chests that were made years ago to store sheet music.

This chest was assembled with butt joints and screws. The screws were countersunk and the holes plugged with $\frac{3}{8}$" redheart plugs. The drawer pulls are also redheart, which were cut using a $\frac{1}{2}$" plug cutter.

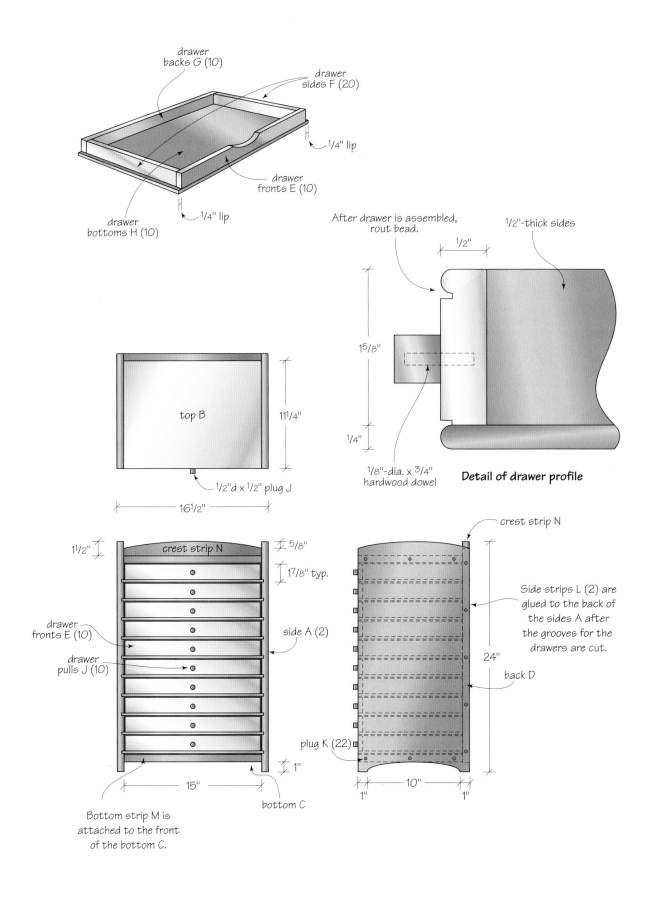

drawer
backs G (10)

drawer
sides F (20)

¼" lip

drawer
fronts E (10)

drawer
bottoms H (10)

¼" lip

After drawer is assembled,
rout bead.

½"

½"-thick sides

15/8"

¼"

1/8"-dia. x 3/4"
hardwood dowel

Detail of drawer profile

top B

11¼"

½"d x ½" plug J

16½"

1½"

crest strip N

5/8"

17/8" typ.

drawer
fronts E (10)

drawer
pulls J (10)

side A (2)

plug K (22)

15"

bottom C

Bottom strip M is
attached to the front
of the bottom C.

crest strip N

Side strips L (2) are
glued to the back of
the sides A after
the grooves for the
drawers are cut.

24"

back D

10"

1"

1"

1"

156

materials list

REFERENCE	QUANTITY	PART	STOCK	THICKNESS	WIDTH	LENGTH	COMMENTS
A	2	sides	qs white oak	3/4	12	24	qs = quarter-sawn
B	1	top	qs white oak	3/4	11 1/4	15	
C	1	bottom	plywood	3/4	11 1/4	15	
D	1	back	plywood	3/4	15	23	top crown is 2 1/4"-wide qs white oak
E	10	drawer fronts	qs white oak	1/2	1 5/8	14 15/16	
F	20	drawer sides	poplar	1/2	1 5/8	10 1/4	
G	10	drawer backs	poplar	1/2	1 5/8	14 15/16	
H	10	drawer bottoms	plywood	1/4	11 1/4	15 1/2	trim sides to fit after drawers are assembled
J	10	drawer pulls	redheart	1/2 dia		1/2	cut with 1/2" plug cutter
K	22	plugs to cover screws	redheart	3/8 dia		1/4 +/-	cut with 3/8" plug cutter
L	2	side A strips	qs white oak	3/8	3/4	24	
M	1	bottom C strip	qs white oak	3/8	3/4	15	
N	1	crest strip	qs white oak	3/4	2 1/4	15	
P	10	dowel rods	hardwood	1/8 dia		3/4	

MILLIMETERS

REFERENCE	QUANTITY	PART	STOCK	THICKNESS	WIDTH	LENGTH	COMMENTS
A	2	sides	qs white oak	19	305	610	qs = quarter-sawn
B	1	top	qs white oak	19	285	381	
C	1	bottom	plywood	19	285	381	
D	1	back	plywood	19	381	584	top crown is 57mm-wide qs white oak
E	10	drawer fronts	qs white oak	13	41	379	
F	20	drawer sides	poplar	13	41	260	
G	10	drawer backs	poplar	13	41	379	
H	10	drawer bottoms	plywood	6	286	394	trim sides to fit after drawers are assembled
J	10	drawer pulls	redheart	13 dia		13	cut with 13mm plug cutter
K	22	plugs to cover screws	redheart	10 dia		6 +/-	cut with 10mm plug cutter
L	2	side A strips	qs white oak	10	19	610	
M	1	bottom C strip	qs white oak	10	10	381	
N	1	crest strip	qs white oak	19	57	381	
P	10	dowel rods	hardwood	3 dia		13	

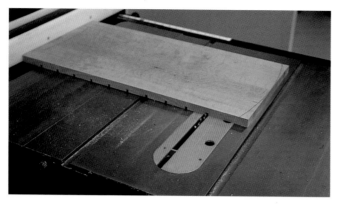

step 1 • Cut the sides A ⅜" narrower than the finished dimension. Then cut the grooves for the drawers. Glue a ⅜" × ¾" strip L to the back of each side. This strip will cover the ends of the grooves.

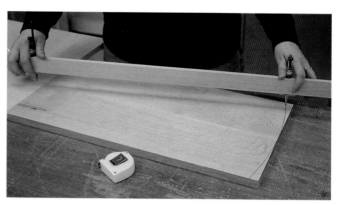

step 2 • Draw the top arc on each of the sides.

step 3 • When laying out the radii at the bottom of the sides, use a small, round object to draw the small radius that defines each foot.

step 4 • Connect these two small radii with an arc that is 1" high from the bottom of the side. Trammel points mounted on a stick are great for drawing arcs. A little trial and error is involved here unless you can figure the radius using math. I try connecting the dots, moving the pencil up or down the stick until I find the radius that works. If you don't have trammel points, drive a nail through a stick at one end. This is your fixed point. Use a small clamp or rubber band to hold a pencil anywhere you need to along the length of the stick to draw your arc.

step 5 • Drill holes with the same radius as the small arcs and connect them by cutting the larger arc with a jigsaw or band saw.

step 6 • Smoothing and shaping is easily done with a rat-tail file or curved rasp.

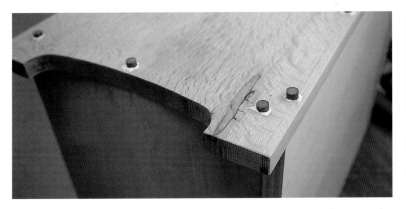

step 8 • If you like, you can cut the crest arc with a bevel to match the arc of the sides. You could go one step further and put a bevel on the side arcs to match the arc of the crest. These little details will make the sides and back flow together nicely.

step 7 • Glue the crest strip N on the top of the back panel D. Make the arc on the crest as you've done for the sides. Cut the top B and bottom panels C to size, then glue a ³⁄₈" × ³⁄₄" strip M on the front of the bottom panel. Assemble the chest using 2" screws. Cut the plugs K and glue them in place to cover the screw heads.

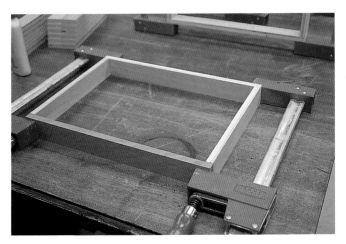

step 9 • Cut all the drawer parts E, F, G and H to size. The sides F are captured between the front E and back G parts, so glue-up can be done with two clamps. I just used glue on these butt joints. I know what you're thinking: Why would he use just glue and no fasteners or other joinery to strengthen this joint? Well, after the bottoms are glued in place, the drawers are quite strong. (If you would like to use fasteners, please do so. Screws or tenons would work well.)

step 10 • I use bench horses all the time to hold parts for gluing. Several drawers can be glued at one time. After applying glue to the bottoms H, hold them in place with a few small brads or nails. Then stack up a few drawers and clamp them while the glue dries. This also helps keep the drawers flat.

step 11 • When the glue has dried on the drawers, rout the beading on the top and bottom of the drawer fronts. The drawer bottoms are the perfect thickness to accept the radius of the bead. (See the technical illustration drawer detail.)

step 12 • If necessary, fit the drawers by planing or sanding the sides of the bottoms that fit into the grooves to ensure the drawers slide smoothly. Then cut the plugs for the drawer pulls J. I attached the pulls with a ¹⁄₈" dowel rod P. Drill a hole in the center of the plug, and a matching hole in the drawer front. Glue the pulls in place, then sand and finish the chest and drawers.

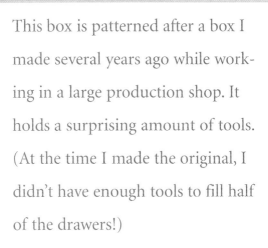

jim's toolbox

This box is patterned after a box I made several years ago while working in a large production shop. It holds a surprising amount of tools. (At the time I made the original, I didn't have enough tools to fill half of the drawers!)

One feature deviates a little from traditional cabinetry: The divider is attached to the chest only at the bottom and the back. This makes it possible to put a wide drawer (a standard crosscut handsaw fits in it perfectly) at the top of the chest and still have smaller drawers below it. The drawers are made using the same techniques as the drawers for the ten-drawer chest.

I made this chest out of a pallet I found in a warehouse. The wood has nail and screw holes in it, but it still looks neat.

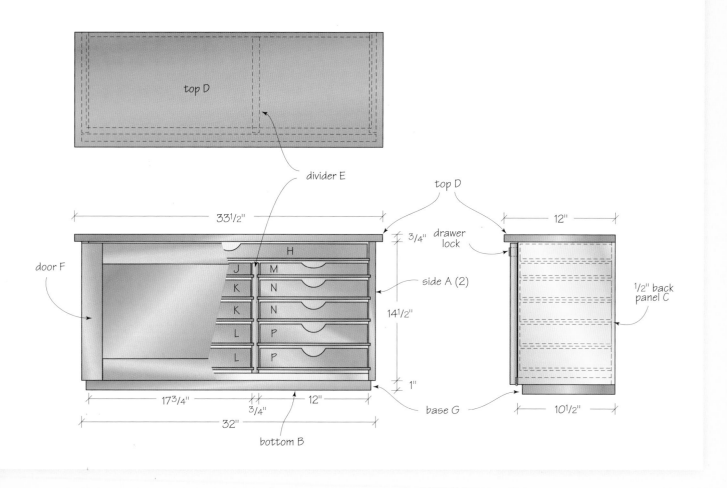

top D

divider E

top D

33¹/₂"

3/4" drawer lock

door F

H

J | M
K | N
K | N
L | P
L | P

side A (2)

14¹/₂"

12"

1/2" back panel C

17³/₄"

3/4"

12"

1"

base G

10¹/₂"

32"

bottom B

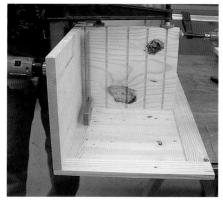

step 1 • After cutting out the parts and assembling the back panel C (see the sidebar "How to Assemble a Frame and Panel" in project seven), glue the bottom B to the back panel. Double-check for squareness.

step 2 • Cut the drawer grooves in the ends A and the divider E. Use a table saw or a router mounted in a router table. Be sure to reference the grooves from the bottoms of the parts. Hold the bottoms against the fence. This will ensure that all the grooves will line up with each other.

step 3 • Glue and screw the vertical divider E to the bottom B, and glue it to the center stile in the back panel C (no screws). Double-check that the divider is square to the bottom panel. This panel will stay in position with very little movement at the front, and the drawers will work just fine.

162

REFERENCE	QUANTITY	PART	STOCK	THICKNESS	WIDTH	LENGTH
A	2	ends	pine	$3/4$	$10^1/2$	$14^1/2$
B	1	bottom	pine	$3/4$	10	$30^1/2$
C	1	back panel	pine	$1/2$	$30^1/2$	$14^1/2$
	2	back C stiles	pine	$1/2$	$2^1/4$	$14^1/2$
	1	back C center stile	pine	$1/2$	$2^1/4$	11
	2	back C rails	pine	$1/2$	$2^1/4$	27
	2	back C panels	pine	$3/16$	$12^5/8$	11
D	1	top	pine	$3/4$	12	$33^1/2$
E	1	divider	pine	$3/4$	10	$11^1/2$
F	1	door	pine	$3/4$	32	$14^3/8$
	2	door F stiles	pine	$3/4$	$2^1/4$	$14^3/8$
	2	door F rails	pine	$3/4$	$2^1/4$	$28^1/2$
	1	door F panel	pine	$1/4$	$10^5/8$	$28^1/2$
G	1	base	pine	1	10	31
	2	base G side rails	pine	1	2	10
	1	base G front rail	pine	1	2	31
	1	base G back rail	pine	1	2	27
H	1	top drawer	pine/ply	$1^3/4$	10	31
	2	drawer H sides	pine	$1/2$	$1^1/2$	9
	2	drawer H frnts & bcks	pine	$1/2$	$1^1/2$	$30^7/16$
	1	drawer H bott	plywood	$1/4$	10	31
J	1	drawer	pine/ply	$1^1/2$	10	$18^1/4$
	2	drawer J sides	pine	$1/2$	$1^1/4$	9
	2	drawer J frnts & bcks	pine	$1/2$	$1^1/4$	$17^{11}/16$
	1	drawer J bott	plywood	$1/4$	10	$18^1/4$
K	2	drawers	pine/ply	2	10	$18^1/4$
	4	drawer K sides	pine	$1/2$	$1^3/4$	9
	4	drawer K frnts & bcks	pine	$1/2$	$1^3/4$	$17^{11}/16$
	4	drawer K botts	plywood	$1/4$	10	$18^1/4$
L	2	drawers	pine/ply	$2^1/4$	10	$18^1/4$
	4	drawer L sides	pine	$1/2$	2	9
	4	drawer L frnts & bcks	pine	$1/2$	2	$17^{11}/16$
	2	drawer L botts	plywood	$1/4$	10	$18^1/4$
M	1	drawer	pine/ply	$1^1/2$	10	$12^1/2$
	2	drawer M sides	pine	$1/2$	$1^1/4$	9
	2	drawer M frnts & bcks	pine	$1/2$	$1^1/4$	$11^{15}/16$
	1	drawer M bott	plywood	$1/4$	10	$12^1/2$
N	2	drawers	pine/ply	2	10	$12^1/2$
	4	drawer N sides	pine	$1/2$	$1^3/4$	9
	4	drawer N frnts & bcks	pine	$1/2$	$1^3/4$	$11^{15}/16$
	2	drawer N botts	plywood	$1/4$	10	$12^1/2$
P	2	drawers	pine/ply	$2^1/4$	10	$12^1/2$
	4	drawer P sides	pine	$1/2$	2	9
	4	drawer P frnts & bcks	pine	$1/2$	2	$11^{15}/16$
	2	drawer P botts	plywood	$1/4$	10	$12^1/2$

hardware

- 1 continuous hinge $3/16" \times 1^1/2" \times 32"$
- 1 drawer lock

REFERENCE	QUANTITY	PART	STOCK	THICKNESS	WIDTH	LENGTH
A	2	ends	pine	19	267	368
B	1	bottom	pine	19	254	775
C	1	back panel	pine	13	775	368
	2	back C stiles	pine	13	57	368
	1	back C center stile	pine	13	57	279
	2	back C rails	pine	13	57	686
	2	back C panels	pine	5	321	279
D	1	top	pine	19	305	851
E	1	divider	pine	19	254	292
F	1	door	pine	19	813	365
	2	door F stiles	pine	19	57	365
	2	door F rails	pine	19	57	724
	1	door F panel	pine	6	270	724
G	1	base	pine	25	254	787
	2	base G side rails	pine	25	51	254
	1	base G front rail	pine	25	51	787
	1	base G back rail	pine	25	51	686
H	1	top drawer	pine/ply	45	254	787
	2	drawer H sides	pine	13	38	229
	2	drawer H frnts & bcks	pine	13	38	773
	1	drawer H bott	plywood	6	254	787
J	1	drawer	pine/ply	38	254	464
	2	drawer J sides	pine	13	32	229
	2	drawer J frnts & bcks	pine	13	32	456
	1	drawer J bott	plywood	6	254	464
K	2	drawers	pine/ply	51	254	464
	4	drawer K sides	pine	13	45	229
	4	drawer K frnts & bcks	pine	13	45	456
	2	drawer K botts	plywood	6	254	464
L	2	drawers	pine/ply	57	254	464
	4	drawer L sides	pine	13	51	229
	4	drawer L frnts & bcks	pine	13	51	456
	2	drawer L botts	plywood	6	254	464
M	1	drawer	pine/ply	38	254	318
	2	drawer M sides	pine	13	32	229
	2	drawer M frnts & bcks	pine	13	32	303
	1	drawer M bott	plywood	6	254	311
N	2	drawers	pine/ply	51	254	298
	4	drawer N sides	pine	13	45	229
	4	drawer N frnts & bcks	pine	13	45	303
	2	drawer N botts	plywood	6	254	311
P	2	drawers	pine/ply	57	254	298
	4	drawer P sides	pine	13	51	229
	4	drawer P frnts & bcks	pine	13	51	303
	2	drawer P botts	plywood	6	254	311

hardware

- 1 continuous hinge 5mm × 38mm × 813mm
- 1 drawer lock

step 4 • Cut biscuit slots in the ends of the back panel C and matching slots in the end panels A.

step 5 • Using biscuits, attach the ends A to the back/bottom assembly.

step 6 • Cut the necessary biscuit slots in the top edges of the ends and back. Cut matching slots in the top D. (Remember, when cutting the slots in the underside of the top, allow for the top overhang at the sides.)

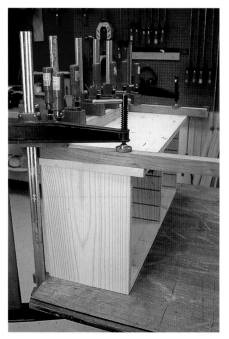

step 7 • This is another view of the top glue-up. Using wooden battens helps distribute the clamping pressure evenly and protects the project from being dented by the clamps.

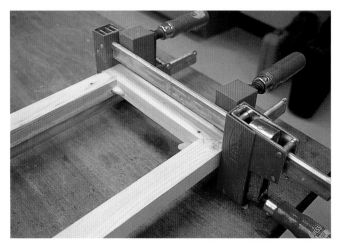

step 8 • Assemble the tool chest base G using biscuits. The two front joints are mitered, and the back joints are butted.

step 9 • Attach the base G to the bottom of the cabinet with screws. Use no glue.

step 10 • Cut out all the drawer parts. Then cut or sand a circular finger pull in the drawer fronts.

step 11 • Assemble the drawers as shown in project four, steps nine and ten. Remember to cut the drawer fronts and backs $\frac{1}{16}$" less than the opening that the drawer will fit into. This will allow plenty of clearance for the drawers to slide freely. This is not a finely tuned set of drawers. They are made to work smoothly and still fit nicely in their respective openings.

step 12 • The drawer bottoms have a $\frac{1}{4}$" lip on each side. Measure the drawer boxes and add $\frac{1}{2}$". Cut the drawer bottoms to this dimension and center the bottoms on the drawer box. The drawers should fit just right. If the drawers do need fitting, shave a little material off the ends of the drawer bottoms. It won't take much, so go easy. If you want to fit the drawers just right, measure the drawer opening from the bottom of each groove, then cut the drawer bottom to this dimension. Assemble the drawer and try the fit. If the drawer bottom fits into the grooves (right to the bottom of the groove), you will have a nicely fitting drawer that will have minimal side-to-side movement.

step 13 • Assemble the frame and panel door. Then, set the continuous hinge into a mortise in the door. This mortise depth should be the same dimension as the thickness of the hinge so the door will close tightly against the front of the chest.

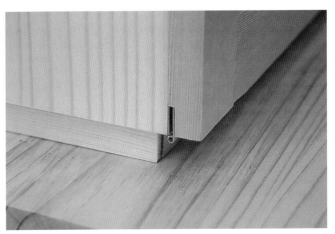

step 14 • This is a view of the closed door. (It looks cleaner if the door seats tightly to the chest.) You could also set the hinge in a stopped mortise if you don't want to see the end of the mortise and the hinge. Finally, install the door lock.

rolling tool cabinet

If you need a place to store hand power tools, this rolling cabinet is a great choice. If you need to move the tools where the work is, no problem. The top of the cabinet also makes a great work surface. The drawers are deep enough for most hand power tools. If you need more room, it's easy to make the drawers larger. I built this cabinet from two pallets. Pallet lumber is good to use because it won't change dimensions much. It has been exposed to the elements for a fair amount of time, so its moisture content is stable.

You can use the tool-box in project five with this cabinet to make a roomy tool storage unit.

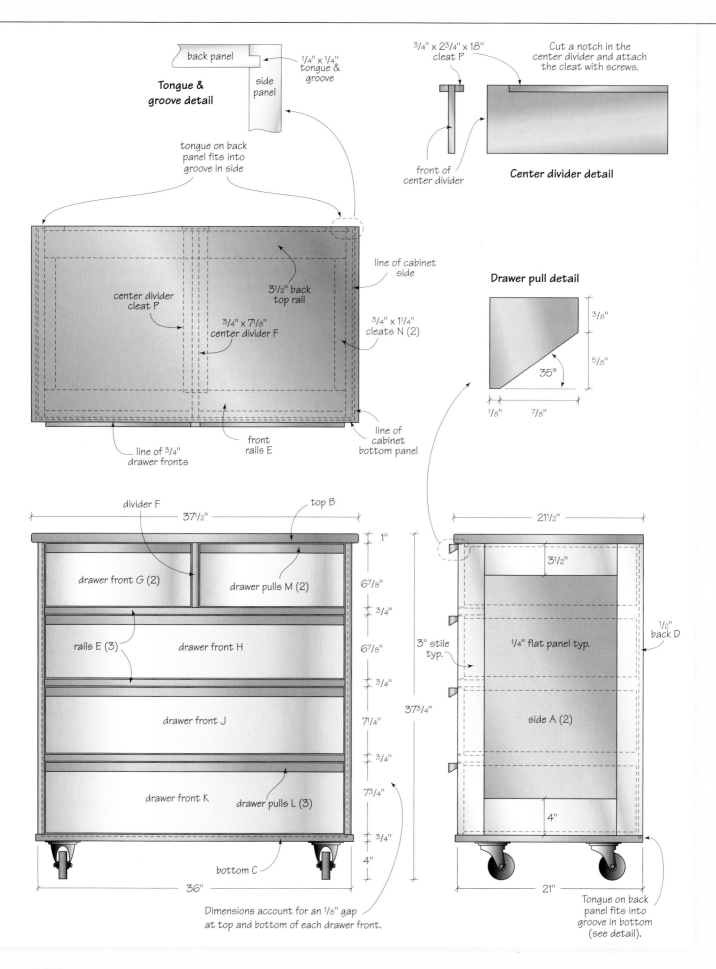

Tongue & groove detail

back panel

side panel

1/4" x 1/4" tongue & groove

tongue on back panel fits into groove in side

3/4" x 2 3/4" x 18" cleat P

Cut a notch in the center divider and attach the cleat with screws.

front of center divider

Center divider detail

line of cabinet side

3 1/2" back top rail

center divider cleat P

3/4" x 7 1/8" center divider F

3/4" x 1 1/4" cleats N (2)

Drawer pull detail

3/8"

5/8"

35°

1/8"   7/8"

line of 3/4" drawer fronts

front rails E

line of cabinet bottom panel

divider F

top B

37 1/2"

1"

drawer front G (2)

drawer pulls M (2)

6 7/8"

3/4"

rails E (3)

drawer front H

6 7/8"

3/4"

drawer front J

7 1/4"

37 3/4"

3/4"

drawer front K

drawer pulls L (3)

7 3/4"

3/4"

bottom C

4"

36"

Dimensions account for an 1/8" gap at top and bottom of each drawer front.

21 1/2"

3 1/2"

3" stile typ.

1/4" flat panel typ.

1/2" back D

side A (2)

4"

21"

Tongue on back panel fits into groove in bottom (see detail).

REFERENCE	QUANTITY	PART	STOCK	THICKNESS	WIDTH	LENGTH		REFERENCE	QUANTITY	PART	STOCK	THICKNESS	WIDTH	LENGTH
A	2	sides	pine	3/4	21	32		A	2	sides	pine	19	533	813
	4	side A stiles	pine	3/4	3	32			4	side A stiles	pine	19	76	813
	2	side A top rails	pine	3/4	3 1/2	16			2	side A top rails	pine	19	89	406
	2	side A bottom rails	pine	3/4	4	16			2	side A bottom rails	pine	19	102	406
	2	side A panels	pine	1/4	15 3/4	25 1/4			2	side A panels	pine	6	400	641
B	1	top	pine	1	21 1/2	37 1/2		B	1	top	pine	25	546	953
C	1	bottom	pine	3/4	21 1/4	36 1/2		C	1	bottom	pine	19	540	927
D	1	back	pine	1/2	32 1/4	35		D	1	back	pine	13	819	889
	2	back D stiles	pine	1/2	3 1/4	32 1/4			2	back D stiles	pine	13	82	819
	1	back D center stile	pine	1/2	3	25 1/2			1	back D center stile	pine	13	76	648
	1	back D top rail	pine	1/2	3 1/2	29 1/2			1	back D top rail	pine	13	89	749
	1	back D bottom rail	pine	1/2	4 1/4	29 1/2			1	back D bottom rail	pine	13	108	749
	2	back D panels	pine	3/16	13 5/8	25 1/2			2	back D panels	pine	5	346	648
E	3	front rails	pine	3/4	3	35		E	3	front rails	pine	19	76	889
F	1	divider	pine	3/4	7 1/8	19 1/2		F	1	divider	pine	19	181	495
G	2	drawer fronts	pine	3/4	6 7/8	16 5/8		G	2	drawer fronts	pine	19	175	422
H	1	drawer front	pine	3/4	6 7/8	34 1/4		H	1	drawer front	pine	19	175	870
J	1	drawer front	pine	3/4	7 1/4	34 1/4		J	1	drawer front	pine	19	184	870
K	1	drawer front	pine	3/4	7 3/4	34 1/4		K	1	drawer front	pine	19	197	870
	4	drawer G box frnts & bcks	Baltic birch ply	1/2	6 3/8	14 7/8			4	drawer G box frnts & bcks	Baltic birch ply	13	162	378
	2	drawer H box frnts & bcks	Baltic birch ply	1/2	6 3/8	32 1/2			2	drawer H box frnts & bcks	Baltic birch ply	13	162	826
	2	drawer J box frnts & bcks	Baltic birch ply	1/2	6 3/4	32 1/2			2	drawer J box frnts & bcks	Baltic birch ply	13	171	826
	2	drawer K box frnts & bcks	Baltic birch ply	1/2	7 1/4	32 1/2			2	drawer K box frnts & bcks	Baltic birch ply	13	184	826
	6	drawer G & H box sides	Baltic birch ply	1/2	6 3/8	19 1/2			6	drawer G & H box sides	Baltic birch ply	13	162	495
	2	drawer J box frnts & bcks	Baltic birch ply	1/2	6 3/4	19 1/2			2	drawer J box frnts & bcks	Baltic birch ply	13	171	495
	2	drawer K box frnts & bcks	Baltic birch ply	1/2	7 1/4	19 1/2			2	drawer K box frnts & bcks	Baltic birch ply	13	184	495
	2	drawer G bottoms	Baltic birch ply	1/2	15 7/8	19 1/2			2	drawer G bottoms	Baltic birch ply	13	403	495
	3	drawer H,J &K bottoms	Baltic birch ply	1/2	33 1/2	19 1/2			3	drawer H,J & K bottoms	Baltic birch ply	13	851	495
L	3	drawer H, J & K pulls	pine	1	1	34 1/4		L	3	drawer H, J & K pulls	pine	25	25	870
M	2	drawer G pulls	pine	1	1	16 5/8		M	2	drawer G pulls	pine	25	25	422
N	2	top cleats	pine	3/4	1 1/4	14 1/4		N	2	top cleats	pine	25	32	362

hardware

- 4 4" swivel casters
- 5 sets 20" full-extension, heavy-duty drawer slides

hardware

- 4 100mm swivel casters
- 5 sets 500mm full-extension, heavy-duty drawer slides

step 1 • Carefully inspect all the wood for nails, screws, staples and any other pieces of metal. Use a small metal detector to find the hidden nails, etc. Once the wood is cleaned up, it's on to building the project!

step 2 • Construct the frame and panel sides A and back D as shown in the sidebar "How to Assemble a Frame and Panel" in project seven. Cut a tongue on the sides and bottom of the back panel. Then cut matching grooves in the sides and bottom C. (See the technical illustration for details.) Lay out the dovetail slots for the front rails E on the insides of the side panels, then make a simple jig as shown to guide the router when cutting the stopped slots.

step 3 • Using the same dovetail router bit, cut the tails on the ends of the front rails E. (Use some scrap wood the same thickness as the rails to make test-cuts when fitting the tails to the stopped slots.) Note the use of a scrap piece of wood to stabilize the rail.

step 4 • When all the parts are fitted properly, add some glue to the slots and tails. Tap the rails E into place.

step 5 • Glue the back panel D into the grooves in the sides A. I let the cabinet hang over the bench so the tongue on the bottom of the back panel could stand proud of the sides.

step 6 • Cut biscuit slots in the bottom panel C as shown.

step 7 • Cut matching biscuit slots in the bottom edges of the cabinet sides A. Put glue on the center biscuit only, set the panel in place and use screws in oversize clearance holes to hold the panel in place. (The extra biscuits are to help align the parts.)

step 8 • Lay the cabinet on its sides to install the drawer slides. Draw a center line square to the front of the cabinet, line up the screw holes in the slide on this line and insert the screws. I prefer to mount side-mount drawer slides toward the top of the drawer box. Use full-extension, heavy-duty slides. You'll be putting heavy tools into these drawers, and you'll want full access to them. Then, install the top cleats N on the inside top of each side panel. Put glue only in the back groove in the top. Use screws installed in oversized holes drilled in the cleats N to attach the top. This allows for seasonal movement of the top.

step 9 • Cut the drawer parts to size and screw the drawer boxes together. I've found that drawers that are screwed together are very strong and are much quicker to make than drawers that involve more complex joinery. Of course, you can make them to your own personal preferences. If you do, remember to make the proper adjustments in the drawer parts' dimensions.

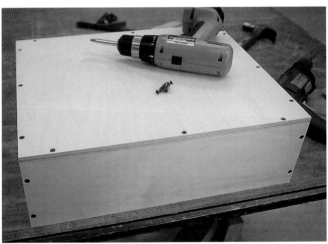

step 10 • Attach the bottoms. The ½"-thick bottoms will support large amounts of weight.

step 11 • Draw a center line on the sides of each drawer box and install the hardware runners. Then put the drawer boxes into the cabinet so you can align and attach the drawer fronts.

step 12 • When mounting the drawer fronts onto the drawer boxes, I've found it's easiest to install two screws toward the top and at each side of the box front. Drive the screws slightly through the drawer box front, align the drawer front on the cabinet and tap it slightly. This will make two dimples on the inside of the drawer front that you can use as guides to drill pilot holes for the screws. Then simply realign the drawer front and screw it into place on the drawer box.

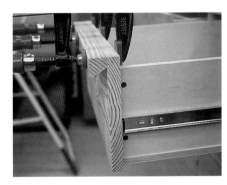

step 13 • These down-and-dirty drawer pulls will stand up to whatever you dish out. Cut each pull's profile on the table saw, sand the pulls smooth and glue them onto the drawer fronts. They'll never bend or come loose!

cabinetmaker's chest

This tool chest is a classic design. I made it out of red oak and stained it a medium-dark color. When closed, the lid pushes a rod into a hole in the top of the drop-front door, holding it closed. If the top is locked, the whole chest is locked. It is easily moved using the handles on the sides.

If you want to make a larger version of this chest, add more drawers or make the top deeper, feel free to do so. This is a basic starter unit for someone with a few screwdrivers, wrenches, pliers and socket sets.

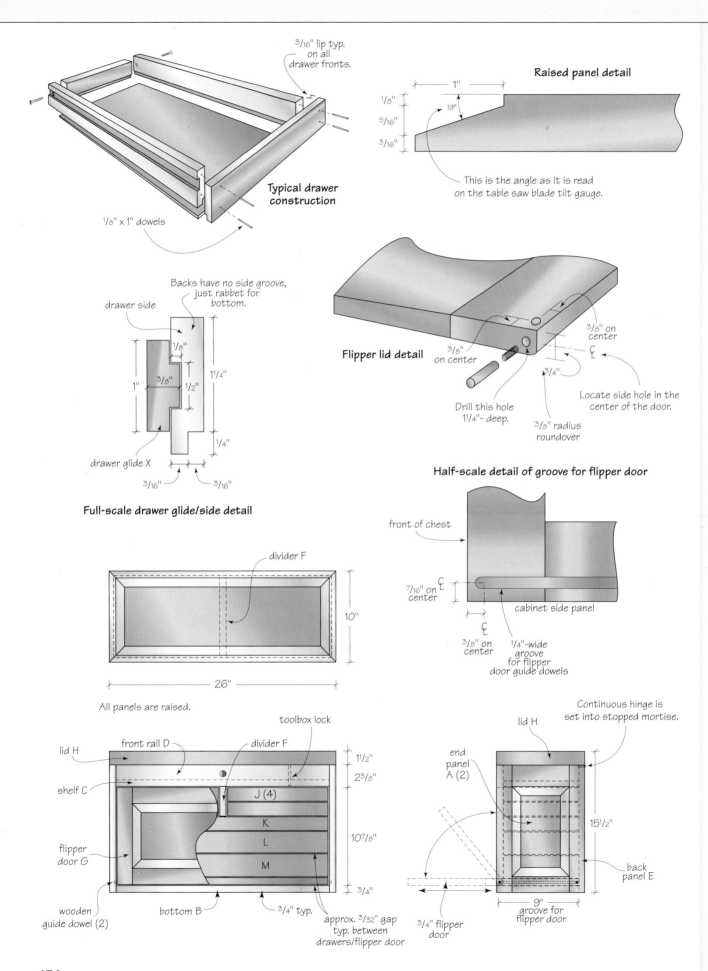

³/₁₆" lip typ. on all drawer fronts.

Typical drawer construction

¹/₈" x 1" dowels

Raised panel detail

1"

¹/₈"

5/₁₆"

³/₁₆"

19°

This is the angle as it is read on the table saw blade tilt gauge.

Backs have no side groove, just rabbet for bottom.

drawer side

¹/₈"

³/₈"

½"

1"

1¹/₄"

¼"

drawer glide X

³/₁₆"   ³/₁₆"

Full-scale drawer glide/side detail

Flipper lid detail

³/₈" on center

³/₈" on center

³/₄"

Locate side hole in the center of the door.

Drill this hole 1¹/₄"- deep.

³/₈" radius roundover

Half-scale detail of groove for flipper door

front of chest

cabinet side panel

7/₁₆" on center

³/₈" on center

¼"-wide groove for flipper door guide dowels

divider F

10"

26"

All panels are raised.

lid H

front rail D

toolbox lock

divider F

1¹/₂"

2³/₈"

J (4)

shelf C

K

L

10⁷/₈"

flipper door G

M

¾"

wooden guide dowel (2)

bottom B

¾" typ.

approx. ³/₃₂" gap typ. between drawers/flipper door

Continuous hinge is set into stopped mortise.

lid H

end panel A (2)

15¹/₂"

back panel E

9"

groove for flipper door

¾" flipper door

materials list

REFERENCE	QUANTITY	PART	STOCK	THICKNESS	WIDTH	LENGTH	COMMENTS
A	2	end panels	red oak	$3/4$	10	14	
	4	end A stiles	red oak	$3/4$	$1^3/4$	14	
	2	end A top rails	red oak	$3/4$	$2^3/8$	$7^1/2$	
	2	end A bottom rails	red oak	$3/4$	$1^3/4$	$7^1/2$	
	2	end A panels	red oak	$1/2$	$7^1/4$	$10^7/8$	
B	1	bottom	plywood	$3/4$	$9^1/4$	$24^1/2$	with $1/4" \times 3/4" \times 24^1/2"$ red oak strip to front edge of bottom
C	1	shelf	plywood	$3/4$	$8^1/2$	$24^1/2$	
D	1	front rail	red oak	$3/4$	$2^3/8$	$24^1/2$	
E	1	back panel	red oak	$3/4$	14	$24^1/2$	
	2	back E stiles	red oak	$3/4$	$1^3/4$	14	
	1	back E top rail	red oak	$3/4$	$2^3/8$	22	
	1	back E bottom rail	red oak	$3/4$	$1^3/4$	22	
	1	back E panel	red oak	$1/2$	$10^7/8$	22	
F	1	divider	plywood	$3/4$	$3^1/4$	$8^1/2$	with $1/4" \times 3/4" \times 3^1/4"$ red oak strip to front edge of divider
G	1	flipper door	red oak	$3/4$	$10^5/8$	$24^3/8$	
	2	flipper door G stiles	red oak	$3/4$	$1^3/4$	$10^5/8$	
	2	flipper door G rails	red oak	$3/4$	$1^3/4$	$21^7/8$	
	1	flipper door G panel	red oak	$1/2$	$7^7/8$	$21^7/8$	
H	1	lid	red oak	$1^1/2$	10	26	
	2	lid H side rails	red oak	$3/4$	$1^1/2$	26	
	2	lid H end rails	red oak	$3/4$	$1^1/2$	10	
	1	lid H panel	red oak	$1/2$	9	25	
J	4	drawer fronts	red oak	$3/8$	$1^1/2$	$11^{11}/16$	
K	1	drawer front	red oak	$3/8$	$1^1/2$	$24^5/16$	
L	1	drawer front	red oak	$3/8$	$2^3/8$	$24^5/16$	
M	1	drawer front	red oak	$3/8$	$2^1/2$	$24^5/16$	
N	10	drawer J & K sides	red oak	$3/8$	$1^1/2$	$7^7/8$	see illustration for drawer glide/side details
P	2	drawer L sides	red oak	$3/8$	$2^3/8$	$7^7/8$	see illustration for drawer glide/side details
Q	2	drawer M sides	red oak	$3/8$	$2^1/2$	$7^7/8$	see illustration for drawer glide/side details
R	4	drawer J backs	red oak	$3/8$	$1^1/2$	$10^9/16$	
S	1	drawer K back	red oak	$3/8$	$1^1/2$	$23^3/16$	
T	1	drawer L back	red oak	$3/8$	$2^3/8$	$23^3/16$	
U	1	drawer M back	red oak	$3/8$	$2^1/2$	$23^3/16$	
V	4	drawer J bottoms	plywood	$1/4$	$8^1/4$	$10^{15}/16$	
W	3	drawer K, L & M bottoms	plywood	$1/4$	$8^1/4$	$23^9/16$	
X	14	drawer glides	red oak	$3/8$	1	$7^7/8$	see illustration for drawer glide/side details

hardware

■	1	continuous hinge	$3/16" \times 1^1/2" \times 24"$
■	1	bullet catch	Rockler #28464
■	1	$5/8"$ sash knob	Rockler #68627
■	1	toolbox lock	Rockler #79236
■	2	brass chest handles	Rockler #25841
■	1	full-mortise lock	Rockler #28241
■	1	small expansion spring	from a ballpoint pen, cut in half to make 2 springs
■	2	wooden guide dowels	$1/4"$ dia. $\times 3/4"$
■	28	wooden drawer dowels	$1/8" \times 1"$

materials list

REFERENCE	QUANTITY	PART	STOCK	THICKNESS	WIDTH	LENGTH	COMMENTS
A	2	end panels	red oak	19	254	356	
	4	end A stiles	red oak	19	45	356	
	2	end A top rails	red oak	19	60	191	
	2	end A bottom rails	red oak	19	45	191	
	2	end A panels	red oak	13	184	276	
B	1	bottom	plywood	19	235	622	with 6mm × 19mm × 622mm red oak strip to front edge of bottom
C	1	shelf	plywood	19	216	622	
D	1	front rail	red oak	19	60	622	
E	1	back panel	red oak	19	254	622	
	2	back E stiles	red oak	19	45	356	
	1	back E top rail	red oak	19	60	559	
	1	back E bottom rail	red oak	19	45	559	
	1	back E panel	red oak	13	276	559	
F	1	divider	plywood	19	83	216	with 6mm × 19mm × 83mm red oak strip to front edge of divider
G	1	flipper door	red oak	19	270	619	
	2	flipper door G stiles	red oak	19	45	270	
	2	flipper door G rails	red oak	19	45	556	
	1	flipper door G panel	red oak	13	200	556	
H	1	lid	red oak	38	254	660	
	2	lid H side rails	red oak	19	38	660	
	2	lid H end rails	red oak	19	38	254	
	1	lid H panel	red oak	13	229	635	
J	4	drawer fronts	red oak	10	38	297	
K	1	drawer front	red oak	10	38	618	
L	1	drawer front	red oak	10	60	618	
M	1	drawer front	red oak	10	64	618	
N	10	drawer J & K sides	red oak	10	38	200	see illustration for drawer glide/side details
P	2	drawer L sides	red oak	10	38	200	see illustration for drawer glide/side details
Q	2	drawer M sides	red oak	10	64	200	see illustration for drawer glide/side details
R	4	drawer J backs	red oak	10	38	268	
S	1	drawer K back	red oak	10	38	589	
T	1	drawer L back	red oak	10	60	589	
U	1	drawer M back	red oak	10	64	589	
V	4	drawer J bottoms	plywood	6	210	278	
W	3	drawer K, L & M bottoms	plywood	6	210	599	
X	14	drawer glides	red oak	10	25	200	see illustration for drawer glide/side details

hardware

▪	1	continuous hinge	5mm × 38mm × 610mm
▪	1	bullet catch	Rockler #28464
▪	1	16mm sash knob	Rockler #68627
▪	1	toolbox lock	Rockler #79236
▪	2	brass chest handles	Rockler #25841
▪	1	full-mortise lock	Rockler #28241
▪	1	small expansion spring	from a ballpoint pen, cut in half to make 2 springs
▪	2	wooden guide dowels	6mm dia. × 19mm
▪	28	wooden drawer dowels	3mm × 25mm

How to Assemble a Frame and Panel

step 1 • Assembly of a frame and panel can be simplified if you proceed as shown in these photos. First, lay out all of the parts, including glue, hammer and clamps. Orient all the parts as you want them put together in the final assembly. It may seem silly to do this for each assembly, but it is easy to make mistakes — for example, turning a panel upside down.

step 2 • Add glue to the end of the first rail and set it in place on the stile. (Note that I cut my stiles a little longer than indicated in the cutting list. I then trim them to length after the frame is assembled. If you cut your stiles to the dimensions as shown in the cutting list, your rail's edges will be flush with the ends of the stiles.)

step 3 • Put the panel in place.

step 4 • Add glue to the end of the other rail and put it in place.

step 5 • Put glue on the ends of both rails and put the other stile in place.

step 6 • Lay the clamps and panel assembly flat; apply light pressure with the clamps. Check the assembly for squareness, adjust if necessary and add a little more pressure with the clamps until the joints are tight. Do not apply any more clamping pressure than is needed because you could distort the joint and it won't stay seated properly.

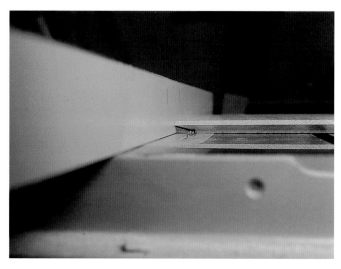

step 1 • Use a ripping blade to cut the bevels on the panels for ends A, back E, flipper door G and lid H. These are cut at 19°. Standard bevels are usually 5° to 9°. I wanted a narrower setoff on the raised part of the panel, so I increased the angle. (This allows the end of the bevel to still fit into the ¼" groove in the frame parts.)

step 2 • After cutting the bevels, set the saw blade square to the table. Lay the panel facedown and cut the cheek on the bevel to set the raised section of the panel. Cut and machine all the frame parts, then glue the panels together. See the sidebar "How to Assemble a Frame and Panel."

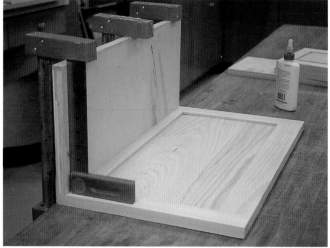

step 3 • Glue the hardwood edging on the front edge of the bottom B. Level the excess edging to the surface of the plywood using a block plane or sand it flush.

step 4 • Glue the bottom B to the back panel E. As always, check for squareness of the parts to each other.

step 5 • Next, glue the shelf C to the back E. Align the bottom of the shelf with the bottom edge of the back's top rail.

step 6 • Cut the stopped grooves (which are the tracks for the guide dowels in the flipper door G) in the end panels A, using a ¼" straight router bit. (See the technical drawing for details.) You can do this as shown on a router table or you can set up a router with a guide fence. Use the bottom of the panel as a reference for the guide fence.

step 7 • Glue the end panels A and front rail D in place.

step 8 • Set up a dado cutter on the table saw and attach a sacrificial fence to your standard fence. Machine the drawer glides X and the drawer sides N, P and Q. Then machine the drawer backs R, S, T and U with just the rabbet for the drawer bottoms.

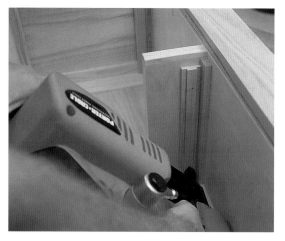

step 10 • Carefully lay out the holes for the guide dowels in the flipper door G. (See the technical drawings.) I used a self-centering doweling jig to drill the holes. I needed to set the holes a little off-center, so I used a shim of cardboard. The grooves in the end panels A should allow the guide dowels to help the front of the flipper door align with the front of the tool chest face.

step 9 • Attach the divider F to the underside of the shelf C with screws, centering it carefully in the chest. Cut the drawer glides X to length and attach them to the inside of the cabinet. Use a spot of glue and staple or screw them into place.

step 11 • Drill an access hole on the inside of the flipper door G. This will allow you to use a sharp point to pull the guide dowel out of the groove and back it into the hole far enough so the door can be removed from the tool chest. I cut a spring (from a ballpoint pen) in half. I inserted one of these halves in each of the holes for the dowels, then inserted the dowel. The spring pushes the guide dowel into the groove in the tool chest sides.

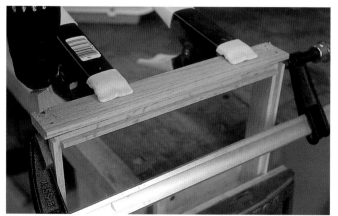

step 12 • Drill the holes for the drawer dowels in the drawer fronts J, K, L and M using the drill press. I used two stops on the drill press table. That way I could drill one hole holding the drawer front against one stop, then move it against the other stop and drill the other hole. Be sure the holes line up where there is solid wood on the ends of the sides. (Avoid the grooves in the drawer sides.)

step 13 • Attach the drawer sides N, P, and Q to the backs R, S, T, and U with screws. Then put the drawer front in place and drill the holes into the fronts of the drawer sides, using the drawer front as a guide. Add glue and insert the drawer dowels. Use clamps to hold the drawer front tight to the sides while the glue dries. Glue the drawer bottoms V and W in place. If the drawers need fitting, pare a little material off the glides in the chest. After the chest is finished (inside and out), the drawers should work perfectly. Apply some paste wax to the glides and the drawer sides if you want.

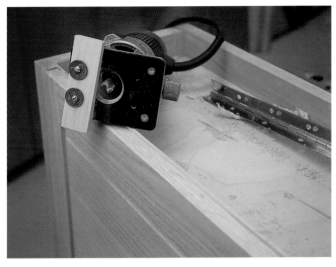

step 14 • Cut 45° miters on the ends of the top's rails and assemble the lid H. Cut a stopped rabbet $3/32$" deep by $3/4$" wide by 24" long in the top edge of the tool chest's back E. Cut a matching rabbet in the lid H's bottom back rail.

step 15 • Square the inside corners of the rabbet and attach the continuous hinge with two or three screws.

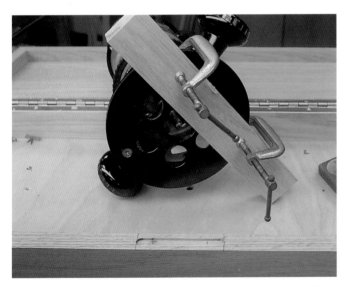

step 16 • Set up a router with the proper size bit (measure the lock you have) and cut a shallow mortise for the full-mortise lock's shoulder plate.

step 17 • Rough out the deep part of the mortise with a drill. Use a chisel to fit the mortise to the lock.

step 18 • When the lock fits, measure and lay out the hole for the key. Drill the hole and size it with a round file if necessary. Finish the chest. Next, install the flipper door G, mark for the toolbox lock and install the lock according to the manufacturer's instructions. Then, install a small bullet catch to hold the flipper door closed. Finally, attach the sash knob on the flipper door, the chest handles on the end panel's top rails and the escutcheon plate on the front rail over the mortise lock's keyhole.

journeyman's tote box

This basic tool tote box has a couple of extras. I've used the basic box before, and I always found myself wishing the handle would swing out of the way so I could easily get to the tools. I put this handle on a couple of swivel bolts, and it works great. Not only does the handle move out of the way, but the box levels itself when you carry it. Because I can never find my tape rule (it always settles to the bottom of the toolbox), I attached a picture-hanging clip on the end of the box to keep it within reach.

Small tools, screws, nails and anything else you might need can be stored in two removable boxes with sliding lids. These boxes fit neatly into the tote.

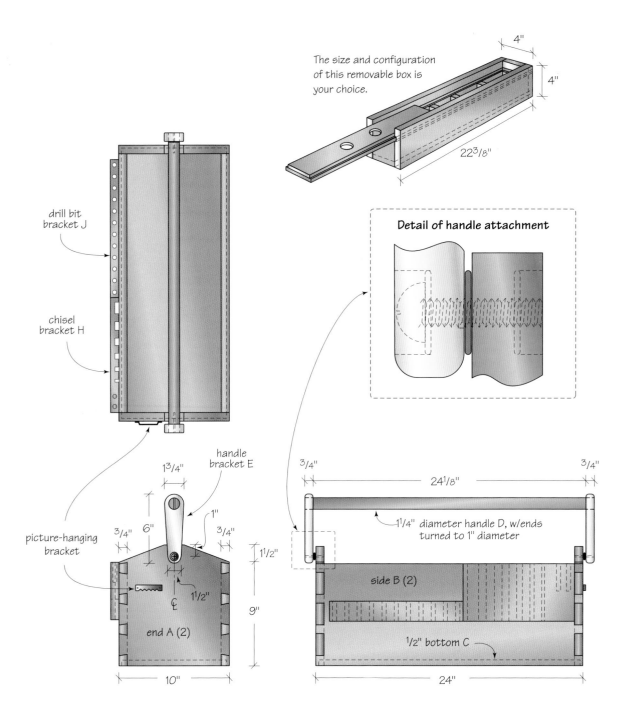

The size and configuration of this removable box is your choice.

4"

4"

22³/₈"

drill bit bracket J

chisel bracket H

Detail of handle attachment

picture-hanging bracket

handle bracket E

1³/₄"

1"

³/₄"

6"

³/₄"

1¹/₂"

¢

1¹/₂"

end A (2)

9"

10"

³/₄"

24¹/₈"

³/₄"

1¹/₄" diameter handle D, w/ends turned to 1" diameter

side B (2)

¹/₂" bottom C

24"

materials list

REFERENCE	QUANTITY	PART	STOCK	THICKNESS	WIDTH	LENGTH	COMMENTS
A	2	ends	poplar	$3/4$	10	$10^1/2$	
B	2	sides	poplar	$3/4$	9	24	
C	1	bottom	plywood	$1/2$	$9^1/2$	$23^1/2$	
D	1	handle	poplar	$1^1/4$ dia.		$25^5/8$	
E	2	handle brackets	plywood	$3/4$	$1^3/4$	6	cut taper as shown in illustration if desired
F	2	removable boxes	plywood	4	4	$22^3/8$	
	4	box F sides	plywood	$1/2$	4	$22^3/8$	
	4	box F ends	plywood	$1/2$	3	4	
	7	box F dividers	plywood	$1/2$	3	$3^3/16$	number of dividers is your choice
	2	box F sliding lids	plywood	$1/2$	$3^1/2$	$22^1/8$	
	2	box F bottoms	plywood	$1/2$	3	$21^3/8$	
G	2	keeper strips	poplar	$1/2$	$1/2$	8	
H	1	chisel bracket	poplar	$3/4$	5	10	
J	1	drill bit bracket	poplar	$3/4$	$1^3/4$	12	

hardware

- 2 $1/4 - 20 \times 1^1/4$" roundhead bolts
- 2 $1/4 - 20$ nuts
- 4 $1/4$" flat washers
- 1 picture-hanging bracket

REFERENCE	QUANTITY	PART	STOCK	THICKNESS	WIDTH	LENGTH	COMMENTS
A	2	ends	poplar	19	254	267	
B	2	sides	poplar	19	229	610	
C	1	bottom	plywood	13	242	597	
D	1	handle	poplar	32 dia.		651	
E	2	handle brackets	plywood	19	45	152	cut taper as shown in illustration if desired
F	2	removable boxes	plywood	102	102	569	
	4	box F sides	plywood	13	102	569	
	4	box F ends	plywood	13	76	102	
	7	box F dividers	plywood	13	76	81	number of dividers is your choice
	2	box F sliding lids	plywood	13	89	562	
	2	box F bottoms	plywood	13	76	543	
G	2	keeper strips	poplar	13	13	203	
H	1	chisel bracket	poplar	19	127	254	
J	1	drill bit bracket	poplar	19	45	305	

hardware

- 2 M6 – 30mm roundhead bolts
- 2 M6 – nuts
- 4 M6 flat washers
- 1 picture-hanging bracket

step 1 • Lay out the pins for the dovetails on the sides B and mark the waste sections. Whether you cut the pins or tails first is your choice. (I think it's easier to fit the tails to the pins, so I cut the pins first.)

step 2 • Cut out the waste on the table saw using the fixture shown in the sidebar, "Table Saw Dovetail Fixture." To cut both sides of the pins, you will need to move the fixture and use the left-hand fence. If you want to speed up the waste removal process, use a dado cutter.

Table Saw Dovetail Fixture

I made this fixture to cut dovetails. One side has fences set at 10° on the left and right ends for cutting the dovetail pins. To use the different fences, the fixture is moved to the left and right on the table saw. (One runner on the bottom fits in the slots on the table.)

To cut the tails, reverse the fixture and set the saw blade to 10°. You need to turn the part to cut each side of the tails. (The blocks on the backs of the fences are for protection from the saw blade.)

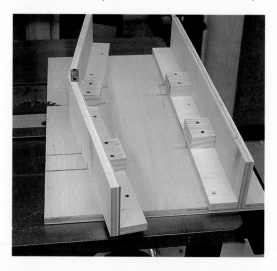

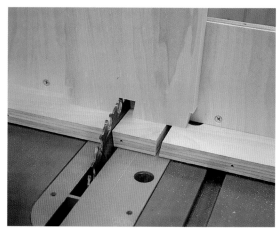

step 3 • After you cut the pins, use them to mark the tails on the ends A. Reverse the fixture, set the saw blade to 10° and remove the waste, leaving the tails. You will need to clean up the corner of the pins with a chisel.

step 4 • Cut the bevels on the top of the ends A. Note that the tails need to be cleaned up in the corners. You can do this easily with a chisel.

Drill the ³⁄₄" seating holes for the flat washers on the insides of the ends A to a depth of ³⁄₈", then drill the ¹⁄₄" through-holes for the bolts in the tops of the ends. See the technical drawing for hole location.

step 5 • When the dovetails have been cut and fit, dry fit the box to be sure all is in order. Then assemble using glue. The sides B and ends A of this box are thick enough that no clamping blocks were needed directly over the joint. Use no more clamping pressure than is needed so the parts don't distort.

Using a rabbet-cutting router bit, cut the ¹⁄₂" × ¹⁄₂" rabbet on the inside bottom of the box. Square out the corners of the rabbet and cut the bottom panel C to fit. Then, glue and screw it into place.

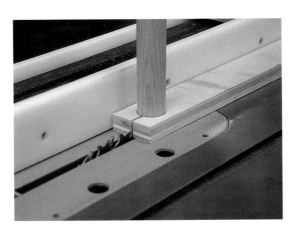

step 6 • Cut, shape and drill the holes in the handle brackets E. Then, turn the handle D so that it is comfortable for your hand and turn the ends of the handle to fit the predrilled holes in the brackets. Drill a 1" hole in a scrap piece of plywood, insert the end of the handle, center the setup over the table saw blade and cut a slot in the ends of the handle.

step 7 • This is a close-up of the slotted handle D and a bracket E. Next, cut a wedge of wood the same width as the diameter of the hole and a little thicker than the width of the slot in the handle. Taper the wedge so it can be inserted into the slot about three-fourths of the way.

Drill the ³⁄₄"-diameter seating hole for the flat washers in the brackets to a depth of ³⁄₈". Then, drill the ¹⁄₄" through-holes for the machine bolts.

tip >> FREQUENT CUTTING OF DOVETAILS ON THE TABLE SAW

If you find you are cutting a lot of dovetails, you might want to have a saw blade sharpened with a 10° bevel on all the teeth. This will eliminate having to clean up the corners of the tails. Be sure to check the blade tilt on your table saw so the bevel will be slanted the correct way.

step 8 • Add glue to the slots and around the ends of the handle. Put the handle assembly together and insert the wedges. Clamp the assembly to a flat surface so that the handle will be properly aligned at both ends. Drive the wedges into place using a clamp as shown. Pulling the wedges into the slots is much easier than trying to drive them in with a hammer.

step 9 • After the handle assembly glue has dried, cut and sand the ends of the handle flush with the brackets. Then attach the handle assembly to the box. See the technical drawing detail for the location of the bolt, washers and nut.

step 10 • This is the inside view of the handle bolts and nut. Recess the nut and be sure the bolt doesn't protrude past the inside surface.

step 11 • Attach the keeper strips G (for the removable boxes) on the inside of the ends, 4" from one side of the box. To keep the box balanced, install the drill bit and chisel brackets on the opposite side of the tote from the removable boxes.

step 12 • I made brackets for a set of chisels H and drill bits J that can be mounted on the outside of the box. Lay out your tools and mark the spacing of the slots for the chisels and the holes for the drill bits. I made a couple of extra holes for a four-way screwdriver and a pencil in the chisel bracket.

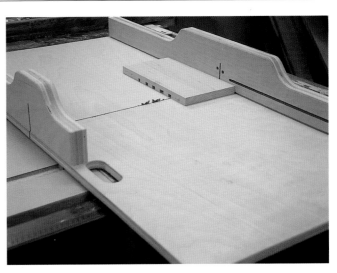

step 13 • Cut the slots for the chisels on the table saw. Then attach the bracket H to the side of the box. Drill the holes for the drill bits and mount that bracket J to the side of the box.

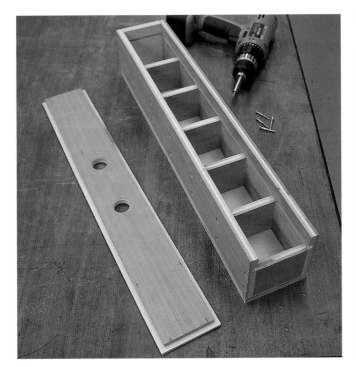

step 14 • The removable boxes F are handy for storing screws, nails, pliers, screwdrivers, wrenches and the like. How many dividers you use is your choice. After cutting the grooves for the sliding lid, I used screws to assemble the boxes. Two 1"-diameter finger holes in the lid will make lifting the boxes easy.

step 15 • This view of the box shows the lid inserted in the grooves.

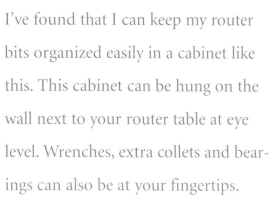

I've found that I can keep my router bits organized easily in a cabinet like this. This cabinet can be hung on the wall next to your router table at eye level. Wrenches, extra collets and bearings can also be at your fingertips.

This cabinet is not very large, so you probably have enough scraps of wood in your shop already to build it. I got lucky and found a pallet with bright red luan mahogany slats on it. I grabbed them immediately and made the doors for this cabinet. The ash handles were a result of the mahogany of the doors being too narrow. I needed extra width on the doors, so I added the ash strips and shaped the pulls right into them. The body is made from scraps of ash.

The construction of this cabinet is simple. I completed the whole project in about four hours.

sliding-door cabinet

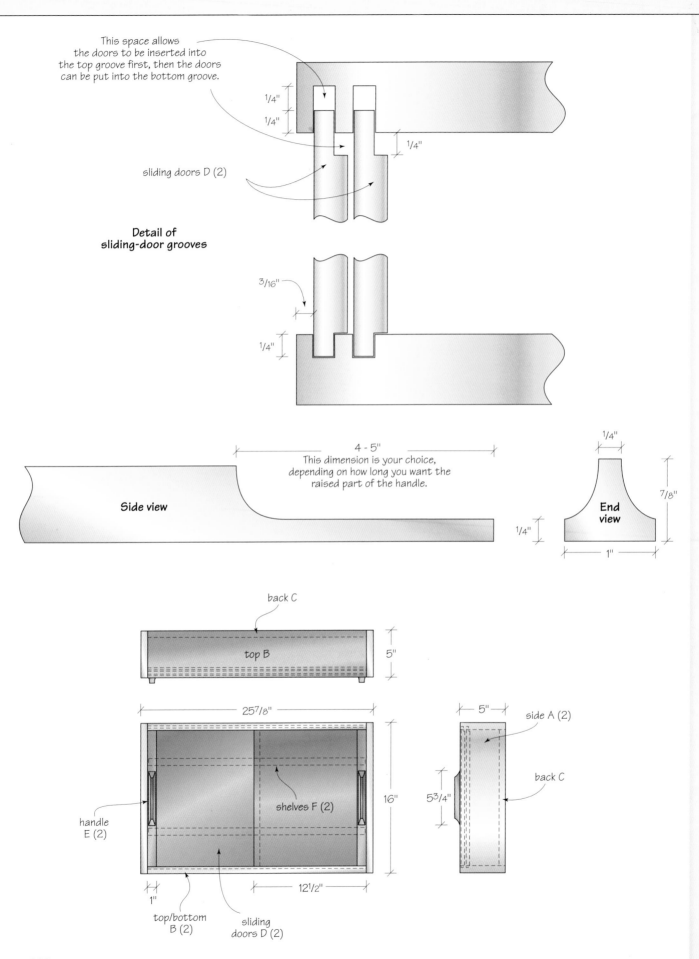

This space allows the doors to be inserted into the top groove first, then the doors can be put into the bottom groove.

1/4"

1/4"

1/4"

sliding doors D (2)

Detail of sliding-door grooves

3/16"

1/4"

4 - 5"
This dimension is your choice, depending on how long you want the raised part of the handle.

Side view

1/4"

1/4"

End view

7/8"

1"

back C

top B

5"

25⁷/₈"

16"

shelves F (2)

handle E (2)

side A (2)

back C

5"

5³/₄"

1"

top/bottom B (2)

sliding doors D (2)

12¹/₂"

materials list

REFERENCE	QUANTITY	PART	STOCK	THICKNESS	WIDTH	LENGTH	REFERENCE	QUANTITY	PART	STOCK	THICKNESS	WIDTH	LENGTH
A	2	sides	ash	3/4	5	16	A	2	sides	ash	19	127	406
B	2	top & bottom	ash	3/4	5	24³/8	B	2	top & bottom	ash	19	127	619
C	1	back	plywood	3/4	14¹/2	24³/8	C	1	back	plywood	19	368	619
D	2	sliding doors	hardwood	3/8	11¹/2	15	D	2	sliding doors	hardwood	10	292	381
E	2	handles	ash	7/8	1	15	E	2	handles	ash	22	25	381
F	2	shelves	poplar	1/2	3³/8	24⁵/16	F	2	shelves	poplar	13	86	618

STEP-BY-STEP construction

step 1 • Cut the parts to size. Then cut the grooves for the sliding doors in the top and bottom B. The grooves in the bottom are ¹/4" deep.

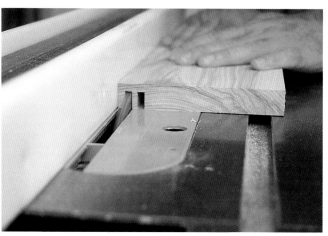

step 2 • The grooves in the top are ¹/2" deep. After the cabinet is assembled, the doors can be lifted up into these grooves and then lowered into the grooves in the bottom panel.

step 3 • Glue the top and bottom panels B to the back panel C. Note the spacers to help hold the assembly square.

step 4 • Cut biscuit slots in the sides A.

step 5 • Cut matching biscuit slots in the ends of the top and bottom panels B.

step 6 • Glue the sides A to the cabinet.

step 7 • The handles E for the doors are made using a $\frac{1}{2}$" cove cutter on the router table. Make the cove cuts on a larger piece of stock.

step 8 • Cut the handles apart on the table saw.

step 9 • Set up a straight-cutting bit on the router table. Mount a stop block to the fence and use it to start the offset cut on the handle. Flip the handle end for end to make the other cut.

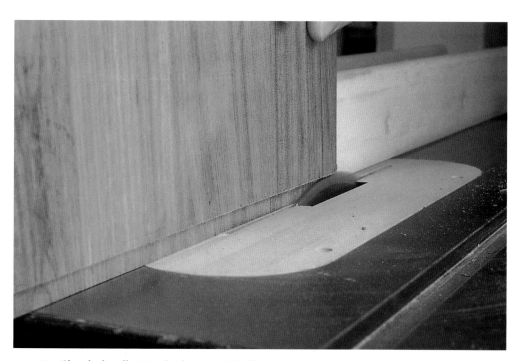

step 10 • Glue the handles E to the door panels D. Then cut the tenons on the doors D to fit into the grooves in the top and bottom of the cabinet. Be sure the door slides freely. Cut the shelves F to size. Lay out all of your router bits (if that's what you're going to store in this cabinet) and drill holes in the shelves to hold the bits in place.

BY CHRIS SCHWARZ

chris's plane cabinet & case

On certain holidays, such as New Year's Day, craftsmen in Japan clean their tools, put them on a shrine and offer them gifts such as sake and rice cakes. It is their way of thanking the tools for the service they have provided and will provide in future days.

As my collection of hand planes grew from a few rusty specimens handed down from my great-grandfather to a small arsenal of high-quality instruments, this Japanese tradition began to weigh heavily on my mind. My planes generally squatted on my workbench when not in use, and I had to constantly move them around to avoid knocking them to the floor as I worked.

After some thought, I decided that a cabinet dedicated to my planes was the best way to protect them from dings and to honor them for the service they provide almost every day of the year.

This cabinet is designed so it can be used either as a traditional tool chest that sits on a bench or a cabinet that hangs on the wall, thanks to a tough French cleat. Because planes are heavy tools, the case is joined using through-dovetails. The lid is a flat panel door assembled using mortise-and-tenon construction. And the dividers inside the cabinet are screwed together so the configuration can be rearranged easily as my collection or needs change.

As you design your own chest, you should measure your planes to ensure there's enough space for everything you own, and plan to own. This cabinet should provide plenty of room for all but the biggest collections.

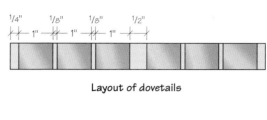

Layout of dovetails

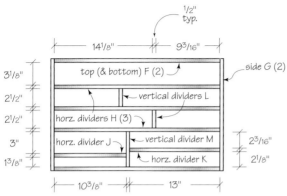

1/2" typ.

14 1/8"   9 3/16"

3 1/8"

top (& bottom) F (2)

side G (2)

2 1/2"

vertical dividers L

2 1/2"

horz. dividers H (3)

3"

horz. divider J

vertical divider M

2 3/16"

1 3/8"

horz. divider K

2 1/8"

10 3/8"   13"

**Elevation
internal dividers**

26 3/8"

7 1/4"

1"

1/4"

3/4"

27 1/8"

Plan

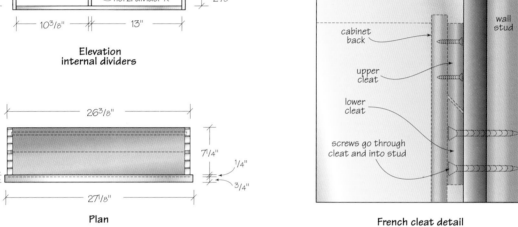

drywall

cabinet
back

upper
cleat

lower
cleat

screws go through
cleat and into stud

wall
stud

French cleat detail

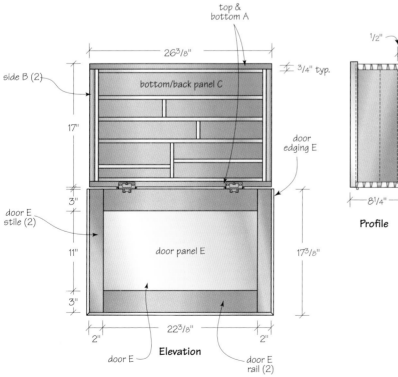

top &
bottom A

26 3/8"

3/4" typ.

side B (2)

bottom/back panel C

door
edging E

17"

door E
stile (2)

11"

door panel E

17 3/8"

3"

3"

2"

22 3/8"

2"

door E

Elevation

door E
rail (2)

1/2"   1/2"

cleats D
(see detail)

8 1/4"

Profile

materials list

REFERENCE	QUANTITY	PART	STOCK	THICKNESS	WIDTH	LENGTH	COMMENTS
A	2	top & bottom	cherry	$3/4$	$7^{1}/_{2}$	$26^{3}/_{8}$	cut $^{1}/_{16}$" long
B	2	sides	cherry	$3/4$	$7^{1}/_{2}$	17	cut $^{1}/_{16}$" long
C	1	bottom/back	plywood	$1/2$	16	$25^{3}/_{8}$	
D	2	cleats	maple	$1/2$	$2^{1}/_{2}$	$24^{7}/_{8}$	cut 45° bevel on one long edge
E	1	door	cherry/poplar	$3/4$	$17^{3}/_{8}$	$27^{1}/_{8}$	
	2	door E rails	cherry	$3/4$	3	$24^{3}/_{8}$	
	2	door E stiles	cherry	$3/4$	2	17	
	1	door E panel	poplar	$3/8$	12	$23^{3}/_{8}$	
		door E edging	cherry	$3/8$	1	65	$^{1}/_{4}$" roundover one edge, cut to lengths as needed
F	2	top & bottom dividers	maple	$1/2$	$2^{1}/_{2}$	$23^{7}/_{8}$	
G	2	side dividers	maple	$1/2$	$2^{1}/_{2}$	$15^{1}/_{2}$	
H	3	horizontal dividers	maple	$1/2$	$2^{1}/_{2}$	$23^{7}/_{8}$	
J	1	horizontal divider	maple	$1/2$	$2^{1}/_{2}$	$10^{3}/_{8}$	
K	1	horizontal divider	maple	$1/2$	$2^{1}/_{2}$	13	
L	2	vertical dividers	maple	$1/2$	$2^{1}/_{2}$	$2^{1}/_{2}$	
M	1	vertical divider	maple	$1/2$	$2^{1}/_{2}$	$4^{7}/_{8}$	

hardware

- 2 no-mortise hinges Lee Valley Tools #00H51.03
- 2 chest handles Lee Valley Tools #06W02.01
- 2 ring pulls Lee Valley Tools #00L02.02
- 2 magnetic catches

REFERENCE	QUANTITY	PART	STOCK	THICKNESS	WIDTH	LENGTH	COMMENTS
A	2	top & bottom	cherry	19	191	670	cut 2mm long
B	2	sides	cherry	19	191	432	cut 2mm long
C	1	bottom/back	plywood	13	406	645	
D	2	cleats	maple	13	64	632	cut 45° bevel on one long edge
E	1	door	cherry/poplar	19	441	689	
	2	door E rails	cherry	19	76	619	
	2	door E stiles	cherry	19	51	432	
	1	door E panel	poplar	10	305	594	
		door E edging	cherry	10	25	1651	6mm roundover one edge, cut to lengths as needed
F	2	top & bottom dividers	maple	13	64	606	
G	2	side dividers	maple	13	64	394	
H	3	horizontal dividers	maple	13	64	606	
J	1	horizontal divider	maple	13	64	264	
K	1	horizontal divider	maple	13	64	330	
L	2	vertical dividers	maple	13	64	64	
M	1	vertical divider	maple	13	64	124	

hardware

- 2 no-mortise hinges Lee Valley Tools #00H51.03
- 2 chest handles Lee Valley Tools #06W02.01
- 2 ring pulls Lee Valley Tools #00L02.02
- 2 magnetic catches

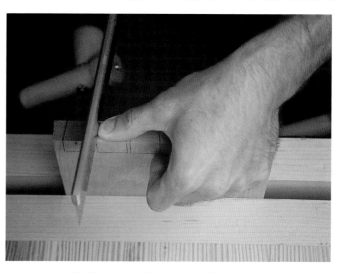

step 1 • Mark the length of your pins and tails on the ends of all your boards A and B. There's some debate as to whether you should mark exactly how long you want your pins and tails, a little less or a little more. I prefer to mark just a little more (no more than $1/32$") so the ends of the pins and tails stick out a bit when the joint is assembled. Then I come back and plane them flush after gluing up the case.

step 2 • As with all things in dovetails, there's a debate as to whether you should cut your tails (the male part of the joint) or the pins (the female part) first. Because I like to have narrow pins and wider tails, it's easier to cut the pins first. Lay out the location of the pins using a sliding T-bevel and cut them with a dovetail saw. Here are my four best tips for sawing straight lines. First, start your cut with the end of your thumb guiding the blade above the teeth.

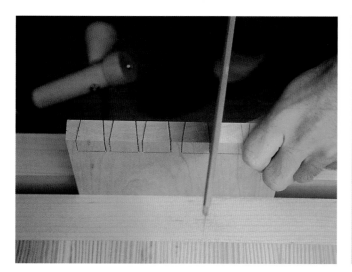

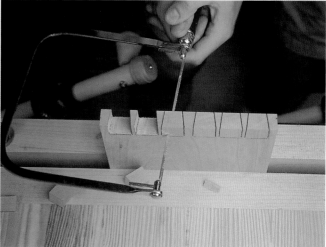

step 3 • Second, once the cut is started, hold the saw handle like you would hold a small bird that you are trying to prevent from flying away. Don't clench the handle; just keep enough pressure to prevent the saw from flying out of your hand. Third, never apply downward pressure with your hand; this will cause your blade to drift left or right. Let the saw do the cutting. And fourth, imagine the saw is longer than it really is so you take long smooth strokes.

step 4 • With the pins defined, get out a coping saw with a fine-tooth blade and remove as much waste as you can from between the pins. The closer you get to the scribed line at the bottom of the joint, the less cleanup you'll have with a chisel. If you overshoot, you're cooked.

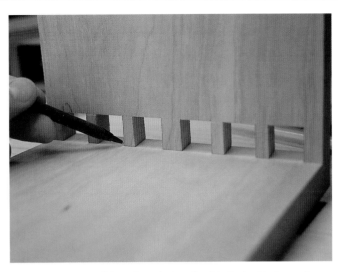

step 5 • Clamp your pin board to a piece of scrap and remove the rest of the waste using a sharp chisel and a mallet. I like to sneak up to the line on one side, sneak up to the line on the other and then clean up any junk in the middle. Clean out the corners of the pins using a sharp knife.

step 6 • Put your tail board on the bench with the inside face pointing up. Position its mate on top of your tail board and mark the locations of the tails using a mechanical pencil. Be careful not to shift either board during this step, or you should erase your lines and start anew.

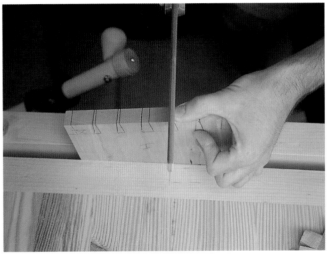

step 7 • Transfer those lines on your tail board across the end using a square and down to the other scribed line on the outside face of the board. Clamp the tail board in a vise. Lately I've found that my joints are better if I skew the board in my vise so I'm actually cutting straight down — though the result is angled. Angle the board one direction and make half of the tail cuts. Remember to cut just ever-so-slightly outside the lines.

step 8 • Then turn the board around and clamp it at the same angle and make the remainder of the tail cuts. Some people say it's easier to clamp the board vertically and go for it. Give both a try and see what works best for you.

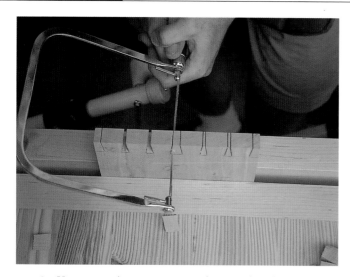

step 9 • Use your coping saw to remove the waste from between the tails. I've always found that short, light strokes are the most accurate and least likely to tear out the grain or overshoot the line.

step 10 • Now you need to slice off the ends of your tail boards. Clamp the board as shown in the photo and again use your thumb to help guide the first couple strokes of your cut. If you have a cross-cut backsaw, use that. Otherwise, your dovetail saw will do the job just fine.

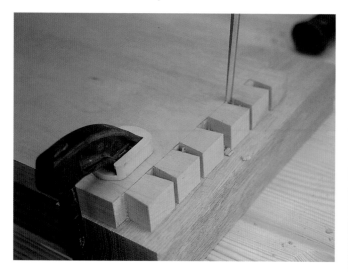

step 11 • Now remove the waste from between the tails using a chisel and a mallet. Remove the waste from the outside face of the board first and then remove the rest from the inside face. This will result in a neater joint if the grain buckles while you are chopping it. Again, clean up your corners with a knife.

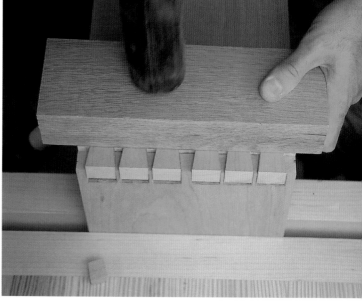

step 12 • Now it's time for a test fit. Assemble the joint using a dead-blow mallet and a backing block to distribute your blows across the entire joint. If your joint is made correctly, you should be able to push it together most of the way using only hand pressure and need only a few taps to seat it in place. If it's too tight (a common malady), try shaving off a little on the inside faces of the pins — parts that will never show in the completed joint. Then ease the inside edges of the tails just a bit.

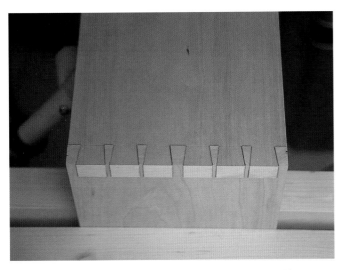

step 13 • This is the completed joint. You can see the pencil lines on my tails and how the ends of the pins and tails stick up just a bit. This makes it easier to trim them flush to the case, but more difficult to clamp up. More on that later. Cut the other joints and then dry assemble the case. Measure its width and length to determine how big your door E should be. You want the door to overhang the case by $^1/_{16}$" on either end and $^1/_{16}$" on the front, so size your parts accordingly.

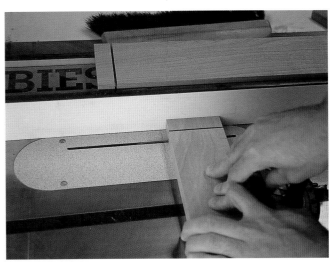

step 14 • As much as I enjoy handwork, I decided to cut the mortise-and-tenon joints for the frame and panel door E using my tailed apprentices (my power tools). I begin making this classic housed joint by cutting a sample mortise with my mortising machine. Then I cut all the tenons. The rule of thumb is that your tenons' thickness should be one-half the thickness of your stock. The door is $^3/_4$" thick, so the tenons are $^3/_8$" thick with $^3/_{16}$" shoulders on the face cheeks. I begin making my tenons by setting the height of a crosscut saw blade to just a shade more than $^3/_{16}$" and setting the fence so it's 1" away from the left edge of my saw blade.

step 15 • Now I raise the blade to $^3/_8$" and define the edge shoulders in the same manner.

step 16 • Now install a dado stack in your table saw. These tenons are 1" long, so I like to put in enough chippers to make a $^5/_8$" cut in one pass. Set the height of the dado stack to $^3/_{16}$" and set the fence so it's 1" away from the leftmost tooth of your dado stack. Make several passes over the blade to remove the waste from the face cheeks.

step 17 • Now turn the rail on its edge and remove the waste from the edge cheeks in the same manner.

step 18 • Test the fit of your tenon in your test mortise. When satisfied with the fit, cut the tenons on all the rails this way, being sure to check the fit after cutting each one.

step 19 • Finally, raise the dado stack to ³⁄₈" and remove the remainder of the waste on the edge cheeks. The bigger edge shoulders ensure that you won't blow out the ends of your mortises while clamping up the door.

step 20 • Now use your tenons to mark exactly where your mortises should go on your stiles. I like this method because there is much less measuring, and therefore less room for error.

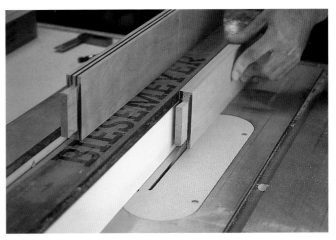

step 21 • Cut $\frac{3}{8}$"-wide by $\frac{11}{16}$"-deep mortises in the stiles. With a hollow chisel mortiser, you need to be careful about how you cut the joint. As you can see from the photo, I cut one hole, skip a space and then cut the next one. Later I come back and clean up the area between. If you cut all your holes right in a row, your chisel is more likely to bend or snap in a cut because it wants to follow the path of least resistance.

step 22 • Now cut the $\frac{3}{8}$" by $\frac{1}{2}$" groove on the door parts that will hold the panel. I use a rip blade in my table saw as shown in the photo. Don't worry about stopping the groove in the stiles. The hole won't show on the front because it will be covered by edging. On the back you'll almost never see it because that is where the hinges go. If the hole offends you, by all means patch it. Assemble the door E and make sure it fits on the case. When all is well, plane down or sand the panel for the door and glue up the door — making sure not to put glue in the panel's groove.

Slick Sole for Smoothing

When using a smoothing plane to prepare wood for finishing, you'll get better results if the plane's sole is waxed. The wax lubricates the sole and allows the plane to skim over the work. You use less effort, and the end result looks better because you're less likely to have to force the plane through the cut. I use inexpensive canning wax you can find at any grocery store that costs a few dollars for a box. Apply the wax in the pattern shown in the photo below. Then start working until you feel the plane becoming harder to move. Reapply the wax and get back to work.

step 23 • Disassemble the case and cut the $\frac{3}{8}$"-deep groove for the $\frac{1}{2}$"-thick bottom C. I made the cut in two passes using a plunge router outfitted with a straight bit and an edge guide. On the pin boards, you can cut the groove through the ends because it won't show. Make sure you put the groove $\frac{1}{2}$" in from the bottom edge of the sides because you need room for the French cleat that attaches the cabinet to the wall.

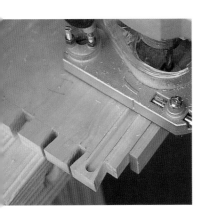

step 24 • On the tail boards you will need to stop the groove in one of the tails as shown in the photo. The dovetail layout shown in the drawing allows you to put the groove solidly into a tail.

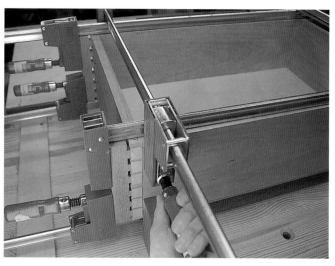

step 25 • Now plane all the case pieces using a smoothing plane. A sharp smoother, such as this #4½", can virtually eliminate sanding. After planing down the case pieces, I'll hit them with some 220-grit sandpaper to remove any ridges left by the plane.

step 26 • You'll need to make some clamping blocks as shown in the photo to clamp the tails firmly against the pin boards. These are easy to make using a handsaw or band saw. Apply a little bit of glue to the tails and knock the case together. Don't forget to slide the bottom in its groove when three sides are in place. Clamp up your case using the clamping blocks and let it sit for at least 30 minutes.

step 27 • When the glue in the case is dry, remove it from the clamps and plane down the dovetail joints. A sharp low-angle block plane is perfect for this job. The low angle is particularly effective with end grain.

step 28 • Now it's time to make the dividers for the planes. This is the easy part. I assembled the dividers using just screws to make sure I could change the configuration in case my plane collection ever changed. The first step is to screw the four outermost pieces together and plane them down so they fit snugly inside the case.

step 29 • As you install the interior dividers, it's a good idea to double-check your initial measurements against the real thing. I had a rude shock when my #4 was wider than I had anticipated. When everything works, screw all the parts together using No. 8 × 1" screws. Then screw the whole thing into the cabinet. I ran the screws in from the back side of the cabinet.

step 30 • The ³⁄₈" by 1" edging creates a dust seal around the edge of your toolbox and gives the piece a nice finished look. I cut a ¹⁄₄" roundover on the inside edge of the edging as you can see in the photo. Miter the ends, then glue and nail the edging to the door's edges.

step 31 • Install the hardware, such as the no-mortise hinges, catches, pulls and chest handles. Don't forget to drill pilot holes for your hardware or your brass screws will self-destruct as you try to drive them.

Planes at Rest: On Their Soles or Their Sides?

One of the big debates among plane users is whether to place hand planes on their soles or their sides when you're not using them at your bench. Traditional carpenters would place them on their sides to protect the plane's iron from becoming dinged. Many woodworkers have picked up this tradition, and it's frequently passed from master to apprentice (as it was to me).

But it might not be necessary. Recently I was convinced by a fellow craftsman that it's better to place planes on their soles when you are working at your bench. Here's the rationale. The old carpenter's saw applied to work on the job site, where you could never be certain about where you were setting your plane (this was back when you might actually see planes on a job site). So placing the plane on its side protected the iron from the grit and gravel that could cover any flat surface in a newly built home. Also, carpenters say putting planes on their sides prevents the iron from being pushed back into the plane's body, which is what could happen when a plane is rested on its sole.

Woodworkers, however, work on a wooden bench — far away from cement dust and gravel. So they say it's best to place an unused plane on its sole to prevent the iron from getting dinged by another tool on the bench. What about the iron getting pushed up into the plane's body? If you think about this statement for a moment, you'll see how ridiculous it is. The plane's iron is secured tightly enough in the plane's body to withstand enormous

pressure as the plane is pushed through your work. It should be child's play for the iron to stay in one place with only the weight of the plane pushing it down.

Other woodworkers have come up with other solutions that work, too, including placing the planes sole-down over the tool well of their bench. Or they rest the sole on a thin wooden strip that holds the iron slightly above the bench. But I don't mess with that. After undoing years of training, I now put my planes sole-down on the bench.

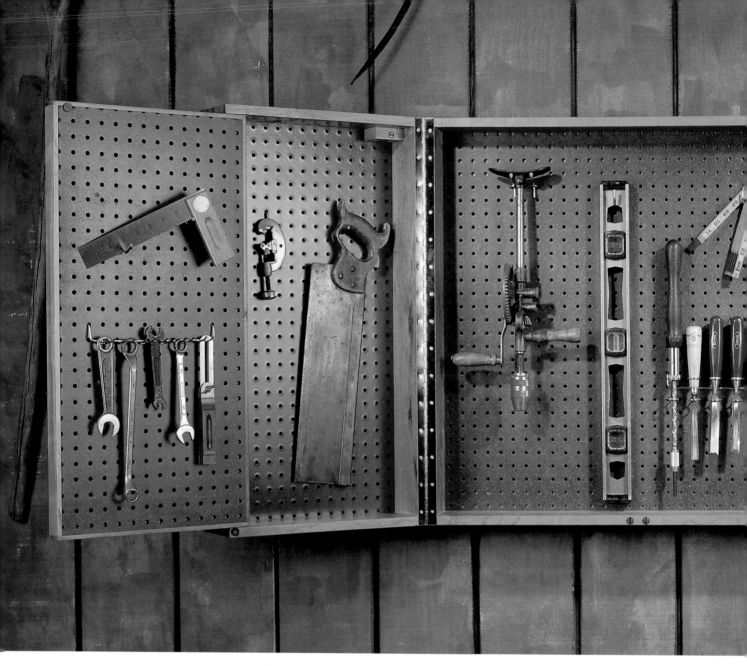

I had access to some gorgeous cherry that had been air-drying for about two years. It came from coworker's backyard and each board was over 20" wide. I used two of the boards for the floating panels in the doors. I trimmed off the white sapwood and left the large cracks. As you can see, it is beautiful!

This cabinet opens up to 9' wide, so there is plenty of room for tools. (The entire cabinet uses about three-fourths of a 4' × 8' sheet of pegboard.) I know home woodworkers who swear by pegboard for storing everything, so this cabinet pays homage to them. The continuous hinges are strong and will support the weight of the tools just fine.

I chose to make the cabinet body and doors using dovetails because of their tremendous strength and because they look cool.

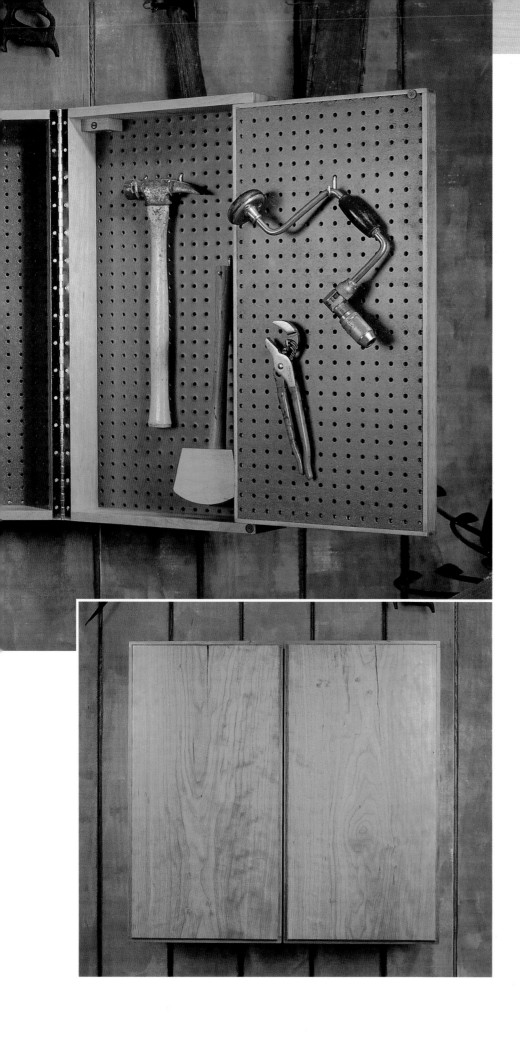

pegboard-lover's cabinet

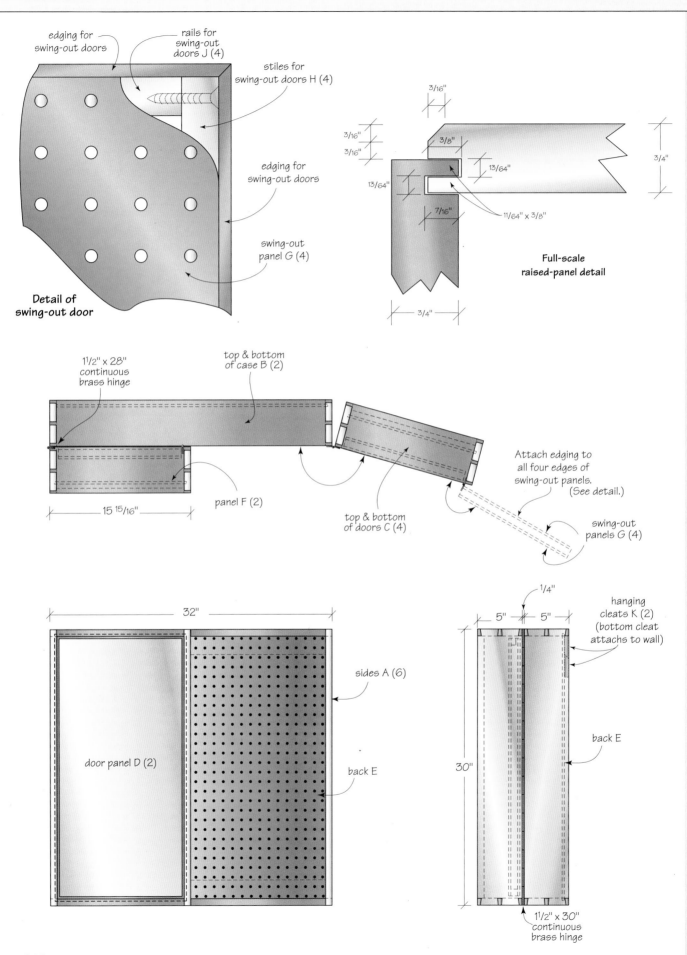

edging for
swing-out doors

rails for
swing-out
doors J (4)

stiles for
swing-out doors H (4)

edging for
swing-out doors

swing-out
panel G (4)

**Detail of
swing-out door**

3/16"

3/16"
3/16"

3/8"

13/64"

13/64"

7/16"

11/64" x 3/8"

3/4"

3/4"

**Full-scale
raised-panel detail**

1¹/2" x 28"
continuous
brass hinge

top & bottom
of case B (2)

Attach edging to
all four edges of
swing-out panels.
(See detail.)

15 ¹⁵/₁₆"

panel F (2)

top & bottom
of doors C (4)

swing-out
panels G (4)

32"

door panel D (2)

sides A (6)

back E

1/4"

5"   5"

hanging
cleats K (2)
(bottom cleat
attaches to wall)

30"

back E

1¹/2" x 30"
continuous
brass hinge

materials list

REFERENCE	QUANTITY	PART	STOCK	THICKNESS	WIDTH	LENGTH	COMMENTS
A	6	sides	cherry	3/4	5	30	
B	2	top & bottom of case	cherry	3/4	5	32	
C	4	top & bottom of doors	cherry	3/4	5	15^{15}/16	
D	2	door panels	cherry	3/4	15^5/16	29^1/8	
E	1	back	pegboard	1/4	31	29	
F	2	panels	pegboard	1/4	14^{15}/16	29	
G	4	swing-out panels	pegboard	1/4	13^7/16	27^1/2	
		edging	cherry	1/4	1^1/4	192	cut to lengths as needed to edge the swing-out doors
H	4	stiles	poplar	3/4	3/4	27^1/2	material for subframe
J	4	rails for swing-out panels	poplar	3/4	3/4	11^{15}/16	material for subframe
K	2	hanging cleats	maple	3/4	2^1/2	30^1/2	cut 45° bevel on one long edge

hardware

- 2 continuous hinges 3/16" × 1^1/2" × 30"
- 2 continuous hinges 3/16" × 1^1/2" × 28"
- 2 magnetic catches

REFERENCE	QUANTITY	PART	STOCK	THICKNESS	WIDTH	LENGTH	COMMENTS
A	6	sides	cherry	19	127	762	
B	2	top & bottom of case	cherry	19	127	813	
C	4	top & bottom of doors	cherry	19	127	405	
D	2	door panels	cherry	19	389	721	
E	1	back	pegboard	6	787	737	
F	2	panels	pegboard	6	379	737	
G	4	swing-out panels	pegboard	6	341	699	
		edging	cherry	6	32	5m	cut to lengths as needed to edge the swing-out doors
H	4	stiles	poplar	19	19	699	material for subframe
J	4	rails for swing-out panels	poplar	19	19	303	material for subframe
K	2	hanging cleats	maple	19	64	775	cut 45° bevel on one long edge

hardware

- 2 continuous hinges 5mm × 38mm × 762mm
- 2 continuous hinges 5mm × 38mm × 711mm
- 2 magnetic catches

STEP-BY-STEP construction

step 1 • This was some very nice cherry I lucked into. I cut off one edge and straightened it on the jointer. I was then able to cut door panels that were over 15" wide. The wood hadn't been stickered and stacked properly to dry, so I had to remove a fair amount of material to get the panels flat.

Cut out all the cabinet and door parts, then lay out and cut the dovetails. See project eight, steps one through three for details on using the table saw to cut dovetails. Then cut the grooves for the back panel. When gluing the cabinet together, be sure to install the back panel at the same time.

step 2 • After installing the back panel, glue the hanging cleat K to the back E and top panel B. Then, for extra strength, insert screws through the top panel into the cleat. Countersink the screws and use plugs to cover the screw heads.

step 3 • Offset the door panels D by cutting a groove in the edge of the door panel. For this cabinet, I just used a square-toothed blade and reset the fence until I had the proper groove width. Cut the corresponding grooves in the door tops C, bottoms C and sides A at the same time. See the technical drawing detail.

step 4 • Tilt the saw blade to 45° and cut the bevel on the top edges of the door panels. My saw blade tilts to the right, so this might look a little awkward to you right-handers. (Of course, if your saw blade tilts to the left, your setup would look just the opposite of the one shown above.) You could also use a block plane to cut the bevels. Assemble the doors as you did the cabinet body. Be sure to capture the panels in the grooves in the door tops, sides and bottoms as you glue the door together. Do not apply any glue to the panels.

step 5 • I know what you're thinking — where does he get all those clamps? Suffice it to say, you can never have too many clamps. Cut the frame parts for the hinged panels to length. Using butt joints, screw or staple them together. Then, cut the pegboard panels ¼" oversize and glue them to the frames. You can glue all four panels to the two frames at the same time, using your trusty bench horses. I put paper between the panels so that any glue that happened to leak through the pegboard holes wouldn't stick everything together. If you spread the glue evenly on the frame members and let it sit for a minute, it gets slightly tacky and has much less of a tendency to seep into other areas. When the glue dries, trim the pegboard flush to the edges of the frames. Then glue the cherry edging to the frames. I glued opposite edges on at the same time, trimmed the ends flush, then glued the other opposing edges to the frame. You could miter the ends of the cherry edging if you prefer.

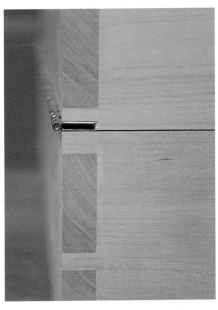

step 6 • Cut a rabbet in the door the same depth as the thickness of the continuous hinge. Attach the hinge with three screws each (top, middle and bottom) in the door and the cabinet. Close the door and check the alignment. Adjust by installing screws in different holes. Check alignment again. Mark the holes so you'll know which ones to put the screws into first after you've finished the cabinet and are putting it back together.

step 7 • This shows the cabinet door in its closed position.

step 8 • Attach the continuous hinge (for the swing-out panels G) to the inside face of the door with three screws.

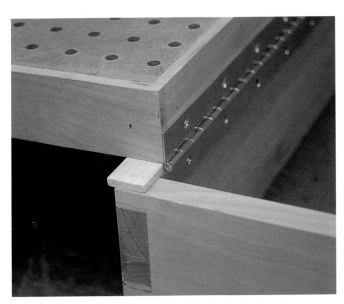

step 9 • Cut a spacer the same thickness as the hinge and put it between the face of the door and the swing-out panel. This will hold the panel in alignment while the screws are inserted into the edge of the swing-out panel.

step 10 • When the swinging door is attached, it should close flush with the inside face of the door. The barrel of the hinge will be proud to the surface of the inside door face. This allows the swing-out panel to open fully.

fly-tying box

This box isn't exactly a tool chest, but I know lots of woodworkers who are fly fishermen (and women). There are some very specialized tools and supplies for tying flies, and I haven't seen too many boxes made in which you could store all these supplies.

This box is made of Baltic birch plywood, which is very solid, so you don't have to worry about wood movement. It's made to take out in the field. If a rainstorm comes up or you just want to take a break, you can relax under shelter and tie some flies and other bugs!

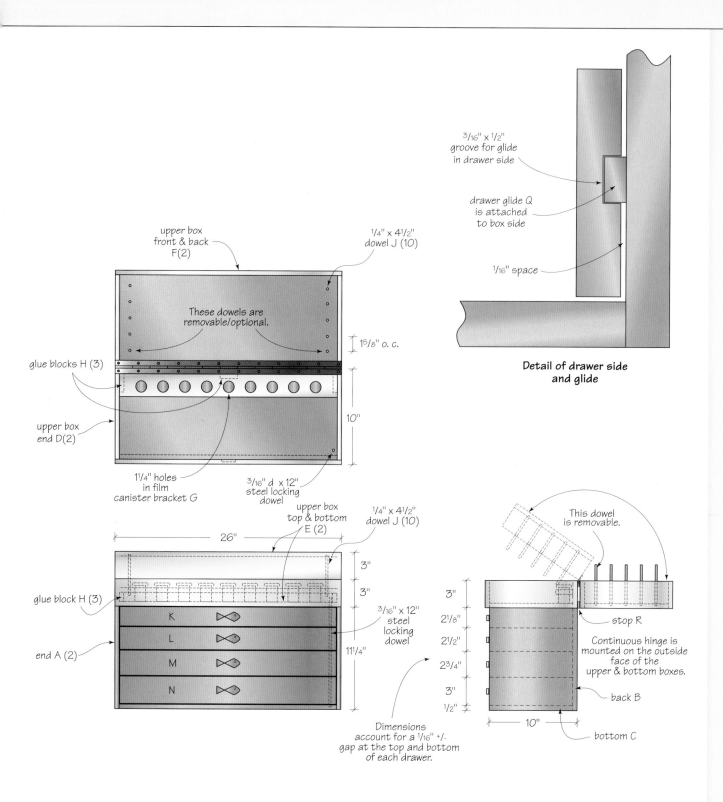

upper box
front & back
F(2)

¹/₄" x 4¹/₂"
dowel J (10)

These dowels are
removable/optional.

1⁵/₈" o. c.

glue blocks H (3)

upper box
end D(2)

10"

1¹/₄" holes
in film
canister bracket G

³/₁₆" d x 12"
steel locking
dowel

³/₁₆" x ¹/₂"
groove for glide
in drawer side

drawer glide Q
is attached
to box side

¹/₁₆" space

**Detail of drawer side
and glide**

upper box
top & bottom
E (2)

¹/₄" x 4¹/₂"
dowel J (10)

26"

3"

3"

glue block H (3)

³/₁₆" x 12"
steel
locking
dowel

end A (2)

K

L

M

N

11¹/₄"

This dowel
is removable.

stop R

Continuous hinge is
mounted on the outside
face of the
upper & bottom boxes.

back B

bottom C

3"

3"

2¹/₈"

2¹/₂"

2³/₄"

3"

¹/₂"

10"

Dimensions
account for a ¹/₁₆" +/-
gap at the top and bottom
of each drawer.

materials list

REFERENCE	QUANTITY	PART	STOCK	THICKNESS	WIDTH	LENGTH	COMMENTS
A	2	ends	Baltic birch ply	$1/2$	10	$11^1/4$	
B	1	back	Baltic birch ply	$1/2$	$11^1/4$	25	
C	1	bottom	Baltic birch ply	$1/2$	$9^1/2$	25	
D	2	upper box ends	Baltic birch ply	$1/2$	6	9	upper box will be cut in
E	2	upper box top & bottom	Baltic birch ply	$1/2$	9	25	half to create the upper
F	2	upper box front & back	Baltic birch ply	$1/2$	6	26	bin and lid
G	1	film canister bracket	Baltic birch ply	$1/2$	$2^1/2$	25	drill 9, $1^1/4$"-dia. holes, evenly spaced, for canisters
H	3	glue blocks	Baltic birch ply	$1/2$	1	2	locate one at each end of canister bracket and one in middle of bracket
J	10	dowel rods	hardwood	$1/4$ d		$4^1/2$	
K	1	drawer front	Baltic birch ply	$1/2$	$2^1/8$	$24^7/8$	
	1	drawer K back	Baltic birch ply	$1/2$	$2^1/8$	$23^7/8$	
	2	drawer K sides	Baltic birch ply	$1/2$	$2^1/8$	9	
L	1	drawer front	Baltic birch ply	$1/2$	$2^1/2$	$24^7/8$	
	1	drawer L back	Baltic birch ply	$1/2$	$2^1/2$	$23^7/8$	
	2	drawer L sides	Baltic birch ply	$1/2$	$2^1/2$	9	
M	1	drawer front	Baltic birch ply	$1/2$	$2^3/4$	$24^7/8$	
	1	drawer M back	Baltic birch ply	$1/2$	$2^3/4$	$23^7/8$	
	2	drawer M sides	Baltic birch ply	$1/2$	$2^3/4$	9	
N	1	drawer front	Baltic birch ply	$1/2$	3	$24^7/8$	
	1	drawer N back	Baltic birch ply	$1/2$	3	$23^7/8$	
	2	drawer N sides	Baltic birch ply	$1/2$	3	9	
P	4	drawer bottoms	plywood	$1/2$	$8^1/2$	$23^7/8$	
Q	8	drawer glides	maple	$1/4$	$15/32$	9	
R	1	stop	maple	$3/16$	$3/4$	26	

hardware

- 4 drawer pulls (fish-shaped if you like)
- 1 $3/16$" dia. × 12" steel dowel rod
- 1 continuous hinge
- 2 sash handles
- 2 drawbolts

STEP-BY-STEP construction

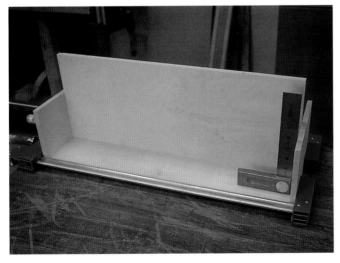

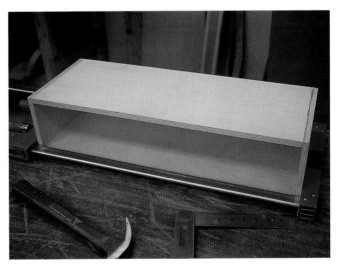

step 1 • Cut all parts to dimensions. Glue the upper box ends D to the upper box top E. Use the upper box bottom E as a spacer to hold the ends square. If the top panel is slightly bent, put the bend to the inside of the assembly.

step 2 • Glue the upper box bottom E to the top/ends assembly. If the bottom panel is slightly bent, put the bend to the inside of the assembly.

REFERENCE	QUANTITY	PART	STOCK	THICKNESS	WIDTH	LENGTH	COMMENTS
A	2	ends	Baltic birch ply	13	254	285	
B	1	back	Baltic birch ply	13	285	635	
C	1	bottom	Baltic birch ply	13	242	635	
D	2	upper box ends	Baltic birch ply	13	152	229	upper box will be cut in half to create the upper bin and lid
E	2	upper box top & bottom	Baltic birch ply	13	229	635	
F	2	upper box front & back	Baltic birch ply	13	152	660	
G	1	film canister bracket	Baltic birch ply	13	64	635	drill 9, 32mm-dia. holes, evenly spaced, for canisters
H	3	glue blocks	Baltic birch ply	13	25	51	locate one at each end of canister bracket and one in middle of bracket
J	10	dowel rods	hardwood	6 d		115	
K	1	drawer front	Baltic birch ply	13	54	632	
	1	drawer K back	Baltic birch ply	13	54	606	
	2	drawer K sides	Baltic birch ply	13	54	229	
L	1	drawer front	Baltic birch ply	13	64	632	
	1	drawer L back	Baltic birch ply	13	64	606	
	2	drawer L sides	Baltic birch ply	13	64	229	
M	1	drawer front	Baltic birch ply	13	70	632	
	1	drawer M back	Baltic birch ply	13	70	606	
	2	drawer M sides	Baltic birch ply	13	70	229	
N	1	drawer front	Baltic birch ply	13	76	632	
	1	drawer N back	Baltic birch ply	13	76	606	
	2	drawer N sides	Baltic birch ply	13	76	229	
P	4	drawer bottoms	plywood	13	216	606	
Q	8	drawer glides	maple	6	12	229	
R	1	stop	maple	5	19	660	

hardware

- 4 drawer pulls (fish-shaped if you like)
- 1 5mm dia. × 305mm steel dowel rod
- 1 continuous hinge
- 2 sash handles
- 2 drawbolts

PROJECT 12 | **FLY-TYING BOX (CONTINUED)**

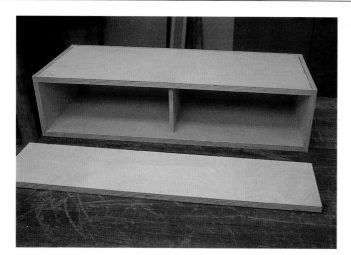

step 3 • Put a temporary spacer in the middle of the assembly. This will push the top and bottom panels flat (if you have assembled the box with the bends to the inside). After this assembly is cut in half to create a lid and upper bin section, you can remove the temporary spacers.

step 4 • Glue the upper box front and back panels F to the box assembly. I am using butt joints throughout this assembly. With the multiple sides coming together, the assembly is quite strong. If it was dropped off a building, yes, it would probably come apart, but for a fly-tying box the joinery is adequate.

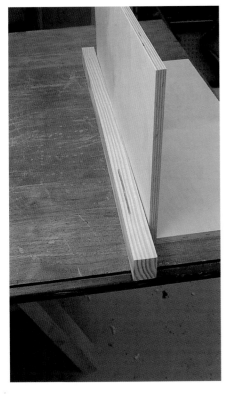

step 5 • When gluing the back B to the bottom C of the lower box, use a caul that is curved. Note the space at the ends of the caul. When the clamps are applied, the caul will be pulled to the back, applying pressure to the center of the panel and at the ends. Only two clamps are needed.

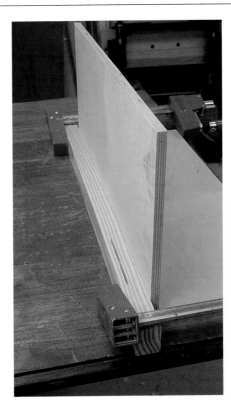

step 6 • When the space is gone between the ends of the caul and the back B, you've got enough clamping pressure.

step 7 • Glue the ends A to the bottom/back assembly. Be sure all edges align.

step 8 • Now, cut the upper box (the one you assembled in steps one through four) in half, creating a lid and upper bin section. This photo shows biscuit slots being cut into the bottom of the upper bin. Cut matching slots in the top edges of the side and back panels of the lower assembly. Attach the upper bin to the lower box assembly with #10 biscuits.

step 9 • Make the film canister bracket G as illustrated in the technical drawings and materials list. Locate and glue the three glue blocks H in place as shown in the drawing, then install the canister bracket.

step 10 • To build drawers K, L, M and N, first glue the drawer bottoms P to the drawer backs. I used some scrap plywood for the drawer bottoms, but you certainly could cut them out of the Baltic birch.

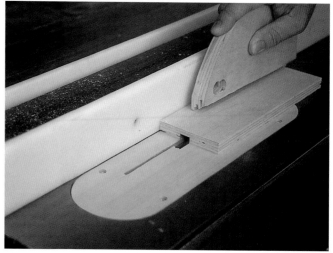

step 11 • Cut the grooves in the drawer sides for the drawer glides Q.

step 12 • Glue the sides to the drawer bottom/back assembly.

step 13 • Finally, glue the drawer fronts to the rest of the drawer box assembly.

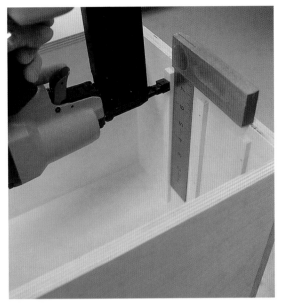

step 14 • Carefully lay out the location of the drawer glides Q. I assembled the drawers first, then I was able to accurately locate the drawer glides. Glue and pin (or screw) them in place. Be sure the glides are square to the front of the cabinet. Take your time.

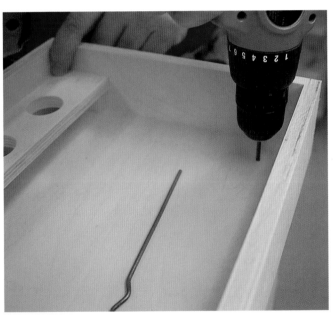

step 15 • Drill a ³/₁₆"-diameter hole toward the front of the upper bin. Continue the hole down through each drawer bottom. Then drill a hole halfway through the bottom C. Measure carefully so that all these holes line up with each other. Thread a ³/₁₆" steel dowel through the holes in the top bin, all the drawer bottoms and into the bottom panel. This will keep the drawers from coming open while moving the box.

step 16 • After drilling the hole in the upper bin bottom, I used a rod to mark the first hole in the top-drawer bottom. After that, measuring where the holes are located will work just fine. Drill holes for the wooden dowels in the lid. Then finish the box. Attach the lid with a continuous hinge. I located the hinge flat on the outside back of the box. This allowed screws to be inserted into the plywood through the layers of the plies, which gives a much better purchase for the screws, rather than inserting them into the end grain of the plywood. When the lid is opened, it rests against the wooden stop R attached to the back of the upper bin section. This stop holds the lid level with the upper bin, creating a nice workspace. Attach the drawer pulls of your choice. I chose some wooden fish pulls. (I believe they're smallmouth bass.) Finally, attach the sash handles and the drawbolts.

This chest will hold a ton of hand power tools. There is also a drop-in box that either can serve as a sliding box inside the chest or, with a handle inserted, can be used as a tool tote.

The Southwestern style is one you can choose to copy, or you can make this in a Shaker, Arts & Crafts or contemporary style to suit your own personal tastes. After all, a tool chest should reflect and incorporate the personality of its builder.

I had a lot of fun laying out and carving the pattern in the lid. I used sugar pine to build the chest because it's easy to carve and it's light in weight. If you use a heavier wood, such as oak or cherry, you might want to put casters on the feet so you can move it easily.

The carved horse in the photo at left was inspired by the Palomino restaurant's logo. It took me three weeks over a four-year time span to carve the horse. I didn't want to rush myself!

southwestern chest

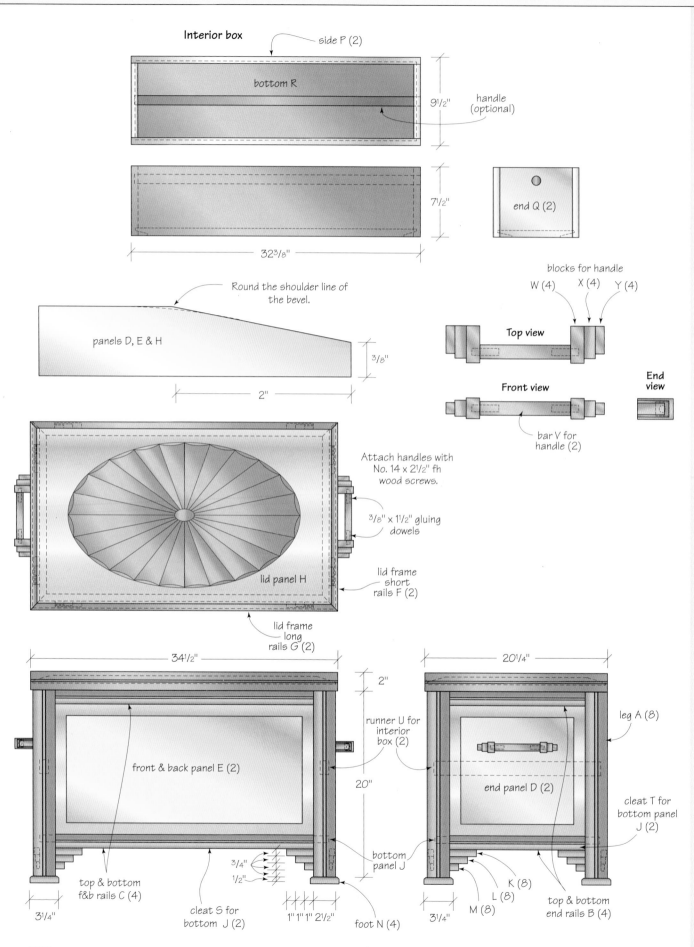

Interior box

side P (2)

bottom R

handle (optional)

9 1/2"

7 1/2"

end Q (2)

32 3/8"

Round the shoulder line of the bevel.

panels D, E & H

3/8"

2"

blocks for handle

W (4)   X (4)   Y (4)

Top view

Front view

bar V for handle (2)

End view

Attach handles with No. 14 x 2 1/2" fh wood screws.

3/8" x 1 1/2" gluing dowels

lid frame short rails F (2)

lid panel H

lid frame long rails G (2)

34 1/2"

2"

runner U for interior box (2)

20"

front & back panel E (2)

20 1/4"

leg A (8)

end panel D (2)

cleat T for bottom panel J (2)

bottom panel J

3/4"
1/2"

top & bottom f&b rails C (4)

3 1/4"

cleat S for bottom J (2)

1" 1" 1" 2 1/2"

foot N (4)

3 1/4"

K (8)

L (8)

M (8)

top & bottom end rails B (4)

224

materials list

REFERENCE	QUANTITY	PART	STOCK	THICKNESS	WIDTH	LENGTH	COMMENTS
A	8	legs	pine	$3/4$	$2^{1}/_{2}$	20	45° miter cut on one long edge
B	4	top & bottom end rails	pine	$3/4$	$1^{1}/_{2}$	16	
C	4	top & bottom f&b rails	pine	$3/4$	$1^{1}/_{2}$	30	
D	2	end panels	pine	$3/4$	$14^{3}/_{4}$	16	
E	2	front & back panels	pine	$3/4$	$14^{3}/_{4}$	30	
F	2	lid frame short rails	pine	$3/4$	2	$20^{1}/_{4}$	45° miter cuts on both ends
G	2	lid frame long rails	pine	$3/4$	2	$34^{1}/_{2}$	45° miter cuts on both ends
H	1	lid panel	pine	$3/4$	$19^{1}/_{2}$	34	
J	1	bottom panel	pine	$3/4$	$18^{1}/_{4}$	$32^{1}/_{2}$	
K	8	moulding pieces at feet	pine	$3/4$	$5/8$	3	
L	8	moulding pieces at feet	pine	$3/4$	$1/2$	2	
M	8	moulding pieces at feet	pine	$3/4$	$3/8$	1	
N	4	feet	pine	$3/4$	$3^{1}/_{4}$	$3^{1}/_{4}$	
P	2	sides for interior box	pine	$3/4$	$7^{1}/_{2}$	$32^{3}/_{8}$	
Q	2	ends for interior box	pine	$3/4$	$7^{1}/_{2}$	8	
R	1	bottom for interior box	pine	$3/4$	$8^{3}/_{4}$	$31^{7}/_{8}$	
S	2	cleats for bottom panel J	pine	1	1	$32^{1}/_{2}$	
T	2	cleats for bottom panel J	pine	1	1	$16^{1}/_{4}$	
U	2	runners for interior box	pine	1	$1^{1}/_{2}$	$18^{1}/_{2}$	
V	2	bars for handle	pine	$3/4$	$3/4$	$5^{1}/_{2}$	
W	4	blocks for handle	pine	$3/4$	$1^{1}/_{8}$	2	
X	4	blocks for handle	pine	$5/8$	$7/8$	$1^{3}/_{4}$	
Y	4	blocks for handle	pine	$1/2$	$5/8$	$1^{1}/_{2}$	
Z	4	filler blocks for legs	pine	$1^{3}/_{4}$	$1^{3}/_{4}$	3	
AA	8	cleats at feet	pine	$1/2$	$1/2$	2	
BB	8	cleats at feet	pine	$1/2$	$1/2$	2	45° miter cut on one end

hardware

- 1 pair trunk strap hinges   Rockler #50732
- 1 chain for lid
- 1 broom handle (optional)
- 4 $3/8" \times 1^{1}/_{2}"$ gluing dowels
- 4 No. 14 $\times$ $2^{1}/_{2}"$ flathead wood screws

STEP-BY-STEP construction

step 1 • Cut the leg parts A. Then, tape the mitered edges as shown in the technical illustration for project one. Here is another way to hold the parts while the glue dries.

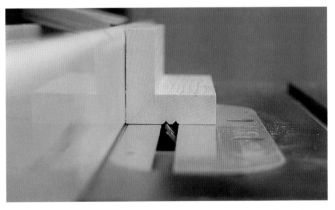

step 2 • Tilt your table saw blade to 45°. Set the blade height so that the blade edge is barely above the tabletop. Run some test pieces to find the V-groove depth that you like. By setting the fence properly, you can make one cut, flip the piece end for end and make the second cut. This assures that the V-groove pattern is centered on the legs. Do the same on all the rail parts B, C, F and G. (You will need to reset the fence to get the pattern centered on the rails because they are narrower.) This technique works best with a square-toothed ripping blade.

REFERENCE	QUANTITY	PART	STOCK	THICKNESS	WIDTH	LENGTH	COMMENTS
A	8	legs	pine	19	64	508	45° miter cut on one long edge
B	4	top & bottom end rails	pine	19	38	406	
C	4	top & bottom f&b rails	pine	19	38	762	
D	2	end panels	pine	19	375	406	
E	2	front & back panels	pine	19	375	762	
F	2	lid frame short rails	pine	19	51	514	45° miter cuts on both ends
G	2	lid frame long rails	pine	19	51	876	45° miter cuts on both ends
H	1	lid panel	pine	19	495	864	
J	1	bottom panel	pine	19	464	826	
K	8	moulding pieces at feet	pine	19	16	76	
L	8	moulding pieces at feet	pine	19	13	51	
M	8	moulding pieces at feet	pine	19	10	25	
N	4	feet	pine	19	83	83	
P	2	sides for interior box	pine	19	191	822	
Q	2	ends for interior box	pine	19	191	203	
R	1	bottom for interior box	pine	19	222	810	
S	2	cleats for bottom panel J	pine	25	25	806	
T	2	cleats for bottom panel J	pine	25	25	412	
U	2	runners for interior box	pine	25	38	470	
V	2	bars for handle	pine	19	19	140	
W	4	blocks for handle	pine	19	29	51	
X	4	blocks for handle	pine	16	22	45	
Y	4	blocks for handle	pine	13	16	38	
Z	4	filler blocks for legs	pine	45	45	76	
AA	8	cleats at feet	pine	13	13	51	
BB	8	cleats at feet	pine	13	13	51	45° miter cut on one end

- 1 pair trunk strap hinges   Rockler #50732
- 1 chain for lid
- 1 broom handle (optional)
- 4 10mm × 38mm gluing dowels
- 4 No. 14 × 64mm flathead wood screws

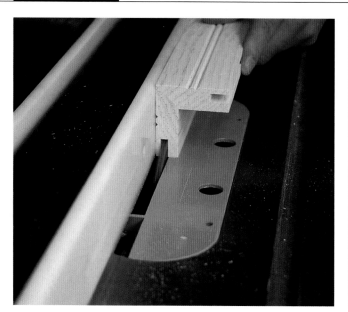

step 3 • Set up a dado cutter to cut a ¼"-wide by ½"-deep groove in the legs and all rails.

step 4 • Use the same dado head to cut the tenons on the rails.

step 5 • Set the saw blade tilt to 5° and cut the bevels on the ends D, front and back E, lid H and interior box bottom R panels. Don't make the shoulder offset cut on the end panels D and front and back panels E. (I did make the offset cut on panel R. No reason, I just chose to do it that way.) Sand the shoulders smooth on the panels. (See detail in technical illustration.) This is a scary-looking setup. Use your guards and be careful!

step 6 • Cut rabbets on the panels to create a tenon that will fit into the grooves of the frame parts.

step 7 • Assemble the front and back panels E with the rails C and the legs A.

step 8 • Clamping is very easy in this operation.

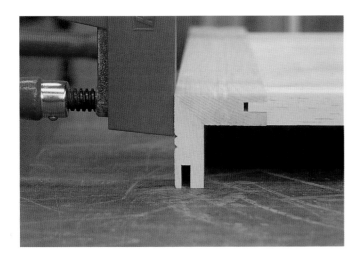

step 9 • Be sure the legs A are square to the frame rails C.

step 10 • When the glue on the front and back panels E is dry, connect the two panels with the end panels D and rails B. When I assembled this framework I put a spot of glue at the center of the ends of the floating panels. This helps hold the panels in place, but still allows them to move with seasonal changes. (The center will always stay fixed.)

step 12 • I found it easier to cut the grooves in step three along the entire length of the legs and later fill in the exposed grooves with some strips of wood.

step 11 • Cut four 1¾" × 1¾" × 3" blocks Z. Glue them inside the legs at the bottom. This helps strengthen the legs.

step 13 • Cut all the small mouldings K, L and M in long strips, then cut them to length. I glued the three stacked mouldings together first, then I glued them in place and added the cleats AA and BB.

step 14 • This is what the mouldings look like from the front. The small pieces are flush to each other on the back, but because they are different widths, this creates the offset, stair-stepped look. It creates a nice visual pattern that has lots of movement and shadow lines. Add the feet blocks N at this time. Don't glue the blocks, just screw them into place on the ends of the legs.

step 15 • Attach the 1" × 1" cleats S and T to the bottom inside edges of the bottom front and back rails C. Then, set the bottom panel J on these cleats and attach it with screws inserted into oversize pilot holes. Also, leave a ⅛" space on either side of the panel. This will allow the panel to move with seasonal changes.

step 16 • Glue and screw the runners U in place. Yes, you can glue them to the floating panel and to the legs. These runners are located in the center of the end panels D. The panels will still be able to move with the seasons. By securing the runners this way, it will hold the panels solid, so the handles can be attached to the panel. The chest can be lifted with no worries of the panels moving and putting undue pressure on the upper rails.

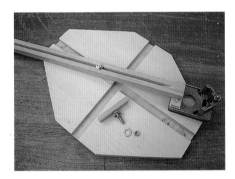

step 17 • After I drew the pattern on the lid panel H, I needed to find a way to cut a perfect ellipse with a V-grooving router bit. I made this jig, which worked flawlessly. (Sometimes you just get lucky.) See the technical drawings for details.

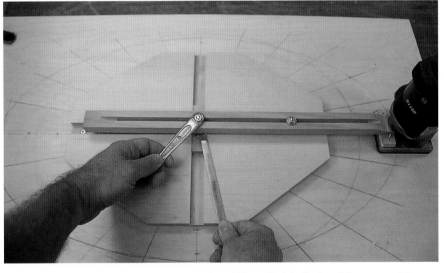

step 18 • The key to using this jig is setting the width and height limits of the pattern. The router will then follow the paths set by the sliding blocks. An ellipse is an angled cross section of a cone and has constantly changing radii. This jig will create a perfect ellipse.

step 19 • I screwed the jig to the panel. The holes mostly disappeared when I routed the straight-line V-grooves in the next step. Rout the ellipse, then remove the jig from the panel.

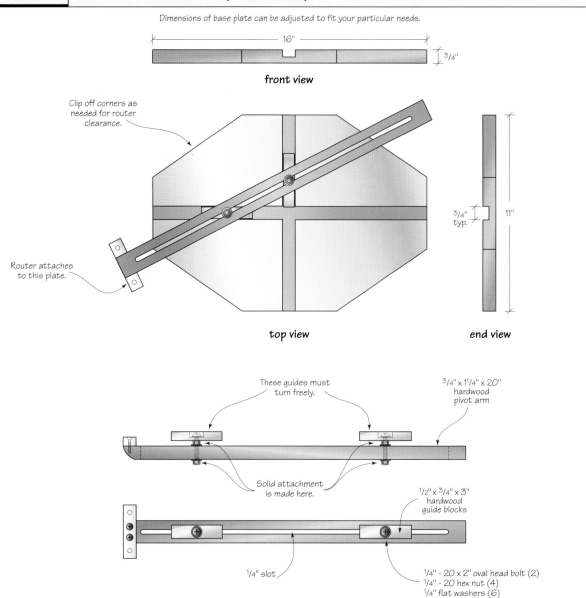

Dimensions of base plate can be adjusted to fit your particular needs.

16"

3/4"

front view

Clip off corners as needed for router clearance.

Router attaches to this plate.

top view

3/4" typ.

11"

end view

These guides must turn freely.

3/4" x 1 1/4" x 20" hardwood pivot arm

Solid attachment is made here.

1/2" x 3/4" x 3" hardwood guide blocks

1/4" slot

1/4" - 20 x 2" oval head bolt (2)
1/4" - 20 hex nut (4)
1/4" flat washers (6)

step 20 • I then routed straight-line V-grooves. Stop at the outer edges of the ellipse line and don't rout across the small ellipse in the center of the pattern.

step 21 • When carving the fan pattern, I found it helpful to turn off the overhead lights and use just one incandescent bulb to create shadows. These shadows clearly show how smooth or rough the surfaces are. As you carve the fan pattern, the center ellipse will start to form.

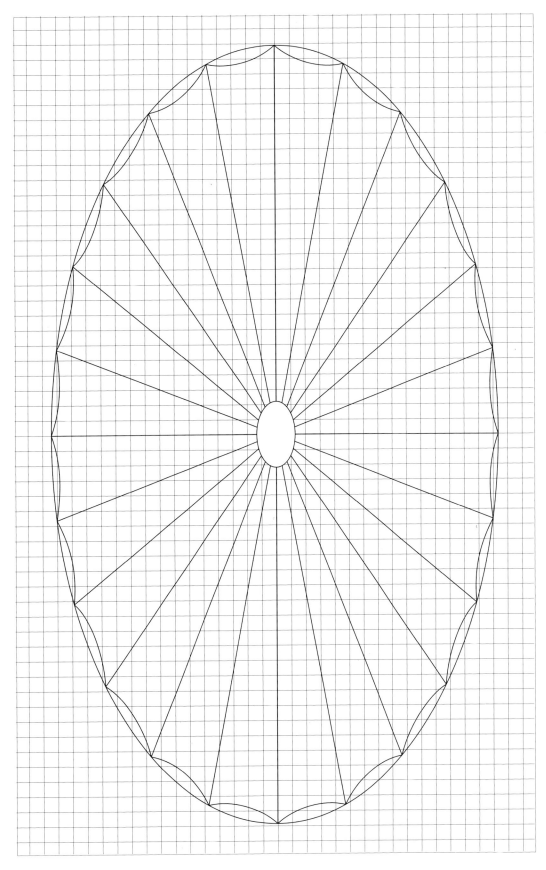

Each square represents 1/2".

For full-size pattern enlarge 320%.

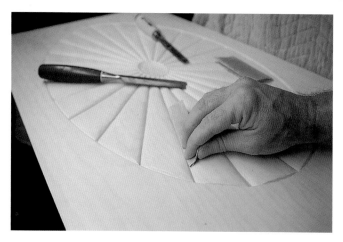

step 22 • I chose to sand the pattern smooth rather than leaving the tool marks, as I had originally intended.

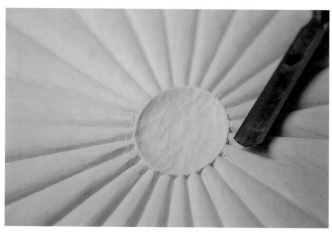

step 23 • The angle of this photo makes the center ellipse look almost round, but it is indeed a true ellipse. I chose to use a small gouge and scoop out the shape. I did leave the tooling marks here.

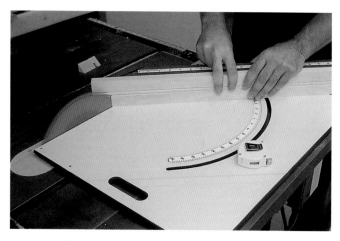

step 24 • After the pattern is carved in the lid panel H, cut the miters on the ends of the rails F & G.

step 25 • You can strengthen the miters by inserting a biscuit at each miter joint.

step 26 • Clamp the miters from two directions to close the joint tightly. This will be a strong joint.

step 27 • Cut the interior box parts P and Q to size. Cut the groove for the bottom panel R, and glue and screw the box together, capturing the bottom.

step 28 • I wanted to put a raised-panel bottom in the box. I don't know why; it just seemed like the thing to do!

step 29 • I cut off a broom handle, sanded off the green paint and rounded the ends slightly. Drill a through-hole in one end of the box and a stopped hole in the other end. Insert the handle in the box, and you've got a tool tote you can use to carry the tools you need for a job outside of the shop.

step 30 • Glue the blocks W, X and Y together to form the ends of the handles. Then drill a ³⁄₈" hole in the assembly and in the ends of the bars V. See the technical drawing for details.

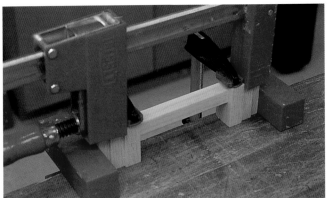

step 31 • Use ³⁄₈" × 1¹⁄₂" gluing dowels to attach the end block assemblies to the bars V. After you've applied the finish to the box and handles, attach the handles to the end panels. Then, set the lid on the box, align it and attach the trunk strap hinges. The trunk strap hinges are made to automatically stop the lid a little past 90° when it is opened. I installed a chain on the inside of the lid and chest so the lid wouldn't open too far and bend the hinges. If you plan on storing heavy tools in the chest, I would recommend putting casters on the feet.

tip >> A WHITEWASHED FINISH

The finish for this chest was not difficult to do, and it added a lot to the overall look and feel of the chest. I wanted to add some depth to the wood, the V-grooves, the mouldings and the carving.

After sanding, apply a coat of sealer. After it dries, sand it smooth. Then stain the chest with a medium-dark brown oil-based stain. Because the wood is partially sealed, the stain will be absorbed evenly. Let the stain sit for 1 minute, then wipe off the excess completely with a clean rag. This will add just the right amount of color to serve as a background for the white stain to be applied later.

After the stain has dried overnight, apply a whitewash oil-based stain. Apply this stain liberally and let it sit for 2 to 3 minutes. The whitewash might pickup traces of the brown stain. That's ok. Wipe off the color gently, leaving some of it in the V-grooves, at the corners where the mouldings butt up to the legs and in the nooks and crannies of the carving. Also, leave enough of this stain to give the whole piece a whitish, weathered look. Let this stain dry overnight.

Finally, apply two or three top coats. The more top coats you apply, the shinier the finish will become.

When I started this book, this was the first project I built. I knew it would be involved. The chest itself is a basic two-door box with some drawers.

What makes the chest what it is, is the curved front — which led to the overall design. The rounded edges of the top, bottom and feet soften the look and feel of the chest. When the curved doors are opened, they in-vite you to open the drawers.

I had been saving this walnut and curly maple for just the right project. Whenever I looked at the wood, I just couldn't bring my-self to cut into it. Then I realized that this was the project for this wood! There comes a time when you have to decide that this is it, and go for the project. I wasn't disappointed in the least and never looked back.

curved-front chest

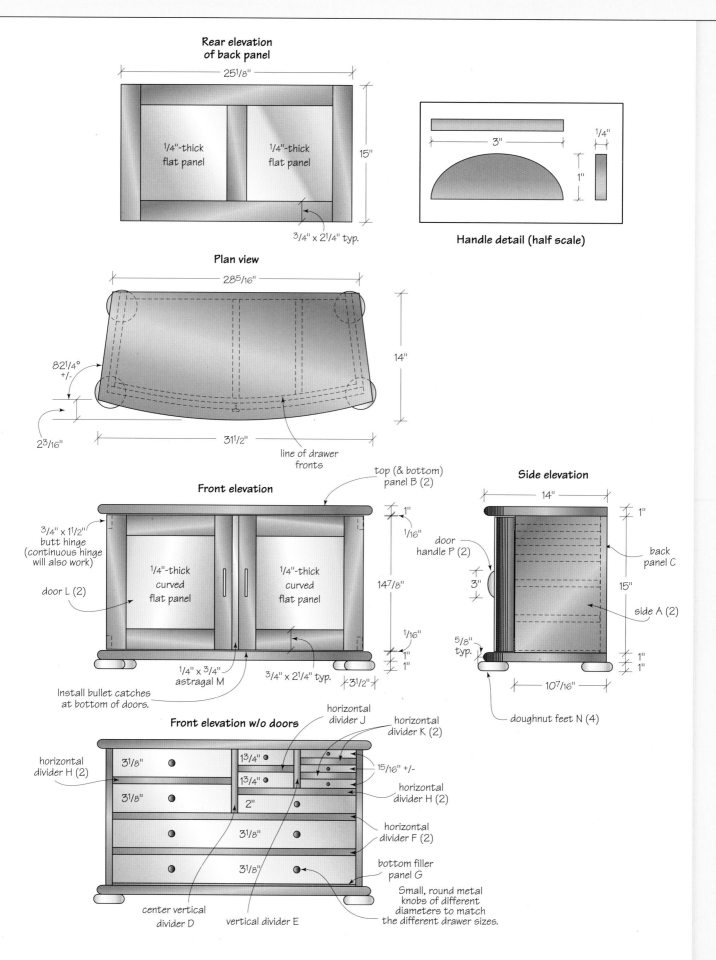

Rear elevation of back panel

25¹/₈"

15"

¹/₄"-thick flat panel

¹/₄"-thick flat panel

³/₄" x 2¹/₄" typ.

Handle detail (half scale)

3"

¼"

1"

Plan view

28⁵/₁₆"

14"

82¹/₄° +/-

2³/₁₆"

31¹/₂"

line of drawer fronts

Front elevation

top (& bottom) panel B (2)

³/₄" x 1¹/₂" butt hinge (continuous hinge will also work)

door L (2)

¹/₄"-thick curved flat panel

¹/₄"-thick curved flat panel

1"

1/16"

14⁷/₈"

1/16"

1"
1"

3¹/₂"

¹/₄" x ³/₄" astragal M

³/₄" x 2¹/₄" typ.

Install bullet catches at bottom of doors.

Side elevation

14"

1"

door handle P (2)

3"

back panel C

15"

side A (2)

5/8" typ.

1"
1"

10⁷/₁₆"

doughnut feet N (4)

Front elevation w/o doors

horizontal divider J

horizontal divider K (2)

horizontal divider H (2)

3¹/₈"

1³/₄"

15/16" +/-

1³/₄"

horizontal divider H (2)

3¹/₈"

2"

horizontal divider F (2)

3¹/₈"

bottom filler panel G

3¹/₈"

Small, round metal knobs of different diameters to match the different drawer sizes.

center vertical divider D

vertical divider E

materials list

REFERENCE	QUANTITY	PART	STOCK	THICKNESS	WIDTH	LENGTH	COMMENTS
A	2	sides	walnut	$3/4$	$10^1/2$	15	bevels will be cut on the sides to finished size
B	2	top & bottom	walnut	1	14	$31^1/2$	
C	1	back panel	walnut	$3/4$	15	$25^1/8$	bevels will be cut on the sides to finished size
	2	back panel C stiles	walnut	$3/4$	$2^1/4$	15	
	1	back panel C stile	walnut	$3/4$	$2^1/4$	$11^1/2$	
	2	back panel C rails	walnut	$3/4$	$2^1/4$	$21^5/8$	cut the rails long, assemble panel and cut to size
	2	back panel C panels	curly maple	$1/4$	$10^1/16$	$11^1/2$	
D	1	center vertical divider	poplar/curly maple	$3/4$	$10^7/8$	7 H	grain runs vertically, width includes $1/4" \times 3/4"$ curly maple strip on front edge of panel
E	1	vertical divider	poplar/curly maple	$3/4$	$10^3/8$	$4^1/4$ H	grain runs vertically, width includes $1/4" \times 3/4"$ curly maple strip on front edge of panel
F	2	horizontal dividers	poplar/curly maple	$3/4$	$10^7/8$	$27^{13}/16$	
G	1	bottom filler panel	poplar/curly maple	$1/4$	$10^7/8$	$27^{13}/16$	all the horizontal dividers are edged with curly maple
H	2	horizontal dividers (l&r)	poplar/curly maple	$3/4$	$10^7/8$	$13^1/2$	and the grain runs left to right (or right to left);
J	1	horizontal divider	poplar/curly maple	$3/4$	$6^7/16$	$10^7/8$	this allows the solid-wood top, bottom, vertical and horizontal
K	2	horizontal dividers	poplar/curly maple	$3/4$	$6^1/4$	$10^5/16$	dividers to move together with seasonal changes
L	2	doors	walnut/curly maple	$3/4$	$14^5/8$	$14^7/8$	
	4	door L stiles	walnut	$3/4$	$2^1/4$	$14^7/8$	
	4	door L curved rails	walnut	$3/4$	$2^1/4$	$11^1/8$	
	2	door L curved panels	curly maple	$1/4$	$10^7/8$	$11^3/8$	
M	1	astragal	curly maple	$1/4$	$3/4$	$14^7/8$	
N	4	doughnut feet	curly maple	1	$3^1/2$dia		
P	2	door handles	curly maple	$1/4$	1	3	see illustration for handle detail

hardware

- 2   pairs butt hinges $3/4" \times 1^1/2"$
- 2   bullet catches
- 6 $3/4"$ dia. sash knobs
- 1 $5/8"$ dia. sash knob
- 2 $1/2"$ dia. sash knobs
- 3 $3/8"$ dia. sash knobs

---

tip >> MAKING DRAWERS FOR THE CURVED-FRONT CHEST

All of the drawers have $1/2"$ plywood bottoms, poplar sides and laminated poplar and white oak fronts. (If you have another species of wood you would like to put on the drawer fronts, that's your option!) Drawer sizes are determined by measuring the assembled chest. I did not use any drawer runners. If you want to use drawer runners, cut a groove in the bottom of the drawer and attach a hardwood strip to the bottom of each drawer space. I would recommend doing this before assembling the cabinet or the drawer cases.

REFERENCE	QUANTITY	PART	STOCK	THICKNESS	WIDTH	LENGTH	COMMENTS
A	2	sides	walnut	19	267	381	bevels will be cut on the sides to finish size
B	2	top & bottom	walnut	25	356	800	
C	1	back panel	walnut	19	381	638	bevels will be cut on the sides to finish size
	2	back panel C stiles	walnut	19	57	381	
	1	back panel C stile	walnut	19	57	292	
	2	back panel C rails	walnut	19	57	549	cut the rails long, assemble panel and cut to size
	2	back panel C panels	curly maple	6	256	292	
D	1	center vertical divider	poplar/curly maple	19	276	178 H	grain runs vertically, width includes 6mm x 19mm curly maple strip on front edge of panel
E	1	vertical divider	poplar/curly maple	19	264	108 H	grain runs vertically, width includes 6mm x 19mm curly maple strip on front edge of panel
F	2	horizontal dividers	poplar/curly maple	19	276	706	all the horizontal dividers are edged with curly maple and the grain runs left to right (or right to left); this allows the solid-wood top, bottom, vertical and horizontal dividers to move together with seasonal changes
G	1	bottom filler panel	poplar/curly maple	6	276	706	
H	2	horizontal dividers (l&r)	poplar/curly maple	19	276	343	
J	1	horizontal divider	poplar/curly maple	19	164	276	
K	2	horizontal dividers	poplar/curly maple	19	158	262	
L	2	doors	walnut/curly maple	19	371	378	
	4	door L stiles	walnut	19	57	378	
	4	door L curved rails	walnut	19	57	282	
	2	door L curved panels	curly maple	6	276	289	
M	1	astragal	curly maple	6	19	378	
N	4	doughnut feet	curly maple	25	89	89	
P	2	door handles	curly maple	6	25	76	see illustration for handle detail

hardware

- 2   pairs butt hinges 19mm × 38mm
- 2   bullet catches
- 6   19mm dia. sash knobs
- 1   16mm dia. sash knob
- 2   13mm dia. sash knobs
- 3   310mm dia. sash knobs

STEP-BY-STEP construction

step 1 • Before starting this project, study the technical drawings carefully. Try to visualize how all the parts will fit together and how they relate to each other. Draw the outline of the top B on your wood and cut it out as accurately as you can. Smooth the curved front edge, then trace the bottom B, using the top as a pattern. Rough-cut it out and use the top as a routing template.

Draw all the side, divider, door, drawer and back panel lines on the top panel. (See the plan view in the technical drawings.) This will be your guide for sizing all the parts for the rest of the project. Use the front, curved edge of the top as a reference to draw the lines for the doors, drawer fronts and horizontal divider front edges. (A combination square or marking gauge works best for doing this.)

step 2 • Glue a 2"- to 3"-wide strip of curly maple (or the decorative wood of your choice) to the front edge of these pieces. Using your top as the guide for sizing, cut out the vertical dividers D and E, the horizontal dividers F, H, J and K, and the bottom filler panel G.

step 3 • After you've created all the dividers, start with the right-hand set and assemble them using biscuits.

step 4 • Cut the sides A to size. Again, use the top as your guide for determining the bevel angles on the front and back edges. Use the divider assembly (from step three) as a template to locate the biscuit slots in the right-hand side.

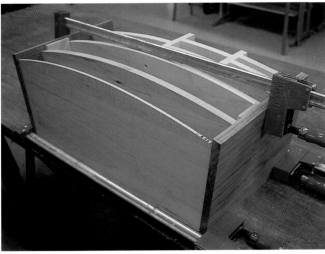

step 5 • Glue the rest of the drawer body together using biscuits. Note the spacers between the horizontal dividers. These assure the assembly is the same on both sides. (There is a very slight amount of adjustability, if needed, when using biscuits.)

step 6 • Cut out the frame parts for the back panel C. I usually use a single, square-toothed ripping blade to cut grooves for frame and panel construction. Adjust the fence so you can flip the parts end for end and end up with a ¼" groove. This ensures the groove will be centered in the frame parts.

step 7 • I use the same square-toothed blade to cut the tenons on the rails and center stile. Set the fence to the required tenon length and set the blade height, so that when you flip the part face for face you will have a centered tenon that is the correct thickness.

step 8 • After the back panel C is assembled, fit it between the side panels A. Then, glue it in place. Round over the side and front edges of the top and bottom panels B. Then, using biscuits, attach the bottom B to the drawer case assembly. Fit the bottom filler panel G into the bottom of the chest and glue it in place. Finally, attach the top B to this assembly using the same setup as shown in the photo.

step 9 • Make the doughnut feet N (without the holes!). Draw circles on the material and rough-cut the feet using a band saw or jigsaw. If you have access to a stationary sander, this is a simple way to perfectly round the feet: Drill a hole in the center of the foot. Drive a 16d nail into a scrap board and clamp the board to the sander's table. Insert the nail into the foot, and set the jig so the wood barely touches the sanding belt. Start the sander and slowly turn the foot. You could rig your belt sander to do the same procedure. Clamp the sander sidewise in your bench vise and use the benchtop as the sander table.

step 10 • Round over the edges of the feet to create the bullnose. Do this in two or three steps, raising the bit a little higher for each cut. If you are not comfortable with this setup, use a wood rasp to round over the edges. (Actually, this setup is safe. The ends of the fences are set as close to the router bit as possible to keep the opening very small. The right-hand fence acts as a brace to steady the work and your hands.)

step 11 • To finish-sand the feet, thread a $^3/_{16}$" hanger bolt into the hole in the center of the foot. Chuck the machine-threaded end of the hanger bolt into a power hand drill. Clamp the drill in your vise. Turn on the drill and lock it. Sand the feet, progressing to 220-grit sandpaper. This fine sanding really brings out the grain of the curly maple! Attach the feet to the chest using a screw through the center hole. Use no glue.

step 12 • Check your drawing on the top of the top panel B. Make a bending jig to the correct radius for the drawer fronts. To save wood, I laminated three layers of $^{1}/_{8}$"-thick poplar and used one layer of $^{1}/_{8}$"-thick white oak to make the drawer fronts. You can use whatever wood you like for the drawer fronts. I used white oak because it bends better than the walnut or curly maple, and I just happened to have some scraps of it in my wood stash. As I've said before, these are your personal tool chests, so do what you like!

step 13 • Before fitting the drawer fronts, cut the plywood drawer bottoms and fit them into their respective openings. Allow for the thickness of the drawer fronts. Then, fit each of the drawer fronts. When you are happy with the fit, cut the drawer sides and backs. Use the drawer bottoms as your template for cutting these parts. (The sides and backs will be glued on the top of the bottoms.)

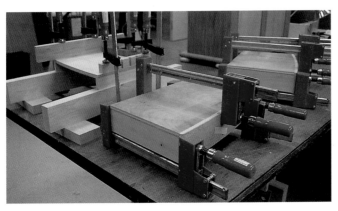

step 14 • The back and sides are being glued to the drawer bottom in the upper left of this photo. The curve of the bottoms and the inside radius of the drawer fronts should match. This means that very little stress is placed on the drawer fronts when they are glued into place, as shown on the other two drawers. If there is too much stress on the drawer fronts, they could come unglued from the bottoms.

step 15 • Cut $^{1}/_{8}$"-thick strips of walnut for the curved rails for the doors L. Laminate them using the same method as you used for gluing the drawer fronts. (However, you will need a different lamination jig with a different radius.) While you're gluing the rails, make some scrap rails to use for practicing your grooving and cutting. After you have sized the rails, cut the groove for the curved panel using a straight-cutting router bit. You don't need a curved fence for this operation. The point of contact on the fence behind the router bit will be just fine. Slowly feed the rail through the setup. I would recommend that you practice on some scrap material if you don't feel totally comfortable with this operation.

step 16 • Cut the rails to length. Hold the rail "flat," right next to the saw blade and make the cut. Butt the ends of the rails to the stiles and hold them on your drawing. If the joint looks like it will match the curve, then you're ready to cut the tenons on the ends of the rails. When I say that the joint looks like it matches the curve, remember that you will need to shape the stiles to continue the curve of the rail through the rest of the door.

step 17 • Cut the tenons on the curved rails. Using a tenoning jig is the easiest. Hold the end of the rail flat on the saw table next to the tenoning jig and simply measure the distance from the top of the jig to the rail. Cut a spacer to fit and you're all set.

step 18 • Set a stack of wedges against the miter gauge fence and under the rail so the end rests squarely against the saw fence. Then make the outside cheek cut for the tenon.

step 19 • Cutting the cheeks on the inside of the rails is just the opposite of the previous step. Put a spacer under the end of the rail and secure it to the miter gauge fence.

step 20 • Now for the fun part — making the curved panels. I created the ¼"-curved panel by coopering it. First, thickness the flat panels to ⁵⁄₃₂". Plane some scrap wood to the same thickness, then slice the curly maple and the scrap wood into 1¼"-wide strips. I know there is a mathematical way to determine the bevel angle that should be cut on the edges of the strips, but I just used the scrap-wood strips in a trial-and-error method. Use your full-scale drawings on top B to be sure the curve is correct by placing the strips on end, butted together. When all is correct, cut the bevels on all the maple strips. Be sure to keep the strips in order, so the grain pattern will match when you glue the strips together. You can cut these bevels either on the table saw or on the jointer. Lay all the strips faceup and tape all the edges together. (See project one, steps three and four and the technical illustration.) Then turn the assembly facedown and apply glue in the bevel joints.

step 21 • Lay out your clamps on a flat surface and lay the panel face-down on the clamps. Apply just enough clamping pressure to pull the bevels together. The panel will begin to arch, but the tape will keep the strips aligned. By putting a little weight in the middle of the panel, you can counter the outward pressure and pull the bevel joints tightly together. After the glue has dried, use a low-angle block plane or scraper to smooth the peaks of the bevel joints. Use a curved scraper for the inside of the panel to hollow the strips so the curve becomes smooth. A random-orbit sander works well to sand it all smooth. When sanding the inside of the curve, let the panel rock back and forth as you sand across it with the sander. Sanding the outside or front of the panel is much easier. Check the fit of the panels in the curved rail grooves. Carefully scrape or sand the panels until they fit into the grooves.

step 22 • Layout the door stiles and clamp them together. Mark where the rails will join the stiles. This helps keep the framework square when gluing it all together.

step 23 • Dry assemble the frames and panels before you apply the glue. Make sure all the parts fit together. At final glue-up, make sure the doors are perfectly square and flat. A curved door can multiply these little errors at fitting time.

step 24 • I used two butt hinges at the very top and bottom of the doors. A continuous hinge would look nice on this chest, also. Lay the hinge on the front edge of the chest's side and draw around its plate. Score the cutout with a utility knife. Use a chisel to cut the mortise.

step 25 • By putting the hinges up in the corners, they are less noticeable.

step 26 • Sometimes the simplest solution is the best. I fussed and fussed with handles for this chest. I finally decided that a simple, half-round piece of curly maple with the edges rounded over just like the top and bottom panels was the solution. I put two small nails in the handle with the sharp ends protruding a little to keep the pulls from moving.

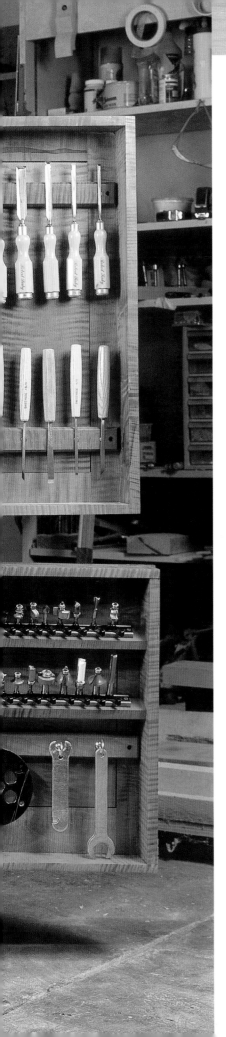

21st-century tool cabinet

BY GLEN HUEY

I've been making a living building fine furniture with my dad Malcolm in a too-small shop for the past ten years, and we have finally decided to move the business into a larger shop. As potential clients would be visiting the location, we decided to build a piece to show off our work.

That's how this tool cabinet came about. We decided the cabinet should be for a 21st-century woodworker. With space for modern and antique tools, this tool cabinet will keep things in order for another 100 years.

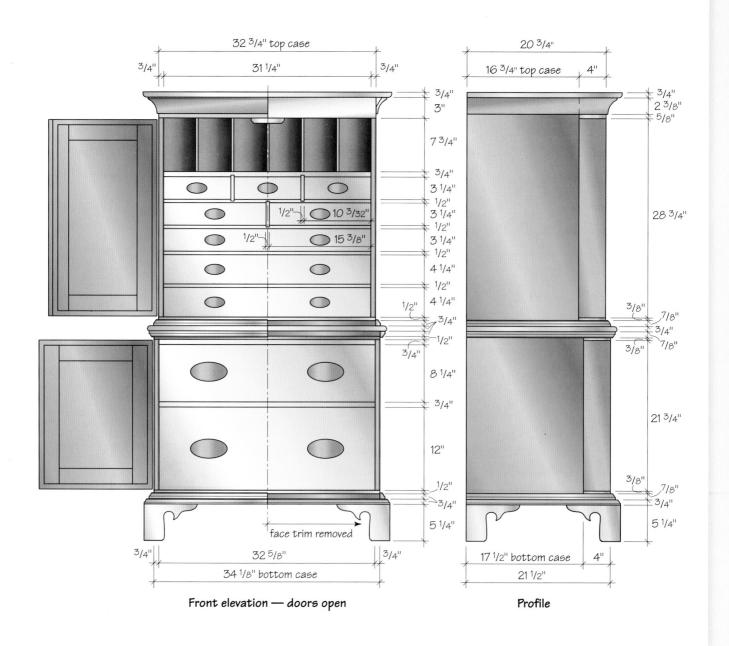

32 3/4" top case

31 1/4"

3/4"   3/4"

20 3/4"

16 3/4" top case   4"

3/4"
3"

7 3/4"

3/4"
2 3/8"
5/8"

3/4"
3 1/4"
1/2"
3 1/4"
1/2"
3 1/4"
1/2"
4 1/4"
1/2"
4 1/4"

1/2" ⊙ 10 3/32"

1/2"   ⊙ 15 3/8"

28 3/4"

1/2"
3/4"
1/2"
3/4"

8 1/4"

3/4"

12"

1/2"
3/4"

5 1/4"

3/8"
7/8"
3/4"
3/8"
7/8"

21 3/4"

3/8"
7/8"
3/4"

5 1/4"

face trim removed

3/4"   3/4"

32 5/8"

34 1/8" bottom case

17 1/2" bottom case   4"

21 1/2"

Front elevation — doors open

Profile

After a number of discussions we determined that the case should be two pieces, an upper and a lower cabinet, with four deep-set doors for storing tools, as well. When opened, the cabinet would array our most-used tools with easy access, while less-attractive and less-used tools would be stored in drawers. We decided I would build the upper section and Dad would build the lower case.

Much like the process when the Transcontinental Railroad was built, Dad and I eventually decided to work separately on our individual pieces, knowing that they were supposed to meet in the middle. Happily, it worked.

This project should be adapted to your tool needs. While you can follow the construction and concepts, the sizes are likely to be different for your shop.

materials list

Lower Cabinet

QUANTITY	PART	STOCK	THICKNESS	WIDTH	LENGTH	COMMENTS
2	sides	maple	$3/4$	$17^1/2$	$24^1/4$	
2	top & bottom	poplar	$3/4$	$21^1/2$	$34^1/8$	
1	bottom filler	maple	$1/2$	$7^1/4$	$34^1/8$	
1	top filler	maple	$1/2$	$7^1/4$	$34^1/8$	
1	front drawer divider	maple	$3/4$	3	$33^1/8$	
1	rear drawer divider	poplar	$3/4$	3	$33^1/8$	
1	base frame front	maple	$3/4$	3	$37^1/8$	45° both ends
2	base frame sides	maple	$3/4$	3	23	45° both ends
1	base frame back	poplar	$3/4$	$2^1/2$	$34^1/8$	$1^1/2$" TBE
6	front & side feet	maple	$3/4$	8	$5^1/4$	
2	rear feet	poplar	$3/4$	7	$5^1/4$	
4	door extension sides	maple	$3/4$	$3^1/4$	$21^1/2$	
4	door ext top & bottom	maple	$3/4$	$3^1/4$	$16^1/2$	
4	door front stiles	maple	$3/4$	3	$21^1/2$	
2	door front rails	maple	$3/4$	$3^7/8$	$14^1/8$	$1^1/4$" TBE
2	door front rails	maple	$3/4$	$2^7/8$	$14^1/8$	$1^1/4$" TBE
2	door panels	maple	$1/2$	12	$15^3/8$	$1/4$" × $3/8$" rabbets
1	waist moulding, front	maple	$3/4$	$3^3/4$	36	45° both ends
2	waist moulding, sides	maple	$3/4$	$3^3/4$	$22^1/2$	45° one end
1	moulding under waist	maple	$3/4$	$7/8$	84	cut to fit
1	moulding above feet	maple	$3/4$	$7/8$	84	cut to fit
2	upper drawer sides	poplar	$1/2$	8	$14^1/4$	
2	upper drwr front & back	poplar	$1/2$	8	$31^3/4$	
1	upper drawer face	mahogany	$3/4$	$8^1/4$	$32^1/2$	
2	lower drawer sides	poplar	$1/2$	$11^5/8$	$14^1/4$	
2	lower drwr front & back	poplar	$1/2$	$11^5/8$	$31^3/4$	
1	lower drawer face	mahogany	$3/4$	12	$32^1/2$	
2	drawer bottoms	plywood	$1/2$	14	$31^1/4$	
1	back	poplar	$1/2$	$22^3/4$	$33^3/8$	4 boards

Upper Cabinet

QUANTITY	PART	STOCK	THICKNESS	WIDTH	LENGTH	COMMENTS
1	moulding above waist	maple	$3/4$	$7/8$	84	cut to fit
2	sides	maple	$3/4$	$16^3/4$	33	
2	top & bottom	poplar	$3/4$	$20^3/4$	$32^3/4$	
1	subtop	maple	$3/4$	20	$31^5/8$	
1	bottom front filler	4"maple/ $2^1/8$"mahog	$1/2$	8	$31^1/4$	
1	cubby bottom	ply w/ $2^1/8$"mahog	$3/4$	$14^3/4$	32	
5	cubby dividers	maple	$3/8$	12	$8^1/8$	
4	drawer dividers	mahogany	$1/2$	$2^1/4$	$31^5/8$	
3	vertical drawer dividers	mahogany	$1/2$	1	$3^3/4$	
3	center drawer runners	poplar	$1/2$	2	13	half-lap w/divider
3	center drawer guides	poplar	$1/2$	$5/8$	$11^1/2$	
6	side runners	poplar	$1/2$	$3/4$	$12^3/8$	
4	housed side runners	poplar	$1/2$	$3/4$	12	
2	rear drawer dividers	poplar	$1/2$	$2^1/4$	$31^5/8$	

Upper Cabinet cont'd

QUANTITY	PART	STOCK	THICKNESS	WIDTH	LENGTH	COMMENTS
1	vertical back support	poplar	$3/4$	3	$13^3/8$	
1	filler @ crown	maple	$1/2$	$2^1/4$	48	cut to fit
1	crown	maple	$3/4$	3	90	cut to fit
1	cornice top moulding	maple	$3/4$	$3^1/4$	90	cut to fit
4	door extension sides	maple	$3/4$	$3^1/4$	$28^5/8$	
2	right door ext top & bott	maple	$3/4$	$3^1/4$	$16^3/8$	
2	left door ext top & bott	maple	$3/4$	$3^1/4$	$15^1/8$	
4	door front stiles	maple	$3/4$	3	$28^5/8$	
4	door front rails	maple	$3/4$	3	13	$1^1/4$" TBE
2	door panels	maple	$1/2$	11	$23^1/4$	$1/4$" × $3/8$" rabbets
12	top/2nd/3rd drawer sides	poplar	$1/2$	$3^1/8$	12	
3	top drawer backs	poplar	$1/2$	$2^1/2$	10	
3	top drawer fronts	mahogany	$3/4$	$3^1/4$	10	
3	top drawer bottoms	plywood	$1/4$	12	$9^1/2$	
2	2nd-row drawer backs	poplar	$1/2$	$2^1/2$	$15^5/16$	
2	2nd-row drawer fronts	mahogany	$3/4$	$3^1/4$	$15^5/16$	
2	2nd-row drawer bottoms	plywood	$1/4$	12	$14^3/4$	
1	3rd-row drawer back	poplar	$1/2$	$2^1/2$	$31^1/2$	
1	3rd-row drawer front	mahogany	$3/4$	$3^1/4$	$31^1/8$	
1	3rd-row drawer bottom	plywood	$1/4$	12	$30^1/2$	
4	4th/5th drawer sides	poplar	$1/2$	$4^1/8$	12	
2	4th/5th drawer backs	poplar	$1/2$	$3^1/2$	$31^1/8$	
2	4th/5th drawer fronts	mahogany	$3/4$	$4^1/4$	$31^1/8$	
2	4th/5th drawer bottoms	plywood	$1/4$	12	$30^1/2$	
1	back	poplar	$1/2$	32	$31^3/8$	5 boards

Drawer Edge Inlay

QUANTITY	PART	STOCK	THICKNESS	WIDTH	LENGTH	COMMENTS
	top three rows	maple	$1/8$	$1/2$	240	cut to fit
	4th & 5th rows	maple	$1/8$	$3/4$	144	cut to fit
	lower section	maple	$1/8$	1	180	cut to fit
11	upper section ovals	walnut	$1/8$	$1^1/2$		
4	lower section ovals	walnut	$1/8$	$2^3/4$		

KEY: TBE = tenon on both ends

hardware

- 2 Accuride 14" full-extension slides — Rockler #32805
- 1 $1^1/2$" × 48" continuous hinge (lower section) — Rockler #19291
- 1 $1^1/2$" × 72" continuous hinge (upper section) — Rockler #19316
- 2 barrel bolts — Rockler #30923
- 4 rosette pulls w/1" backplate, 3" bore — Horton Brasses # H-10S
- 11 stirrup pulls w/1" backplate — Horton Brasses # H-83
- 2 latches — Horton Brasses # SL-3
- 2 $1/4$" washers
- rare earth magnets — Lee Valley Tools

Lower Cabinet

QUANTITY	PART	STOCK	THICKNESS	WIDTH	LENGTH	COMMENTS
2	sides	maple	19	445	616	
2	top & bottom	poplar	19	546	867	
1	bottom filler	maple	13	184	867	
1	top filler	maple	13	184	867	
1	front drawer divider	maple	19	76	841	
1	rear drawer divider	poplar	19	76	841	
1	base frame front	maple	19	76	943	45° both ends
2	base frame sides	maple	19	76	584	45° both ends
1	base frame back	poplar	19	64	867	38mm TBE
6	front & side feet	maple	19	203	133	
2	rear feet	poplar	19	178	133	
4	door extension sides	maple	19	82	546	
4	door ext top & bottom	maple	19	82	419	
4	door front stiles	maple	19	76	546	
2	door front rails	maple	19	98	359	32mm TBE
2	door front rails	maple	19	73	359	32mm TBE
2	door panels	maple	13	305	391	6mm × 10mm rabbets
1	waist moulding, front	maple	19	95	914	45° both ends
2	waist moulding, sides	maple	19	95	572	45° one end
1	moulding under waist	maple	19	22	2134	cut to fit
1	moulding above feet	maple	19	22	2134	cut to fit
2	upper drawer sides	poplar	13	203	362	
2	upper drwr front & back	poplar	13	203	806	
1	upper drawer face	mahogany	19	209	826	
2	lower drawer sides	poplar	13	295	362	
2	lower drwr front & back	poplar	13	295	806	
1	lower drawer face	mahogany	19	305	826	
2	drawer bottoms	plywood	13	356	793	
1	back	poplar	13	578	848	4 boards

Upper Cabinet

QUANTITY	PART	STOCK	THICKNESS	WIDTH	LENGTH	COMMENTS
1	moulding above waist	maple	19	22	2134	cut to fit
2	sides	maple	19	425	838	
2	top & bottom	poplar	19	527	832	
1	subtop	maple	19	508	803	
1	bottom front filler	102mm maple/ 54mm mahog	13	203	793	
1	cubby bottom	ply w/ 54mm mahog	19	375	813	
5	cubby dividers	maple	10	305	206	
4	drawer dividers	mahogany	13	57	803	
3	vertical drawer dividers	mahogany	13	25	95	
3	center drawer runners	poplar	13	51	330	half-lap w/divider
3	center drawer guides	poplar	13	16	292	
6	side runners	poplar	13	19	315	
4	housed side runners	poplar	13	19	305	
2	rear drawer dividers	poplar	13	57	803	

Upper Cabinet cont'd

QUANTITY	PART	STOCK	THICKNESS	WIDTH	LENGTH	COMMENTS
1	vertical back support	poplar	19	76	340	
1	filler @ crown	maple	13	57	1219	cut to fit
1	crown	maple	19	76	2286	cut to fit
1	cornice top moulding	maple	19	82	2286	cut to fit
4	door extension sides	maple	19	82	727	
2	right door ext top & bott	maple	19	82	416	
2	left door ext top & bott	maple	19	82	384	
4	door front stiles	maple	19	76	727	
4	door front rails	maple	19	76	330	32mm TBE
2	door panels	maple	13	279	590	6mm × 10mm rabbets
12	top/2nd/3rd drawer sides	poplar	13	79	305	
3	top drawer backs	poplar	13	64	254	
3	top drawer fronts	mahogany	19	82	254	
3	top drawer bottoms	plywood	6	305	242	
2	2nd-row drawer backs	poplar	13	64	389	
2	2nd-row drawer fronts	mahogany	19	82	389	
2	2nd-row drawer bottoms	plywood	6	305	375	
1	3rd-row drawer back	poplar	13	64	800	
1	3rd-row drawer front	mahogany	19	82	790	
1	3rd-row drawer bottom	plywood	6	305	775	
4	4th/5th drawer sides	poplar	13	105	305	
2	4th/5th drawer backs	poplar	13	89	790	
2	4th/5th drawer fronts	mahogany	19	108	790	
2	4th/5th drawer bottoms	plywood	6	305	775	
1	back	poplar	13	813	797	5 boards

Drawer Edge Inlay

QUANTITY	PART	STOCK	THICKNESS	WIDTH	LENGTH	COMMENTS
	top three rows	maple	3	13	6096	cut to fit
	4th & 5th rows	maple	3	19	3658	cut to fit
	lower section	maple	3	25	4572	cut to fit
11	upper section ovals	walnut	3	38		
4	lower section ovals	walnut	3	70		

KEY: TBE = tenon on both ends

hardware

▦ 2	Accuride 356mm full-extension slides	Rockler #32805
▦ 1	38mm × 122cm continuous hinge (lower section)	Rockler #19291
▦ 1	38mm × 183cm continuous hinge (upper section)	Rockler #19316
▦ 2	barrel bolts	Rockler #30923
▦ 4	rosette pulls w/25mm backplate, 76mm bore	Horton Brasses # H-10s
▦ 11	stirrup pulls w/25mm backplate	Horton Brasses # H-83
▦ 2	latches	Horton Brasses # SL-3
▦ 2	6mm washers	
▦	rare earth magnets	Lee Valley Tools

Everything In Its Place

The case pieces were dovetailed together, with the solid-wood shiplapped backs set into rabbets. Many of the drawers are divided by, and glide on, individual mortise-and-tenon web frames that are dadoed into the sides.

After looking at the tools that we wanted to store, we determined that the best use of the case storage area was mostly drawers. Shelves are easier to make, but tools tend to wander toward the back of the cabinet. Drawers allow you to look down into the storage area and quickly find the tool you're looking for. They also give the cabinet a cleaner look.

Rather than risk hanging the planes on the doors (where they could fall off if the door was jostled), we designed spaces for the four larger bench planes we use often (and room to add two more) above the drawers at the top of the cabinet.

All the smaller tools went into the doors, with a variety of ways to hang or store them. Router bits are stored in a bit holder that fits onto a ledge in the doors. Cup hooks were used to hang some drawknives and scrapers, and the drill bits are stored in a box temporarily attached to the door with rare earth magnets. Also, chisels and gouges are firmly suspended using these magnets. (The magnets are countersunk into a wood strip so they are hidden.)

The Shaker pegs attached to the lower left door offer a great storage answer for sanding belts and many other "hanging" tools. Also, a Shaker candle box has been adapted in size to hold random-orbit sanding discs.

A $\frac{1}{4}$"-tall riser block has been added to the back of each plane cubby to lift the front end of the plane far enough to keep the blade from touching the bottom of the cubby. With shorter-length planes, you can make the riser block in an "L"-shape that will keep the plane's handle within easy reach of the front of the cabinet, rather than sliding too far

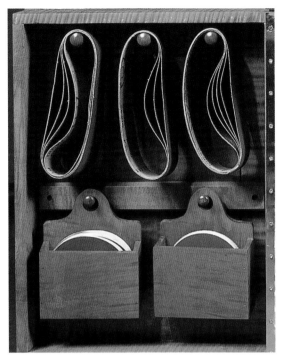

into the cubby.

If you need a visual image to help you lay out your door storage, start with a blank piece of paper that is the size of the door interiors and lay your tools on it until you're happy with the arrangement and spacing.

Rare earth magnets, buried in the strips attached to the right-hand door, hold the chisels and gouges to the door tightly, but allow easy removal. The drill bit holder, lower left, is also held in place with magnets. The cubby-holes for planes keep everything tidy but accessible, and also do double duty for a brad nailer.

CONSTRUCTION

The rear view and enlarged view in the technical drawings show many of the details of the construction and simplify the built-up mouldings.

Start construction by gluing up and trimming to size the panels for the sides, tops and bottoms for both sections.

After the panels are sized, cut dadoes in the sides to accommodate the drawer runners. Use the diagrams to locate the dividers and cut the dadoes in the sides.

Both cabinets have $\frac{1}{2}$"-thick shiplapped backs made from multiple boards. To accommodate the back thickness, cut a $\frac{1}{2}$" × $\frac{5}{8}$" rabbet on all four sides.

Next, cut through-dovetails to join each cabinet's sides, tops and bottoms. Glue up both carcasses; be sure to check them for squareness as you go.

Glue the front and rear drawer dividers in place on the lower cabinet. Unlike the upper cabinet, the drawers in the lower unit use heavy-duty full-extension drawer slides.

When you attach the dividers, glue the front divider in place, but leave the runners and rear divider joint loose. This will allow for seasonal wood movement in the sides of the case.

The cubby bottom also serves as the top divider of the drawer section, so the leading edge should be mahogany to match the other dividers. You can also make the bottom front filler, which is made up of a maple and a mahogany piece.

Next, mark and cut the dadoes for the cubby dividers in the subtop and the cubby bottom. Also, the top and second rows of drawers require three drawer runners that are half-lapped onto the dividers — two for the top tier of drawers, and one for the second tier. The front dividers are half-lapped only to the rear of the rail, and then dadoed to accept the vertical drawer dividers, visible from the front of the cabinet. You also can cut the mating half-laps on the drawer runners at this time.

Dry fit all the parts. Start with the plane cubbyhole section, then work down to the two upper tiers of drawer dividers. Finally place the lower drawers, front dividers and the runners in place. If everything fits well, take it apart and do it all again with glue.

As with the lower cabinet, seasonal wood movement is a concern, so glue the front dividers and guides in place, but leave the rear dividers loose. On the lower runners, use screws in slotted holes to let the wood move.

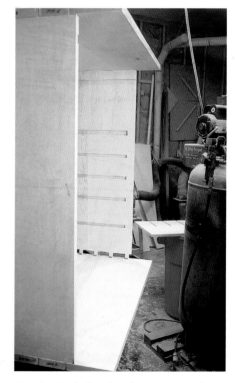

step 1 • Ready for glue, the upper case shows the extended top and bottom, the dovetailed sides and the dado grooves for the drawer dividers.

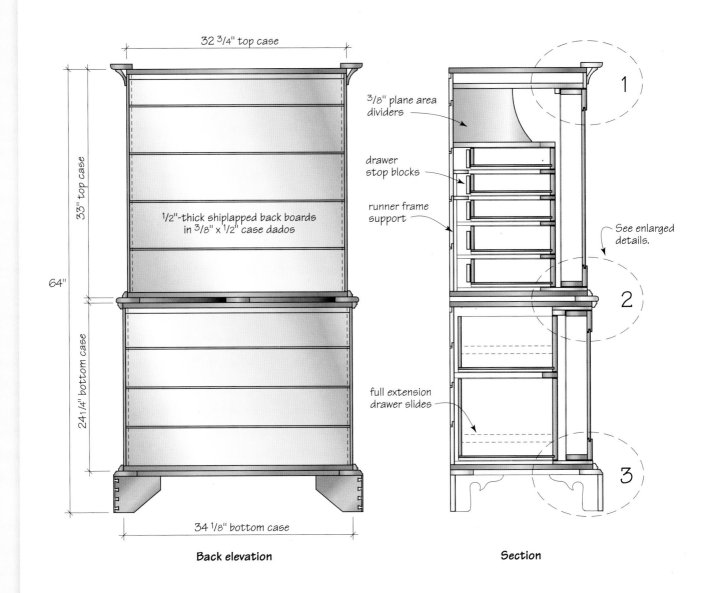

32 3/4" top case

33" top case

64"

24 1/4" bottom case

1/2"-thick shiplapped back boards
in 3/8" x 1/2" case dados

34 1/8" bottom case

Back elevation

3/8" plane area
dividers

drawer
stop blocks

runner frame
support

full extension
drawer slides

See enlarged
details.

1

2

3

Section

step 2 • Note the subtop panel at the top of this photo taken from the back. The space formed by the subtop allows room to mount the crown moulding without affecting the interior function of the cabinet. You can also see the front drawer dividers, side runners and rear drawer dividers in place.

DRAWERS

The drawers in the upper section are built with the fronts attached to the sides using half-blind dovetails. The drawer backs attach to the sides with through-dovetails. The bottoms of the drawers are inserted into grooves cut in the sides and fronts, $\frac{1}{2}$" up from the bottom edge. The bottoms slide below the lower edge of the drawer back, and then are nailed in place to the drawer backs.

While the upper drawers ride on, and are supported by, drawer runners attached to the cabinet sides, the lower drawers ride on full-extension drawer slides. Because of this, the drawer fronts, or faces in this case, extend $\frac{1}{2}$" beyond the drawer sides on either side to hide the drawer slides. The easiest way to do this was to simply make a drawer box, with dovetailed $\frac{1}{2}$"-thick sides, front and back and the same bottom arrangements as on the upper drawers. The $\frac{3}{4}$"-thick mahogany, maple and walnut drawer fronts are then screwed to the drawer box front once the proper spacing is determined.

step 3 • The lower cabinet is shown with the left door held in place while the hinge is attached. The doors themselves are small cabinets, with a frame and panel door front attached to a dovetailed frame. Because the door is captured by the cabinet (top and bottom), and flush to the sides, you want to make sure you've got the door the right size before you glue it up. Adjusting afterward is tricky. To give yourself a little room, notice that the door front overhangs the frame a little to allow some fitting. Also, the doors' faces extend beyond the dovetailed extension at the center of each pair. This leaves room for the barrel slide catches holding one of each pair of doors.

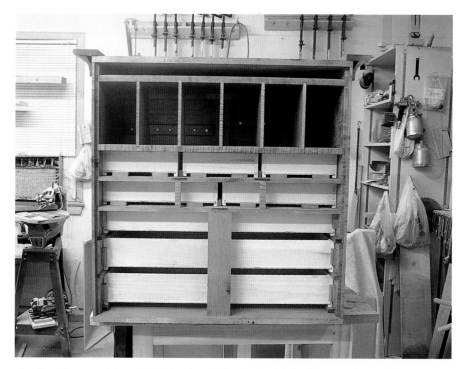

step 4 • After assembly and finishing, but before the back is in place, you have a chance to see all the pieces come together from their less-attractive angle. The smaller drawer dividers and supports are plainly visible here.

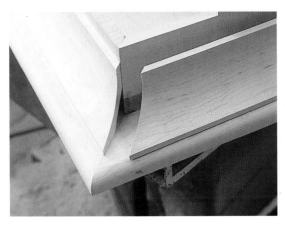

step 5 • With the upper case flipped over, you can see the top and subtop extending beyond the cabinet, with the filler, top cornice moulding and crown moulding ready to be put in place.

step 6 • The color for the piece is a water-based aniline dye (Moser's Golden Amber Maple from Woodworker's Supply, 800-645-9292 or www.woodworker.com). Then top-coat the piece with multiple coats of sprayed-on satin-finish clear lacquer. One note: To achieve the natural tiger maple detail on the drawer fronts, finish with Danish oil. The left-hand doors are held in place with a sliding catch.

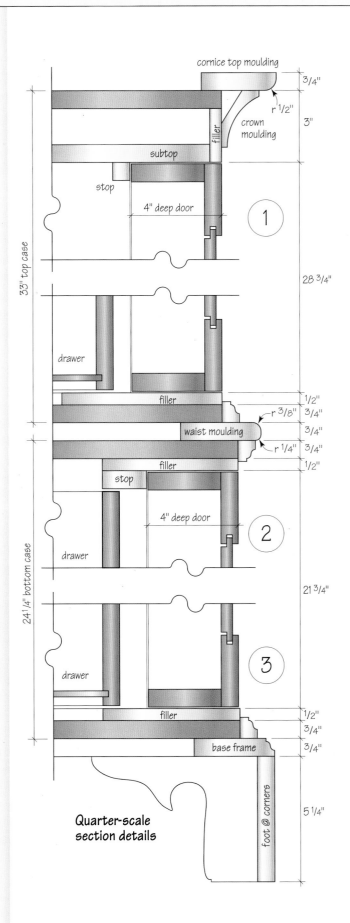

cornice top moulding
3/4"
r 1/2"
crown moulding
3"
filler
subtop
stop
4" deep door
①
33" top case
28 3/4"
drawer
filler
1/2"
r 3/8" 3/4"
waist moulding 3/4"
r 1/4" 3/4"
filler 1/2"
stop
4" deep door
②
24 1/4" bottom case
drawer
21 3/4"
③
drawer
filler 1/2"
3/4"
base frame 3/4"
Quarter-scale section details
foot @ corners
5 1/4"

ADAMS & KENNEDY – THE WOOD SOURCE
6178 Mitch Owen Road
P.O. Box 700
Manotick, Ontario, Canada K4M 1A6
613-822-6800
www.wood-source.com
Wood supply

BALL AND BALL
463 West Lincoln Highway
Exton, Pennsylvania 19341
800-257-3711
www.ballandball-us.com
Hardware reproductions

CONSTANTINES WOOD CENTER
1040 East Oakland Park Boulevard
Fort Lauderdale, Florida 33334
800-443-9667
www.constantines.com
Tools, woods, veneers, hardware

DELTA MACHINERY
P.O. Box 2468
Jackson, Tennessee 38302
800-223-7278 (U.S.)
800-463-3582 (Canada)
www.deltawoodworking.com
Woodworking tools

EXAKTOR PRECISION WOODWORKING TOOLS, INC.
4 Glenbourne Park
Markham, Ontario, Canada L6C 1G9
800-387-9789
www.exaktortools.com
Accessories for the table saw

FORREST MANUFACTURING COMPANY, INC.
461 River Road
Clifton, New Jersey 07014
800-733-7111
forrest.woodmall.com
Carbide-tipped saw blades, dado sets, sharpening

FREUD TOOLS
218 Feld Avenue
High Point, North Carolina 27263
800-334-4107
www.freudtools.com
Carbide-tipped saw blades, dado sets, tooling

THE HOME DEPOT
2455 Paces Ferry Road
Atlanta, Georgia 30303
800-553-3199
www.homedepot.com
Tools, paint, wood, electrical, garden

HORTON BRASSES, INC.
49 Nooks Hill Road
Cromwell, Connecticut 06416
800-754-9127
www.horton-brasses.com
Hardware for antique furniture; Hepplewhite, Chippendale and Victorian brass hardware; hand-forged iron hardware

LEE VALLEY TOOLS LTD.
U.S.:
P.O. Box 1780
Ogdensberg, New York 13669-6780
800-267-8735
Canada:
P.O. Box 6295, Station J
Ottawa, Ontario, Canada K2A 1T4
800-267-8761
www.leevalley.com
Fine woodworking tools and hardware

LOWE'S HOME IMPROVEMENT WAREHOUSE
P.O. Box 1111
North Wilkesboro, North Carolina 28656
800-445-6937
www.lowes.com
Tools, paint, wood, electrical, garden

LRH ENTERPRISES, INC.
9250 Independence Avenue
Chatsworth, California 91311
800-423-2544
www.lrhent.com
Magic Molder

PORTER-CABLE
4825 Highway 45 North
P.O. Box 2468
Jackson, Tennessee 38302-2468
800-487-8665
www.porter-cable.com
Woodworking tools

ROCKLER WOODWORKING AND HARDWARE
4365 Willow Drive
Medina, Minnesota 55340
800-279-4441
www.rockler.com
Woodworking tools and hardware

WOLFCRAFT NORTH AMERICA
1222 West Ardmore Avenue
P.O. Box 687
Itasca, Illinois 60143
630-773-4777
www.wolfcraft.com
Woodworking hardware and accessories

WOODCRAFT
P.O. Box 1686
Parkersburg, West Virginia 26102
800-225-1153
www.woodcraft.com
Woodworking hardware and accessories

WOODWORKER'S SUPPLY
1108 North Glenn Road
Casper, Wyoming 82601
800-645-9292
www.woodworker.com
Woodworking tools and accessories; finishing supplies; books and plans

How to Design and Build Your
Ideal
WOODSHOP
REVISED EDITION

Bill Stankus

POPULAR
WOODWORKING
BOOKS

CINCINNATI, OHIO
www.popularwoodworking.com

table of contents

introduction

Just how are we to determine what is an ideal woodshop?

Old photographs and old line drawings can only show how historical woodshops looked. And modern-day woodshops are mostly seen via TV documentaries. There are almost no apprenticeship woodshops existing that have a master craftsman passing on skills while at the same time producing objects for sale. Despite these limitations, most modern woodworkers seem to believe they have a grasp of what it takes to make an ideal woodshop.

Of course, each of us has a different starting point when setting up a woodshop. Some of us have shop training from art schools, trade schools or family heritages. There are those of us with tight budgets and those with unlimited funds for setting up a woodshop. A few lucky individuals might inherit tools from previous generations, while others spend a lifetime searching for their tools.

Many new woodworkers have been motivated by the Pied-Piper-like flood of PBS-type home-improvement programs, or by the amazing amount of woodworking magazines. Then, too, there is the siren song of manufacturers and tool catalogs.

Are there any connections amidst all this diversity? There certainly seem to be quite a few people interested in something. The proliferation of clubs, guilds and traveling roadshows all indicate that woodworking isn't a single-topic event with an audience interested in "less is more."

A recurring dichotomy seems based in stubbornness and passion. Old ideas and new stuff. Is there only one "right" way to achieve your goals? The flood of interest in the old ways has produced high-powered machines and intricate accessories for seemingly obscure uses. Does the mastery of 19th-century British woodworking really mean anything if you use a powerful compound miter saw or router? Certainly there is a background litany about good work, accuracy and organization, while at the same time there is a looseness to the definition of woodshop functionality. We use tools to make things: We seek the impersonal precision of milling machines and laser-like cuts in our craft, and yet we still use handheld tools.

How many woodworkers feel that an imprecise joint is a failure? Are they obsessing over trivia rather than content?

It may be simplistic, but to design, build and set up your ideal woodshop requires a raft of diverse information — both historical and modern. You have to adapt every piece of the puzzle to your own situation.

I have never been that interested in electrical, plumbing or other construction skills, but I have had to cope with these elements in order to have a woodshop. More than 25 years ago, I began to build furniture. For many years, every moment produced new mysteries and more learning experiences. Even now, I don't have the so-called perfect woodshop. But I do enjoy work-

ing in the one I have — simply because I have tools and I can work in my shop to make things.

Learn from the past and adapt with the new. Question the pundits but realize the value of learned opinion. Don't build a woodshop only for the sake of building a picture-perfect shop. Take a lifetime to create your dream woodshop — and use it daily to make as many wonderful wooden objects as you can.

The reality is that the woodshop is a tool, and it is the craftsman's achievement to use that tool successfully.

In this new edition, there are many new photographs and each chapter has been revised. There is also a new chapter about the environment that you can create within your ideal woodshop.

chapter *one*

Building Safety Into Shop Design

BEFORE SETTING OUT TO DESIGN your ideal woodshop, safety should be foremost in your mind, since safety is a factor that has extraordinary consequences in both the present and future.

Is your woodshop a safe place? Think about this: Some of the most dangerous objects and materials that you will ever come across are in the woodshop. This includes just about everything that is used in the woodshop: machines, hand tools, solvents, wood and sawdust. The physical activity of lifting or moving heavy objects, breathing solvent fumes, touching various chemicals, listening to high-decibel sounds, holding vibrating electrical tools and climbing on stepladders are some of the obstacles that need to be safely managed. In fact, they are at the core of how you should design and build your woodshop.

There is a certain disconnect most beginners have regarding today's woodworking. Most beginners have never had years of instruction or the hands-on traditions of trade schools or apprenticeships. But let's assume that the beginner has the de-

sire and abilities to set up a woodshop, and that person comes from some unrelated background: computer programming, business, sales and so on. Where does this beginner get the information necessary for woodworking? Most likely from books, magazines, videos and hardware store salespeople. But is that enough to really understand the relationships of the many facets of woodworking and safety? Does the beginner have the correct information necessary to judge appropriate products? Is the salesperson or magazine writer or video personality free of vested interests? Probably not. If the information is from a company, you can bet their legal and advertising departments have influenced their information. If the information is from a magazine or store, the information is potentially biased by advertiser or supplier influences. And, product review magazines rarely deal with the interrelationships of diverse products.

The essential question of safety is often obvious and also it is more than likely to be very subtle. Furthermore, there are other complications

to essential safety that historic woodworkers never dealt with: an array of plastics, man-made building materials, volatile liquids, environmental issues, building codes and regulations and so on. Today, it is not enough to know how to cut dovetails: Do you understand the complexities of mixing heat, chemical and dust fumes, synthetics, sharp things and electricity with flesh and blood?

It's possible that we could one day see the advent of safety inspectors for the home woodshop. Woodworkers, especially those with home woodshops, have had a long history of not being monitored by the agencies that scrutinize commercial woodshops. However, if you notice modern safety trends, there probably are (or will be) people and organizations that want to codify what goes on in home woodshops. While there has been a trickling down of valuable safety products to the home woodshop, I can't imagine that many people want to have outside groups dictating home woodshop procedures and necessities. Having said that, most woodworkers are doing a good job of learning how to do woodworking, and they are generally buying tools and machinery that have been tested for safe use. Of course, there are many old, worn-out or poorly modified tools sold at garage sales or passed down through families. And these should be identified and gotten rid of so that accidents won't happen. However, in addition to operating machinery safely, we should also improve our handling of heavy materials (thus reducing bodily sprains and strains) and our use of chemicals (solvents and finishing products). More or less, the amateur woodworker and the one-person small-business woodshop want the best of two different worlds: the freedom of the hobby and craft world, and the tools, materials, techniques and business of the professional and commercial world. While this may seem fair if you are a home woodworker, the problem is that there are potentially unsafe woodshop situations not being corrected.

It is up to each of us to be individually responsible for having safe woodshops. Don't pretend that your woodshop is safe or that it's too expensive to do the right thing, or don't come up with some other rationalization that keeps you from upgrading questionable situations. Make your woodshop safe, learn proper woodworking techniques and never attempt to use tools or supplies in unsafe ways. Stay current on new tools, accessories and supplies. For example, router bits are now available in bright colors that are visible when the router is operating. Manufacturers often improve their products to comply with new safety guidelines. A few manufacturers actually make their products safer because of consumer demands.

SAFETY CHECKLIST

The initial steps toward woodshop safety begin with the idea that you have to be aware of your surroundings.

- Always look for the accident that's about to happen.
- Don't ignore potential accidents or dangerous conditions.
- Always evaluate the situation and ask yourself, "Is this the best way of doing something or is there a safer way?"
- If there's a potential safety problem, take the appropriate steps to correct it.
- Periodically review all woodshop safety considerations.
- If you have older machines, compare them to their modern counterpart's safety features.

General Safety Concerns

This list, though not definitive, is meant as a basic overview and a starting point for your own quest for a safe woodshop.

- Never work when you are tired.
- Never use tools and machinery when under the influence of alcohol, drugs or medications.
- Wear suitable work clothing that is not loose fitting or with floppy or dangling sleeves, ties, etc.
- Remove all jewelry, ties and scarves, and tie up long hair.
- Wear safety goggles or safety glasses that have side guards.
- Wear hearing protection when operating machinery and power tools.
- Have approved and fully charged fire extinguishers in the woodshop.
- Don't wear gloves while operating tools and machinery.
- Keep up-to-date insurance information on yourself, others using the woodshop and the woodshop itself. Check with your insurance company on policy coverage relating to accidents and other woodshop misfortunes.
- Keep a list of emergency telephone numbers near the telephone.
- Know where to go for emergency medical treatment.
- Stay current on codes, laws and other regulations pertaining to safety and hazardous materials, equipment and procedures.

Safety Preparation and Maintenance

- Read, understand and follow all instructions in the owner's manual for all machines and tools.
- Keep all owner's manuals in a handy location.
- Maintain all machines and tools to the manufacturer's recommendations.
- Use machine safety guards provided by the manufacturer.
- Don't modify safety guards or other safety-related equipment.
- Be sure that any modification to a tool or machine is either approved by the manufacturer or within the design limits of the tool.
- Before adding any accessory to a tool or machine, be sure that it is both acceptable and safe.
- Use tools and machines for their intended purposes.
- Periodically review owner's manuals for safe operating procedures.
- Periodically inspect cutting tools, such as tungsten-carbide table saw blades and router bits, for damage or cracks. Replace as necessary.
- Keep cutting tools sharp.

Work Area Safety

- Do not work with a cluttered floor or with unstable piles of tools and materials.
- Wheels on mobile bases must be secured before using the machine.
- Prevent unauthorized use of the woodshop by installing lockable on/off switches on all machines.
- Have proper lighting and ventilation.
- Read and follow label information, including all warnings and cautions, prior to using solvents,

finishing products or other chemicals, and follow all recommended use and safety procedures. If you have any concerns about products, call the manufacturer, your own physician or health agencies of the EPA.

- Not all rubber gloves are the same. Use the correct type when working with solvents, finishing products, paint strippers, etc.
- Never dispose of oily rags in sealed trash cans that will be exposed to heat or direct sunlight.
- Store solvents and other flammable materials in approved storage units.
- Never use flammable solvents or other flammable finishing products near water heaters or any other high-temperature device or open flame.

Equipment Safety

- Use vises, clamps or other safe holding devices to firmly hold work material.
- If you are considering buying used equipment, be very cautious about missing parts, modifications, wobbly shafts and belts, and any other loose, damaged, bent or out-of-the norm condition. When possible, ask for owner's manual and parts list.
- Don't buy used air compressors. The problem is that you can't see rust and corrosion inside the air tank.
- Absolutely never consider buying an air compressor that has patched pinholes in the air tank.

Safety with Chemicals

I feel compelled to repeat myself: Read the labels on all finishing products and follow all recommended use and safety procedures. If you have any concerns about products, call the manufacturer, your own physician, health agencies or the EPA. Take no unnecessary risks relating to the handling and use of chemicals; design

Electrical Hazards Checklist

Make a copy of this list and check your woodshop for the following electrical hazards:

— Comply with local electrical codes concerning wiring type, conduits, hookups, service panels and other electrical features.

— Have the correct amperage and type fuses or circuit breakers installed in the electrical service.

— Light fixtures should have bulbs with the correct wattage.

— Halogen type lights generate considerable heat and should be kept away from accidental bumping and flammable materials.

— Electrical motors, power tools and machines should have their technical information plates attached.

— Electrical motors, power tools and machines should have labeling indicating that the product has been tested by a nationally recognized testing laboratory.

— Replace frayed or worn electrical cords.

— Replace electrical cords that have worn or bent plugs.

— Replace electrical cords nicked by sharp tools.

— There should be no standing water or moisture where electrical devices are used.

— Don't use unnecessary or overloaded extension cords.

— If extension cords are used, be sure to use correct wire gauge.

— Don't use modified adapter plugs: All three prongs should be intact.

— Don't use adapters that have a missing ground prong or grounding wire.

— Electrical cords shouldn't be placed in walkways or traffic areas.

— Don't have heavy objects resting on electrical cords.

— Electrical cords should be positioned well away from spinning or operating machinery.

— Unplug electrical cords when adjusting or performing maintenance on machines and power tools.

— Electrical cords shouldn't be fastened down with nails or staples.

— The woodshop should have a sufficient number of well-placed electrical receptacles.

— All outlets must work properly.

— Unused outlets should have safety covers placed in receptacle openings.

— GFI (ground fault circuit interrupters) outlets should be installed near sinks or other wet areas.

— Never use sparking electrical motors or tools near dust, oily rags or solvent fumes.

— Ventilation fans must be nonsparking and certified for venti-lation of flammable fumes.

— There should be air circulation around electrical tools.

— Portable heaters must be listed as tested and approved for use in woodworking environments.

— Never use portable heaters near flammable materials such as rags, dust, scrap wood, finishing supplies, paper and drapes.

— Position approved portable heaters so that they can't be tipped over.

— Check for unnecessary machinery vibrations that can cause wear or stress on electrical wiring.

— Never leave woodburning tools, soldering irons, hot-glue guns, heat guns or other high temper-ature tools unattended, and unplug these tools immediately after using them.

your woodshop to be user-friendly and safe.

Working with Hazardous Materials

- Read product labels and understand their implications.
- Have operational smoke detectors within the woodshop.
- Most vapors are invisible. And it is difficult to know how much vapor is too much. Ventilate the room.
- If the woodshop is located within a garage which has a gas water heater and parked automobiles, install a carbon monoxide detector and natural gas and propane gas detectors.
- If the woodshop is located in a garage or basement which has cracked concrete floors, then you should periodically use a radon detection kit.
- Have fully charged fire extinguishers rated ABC or BC and know how to properly use them. Consult with your local fire department for fire extinguisher training classes.
- Do not pour water on chemical fires.
- Never mix ammonia with household bleach. The resulting solution produces a deadly gas.
- Use safety goggles, dust masks, multi-purpose respirators and rubber gloves.
- Be aware that standard clothing can retain vaporous fumes.
- Know the telephone number and location of a local Haz-Mat office.

FIRST AID

I have visited with manufacturers and their lawyers enough to realize that there are quite a few people who have gotten hurt by doing things that perhaps they shouldn't. A standard knowledge of first aid should be a priority for you, both in and out of the woodshop. But within the shop, you'll most likely face two types of trauma — cuts and electrical shock.

Treating Chemical Burns

Numerous solvents, oils, paint strippers, bleaches and dyes are dangerous, and their labels offer information regard-ing their uses and side effects. The fol-lowing is the standard first aid procedure for treating chemical burns.

1. Immediately call for medical aid and rescue. If possible, tell the operator what kind of chemical has caused the burns.
2. As quickly as possible, flood the affected chemical burn area with water. Continue with the water for at least 15-30 minutes so that all traces of the chemical are removed.
3. If the chemical has gotten into the eyes, gently spray clean water into the eyes. If a water spray is unavailable, have the victim lay flat and then gently pour water into the eyes. Continue the eye washing for a minimum of 5 minutes.
4. Clothing can absorb spilled chemicals so remove the victim's clothes.
5. If available, place a clean pad over the chemical burn area.

Making a First Aid Kit

To make a first aid kit, get yourself a sealed container, such as a tool box, and paint the red cross symbol on all sides so that it is easily identified by anyone. Remember to replace all supplies as they are used. Include the following:

- 5" x 8" card, preferably laminated, with street address and driving directions to the woodshop. This saves time when speaking with an emergency operator. This card should also include any medical conditions, such as diabetes, heart disease, allergies, reactions to medications and so on. Include name of personal physician.
- Box of assorted bandages
- 12 each 2" x 2" sterile pads
- 12 each 4" x 4" sterile pads
- 2 each 2" roller bandages
- 2 each 1" roller bandages
- Roll of 1" adhesive tape
- 6 each 3" to 6" wide elastic bandages
- Scissors
- Tweezers, a nice version has an attached magnifying glass
- Safety pins
- Box of alcohol swabs
- Several pairs of latex gloves
- Antiseptic solution and wipes
- Eye goggles
- Resuscitation mask or face shield

Other useful items:
- Hand soap
- Flashlight
- Additional sterile or clean strips of cloth
- Plastic quart or liter bottle filled with water
- Survival blanket — it compacts to size of a fist, but will give warmth to shock victim
- Ice bag or chemical ice pack

Treating Severe Cuts and Bleeding

Steel is indifferent to flesh. Neither minor nor major cuts should be taken lightly. Severe bleeding can result in death. I suggest that, at the minimum, you read a first aid book and that the appropriate techniques for cut treatment are understood and practiced. I purchased a useful first aid book at a local community college titled *American Red Cross First Aid, Responding to Emergencies* by

American Red Cross, Health and Safety Services (Mosby Lifeline 1996). I know from experience about the blink-of-the-eye speed in which accidents occur and about the trauma of bleeding cuts. Believe me, that is not the time to wonder "Gee, what do I do?" I still have all my fingers, but there are a few scars left over from unnecessary accidents.

Treating Electrical Shock

- Never put yourself in danger when considering the rescue of a person endangered by electrical current.
- If the victim is immobilized by live current, knock him free using a stout wooden implement.
- Monitor the victim's life signs.
- Have someone immediately call for medical support.

Using Fire Extinguishers

Fire extinguishers give the appearance of something that is self-evident and as easy to use as "pull the trigger and spray." The truth is, there is more to it than that, and I recommend that you read further about the use of fire extinguishers and talk with your local fire department about instructions in the proper use of fire extinguishers. Imagine this scene — a shop fire being spread further by incorrect use of a fire extinguisher.

Install fire extinguishers that have a gauge and use the PASS technique:

P — Pull the pin on the fire extinguisher.

A — Aim the fire extinguisher at the base of the fire.

S — Squeeze the handle of the fire extinguisher.

S — Sweep the fire extinguisher back and forth repeatedly to cover the base of the fire.

(From: Kidde Safety, Mebane, NC)

- Locate any burns where the electricity entered and exited the victim. These burns are often found at jewelry locations, belt buckles or where there was contact with the electrical wire.
- Treat entrance and exit burns as third-degree burns.
- The victim should be lying down and with the feet slightly raised.
- If the victim has no pulse, or the pulse is weak or irregular, a qualified person should administer CPR (cardiopulmonary resuscitation).
- If the victim is not breathing, or has uneven or very shallow breathing, administer artificial respiration.
- Keep the victim warm with blankets or jackets placed on top and under so that body heat loss is minimized.

WOODSHOP SECURITY

I am not someone who wants to live in a bunker. But I also know we live in a tough world. Prudence is an important value, and it is wise to at least review your work area's current security. The following list also is an approach for reviewing the windows, doors, lighting and safety procedures of your woodshop.

Inexpensive Security Devices

- standard dead bolts
- dead bolts with attached alarmed rim; a battery-powered unit that will sound when the locked door is forced
- wide-angle door viewers
- keyed security bolt for sliding door
- any of a variety of window locks designed for different-style windows
- security bar for sliding doors and sliding windows
- metal lock reinforcers which fit on both sides of the doorknob and dead bolt areas
- a third hinge added to doors

- a rechargeable flashlight kept near a door or in an easy-access location
- for increased fire safety, lock sets can be installed to interconnect the doorknob mechanism with the dead bolt
- nightlights can be installed at appropriate outlets
- three-way wall switches can be installed so that lights can be turned on and off at the top and bottom of stairs or at opposite sides of a room
- telephones programmed with emergency numbers
- inventory your tools and accessories and keep a record of their models and serial numbers in a location other than in your woodshop
- have a proper insurance policy, including coverage for loss, accidents or disasters; ask your insurance agent about riders for additional coverage

Advanced Security Methods

- Replace basement windows with glass blocks. These will create a distorted image to anyone attempting to look in from the outside.
- Windows can be covered with a specialized security film that laminates glass with a tough transparent coating. This film resists penetration and will hold broken glass, more or less in place — a jagged window hole.
- There are many types of sophisticated alarm systems that can be customized for woodshops.
- Monitor the woodshop via closed-circuit TV. If you work alone and the woodshop is distant from the main living area, this allows a family member to periodically check that all is well.
- Install an intercom system for instant communication with remote areas.
- If you spend sufficient time

Plants That Provide Security

Holly
Hawthorn
Rose
Barberry
Blackberry
Oregon Grape
Flowering Quince
Cactus
Yucca
Locust
Bougainvillea
Red Currant or Gooseberry

working while it is dark, install sound- or motion-activated light switches.

Exterior Security

Many security experts recommend using exterior devices and systems for home security simply because they are meant to keep trouble from entering your house and woodshop. There are far more choices than this list — these are meant to be suggestions of possible methods of securing your property.

- Install fencing around the grounds or yard. A minimum height of 40" is recommended.
- Do you like dogs? Dogs have keen hearing and are protective of their turf. They offer some protection against prowlers and thieves.
- If you don't own a dog, you can still install "Beware of Dog" signs or place a dog water bowl and resting pad outside on a porch or walkway.
- There are alarm systems that respond to motion detection with the sound of barking dogs. The sensors track any motion, and once the motion ceases, the barking stops.
- Have bright exterior lighting at doors, driveways and walkways. Place lighting on sides of buildings, on posts, under eaves or under windows.
- Motion detection lights will give visual warning that someone is outside.
- There are a variety of plants that have thorns or sharp leaves that can be planted under windows or near fences and walkways — consult your local nursery or garden center for plant hardiness in your climate zone (see "Plants That Provide Security" sidebar).

chapter *two*

The Woodshop Environment

WHY IS IT THAT WOODWORKERS — a group of people with great skills, wonderful problem-solving capabilities and powerful insights into all the world's problems — often set up woodshops that have exposed framing, creaky windows, no insulation, no ventilation or no heat? There is no reason for working in a cold, damp or stuffy woodshop. Want a cozy woodshop? Start by performing a woodshop energy evaluation.

- Is the attic well-ventilated?
- Is the attic insulation adequate?
- Is the wall insulation sufficient?
- Are the windows single or double pane?
- Are there storm doors?
- Are the windows caulked?
- Are the foundations caulked?
- Are heating ducts and hot water pipes insulated?

The uniformity of a well-insulated wall is interrupted by windows and doors; though necessary, they are the main cause of outside weather entering the woodshop. OK, that's obvious, but what may not be is that there are many new items available to keep your shop environmentally comfortable.

WINDOW GLASS
There are many types of glass and new types are constantly being manufactured. However, I would like to make note of just a few special types of glass: reflective, heat-absorbing and tinted.

Reflective Glass
There are several types of reflective glass, some of which do look like mirrors from the outside. However, for the woodshop, I'm only interested in the type that looks like normal window glass — and has insulating properties. High-performance reflective glass has a transparent film coating, sometimes only molecules thick, and it has unique insulation properties because of the unique coating designed to reflect solar radiation, reduce heat transfer and still allow light into a room. Let's look at two types of high-performance reflective glass: Low-E and Heat Mirror.

Low-E (low emissivity) windows have two or more panes, a gas buffer, and a heat-reflective coating that helps keep the glass warm and can reduce energy loss by as much as 30% to 50%. Low-E windows also

Rob Girdis' woodshop window with double-pane glass, wood frame and insulating blinds.

block about 75% of ultraviolet radiation from entering a room.

Heat Mirror glass has a reflective film which acts as a transparent insulation. It blocks about 99% of ultraviolet radiation (thus reducing the fading of interior items) and reduces noise levels by 50% — compared to a standard double-paned window. There are different types and styles of Heat Mirror glass. Manufacturers have claimed R-4 to R-7 insulation values for some of these windows.

There is a new generation of efficient windows just now showing up in the marketplace. Some are so new that only a few window installers are even aware of them. These new windows are being referred to as "super-windows." They have very high thermal resistance because of multiple Low-E coatings, specialized gas fillings, reduced convective circulation of the gas fillings, and insulated frames. There are claims of R-8 to R-12 values for these windows.

Heat-Absorbing Glass

This glass contains metallic oxides which absorb solar energy, thus reducing heat gain. The absorbed sunlight is convected as heat to either the inside or the outside — depending on which side is cooler. This means that during the winter more heat is dissipated to the outside and during the summer more heat is dissipated to the cooler interior. While this may

seem contrary to the cooling or warming of a room, there is still an overall benefit because substantially less heat-producing sunlight is admitted through heat-absorbing glass. Heat-absorbing glass reflects only a small percentage of visible light and therefore does not have the mirror-like appearance of reflective glass.

Tinted Glass

Color elements, such as bronze, gray, gold, green or blue are added to molten glass to create various tint colors. It can be made to either reduce light, absorb heat, or both. Tinted glass is most often used for indoor visual comfort or design purposes. Generally, it is not considered as an insulation type of glass.

Having the proper glass is only part of the insulation process. Window-frame material and ill-fitting window frames allow unwanted temperature or air into a room that will instantly reduce the energy savings of efficient glass. In fact, if the frame is temperature-conductive, the R-value can drop from R-4 to less than R-1.

TYPES OF WINDOW FRAMES

Metal frames, usually aluminum, easily transmit outside temperatures to the inside and are often the cause of window condensation.

Vinyl frames have excellent resistance to heat loss and weathering. They are available in a limited color selection. For remodeling purposes, they are nearly impossible to repaint.

Wood frames offer excellent insulation but are susceptible to warping, shrinkage and wood rot. Wood frames also require maintenance with protective coats of paint or preservatives.

Fiberglass frames are fairly new but offer some of the best features sought for window construction.

One entire wall of this workshop has windows offering a wonderful view.

Fiberglass has excellent insulation properties and can be cut, sanded and painted. Some fiberglass frames are of solid thickness, and there are some that have hollow cores which may be empty air pockets or stuffed with insulation.

WEATHERSTRIPPING AND CAULKING

Windows and doors are breaks in the continuity of walls. Thus, they are significant sources of air and sound leakage.

Weatherstripping is the answer for the interface of a moving window or door. Factory-made windows and doors usually include weatherstripping. However, if you are remodeling, you should choose the type of weatherstripping that meets your needs.

NONREINFORCED, SELF-ADHESIVE FOAM This is easy to apply on clean surfaces, good for the inside of door-jambs and window tops and sills. Some foams will hold moisture.

NONREINFORCED FELT This is nailed in place and can resist abrasion. Best used where not exposed to the weather.

REINFORCED VINYL, FELT AND FOAM This is reinforced with metal or plastic strips. Good for attaching to windows and doors.

SPRING STRIPS, S- OR V-SHAPED These are for window and door applications, can be either self-adhesive or nailed.

TUBULAR GASKETS These come in a variety of types, hollow or filled with foam, nailed to windows or doors.

DOOR AND GARAGE DOOR BOTTOMS (SHOES) There are numerous shapes and sizes of these. They are usually metal with tubular or rubber strips and are nailed in place.

WALL OUTLET SEALS These are specialized gasketlike shapes that conform to the wall outlet. Often fiberglass insulation is also stuffed around the wall box.

Other Methods for Maximizing Energy Efficiency

REFLECTIVE FILMS These are thin films, available in various-size rolls that can be applied to windows. They typically block more light than heat; however, they do slow the transmission of heat. Because they are very effective at blocking light, the inside room is darker than normal.

WINDOW TREATMENTS These are insulated window shades, shutters and blinds that will prevent heat loss through glass windows. Very applicable in an unheated woodshop during the night hours.

CAULKING EXTERIOR SEAMS There are many types to choose from, but silicon acrylic latex caulk is the better type for most applications. Expanding polyurethane foam, dispensed from an aerosol can, is useful for larger gaps and is ideal for air pockets around pipes and other irregular openings.

SOUND REDUCTION

To minimize noise from woodworking machines, you must interrupt the movement of sound. This is normally done by either reflection or absorption. Nonporous barriers are the principal methods of reflecting sound, and insulation materials are used to absorb sound. Combining both reflective and absorbing materials usually offers the best properties for sound reduction.

The main physical features you should review for reducing sound are walls, windows, doors and ceiling construction. If there are any holes or open spaces air can pass through, then so can sound.

Walls

Generally, the more solid a wall the more it will reflect sound. Concrete obviously offers the best in sound reduction. Since not all woodshops are in basements or have concrete walls, I will only discuss how to reduce

sound in a framed room.

Most rooms are now sealed with drywall. Because the density of a layer is important, ⅝"-thick drywall is better than ½"-thick drywall for sound insulation. I know that there are many woodshops with open frame walls having no insulation, but it is the worse of possible sound controls. Since this is meant to be an overview, I will describe several methods for making walls more soundproof.

- Fill uninsulated walls with sound-absorbing batts, and cover with drywall. A good example of this type is John Manville's ComfortTherm Sound Control Batts which are made of polywrapped, encapsulated, low-density 3½"-thick fiberglass insulation. Standard insulation batts will also work.

- Attach a second layer of ⅝" drywall over the first layer of drywall. This method can be further improved by first attaching furring strips to the room side of the first layer of drywall and then attaching the second layer. This creates an air space that breaks sound wave movement through the wall.

- Stagger drywall seams so that a stud doesn't have more than one seam nailed to it.

- Some experts recommend using type X drywall as this second layer. Type X refers to the fact that the drywall is made to resist fire transmission through a wall for a certain time period. It is composed of gypsum and fiberglass strands, making it ideal for sound reduction.

- There are complicated construction techniques involving building staggered wall studs. This advanced technique should be discussed with contractors specializing in building soundproof rooms. Your local library will also have books dealing with this technique.

- Stuff all open seams and holes with insulation materials. This is usually at the bottom and top of walls and around pipes.
- If there are electrical outlet boxes on both sides of a wall, offset them from each other.
- Caulk all seams and gaps. Remember the rule of thumb: If air can get through, so can sound.

Windows

- Single-pane windows easily transmit sound. Install double- (or triple-) pane windows, which are designed with an air pocket, to reduce sound transmission. Before purchasing new windows, check the specifications for their sound-reduction capabilities.
- Laminated glass sandwiches a soft vinyl-type layer between sheets of glass. It is made so that if the glass breaks, the shards are kept in place by the soft vinyl. However, the lamination also acts as a sound barrier and will reduce the transmission of shop noise to the outside.

Doors

Doors are difficult to soundproof, and it is also difficult to make doors as soundproof as the surrounding walls.

- Hollow-core doors easily transmit sound so they should be replaced with thick solid wood doors.
- High-quality weatherstripping should be installed around the door, even if it is an interior door. There are special acoustical door seals made for stopping sound.
- Music studios often have double doors. Imagine the cross section of a door frame: a solid door, an air space and another solid door. Both doors should have weather-stripping seals.

Ceilings

- If the ceiling has exposed joists, fill with insulation and then cover with drywall.
- Stuff insulation around light fixtures.
- If you have a drop-down ceiling with acoustic tiles, put insulation batts on top of the ceiling tiles.

HEATING THE WOODSHOP

Garages, basements and secondary buildings are often uninsulated and unheated. A warm woodshop is a pleasant place to be when the weather is wet and cold. For some, when there is no yard work or outdoor activity they go to the woodshop. Others are in the woodshop many hours a day because they have things to build. Either way, it is a wearisome task to warm a woodshop only by toil and sweat.

The Best Ways to Heat the Woodshop

FORCED AIR This is available in many shapes and sizes with the useful options of humidity control and air filtration. Gas- or oil-fired systems are very efficient, but space is needed for the duct work.

RADIANT HOT WATER Hot water is circulated via pumps through pipes into a radiator or under-floor tubing; no hot spots or open flame, except within the furnace boiler. Gas and electrical versions are available; an efficient system that is ideal when remodeling.

PASSIVE SOLAR Glass windows are positioned to absorb solar radiation. Best as supplemental source in colder climates, nice in milder climates. Carefully choose the correct glass.

HEAT PUMP This is efficient, but might require an expensive installation and may not be ideal in colder weather environments. It is better suited to areas needing more air conditioning than heating, since it does both. It also comes with air filtration and humidity control.

CERAMIC HEATER This is a portable, convection-style heater with a fan that blows air from a heated ceramic unit. It's reasonably safe, but has a slow response when changing temperature.

Other Possible Heaters

Reserve your judgment until reviewing the specific safety features of a particular heater model.

CONVECTION HEATER This is portable, and becomes very hot; keep away from flammables. Certain models can be used in woodshops. Available in baseboard and upright styles.

RADIANT HEATER This is also a portable heater. Use caution if it focuses heat in one direction; otherwise, it can warm quickly. A radiant heater has a high operating cost.

Not Recommended

WOOD STOVE This is expensive, requires frequent monitoring, has no thermostat, has large surface areas of hot metal, has open flame, can produce fumes within the room, takes up considerable floor/wall space, is messy with both ash and firewood debris, requires annual chimney inspection and cleaning, and releases outdoor air pollution. Check your local building codes before installing one in a woodshop. I have visited shops that have wood stoves as the primary heating source, but in each case the woodshop was not typical in size, use or location. Because there are so many variables related to wood stoves, I don't recommend them for the average woodshop.

LIQUID-FILLED HEATER This unit is filled with oil or water and looks like an old-fashioned radiator. These are often top-heavy and are not that efficient for woodshops.

KEROSENE HEATER This can be a source of carbon monoxide, and requires refilling with a liquid fuel. Keep away from flammables.

If you have concerns about a heater's ability to function in a woodshop environment, call the manufacturer for advice and recommendations. The reality is that heating systems often require customization in order to meet the needs of the woodshop and woodworker. It is advised that a heating-and-air master technician be consulted when designing and installing a heating system. Always check with your local safety and fire departments about what is permitted in your area.

RADON

Radon is not the home planet of a superhero. Instead, it's an invisible, tasteless and odorless naturally occurring radioactive gas formed by the breakdown of radium, a decay product of uranium, in the earth's rock and soil. All rocks contain some uranium, although in most rocks it is a very small amount. Some rocks have higher than average amounts of uranium. This includes granite, dark shale, pitchblende, light-colored volcanic rocks, sedimentary rocks containing phosphate, and metamorphic rocks derived from these rocks.

Radon gas percolates upward through soil and rock and enters homes and woodshops through gaps and cracks in the building's foundation or through sump pump holes, drains, pipes and any other openings. Once radon gas has migrated into a closed room, it will remain there until it is vented out.

The surgeon general, the U.S. Environmental Protection Agency (EPA), the National Academy of Sciences and the American Medical Association have all identified indoor radon as a national health problem. The American Lung Association estimates that indoor radon exposure is the second leading cause of lung cancer in the United States. Radon effects are mostly long-term, and it apparently does not cause any short-term health effects, such as shortness of breath, coughing, headaches or fever. The EPA estimates that approximately one out of every 15 U.S. homes has indoor radon levels at or above the EPA's recommended levels.

So what's the big deal? What does radon have to do with woodworking? The answer is that most woodshops are located in homes, in basements, in garages or secondary ground level buildings. Most woodworkers spend hours in their woodshops and these woodshops generally are closed when there's work being done, so there is plenty of time for breathing radon.

The only way to know if radon is a problem in your home and woodshop is by measuring the actual levels. If your neighbors have had their homes tested, that is of no use to you. Rock and soil conditions vary and the percolating radon will follow the paths of least resistance to the surface. A single house with high radon levels can be surrounded by houses with low radon levels.

There are two types of testing: short-term and long-term. Short-term tests take from two to 90 days, and long-term tests take from 90 days to a year. Radon levels in a room also vary with the different seasons. The levels are generally higher in the winter months due to a larger differential between indoor and outdoor pressures. Also, houses are closed and less ventilated during the winter. The long-term test will give a better evaluation of average radon levels. Short-term tests are good indicators of whether additional testing is necessary.

Radon is measured in picocuries per liter of air (pCi/L). The EPA recommends that some sort of action be taken if radon levels are greater than 4 pCi/L. The average indoor level is 1.3 pCi/L and outside air is about 0.4 pCi/L. If your home or woodshop tests at values greater than 4 pCi/L, then you will have to find ways to lower that value.

Reduce radon to safe levels by filling in floor and foundation cracks, covering sump pump holes or venting the room to the outside. The process of subslab depressurization uses pipes and fans to remove radon gas from beneath concrete floors and venting it outside. Once the modifications are in place, the room will need to be tested again.

If you are considering testing your home and woodshop, you can either purchase test kits or hire a service to perform the tests. Check in the telephone book yellow pages under "Radon," or call a local real estate office for the name of a certified testing company. You can also call the EPA at 1-800-557-2355 or the American Lung Association at 1-800-LUNG-USA for assistance.

This information about radon is from the Environmental Health Center, a division of the National Safety Council, Washington, D.C.

chapter *three*

Planning Your Ideal Woodshop

YOUR WOODSHOP WILL REFLECT your type of woodworking. Usually that means you're either a generalist or a specialist. Whether you are setting up a new woodshop or enhancing an existing shop, it is of utmost importance to maintain a realistic goal, similar to when buying or remodeling a house. Having expectations and making subsequent changes in design often result in unforeseen adventures.

There are several principles that motivate and drive the desire for a woodshop. First is wanting to build something. Second is having the finances to set up the woodshop. Third is having a location for the woodshop. What is often missing is having some background or experience that forges and shapes the generalizations we think are the foundations of woodworking. Unfortunately, many of us reinvent the wheel when we are attempting to design and set up a woodshop. Sometimes it's impossible to separate the wheat from the chaff when your own reference points are vague. And sometimes it's difficult to ask the right questions simply because you haven't learned the vocabulary. Consequently, we are often

making do or working with the wrong equipment in an inappropriate space.

Many of us set up woodshops without a reference point, such as that provided by a trade school or a master craftsman. The advantage of not having had years of training from a master craftsman is being free to pick and choose everything from adzes to zebrawood — and using them for whatever seems appropriate. The disadvantage is that we don't have someone's hard-earned experiences to guide us. Being self-taught, we can't call upon traditions to specify project design or answer questions such as, "Should I buy a table saw or a band saw first?" And therein is the crux of the problem. How does one design and organize a woodshop? It's a tough question that, when answered, can lead one through the full spectrum from happiness to misery.

If you are fortunate, you will have friends with useful woodshop experiences and you will have ideas about what you want to do in a woodshop. Most areas have clubs or guilds that are a great resource center because their main purpose is advanc-

ing woodworking knowledge. Their members are motivated by an interest in woodworking and a desire to socialize with other woodworkers. While there are clubs which focus on general woodworking, there are also specialized clubs for carvers, lathe turners, model makers and other unique endeavors. Visit these clubs both for problem-solving information and for camaraderie.

FINDING THE PERFECT WOODSHOP

The thorny issue of using master woodworkers as sources of information must be addressed. There is no question that a skilled craftsman can inspire, motivate and educate. I can think of no better person to go to for learning about cutting dovetail joints, applying lacquer, carving or lathe turning. These individuals have spent a lifetime learning the skills that most of us cherish. However, some caution is in order when looking at their woodshops. I would suggest that the woodshop of a seasoned craftsman or master woodworker is akin to a comfortable, but worn, pair of leather shoes, which fit only one person.

Anyone else who tries to wear those shoes will get pinched toes, sore ankles or fallen arches. So, too, is the woodshop of the craftsman: The shop is an extension of that person. The layout, the equipment and the open space all reflect personal interests, habits and projects. Additionally, the temperament, rationalizations and judgments of a craftsman are imperfect. Even the masters have learned from a limited sampling of woodworking experiences. A person taught to use computer-controlled machines in a German trade school probably hasn't experienced the portability of a traditional Japanese craftsman's tool chest. Nor is the proponent of wooden planes necessarily interested in using an air gun nailer.

Setting aside the meticulousness of engineers and patternmakers, I don't know of any woodworker who approaches woodshop organization using the scientific method. Nor do I know of anyone using a consumer's research system or product review method to identify woodshop organization in a precise and controlled way. Instead, we organize in a facile and casual manner and let our pocketbook and free time steer us into tools, storage and gizmos. However, because we are spending our hard-earned time and money, we should try to be somewhat methodical and logical when organizing the woodshop. Ignorance might be blissful, but it's not the best approach when organizing the woodshop.

The old expression "jack of all trades and master of none" does indeed apply to woodshop organization. Typically, the novice woodworker thinks that there is a particular set of tools and equipment that should be in any woodshop. The scenario develops something like, "I need a table saw, band saw, jointer, planer, drill press, router table or shaper, dust collector, air compressor, disc and belt sanders, workbench, tool chests, all portable power tools (including

three routers) and every clamp known to mankind. After all," you say to yourself, "there must be a reason for a hundred different router jigs and templates being in the marketplace and don't the toolmakers and sellers know more about all of this than I do?" My advice is to show restraint and buy tools and equipment with caution and prudence. In fact, if you want to include a tool in your woodshop because it was used on a TV woodworking show or demonstrated at a woodworking seminar, be wary, that tool might have been shown simply as a sales and marketing ploy.

The media has also fostered the notion that there is a "perfect" woodshop complete with stationary and portable tools, uncluttered storage and room left over for the car, water skis and a winter's worth of firewood. There are so many references to the ideal positioning of equipment and workbenches, and the systematic flow of work from machine to machine, that it seems the goal is to have an efficient production business instead of a neat and useful woodshop. I have never seen a woodshop plan that matches my woodshop with regard to type of machines, size of workbench, available wall storage or family cooperation about not parking their bicycles in the shop. However, we do need to begin the planning and organization of the woodshop with some type of personal perspective; otherwise, the woodshop might end up looking like a hardware store. There should be a reference back to the three guiding principles: woodworking inclination, money and space. Ask yourself these questions: "What do I want to build? What do I want to spend? Where will I do the work?"

TYPICAL WOODSHOPS
Some of the basic requirements for a woodshop are sufficient room size, machines, hand and power tools,

workbench, lumber storage, tool storage, assembly area, dust collection, air circulation and ventilation and proper lighting. Each of these requirements has some application to all woodworking endeavors. How these requirements apply are a function of your woodworking interest. Tool storage, for example, is different for carvers and turners. And side lighting, although useful for carvers, isn't generally useful when making cabinets. One more thought before I outline the various types of woodworking and woodshop peculiarities: The majority of tools are designed for general-purpose use. Everything from band saws to mallets has to be reviewed as it applies to your needs.

The Cabinetmaker's Woodshop
If there is such a thing as a general-purpose woodshop, the furniture or cabinet woodshop might be it. Here is where we find the most general-purpose machines, tools and accessories. Why? Because furniture-making and cabinetmaking require basic cuts and joinery that are thought to be the domain of the basic power tool group (whatever that is). It's worth noting that tool and machine manufacturers rarely state that their products are designed for specific constructions. Their product information emphasizes the general nature or usefulness, accuracy or precision of nonspecific functions. That is because companies deliberately design these products for general use. The exceptions are the tools designed for a specific function, such as biscuit joiners or dovetail jigs. Generally, someone who has been building furniture or cabinets for years has a repetitive woodworking style and probably has a basic collection of tools to match that repetition. For example, I like to make table legs that have 1" × 2" round tenons that fit 1"-diameter through-mortises in the tabletop. To simplify cutting the round tenons, I made a jig out of ply-

wood to use with a router. The set up is fast and easy and it takes very little time to make a set of legs. Consequently, I find it natural to design furniture using the round-tenon jig and I use it frequently. Thus, the woodshop becomes simplified through the process of repetition.

ROOM SIZE Furniture and cabinet work require a room that permits the safe operation of machines and other tools. There should be safe zones around machines such as table saws, so that the operator and anyone else in the woodshop can stand in an uncluttered and safe location while the machine is running. It is also necessary to allow enough space to move any workpiece to and from a machine without being obstructed. Yellow or orange safety tape stuck to the floor can be used to define this safety zone.

The furniture and cabinet shop should be large enough to accommodate typical machines, a workbench, storage cabinets and lumber storage. Mobile bases can be attached to machines so that they can be stored out of the way when not in use, but remember, even mobile machines require floor area for storage. Although a machine can be moved to create an open area, it still must be stored somewhere. Consider this point when arranging the work area.

An assembly area, or open space, is necessary for putting things together. Think of open space as an object, similar to a workbench or table saw. When designing your woodshop be certain to include enough room for assembling the largest piece of furniture to be built. Factor in the following: moving workpieces for assembly; access to, and positioning of bar clamps; flat and even flooring; and whether the workpiece can be left in this location while other tools or machines are used. Ideally, this open space should be away from stationary machines

and near the workbench and clamp storage. And if the workpiece will have finishes applied at this location, the space should be away from any heat sources (e.g., water heaters, furnaces or sparking motors) to avoid fire danger.

LUMBER STORAGE Lumber storage is typically very low-tech in the furniture woodshop. The most common storage technique is to pile it on the floor or lean it against a wall. Lumber is heavy and, for safety reasons, shouldn't be stored at too great a height. If wall racks are used, care must be taken to build the racks sturdy and strong. There are several commercial wall racks suited for lumber storage. However, suitable storage can be made from 2×4s at a fraction of the cost. A simple storage rack need be nothing more than an open frame structure. If you need to store short lengths, the structure can be shelved in with plywood or particleboard. Another simple lumber storage system consists of 2×4s or 4×4s vertically bolted to wall studs with sturdy dowels or metal rods inserted into holes. Remember not to place heavy loads at the ends of the dowels.

A very real option for the hobby woodworker is to let the lumberyard store the wood. Purchase what you need prior to starting a project. If the environment of your woodshop is significantly wetter, drier, hotter or colder than the lumberyard, purchase the lumber a month or so before you plan to start construction to allow the wood to acclimate to the woodshop. Small pieces of wood (good scrap pieces and cutoff pieces) usually are stored in boxes, bins and on shelves. I believe that there is a Murphy's Law concerning these pieces: "If they are left alone in a box on a shelf, their numbers will multiply and they will never go away!" Some woodworkers actually burn scrap wood in wood-burning stoves.

MACHINERY Never before in the history of the world has there been such a variety of woodworking tools. It would take several football stadiums to display one of each machine model from all of the world's manufacturers. Today's woodworker can own an infinite combination of machines for making furniture. Selecting the machines that best satisfy your requirements is time-consuming and difficult. Most experts suggest the basic furniture-making machines: table saw, radial-arm saw, band saw, lathe, shaper/router table, drill press, jointer and planer. While this a predictable (and expensive) answer, there are other approaches for determining the machinery you need.

Keep in mind what you are planning to build, and avoid the notion that a general-purpose tool might be useful at a later date. Create a budget for machinery and set high and low dollar amounts. Next, visit with friends and acquaintances who enjoy woodworking. Ask questions about favorite machines, warranties, accuracy, maintenance, durability, accessories, spare parts and other concerns of this sort. Obtain specification and price sheets from manufacturers. Use caution when visiting retail stores selling machinery. Using the table saw as an example, no store is large enough to display all of the models from one manufacturer, let alone all of the table saws from all of the manufacturers. Most retail stores are going to attempt to sell you whatever is in stock — but the saw that they don't sell may be the perfect one for your needs.

Once you have a list of potential machines, add up the costs and look at your budget. But don't get discouraged and go out and buy a new truck instead. If the cost exceeds your budget, ask yourself, "Do I need that machine? Is there an alternate way to do the work? Can I use machines at the local school? What about combination machines? Hand tools?"

If you are a beginning furniture or cabinet maker, start with good-quality and reasonably priced machines such as a contractor's 10" table saw, a 14" band saw, a 6" or 8" jointer and a portable 12" planer. Look for sale prices or buy used (but not worn-out) machines. Work with these machines for awhile until you understand their functions, foibles and how they apply to your own work. In time, as your skills improve, you can sell them (there's always a market for used machines) and move up to better or more specialized machines. If you have a limited budget, selling your older machine to buy a newer one is a great way to afford better tools.

Take your time when buying machines. There is nothing wrong with having a five- or ten-year plan. That is, use your machines, complement them with hand tools and plan for future purchases based upon your current woodworking interests. Perhaps a mortising machine or dovetail jig or wide-belt sander might suit your needs once you have spent time making furniture without them. Doing without is a wonderful woodworking process, because it allows you to problem solve and appreciate the real value of a woodworking machine.

HAND TOOLS AND POWER TOOLS Selecting hand tools and power tools requires the same process as that for machinery. The appealing nature and cost of these tools make them easier to purchase and store away. The problem is that, after reading a typical tool catalog, it seems that every tool is necessary for the woodshop. The reasonable thing to do is look at the construction process for your work and then decide whether a monster miter saw or battery-powered router is really necessary. The new home improvement centers (the modern version of hardware stores) are great for browsing and handling tools. It's important to touch hand tools and to experience

their heft, balance and physical nature. But remember, don't buy a tool unless you need it — and need it for more than one work project.

WORKBENCH Furniture and cabinet makers require a workbench. Size, shape and number of vises are matters of personal taste. I know of woodworkers who use their bench as a catch-all surface and others who treat the workbench as a piece of fine furniture. The workbench may be positioned against a wall or located so that it can be accessed from all four sides. The workbench should have the flattest reference surface in the woodshop so that it can also be used as a clamping surface. In my opinion, a traditional workbench is OK for building furniture with traditional hand tools, but if you are using routers, portable belt sanders and other modern tools, the workbench should be designed with those tools in mind.

TOOL STORAGE The shops of furniture and cabinet makers probably have the greatest array of tools, accessories, jigs and fixtures of any woodshop because this type of woodworking requires assorted layout and measuring tools, chisels, saws, sharpening equipment, mallets, hammers and accessories for all the power tools. Generally, these items are stored in chests or drawers, or are hung on walls.

Some potential furniture makers and cabinetmakers get distracted from their goal of making furniture and instead pursue the notion of the "perfect" woodshop: Drawers and cabinets are designed to store (or showcase) pristine tool collections. While there is nothing wrong with collecting, functional storage should be the goal if you plan to use the tools.

DUST COLLECTION Until recently, woodshops with piles of sawdust mounded around table saws and jointers were

the norm. Heaps of chips were a sign that something was being made in the woodshop. Thankfully, times have changed. Furniture and cabinet shops can now be reasonably free of chips and dust because numerous types of dust collection units are available. The portable units take about the same amount of floor space as a band saw; built-in units can be as large as you want or need. Most dust collectors are affordable, so there is no reason to have potentially dangerous and unhealthy dust in the woodshop.

AIR CIRCULATION AND VENTILATION Woodshops need adequate air circulation. Windows, fans, open doors or any other system of venting the room to provide fresh air is a must. If the woodshop is located in a basement, humidity and lack of fresh air can rust tools and cause finishing products to set up poorly. And as the basement environment cycles between dry during the winter when the furnace is operating, and the warm humidity of summer, wood that is stored there will react accordingly. For example, drawers that work smoothly in the winter may swell with the summer's humidity and not open.

Another air-quality problem is radon radiation not dissipating due to poor air circulation. Radon is most commonly found when rooms are located over shale and the radiation seeps upward and into rooms through cracked floors and leaky foundations.

Fumes from finishing products and solvents, when confined to a closed room, are another potential hazard. Furthermore, many finishing products that evaporate into the air are flammable either as a liquid or as a vapor. Using flammable products in a closed room with a furnace or water heater or other heat source near by is a good way to end up with TV coverage of firemen hosing down the rubble of what was once your woodshop.

LIGHTING Ideal lighting should be glare-free, color-balanced and visually comfortable. If it were possible, I would like my woodshop to have every lighting source possible: windows, a skylight, incandescent lights and fluorescent lights. If windows and skylights aren't possible, the best artificial lighting is a combination of incandescent and daylight-balanced fluorescent lights. The fluorescent lights cover the overall woodshop, and incandescent lights enhance specific work areas (e.g., above the workbench and at machines).

The Carver's Workshop

ROOM SIZE Woodcarvers are very fortunate when it come to choosing work areas, as the possibilities are almost unlimited. Carving tools can be packed up in a shoe box and taken to a vacation locale, so a seat under a palm tree becomes the workshop. Or woodcarvers can have beautiful state-of-the art woodshops with room to carve old-fashioned circus wagons. But most woodcarvers work in modest-size shops in garages, spare bedrooms or basement corners. Compact work areas (50 to 100 square feet) are common.

MACHINES The diversity of woodcarving makes it difficult to generalize about the typical machines used. With that said, a modest-sized band saw, scroll saw, drill press and motorized grinding wheel (for sharpening) are the most commonly found machines. Woodcarvers do more rough shaping of wood than the precise type of cutting found in a cabinet shop. Also, carvers can work on thicker or smaller workpieces than are found in a furniture shop. If power rotary carving tools are to be used frequently, a small dust collector or shop vacuum should be included in the woodshop.

HAND TOOLS AND POWER TOOLS Woodcarving tools are generally either traditional chisels and mallets or power rotary tools. And rarely does a woodcarver use only one carving chisel. Generally, chisels are grouped as a complementary set (10mm No. 5 straight, 20mm No. 31 spoon, 12mm V-tool and so forth). Chisels are also long, short, stubby and microsize. Some are meant to be hand pushed; others are to be hit with a mallet. Rotary tools require AC, battery or air power. And there are hundreds of carving burrs and abrasive points from which to choose. What this means is that the carver's shop requires thoughtful storage for easy access to potentially hundreds of tools that vary in size from 1" to 18". Furthermore, there are mallets, sharpening tools, drill bits and assorted knives to use and store.

WORKBENCH One key requirement of a woodcarver's bench is that it must be capable of holding a workpiece rigid. When carving a statue, the workpiece is typically held vertically, and carving is done 360° around the piece. As work progresses, the workpiece needs to be moved so that work proceeds evenly around it. To do this, the workpiece must constantly be clamped, unclamped, repositioned and reclamped. Typical front and end vises are not designed for this type of holding. However, specially designed workpiece holders that mount directly to the workbench and can be rotated 360° are available for carvers.

Typically, woodcarvers use smaller benches than those of cabinetmakers. Some workbenches are about the same size as a bar stool. If using mallet and chisels, the workbench must be heavy enough to absorb the constant vibrations from the mallet blows. Power carving also requires working 360° around the workpiece, but since it doesn't produce heavy mallet hits, it doesn't have to be as stout.

For smaller carving projects (that is, the bird-in-the-hand size), the workbench probably will be used as a place to rest tools while working. A TV tray is actually adequate for small carving work. If you are sitting down, it's large enough to hold a few tools and catch the workpiece chips.

For carvers, the workbench is the assembly area. Carved workpieces are not usually the size of furniture, so a separate area is not required.

WOOD STORAGE I haven't seen many woodcarvers' woodshops that have racks of long lumber. Instead, woodcarvers tend to have boxes and bins of small wood pieces: cutoff pieces, firewood-size chunks, limbs and slabs of wood. Generally, the reasons for racking lumber (flatness, moisture control, etc.) aren't as necessary for woodcarving. Shelves and bins are perfectly acceptable for storing woodcarving wood.

TOOL STORAGE The woodcarvers I have known all have had a similar work environment in one respect: Their work area is like that of a piano player; that is, most of their tools are within easy reach when sitting or standing at the workbench. Consequently, tool chests with plenty of small drawers, tool racks behind the workbench or even coffee cans filled with tools sitting on the workbench are common types of storage. Power carving tools are generally suspended over the workbench or hung on a nail next to the bench, and the grinder for sharpening is equally close at hand.

DUST COLLECTION It's difficult to remove wood chips while carving. The old expression "let the chips fall where they may" still applies. The great thing about using a mallet, chisels and knives is that the chips do fall to the floor and you aren't breathing dust. However, when using power tools, the dust flies through the air and into faces and lungs. It's not uncommon to watch a power carver, using a rotary tool, doing detail work fairly close to the face. Obviously, safety goggles and dust masks should be used, but a dust collector for drawing the dust away from the work area would be ideal.

AIR CIRCULATION AND VENTILATION Several conditions make air circulation and ventilation very important. Paints and other finishing products should be used in a well-ventilated area. Again, many finishing products are potential fire hazards. But even if the finishing products are not flammable, it's best to vent the room so that you (and others) don't have to breathe the chemical fumes. Carvers also enjoy working with unusual and exotic woods, like applewood or cocobolo, that can cause skin irritation, so efforts should be made to work as cleanly as possible.

LIGHTING Since most carving work is done in centralized areas, fewer lighting fixtures are needed than in a cabinet shop. Ideally, the carver's shop should have both incandescent and fluorescent overhead lighting with separate on/off switches. Side light is very useful for the carver. By turning off the overhead lights and using side lighting from a tabletop gooseneck lamp or other type of lamp, the workpiece will have different shadows which helps to visually reveal textures.

The Lathe Turner's Woodshop

Woodturning is aptly named, because every time you turn around there are new lathe and tool innovations and new lathe techniques. The past 20 years have seen incredible developments in woodturning — new lathe designs for turning bowls, spindles and miniatures, new shapes in turning tools and an armada of workpiece-holding devices — and to make it even better, a new generation of

Hobbyist John MacKenzie enjoys lathe turning and having a large air compressor.

woodturning instructors, instructional videos, magazines and woodturner's clubs as sources of information.

ROOM SIZE The basic lathe turner's woodshop can be compact, with enough room for a lathe, other tools, machines and storage. The basic nature of woodturning allows the work project to be started and finished on the lathe, which means there is little need for additional room space for other types of wood processing. Because the lathe is usually located against a wall, with the operator in a more or less static position, the woodturner can easily set up a woodshop in a garage or basement.

MACHINES The traditional wood lathe has undergone considerable design changes because of the heightened interest in bowl turning. In the old days, lathes had long beds with 36" to 48" distances between centers and were mostly used for turning stair spindles and other long pieces. These lathes generally had a 6" distance from centers to bed surface which meant that a 12" bowl was the maximum capacity over the bed. Bowls of greater size were meant to be turned "outboard" on the opposite

side of the head stock, if the lathe had that capacity. Today's turners often use both the head and tail stock for support while turning bowls. That means that the distance from centers to bed should be adequate to turn larger diameter bowls. Many lathes now have this capacity and other useful features, such as DC motors, which permit variable turning speeds starting at zero RPM. AC motor variable speeds usually begin at about 500 RPM.

Other machines common to woodturner's woodshops are band saws, dust collectors and grinders. Table saws, jointers and planers can be useful for wood preparation, but they aren't a necessity.

HAND TOOL AND POWER TOOLS There are many tools and accessories that aid in woodturning. A few of the more important power tools are a cordless drill for attaching face plates, a finish sander for sanding the workpiece while it's still mounted on the lathe, a rotary tool for detail work and sanding, and a jigsaw or saber saw for preliminary shaping. There are many useful measuring devices, such as inside and outside calipers and center finders. If hand tools are used, it's probably for preliminary wood removal or for some detail design work.

WORKBENCH In a sense, the lathe is the workbench. Once the preliminary shaping of the workpiece is done, just about everything else is done at the lathe. The other ongoing activity while turning is sharpening. For convenience, most turners install a grinder next to the lathe. A small workbench or countertop is useful for the odds and ends of setup or take-down work. The workbench is also used for sorting wood and other miscellaneous tasks.

LUMBER STORAGE Depending upon your zealousness, storing wood can range from a few pieces to filling garages, decks and barns with chunks of wood. If you are collecting wood and searching for downed trees in orchards, yards, parks and forests, you will need adequate storage. Not only will you need room to store the freshly cut (often referred to as *green* or *wet*) wood, but you will also need storage areas for the drier pieces. To further complicate the picture, there should be a functional inventory system so that different species can be identified — without leaves, one chunk of wood is difficult to tell from another.

TOOL STORAGE Lathe turning, billiards and golf have one thing in common: They all require easy access to long, thin tools. Neat and tidy storage for lathe tools is indeed similar to racks designed to hold cues. But don't make a rack for 12 tools and then buy 13. One possibility is to make a wall rack that can accommodate a growing tool collection. Another easy storage solution is pegboard-covered walls near the lathe. A roll-around cart also permits easy access to lathe tools, and it's less limited in the number of tools it can hold.

Earl Bartell keeps a small take-apart table near his lathe. The table has rows of holes around its perimeter for holding lathe tools. The type of tool is identified by different colors and numbers of rings on the handles. The table is assembled with oversize knobs for quick assembly. He also uses this table when teaching lathe classes at locations other than his woodshop.

Also in Earl Bartell's shop is this oversized shelf and wall pegboard, located near the lathe. Frequently used chucks, tools and other accessories are within arm's reach of the lathe.

Earl Bartell uses an auxiliary tray mounted to the lathe bed for frequently used tools. The tray is easily repositioned or removed when necessary.

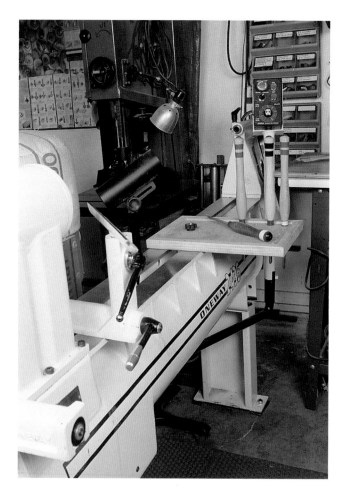

ASSEMBLY AREA The assembly or construction area is at the lathe itself. Off-lathe work consists of activities such as tool sharpening, wood preparation and detailing and finishing work.

DUST COLLECTION Depending on whether dry or wet wood is turned, the debris will come off the turning as long stringy pieces or as smaller bits and dust. A good dust collection system will not only make the lathe work neater and easier, but also keep the debris from traveling many feet away from the lathe. Without dust collection, the debris field (especially that of green or wet wood) looks like a confetti celebration — of carrot peelings. Ideally, a dust collection port should be positioned behind and near the turning area. Articulated ductwork with a port is especially useful when it can be repositioned for any work angle or location. In truth, most

turners will let wet wood peelings pile up on the floor because their dust collectors cannot handle the volume and weight of the debris. If a duct port is positioned at the lathe it is for dust control.

AIR CIRCULATION AND VENTILATION Moving dust and chips away from the work area also means cleaner air for the lathe operator. A simple solution is to position an electric fan near the work, so that it moves air (and dust) away from the operator, preferably toward a window or door.

Many turners use helmets with face guards that have built-in fans and filters. These battery-powered units filter air at the back of the helmet and move clean air across the face area.

LIGHTING Pleasant overhead lighting is a necessity in the wood turner's shop.

It's advantageous to be able to turn different lights on and off so that wood surface textures and features can be easily viewed from different lighting angles. Isolated spotlights aimed at the work area are also useful for watching how cutting tools perform against wood.

The Furniture Restorer's Woodshop

Furniture restoration and repair woodshops have to be more versatile than the typical furniture-making, lathe turning or carving shops. That's because the restorer has to be able to set up the woodshop so that almost every woodworking skill can be performed. For example, replacement chair rungs must be turned on a lathe, broken decorations must be carved, or drawer sides and bottoms must be cut to a specific size and thickness. Even if you specialize in one particular item (chairs), it's difficult to know what demands the next broken piece will make on the woodshop.

ROOM SIZE The type of furniture being restored determines the necessary size of the room. For example, a dining room obviously requires more space than an antique jewelry box; a drop-front desk requires more space than a hall mirror.

The woodshop has to have enough room for three functions: storage of broken pieces, space to fabricate replacement pieces using tools and machines in a woodshop filled with workpieces, and finally, space for cleaning, disassembly, gluing up and reassembly. I spent many years restoring turn-of-the-century Arts and Crafts (mission-style) furniture, and the sizes of those pieces was always a problem. Sideboards and settles (benches) are large, heavy and difficult to move. If several pieces were brought into my woodshop, suddenly the room got smaller. So plan enough space to store works-in-progress as well the machines to work on them.

Here's a view of Doug Matthews' woodshop. The sliding glass doors are often left open in good weather.

MACHINES Unlike furniture and cabinet shops where machines are required for a significant portion of the construction process, the same machines are minimally used for restoration. The chair or table is already made, it just needs a part or two. The emphasis thus shifts to the need for high-quality machines to make occasional replacement parts. If I could assign a proportional value to the need for machines in restoration work, I would say that need is less significant than other factors. Far more important is understanding how to use various joinery techniques, using chemicals or gluing up odd-shaped pieces.

You may use a lathe to make bowls (for your own enjoyment), but very rarely do you need a lathe to restore bowls. Instead, the restorer's lathe will be used to turn replacement spindles, posts and rungs, so its main feature should be bed length (distance between centers).

A high-quality saw blade is the most important feature of a table saw for restoration work, because it's often necessary to make tear-out-free and odd-angle cuts through antique wood. The aim is to waste as little as possible of the irreplaceable original wood. Band saws should have ⅛" or ¼" smooth cutting blades so that clean radius cuts can made easily.

The same kind of careful evaluation should be applied to other machines as well. For example, a planer with a slow feed rate is preferred for planing highly figured wood.

HAND TOOLS AND POWER TOOLS I firmly believe that successful restoration work requires the use of an array of traditional hand tools and power tools. For example, a desk or cabinet from the early 1800s probably was built with hand-cut dovetails. If the piece has boards that are damaged beyond repair, the replacement wood will need hand-cut dovetails made to match the original. That means using a tenon saw, chisels, a marking gauge and a mallet. Or there may be hard-

ened glue in a dowel hole that resists being picked out. Using a rotary tool with a round burr might be the only method of removing the dried glue.

The tool selection for restoration work is eclectic due the variety of potential repairs. Bench planes, moulding planes, routers with specialty cutters, scrapers, chisels, wire brushes, screw extractors, band clamps and putty knives are but a few of the tools that make work easier.

WORKBENCH The traditional workbench with front and shoulder vises is useful to the restorer simply because that prized antique now being restored was originally built at such a bench. And duplicating the original construction process will lead to a better and more valuable restoration. However, if you have the room, a low workbench (approximately 12" to 24" high) is also very useful. A 4' × 8' sheet of ¾" particle board laminated with melamine resting on low sawhorses is ideal for general cleaning and disassembly. Melamine cleans easily, resists most glues and can be turned over for another clean side if it becomes scratched.

LUMBER STORAGE Just what is the lumber in a restoration woodshop? I like to have bins of wood pieces sorted by color — dark, light, reds and tans — so that colors can be quickly matched with the workpiece. And I have storage for pieces from discarded furniture and other devices. I once had to replace a spindle in a Windsor chair that dated to approximately 1795. I searched for months to find a piece of ash that had a similar color and grain pattern. My search ended when I found an old garden rake handle that was a perfect match. Now I save all sorts of wood simply because I never know when it will be useful. I also like to keep veneer pieces stored between plywood covers, an arrangement resembling a scrapbook. Full rolls of veneer should be kept rolled and wrapped in paper to keep it clean and out of the woodshop air.

FINISHING PRODUCTS AND STORAGE Don't be casual about storing finishing materials, finishing products and solvents. Specialized metal cabinets for storing hazardous and flammable materials are available, and there are specialized trash cans for oily rags and other flammable products. Check in the telephone yellow pages under "safety equipment" for a source of storage cabinets. All finishing materials and products should be stored a safe distance away from any heat source or direct, all-day exposure to sunlight. Finally, keep all finishing supplies away from those who aren't trained in their usage.

AIR CIRCULATION AND VENTILATION If you have done any paint stripping or furniture repair, the words methylene chloride should speak volumes to you. Also, lacquer thinner, paint thinner, benzene, MEK, alcohol, turpen-

Commonly Found Woodshop Mistakes

- Floor clutter
- Poor ventilation & poor air circulation
- Poor dust collection design, including collector size, type of pipe and pipe configuration
- Improper storage and handling of volatile and hazardous materials
- No provision for chemical spills
- No provision for disposal of unwanted hazardous materials
- Heavy lumber stored at too great of height
- Removal of safety guards from machines
- Ignoring appropriate use of hearing and eye protection
- No first aid supplies or fire extinguisher
- No contingencies for accidents or emergencies
- Not reading operator's manuals
- Poor quality lighting
- Insufficient electrical supply
- Insufficient number of electrical outlets
- Reliance on electrical extension cords
- Space is too small for the number of machines, benches, etc.
- Little or no open space
- Poor access for moving large and heavy objects into woodshop
- Unrestricted humidity, especially in basement and garage woodshops
- Far too much reliance on the concept of "assuming," as in, "I assumed that it was OK."

tine and wood bleach are all dangerous and should be handled with extreme care. Since the earliest days of the industrial revolution, chemicals have been both a blessing and disaster to man. The phrase "mad as a hatter" referred to those who made hats with poisonous chemicals. The early-day photographers worked with their faces directly over mercury-coated glass plates while developing film plates. These photographers didn't live long; old-time restorers who worked for long periods breathing formaldehyde and other toxic chemicals didn't live to ripe old age either. If having a long and healthy life is important to you, avoid chemical risks and work with intelligence and caution. Know the chemicals that you are using and follow all product safety notices. Store and use all finishing products as if they were the most dangerous liquids in the house (they probably are). Think of your skin and clothes as if they are sponges, ready to absorb any oil, sol-

vent, bleach, dye or stain. Build and set up the woodshop with whatever it takes to be safe.

LIGHTING Restoration work should be done with proper lighting. Ideally, the lighting should be color balanced to simulate the room where the repaired piece will eventually reside in. It is worth asking the question about the room light before starting on any repair/restoration projects. Since there are a variety of different color-balanced fluorescent lights, keep a supply of these available. The lighting tubes can then be replaced according to need.

Restoration work also benefits from side lighting. That is, a strong light source angled from a horizontal location will cast shadows on the work area. These shadows that are created will enhance the wood grain and carved surfaces, and therefore make detailing the work easier.

chapter *four*

Choosing the Right Shop Location

THE IDEAL WOODSHOP LOCATION is the location that you already have. If I could make a wish, like most woodworkers, I would have a separate building with 2,000 square feet, high ceilings, skylights, one or two windows with views of rivers and mountains, an oversize door (maybe even a garage door), wood flooring, heating and air conditioning, plumbing with sinks and a toilet, sound-insulated walls and a smaller secondary room for office needs and for displaying the things I've made.

This is the view from my woodshop. I am surrounded by a forest of Douglas fir, Western red cedar and hemlock trees.

Setting wishes aside, I know that I do have a woodshop for woodworking. And that is perhaps the the most important reality. In fact, this realization should always be the main consideration in the quest for the ideal woodshop. If you have a location or space that is usable, ask yourself which is more important — the woodshop or the things that you make? It's easy to be distracted by pinup pictures of fancy or well-appointed woodshops. What is more difficult to see in the coffee-table woodshop book pictures is that the ideal woodshop is really nothing more than the woodshop that is your own, where you can happily practice your woodworking. You can always improve on fixtures, storage and so on, but those things can evolve as you do your woodworking.

Most of us use the garage or basement for our woodshops. Sometimes, if we are doing less messy work, we might be able to use a second bedroom or part of the laundry room, but the rooms with the most space for a shop are garages and basements. However, organizing a garage or basement is not necessarily a simple task. Garages are storage tunnels, and basements are storage holes. Room proportions and construction materials differ, and the use of either room means displacing specific home utility functions.

THE GARAGE SHOP

Typically, garages are for one or two cars; this translates into approximately 10' × 20' (200 square feet) for one car and about 20' × 20' (400 square feet) for two cars. Garages usually have a garage door, a door into the house and a window. They can also have wall-mounted cabinets, a water heater, a built-in vacuum system for the house, a laundry and overhead storage in attic or open rafters. Garages in newer houses are generally framed but can also be constructed of concrete blocks or brick.

Let me create a hypothetical garage for the sake of solving a space-utilization problem and designing a woodshop. Imagine a two-car garage in which cars are parked at night. In addition, the garage is also used to store bicycles, sports equipment and garden tools. It has one window on a side wall, a door into the house and a door to the outside. Other noteworthy features include open rafters, one 4' × 5' wallhung cabinet, the house electrical service panel, one overhead light and AC outlets on three walls.

Because the car is destined to remain in the garage for a certain number of hours each day, only the walls and the overhead areas can be used for permanent storage. These storage areas will determine the actual design and composition of the woodshop. Remember, even though the car will be outside when machines are placed in the open central area, all equipment must be returned to the wall areas or ceiling when the car is parked inside.

Begin by making a list of all permanent storage: household items, sports equipment and so on. Next, make a list of woodworking machines, tools and supplies that you

Jon Magill converted his garage into a woodshop, and two of the car bays are used for woodworking. When the cars are parked outside, mobile machines and portable workstations are moved into their locations. There is ample open area for most construction projects.

This woodshop is permanently set up in a garage. Note the skylights, indirect lights, air filtration box and the location of the workbench relative to the permanent wall with the storage/countertop area.

own and also a list of things you plan on acquiring. Now, using ¼" graph paper, draw a floor plan of the garage, including doors, windows and steps (use ¼" = 1'). On a separate sheet of graph paper, using the same scale, draw all machines, cabinets and storage containers that you want in the woodshop (or use the icons found on the next page). Cut these drawings out, and place them on the graphed drawing of your garage floor-plan to experiment with spatial arrangement, as shown on page 284.

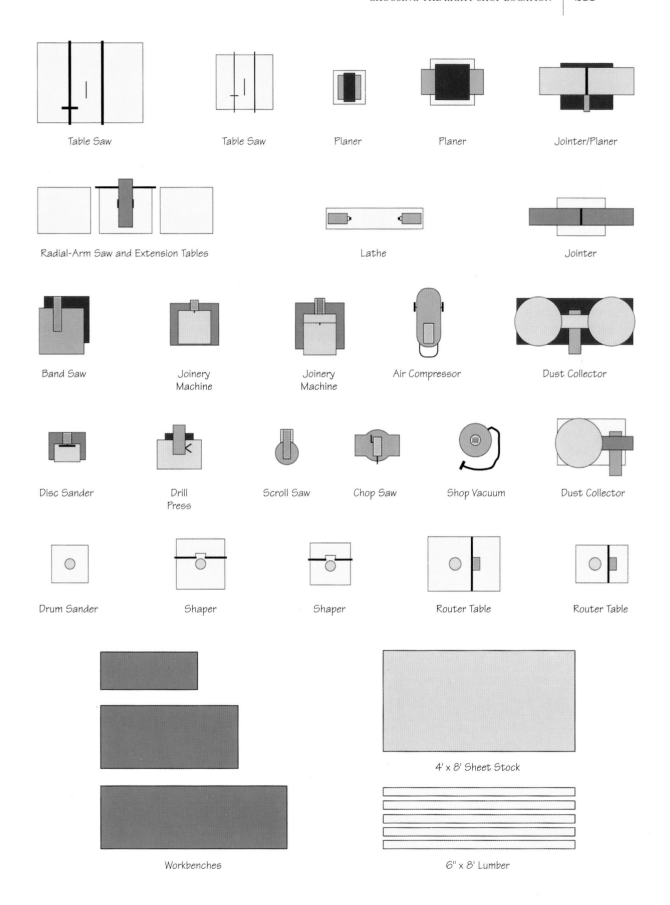

Table Saw

Table Saw

Planer

Planer

Jointer/Planer

Radial-Arm Saw and Extension Tables

Lathe

Jointer

Band Saw

Joinery Machine

Joinery Machine

Air Compressor

Dust Collector

Disc Sander

Drill Press

Scroll Saw

Chop Saw

Shop Vacuum

Dust Collector

Drum Sander

Shaper

Shaper

Router Table

Router Table

Workbenches

4' x 8' Sheet Stock

6" x 8' Lumber

Scale ¼" = 1'. Use ¼" grid paper and copies of these icons to create woodshop layout arrangements.

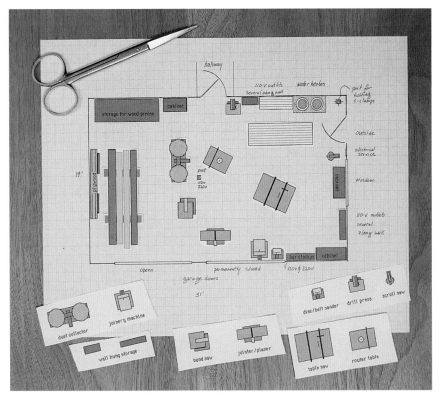

Use the icons on page 283 and lay out your shop on ¼" grid paper.

Typical Dimensions and Areas

ITEM	DIMENSION	AREA (SQ. FT.)
Car	6'x15'	90
Household storage	2'x5'	10
Sports equipment	2'x6'	12
Garden tools	1'x4'	4
Tool cabinet #1	2'x4'	8
Tool cabinet #2	2'x5'	10
Workbench	3'x6'	18
Table saw	4'x4'	16
Band saw	3'x3'	9
Drill press	2'x2'	4
Jointer	1'x4'	4
Planer	2'x2'	4
Dust collector	2'x3'	6
Lumber storage	2'x8'	16

The results of your graphing might look something like what you see above. Use the chart on this page as a quick reference for typical dimensions and areas of woodshop tools and other items.

Now, if you were to place all the items listed in the chart at left, you would have 211 sq. ft. of tools and other objects. But the garage has only 200 sq. ft. of space. Obviously, there is less area available than the floor area required when the car is inside. Judicious wall and overhead storage is necessary to open up the woodshop area. So begin by rethinking the common ideas of storage. Consider ripping out the garage cabinet furnished by the house builders. Don't anticipate using secondhand bookcases, old kitchen cabinets, inexpensive metal shelvings or any other combination of odds and ends, and resist the urge to build new cabinets and storage units until you are reasonably certain of your needs and requirements. Sacrifice all of these things in the name of efficiency. In fact, the best approach might be to develop an overall plan that unifies the entire room using a design that incorporates both house and woodshop items. This plan might include floor-to-ceiling storage units near the garage door consisting of broom-type cabinets for storing rakes and shovels, with compartments for flower pots, located beside cabinets for storing skis and tennis rackets with drawers for storing camping supplies. Similar built-in units could be used for tools and supplies. Specialized features would allow for a lumber rack, a workbench and a clamp rack. Add mobile bases to your machines so they can be stored against the walls and easily moved to the center area when the car is parked outside. This unified design might even create enough open space so that some work (not machine work) can be done at the workbench even when the car is inside. Once there is a workable layout, the details of flooring, wall insulation, electrical service, lighting, ventilation and security can be addressed.

Flooring

If the garage floor is cracked, rough or oil-stained, it should be cleaned, repaired or reconditioned before any other remodeling. Cracked or rough concrete floors make it difficult to move machines and construction projects. Casters are generally too small to roll over wide cracks and mobile bases may not work well on rough or uneven floors. Engine-oil stains, besides being ugly, will contaminate wood and shoes.

There are several options for restoring, repairing or resurfacing concrete floors.

- Remove oil and grease stains with liquid degreaser or have the floor steam cleaned.
- Use concrete patching compounds to patch chips and holes. Cracks should be thoroughly cleaned and then filled with concrete repair caulk or patching

compound.

- If the floor is too rough, consult with a floor finishing company that specializes in applying smooth surface coats.
- Consider alternative flooring materials: rubberized tile squares, wood tile squares, vinyl flooring, epoxy floor paint, solid wood tongue-and-groove strips or planks, and wood-composition tongue-and-groove strips.

A Simple Floor Covering

Here's a rather crafty and simple floor covering: First tear large, irregular pieces of kraft paper. Lay those pieces on the bare concrete and brush on several coats of polyurethane varnish. The result is a warm-colored floor that is also sealed and easy to clean.

Walls

Insulating a garage makes it more energy efficient and helps moderate ambient temperature. Insulation also acts as a sound barrier and reduces machine noise to the inside of the house or externally to the neighbor's house.

If the garage is already finished with wallboard, you will have to make a remodeling decision. One choice would be to remove the wallboard, install insulation between the studs and replace the wallboard. Alternatives to this approach include:

- Hiring an insulating company to drill holes in the wall for blowing insulation into the wall cavities.
- Attaching solid or rigid insulation board (sometimes referred to as *blueboard*) with a vapor barrier directly to the existing wallboard and then covering it with new wallboard (note: this extends the walls outward about 1½").
- Covering the existing walls with plywood or pegboard and paint-

ing them with fire-retardant paint.

- Weatherstripping both interior and exterior doors.
- Insulating the garage door. Be aware that this is not as easy as insulating walls. If the garage door is solid construction, solid insulation board might be attached to it. But don't make the door too heavy. Check with garage door companies regarding appropriate door weight and other methods of insulation.

Electrical Service and Wiring

Not having adequate electrical power in a woodshop is like having a sports car without gasoline. No matter how fine the woodworking machines or how sophisticated the lighting, unless the electrical service is specifically designed for the woodshop, you might as well whittle with a pocketknife. Not only do machines require adequate power for operation, but it is unsafe to use any electrical tool with an inadequate power supply. Underpowered electrical tools will wear out faster, as well as being potential fire hazards.

Typically, the electrical service panel for a house is located in the garage. This makes it easy to check the panel for service voltage to the house and determine whether there are unused circuits. If circuits are available, they can be dedicated to the garage woodshop. For example, if there are three 20-amp breaker circuits not in use, one could be used for lighting, another for the table saw and the third for outlets for hand power tools. An alternative option is to install a second electrical panel that is separate from the house electrical service, often referred to as a subpanel. The subpanel consists of circuit breakers dedicated to the woodshop. Subpanels are relatively easy to install; however, call a licensed electrician if you have any reservations about your ability to

Insulation R-Values

All insulation types are rated with numbers called an R-value, which have been established by the U. S. Department of Energy for walls, floors and ceilings in different climate zones in the United States. Some manufacturers of insulation recommend R-values higher than the Department of Energy's recommendations. These higher R-value recommendations are usually based on the concept that more insulation is more energy efficient. Obviously, wood-shops in Santa Monica, California, require less insulation than wood-shops in Milwaukee, Wisconsin. Check with your local insulation suppliers to determine the correct R-values for your specific climate zone.

If you don't want machine sounds blasting through the garage door, drape sound insulation (and fireproof) curtains in front of the garage door. Or use manufactured garage doors made with insulation materials.

handle the installation.

Almost as important as adequate electrical power is the location of the electrical outlets. There is consensus among woodworkers that outlets should be everywhere in the room, including the ceiling. My suggestion is to first design the location of cabinets, the workbench and machines, and then determine the location of outlets. There should be outlets at either end of the workbench and approximately 5' apart around the open walls. And don't forget to place several outlets at overhead locations near the workbench. Some woodworkers prefer having all outlets approximately 4' from the floor, others prefer lower outlets so that the cords aren't suspended in the air.

Why so many outlets? It's simple: so you can avoid potentially annoying electrical tool scenarios. If there are too few outlets in the woodshop area, you will either be constantly plugging and unplugging AC cords while you work, or you will be tempted to use extension cords with multiple sockets which could potentially damage your tools because the correct voltage is not being supplied.

It's better to have outlets at the ends of a workbench so that power cords are near you and away from the work area. Electrical cords positioned over a workbench can easily smear wet glue and scatter glue bottles, screws and smaller tools as you work with a tool and drag the cord back and forth. AC cords on a workbench also can be accidentally cut or damaged by belt sanders, routers and jigsaws. Finally, an adequate number of outlets means less opportunity for cords to become tangled or to be a problem for foot travel.

Electrical wiring in unfinished basements is simplified if the joists are exposed and there is no ceiling. Finished basements will require remodeling to locate and place new wiring. The type of wiring and conduit used will vary with different building codes. Generally, wiring is routed through the joists and installed in conduit when the wires are routed down the wall surfaces. I would suggest that you select conduit that, while meeting code requirements, is also tough enough to resist being bumped by lumber and other heavy objects. I had electrical contractors install wiring and lights in my woodshop in Syracuse, New York. They drilled holes in the joists and installed Romex cables from the subpanel to both the lights and the 110V and 220V outlet locations. Rigid conduit was used from the top of the basement wall to the outlet location.

Installing Adequate Lighting
Very often lighting is set up haphazardly; that is, the local hardware store will have a sale on 4'-long fluorescent lights and so these become the woodshop lights. Attached to rafters, they are turned on via a pull string. While this does produce light, there are better approaches.

The lighting possibilities for garage woodshops are more numerous than those for basements because of the ease of access to natural light through walls, the ceiling and the garage door. If the garage window is too small, it can be removed and replaced with a larger one.

The simplest replacement types are manufactured windows which are available in many sizes and types. If the garage has open rafters, it's easy to install skylights. Skylights offer wonderful lighting with a quality unlike any artificial lighting. Natural light makes the color of finishing products easier to identify and use, both on and off wood. And during the winter months, the psychological lift of working in sunlight is extremely positive.

Adding windows to garage doors is fairly straightforward. If the garage door is articulated, with frame and panel construction, some of the panels can be removed and replaced with either safety glass, acrylic or Plexiglas. I advise against using standard window glass because garage doors are easily bumped and the opening and closing process usually includes some sort of impact.

House contractors usually install little more than a single bulb with an on/off pull string in basements. Which, of course, is totally wrong for a woodshop. If the basement ceiling is finished, it's tempting to retrofit lights onto the ceiling surface. Although this is easy to accomplish, the effect is a lowered ceiling, which hinders your efforts to move long or tall objects. Consider recessed lights in finished ceilings; if the basement ceiling is unfinished, install 4' or 8' fluorescent lights between ceiling joists.

Garage Woodshop Security

Fear and worry are two different human conditions. Fear is a natural reaction to a terrible and immediate situation. Worry is self-manufactured nervousness. Secure your garage woodshop with common sense. There are a number of devices and procedures to keep everything safe: installing door locks and dead bolts; closing doors and windows; installing machine on/off switch locks; shutting off the circuit breakers to the woodshop; maintaining a low profile and minimizing noise (unwanted advertising); knowing your neighbors; not loaning tools; keeping fire extinguishers and first aid kits handy; and keeping a list of emergency telephone numbers near the telephone.

Garage Shop Ventilation
Fresh air is of paramount importance in a woodshop. Not only do you require clean air for breathing, but air that is too wet, dry, dusty or stale affects the quality of the woodworking project. Poor air causes finishes not to adhere or set up properly. Wet air causes wood to expand (and later shrink when moved to a drier area), as well as rust and stain tools and machines. Stale air contains assorted pollutants that affect wood, tools, finishes — and woodworkers.

The simplest ventilation system is windows and doors. However, some caution is in order. Open windows and doors lead to a degree of interaction with the outside world. Noise and dust will leave the shop and visit the neighborhood. Bugs seem to quickly find open shop doors and may bite you, leave tracks on freshly varnished surfaces or burrow into stacks of wood and lay millions of eggs. Open windows and doors also broadcast the fact that you are a woodworker. While this may be a

To heat this woodshop, a small gas furnace has been placed in the corner.

good form of advertising, you may not want to tell the world that you have expensive tools and machines.

If a ventilation system is deemed a worthy investment for both woodworking and health reasons, it's prudent to consult with ventilation specialists. A system should be designed to bring a continuous flow of fresh air into the shop and to filter the exhausted air. This type of ventilation system is usually designed for specific shops — there are no off-the-shelf systems available. A basic unit will cost between $1,000 and $2,000.

If you decide to install a ventilation fan unit, the type found in most home improvement centers, there are a few cautions. Be certain that the fan motor is explosion-proof and dust-proof. Solvents such as lacquer thinner, alcohol, acetone and paint thinner are very flammable. When these solvents become fumes and are airborne, they are still flammable. It is very dangerous to vent fumes through a fan motor that could spark or that is not made for venting flammable solvents. Fine dust is also

highly flammable and potentially explosive, so enclosed motors that are designed for use around dust should be used.

Also consider that when cold outside air is brought into the shop, the warm inside air is exhausted. If the woodshop is heated, that means higher heating bills due to the constant loss of warm air as it is vented from the shop.

In this day and age, you simply cannot vent fumes and dust into the outside environment without some repercussions. Even home woodshops must — or should — abide by community air quality directives and laws. Furthermore, neighbors generally are not tolerant of noise, dust and clouds of fumes invading their space.

Heating the Garage Woodshop

Heating the woodshop is a difficult issue. Working in a warm room is often thought of as a luxury because heating units are potentially dangerous around woodworking solvents and materials and because a separate heating unit or system is thought of as too expensive. If you live in a warm climate, heating the woodshop might not be necessary. However, a warm, dry woodshop will stabilize humidity, thus keeping lumber at a constant moisture content; the warm air will also help prevent rust. Always check local building codes and with your local fire department regarding the installation of heating units in the woodshop.

THE BASEMENT SHOP

For many years I had basement woodshops, and I can say that although there were many good things about the location, there were also many disadvantages. However, the basement is a reasonable woodshop location, especially when cars, boats and motorcycles are parked in the garage.

There are many benefits to the basement shop. First, the basement

woodshop that is accessed through the house is generally more secure and less apparent to the outside world than a garage. Noise isn't as likely to bother the neighbors. Basement woodshops are warmer during the winter months, and it is both easy and comfortable to work in a basement woodshop at any time of day. For example, on especially hot summer days, basements offer a wonderful escape from the heat. Since there are no large windows and doors, there can be generous amounts of wall storage. Unlike a garage, which is constantly used for storage and foot travel, the basement is somewhat out of the main pathways and can usually be sealed off by closing a single door.

The main problems with basement woodshops are access, stairs, overhead height, ventilation, noise and dust. Moving lumber, heavy machines and finished constructions in and out of basements can be difficult because of basement stairs, hallways, corners, doors and less-than-straight-line pathways to the basement. Moving heavy objects can be further complicated by floor-to-ceiling heights, especially in stairways and around heating ducts, pipes, lights and other overhead projections.

Basement Shop Access

A typical basement might be accessed from the kitchen, often via a hallway and several doors from the garage. If you plan on using lumber, the transportation of that lumber to the basement may well cause serious family discussions! Carrying a single 10' board can easily damage doors and door frames, floor mouldings, walls, shelving, cabinets, picture frames, carpets, windows, lamps, lights and kitchen counters (along with everything on them). It's no wonder that some woodworkers have a radial arm saw in the garage for cutting boards into shorter lengths before moving them to the basement.

Installing Doors

One option for basement access is to install an exterior bulkhead hatch or cellar door. If your basement already has a cellar door, then you are set. However, if you are considering the installation of one, several factors must be considered. The cellar door requires its own foundation, normally to the same depth as the basement. That means that a hole approximately 8' × 8' × 10' will need to be dug, which may compromise existing drainage systems. The cellar door area should not interfere with plumbing pipes and electrical cables, and it should be placed where the grade is the lowest and slopes away from the foundation of the house.

Bulkheads are easier to install if your basement is constructed of cinder block, brick or stone. I considered having a bulkhead installed in our basement. Because the basement walls were solid concrete, I consulted a cellar door specialist. He said the job would not be a problem, but as we proceeded to discuss details a few red flags appeared. It would be necessary to use diamond saws to score the concrete, and both the sawing and the subsequent sledgehammer work would produce volumes of fine dust that would travel throughout the house. We decided that the work area could be isolated with plastic sheeting, but I wasn't thrilled with the idea of concrete dust floating around my stationary machines (downstairs) or my wife's kitchen (upstairs). However, what finally killed the project was that the contractor told me to remove all hanging lamps and wall-hung items from the entire house. When I asked why, he replied that the basement walls were about 12 years old and well-hardened and that the sledgehammer work would not only rattle the entire house but also pop out drywall nails throughout it. That did it. Since I wasn't willing to renail, replaster and repaint all the upstairs rooms, I decided that I could do without an outside entrance to the basement.

Reducing Irritants in the Basement Shop

It takes a very tolerant family to live with machinery noise just below their feet. The constant sound of dust collectors, the screaming sound of routers and the high-pitched whine of table saws all will travel throughout the house. Another invasive woodshop material is dust. Even when using dust collectors, dust seems to migrate to the furthest areas of the house. Fumes and odors from finishes also can permeate an entire house. Noise, dust and fumes are not the sorts of things most people want to have in their home.

Basement Shop Ventilation

Air in a basement woodshop can be damp, dry or stale. Humidity, dust, finishing fumes, mold, mildew, air circulation and ventilation all are related problems in the basement woodshop. The typical basement is more humid during the spring and summer months when the furnace isn't used; when the furnace is used, the basement dries. This alternating cycle of humidity and dryness will affect lumber and joinery by either swelling or shrinking the wood. The only effective method of moderating this cycle is to adequately moderate the air quality. Typically, the things that can be done are to cover sump pump holes, seal basement walls with sealers and basement paints, provide good air ventilation from the outside (windows and fans) and operate dehumidifiers all year long.

Tired of Working in a Gray Basement?

Do you have a basement woodshop with bare concrete walls and are you tired of the drab bomb shelter look? First brush and clean the concrete or masonry walls. If there is efflorescence, that is, a powdery substance, it is likely that moisture is seeping through the wall. Wire brush the efflorescence. It may be further necessary to clean the walls with muriatic acid (carefully follow the product's instructions) or an etching compound, which is usually safer than muriatic acid. If water is seeping through cracks or seams, seal them with a hydraulic cement. After the walls are cleaned and sealed, apply a waterproofer, such as UGL Drylok Waterproofer. This type of waterproofer is a thick paint-like material which is brushed on. It is usually available in white, but it is also available in a limited number of other colors.

One other note, if there is basement moisture and water seepage, check the outside foundation areas for how the water is percolating into the basement. Look at the condition of rain gutters, the grade angle of the soil next to the house, and poorly functioning drainage pipes. Repair the problem.

chapter *five*

Maximizing Your Shop Space

IMAGINE 100 EMPTY COLLEGE dormitory rooms. Each of those rooms has the same dimensional configuration, and each has the same furniture. Now fill those rooms with college students and wait a month or two and those rooms will no longer resemble each other. The unique personalization process will make it difficult to imagine the original sameness of the rooms. Individualism, personal interests, budgets, creativity and experience are just some of the factors that shape those rooms. The same is true in the woodshop. If 100 woodworkers were given the same size room in which to create woodshops, there would be 100 variations on woodshop layout. Be comfortable and enjoy the locale. Personalize your woodshop.

DESIGN WITH YOU IN MIND

Fundamentally, the layout of your shop should be safe, comfortable and reflect your personal style of woodworking. While it's interesting to study another woodworker's woodshop, you must always relate what you see to your own needs, tools, materials and room location. Ultimately,

the ideal woodshop is the one in which you are comfortable. Personal satisfaction is one of the main reasons for woodworking. There are too many references to the perfect woodshop in books and magazines; when I see these woodshops, I always feel that they are impersonal and lack character and individuality. Truthfully, when only you know what's on cluttered shelves and in boxes of odd and ends, or what a curious jig-type object is for, you have achieved that unique woodshop that is yours. The perfect woodshop is a concept, not a real place.

USING THE WORK TRIANGLE

A designer fad that surfaces occasionally is the work triangle. The triangle concept is based on the notion that there is a maximum efficiency pattern to a work area. It is frequently applied to kitchen layouts; that is, the work pattern between sink, refrigerator and range. The best work triangle configuration is when the sides of the triangle are equal (or nearly equal) and the total length of the sides is 14 to 22 feet. This preliminary design layout tool has some

merit when it is applied to the woodshop, if for no other reason than to determine principal work areas and efficient placement of workstations and storage locations. If the work triangle becomes too large or strangely shaped, it may be necessary to reorganize the work area layout. For example, it's of little value to have hand tool storage too far from the workbench or to have tools in an awkward location. Likewise, certain tools, machines and accessories should be located so that the operator can comfortably use them in interrelated processes (for example a bench grinder and a lathe).

In the woodshop, it's important to create a layout that is both comfortable for the woodworker and efficient. However, the work pathway might be circular, triangular or another shape. What is important is to design a layout in which there's a relationship among various work areas, traffic patterns, windows, doors and all the other features of a room. For example, many woodworkers think the workbench is the principal focal point in the woodshop. If that is so, machines, tools

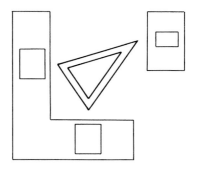

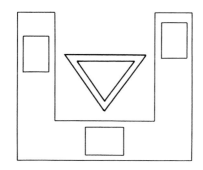

Here are some typical work triangles showing work area layout and the triangular pattern of motion between work locations.

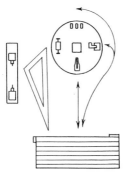

This work triangle includes a workbench, a lathe and round work surface mounted on a post.

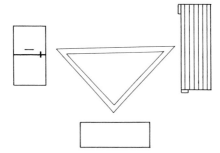

This is a work triangle between a workbench, a cabinet and a table saw.

and accessories that are used the most should be in a direct pathway to the workbench. In this case, in addition to a conveniently placed hand tool storage area, a drill press, miter saw and band saw, which are the significantly used machines, should be located 5' to 10' away from the workbench. The secondary machines — a jointer, table saw or joinery machine — would be slightly further from the workbench. Overlaying the primary and secondary work patterns are factors such as being able to move lumber freely or to avoid stepping on cables, air hoses and dust collector hoses.

BASING LAYOUT ON SEQUENTIAL WORK FLOW

Often, the experts refer to the notion that work should be done sequentially; that is, woodworking procedures can and should be done in a methodical, step-by-step sequence:

1. Rough lumber is cut to length with a radial-arm saw.
2. Rough lumber pieces are flattened, smoothed and thicknessed with a planer.
3. Rough edges are smoothed and straightened with a jointer.
4. Semifinished lumber is resawn with a band saw.
5. Resawn wood is smoothed with a jointer and planer.
6. Smoothed pieces are cut to specific lengths and widths with a table saw.
7. Joinery is done to workpieces with hand tools, router and so on.
8. Workpieces are glued and clamped.
9. Glued-up assembly is sanded.
10. Finish is applied.

If this sequence is properly followed, the layout of machines, tools, accessories and work areas would be

ranked (or used) in this order:

1. Radial arm saw
2. Workbench
3. Planer
4. Workbench
5. Jointer
6. Workbench
7. Band saw
8. Jointer
9. Planer
10. Workbench
11. Table saw
12. Workbench
13. Joinery tools
14. Workbench
15. Assembly and gluing
16. Sanding
17. Finishing

RELATING MACHINE FUNCTION TO LAYOUT CONSIDERATIONS

The recurring feature of this sequential-use list is that the workbench is used repeatedly and most machines are used for unique (limited) functions. The radial arm saw is used for cutting lumber to length, the planer is used for thicknessing and smoothing boards, the jointer is used for squaring edges, the band saw is used for making different thicknesses of lumber (resawing), the table saw is used for the final sizing of boards and joinery machines are used for cutting joints (i.e., dovetails or mortises and tenons). If this process is followed as a regular routine, it can be used as a template for woodshop layout.

Start With Initial Cutting

Begin with the premise that lumber and sheet materials should be near the woodshop entry door; that way it won't be necessary to move heavy and awkward materials through the woodshop. Station the initial cutting machine — probably the radial arm saw, panel saw or sawhorses and a circular saw — near the lumber and sheet material storage.

If a radial arm saw is set up on a long table placed against a wall, the area beneath the saw is often used for storage. I have seen several useful adaptations of this space: storage for roll-around cabinet modules, fixed cabinets and drawers and open-shelf storage for shorter pieces of wood. The size and shape of the woodshop affects which style of storage is used. In large rooms the radial-arm saw is usually some distance from the main work area. This generally makes fixed cabinets and drawers less appealing, because of the walking distance, and makes open-shelf storage more attractive. If the woodshop is small and compact, the use of modular cabinets maximizes storage and tool usage.

Facing Materials

Once lumber is cut to a manageable length, the planer is used. The planer requires an open workspace on either side. The open area is defined by the length of the longest lumber entering and exiting the planer. The traditional stationary planer is large and heavy and is usually oriented on the long axis of the woodshop. The new suitcase (or lunch box) size planers are lightweight, portable and easily moved to an open area. Since the concept of a portable planer is relatively new, most traditional woodworkers haven't gotten accustomed

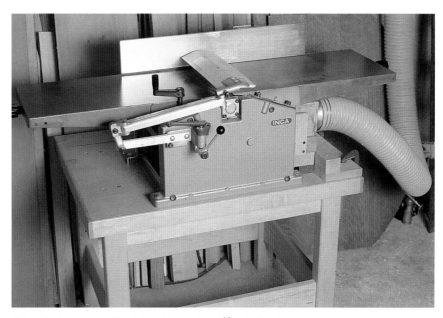

This is the Inca combination jointer/planer with 10¼" knife head.

to the idea that the planer can be stored on a shelf when it's not being used. Newer woodworkers, however, are beginning to use the planer somewhat like a router or circular saw, that is, taking it from the shelf when it's needed and then storing it away.

The jointer is often located against an uncluttered wall because, like the planer, it requires an open area for infeed and outfeed clearance. The most common jointers have 6"-wide cutter heads and 3' to 4'

bed lengths. Both planer and jointer are far more efficient if the machines have cutter heads that are the same width. Oddly, very few planers and jointers are made this way, even when they are from the same manufacturer. This is based upon the (relic) premise that jointers are used for edges and planers are used for surface widths. In reality, the best method for preparing boards (to make them flat) is to first smooth and flatten one board surface on a

Hannes Hase has a commercial business making windows and doors, and his woodshop is in an odd-shaped and odd-sized room. He uses a Felder combination machine that includes a table saw, a jointer and a planer.

The Felder machine rotates upon a swivel base so that each function is easily accessible. Note that the planer tables are raised.

wide jointer. Once the surface is flat, place the flat surface against the planer's flat surface and feed the board into the planer so that the rough side is smoothed by the cutter. This produces dimensionally flat wood, free of twists, cups and distortions. If rough lumber is fed directly into a planer without having one flattened surface, the surfaces will be planed smooth, but the board will have any twists or cups originally found in the rough lumber. The only machine solution for this woodworking dilemma is to have a wide-surface jointer.

Realistically, these machines are rather heavy, large and expensive. A worthwhile alternative is the combination jointer/planer. The advantages of this type of combination machine are twofold. First, you have one machine instead of two. Second, a variety of combination machines with cutter head widths from 10" to 24" are available, making it much easier to work with wider boards.

The basic design of the jointer/planer machine incorporates over and under the cutter head use. Jointing and flattening work is done on the top surface of the machine, as on a standard jointer; planing is accomplished by feeding the board under the table and into the lower area of the cutter head. I strongly recommend the combination jointer/planer, especially if woodshop space is limited and you want dimensionally flat and stable boards.

BAND SAWS The band saw has numerous and valuable applications, including cutting curved edges and resawing. Resawing is possibly the most useful application if only because it is nearly impossible with any other machine. Resawing lumber requires adequate space for the lumber to enter and exit the band saw. Typically, the band saw is positioned near a wall so that the cutting direction is parallel to the wall. However, if the

band saw is too close to the wall, it's difficult to use the machine for cutting curves because the workpiece will most likely rotate into the wall.

One interesting solution is locating the band saw in front of a door. When resawing long lumber is necessary, the door is opened and the cuts are made.

Secondary Cutting and Shaping

PLACING A TABLE SAW The location of the table saw requires careful consideration. The table saw is generally used as both a primary and secondary processing machine. Primarily, it is used to cut long, wide boards to smaller lengths, or to cut full-size sheets of man-made materials to smaller sizes. Secondary work consists of the final shaping of boards, cutting joints, grooves, dadoes and moulding profiles. Each of these elements has specific design requirements. Primary processing requires adequate area around the table saw to permit the handling of large boards and sheets. This means that there should be both infeed and outfeed space for the safe handling of materials. Under no cir-

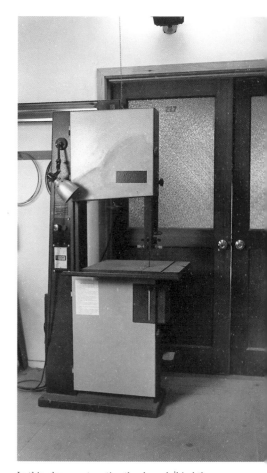

In this placement, notice the doors behind the band saw. They can be opened when the saw is being used for resawing long boards.

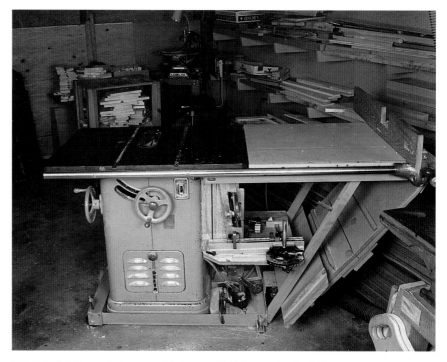

Tom Dailey's table saw features a mobile base and fold-down extension table.

cumstances should material bump, or be deflected by, surrounding tables, cabinets or other woodshop items. The operator should have absolute control of large pieces while using the table saw. Many experienced woodworkers attach support tables on either side and on the outfeed side of the

The Inca saw has a shop-made router table inserted between the saw's main table and extension. The router table compartment is sealed, with a dust collection port mounted on the back side.

table saw to support oversized boards and sheets. Never attempt to cut a full-size sheet of plywood or particleboard on a table saw that doesn't have ancillary support tables. The sheer weight of plywood held suspended in air over the back of the table saw by the operator, plus the spinning saw blade, is an accident waiting to happen. Furthermore, using the table saw to crosscut the ends of long boards is also foolhardy.

DO YOU NEED A SHAPER? Ten to twenty years ago it was fairly common to find shapers as part of the standard woodshop machinery. However, many new woodworkers think that the router table replaces the shaper. I don't think that the router table actually replaces the shaper, but many woodworkers rely on the router table as the principal machine for making dadoes and grooves, shaping edges, joinery and frame and panel constructions. Part of the reason for this popularity is that there are many magazine articles featuring router tables: The router is a very popular tool and there are hundreds of different router bits. The sophistication of the router is a modern success story. Plunge routers with variable speeds and 2 to 5 hp are now very common. And there are now routers specifically designed to work upside down under a router table.

The shaper as a machine of choice has fallen out of favor due to several factors. The shaper hasn't

Dean Bershaw's cabinetmaker's table saw features an oversize table area. This permanently installed table makes the handling and cutting of sheet materials much easier. The table is large enough to also support a planer machine.

Doug Matthews added a modest-size table to his table saw. Note how the Workmate holds an outfeed roller at the back of the table saw.

changed all that much during this time of the router table development, and many hobby woodworkers feel that the shaper is more dangerous than a router table. This fear, distrust and rejection of shapers is, I think, based upon several perceptions: Shapers have large cutters that make large cuts, thus appearing more aggressive (i.e, more dangerous); shaper cutters are more expensive than router bits, and shapers are more expensive than routers; common router functions are improved and made easier when done with router tables; and shapers haven't really been marketed to hobby woodworkers.

A custom stand for a jointer and a sander is in the Dailey shop. Note the dust collection system.

Actually, there are several important and real differences between the two machines. One of the main differences is that, excluding special adapters, shaper cutters are designed to cut board edges. Shapers operate in the 6,000 to 10,000 RPM range; while variable-speed routers run at 8,000 to 24,000 RPM. Also, the more professional shaper models have tilting spindles, forward and reverse switches and interchangeable ½", ¾", 1" and 1½" spindles.

WILL A ROUTER TABLE DO? Router tables allow both edge work and board surface work. However, in spite of the large-diameter router bit trend, routers are limited to ¼", ⅜" and ½" shanks. Even with a router set at 8,000 RPM, I have never felt comfortable using 2" (or greater diameter) router bits. If I do use a larger router bit, I make many light passes, raising the bit ever so slightly until the final cut is made. In my opinion, router tables are very useful with piloted bits and for cutting dadoes, grooves, rabbets, finger joints and other light cuts requiring cutter bit diameters of ¾" or less. The general safety rule is: Use lower RPM speeds for heavier and larger diameter cutters.

PLACING A SHAPER OR ROUTER TABLE Whether it's a shaper or a router table, there are several essential layout considerations. Both of these machines require space for moving wood in and away from the machines. And they both require rock-solid stability: Under no circumstances should these machines be unbalanced when they are used. Many shapers feature right-angle feet attachments so that they are easily bolted to the floor. I have seen few router tables bolted to the floor, and yet, they are used to cut grooves in 8' lengths of plywood. Just imagine the suspended weight of this wood as it exits the cutter and is hanging on the outfeed side of the router table. Shapers are generally constructed with the motor located in the lower areas of the body, creating a lower center of gravity that helps to stabilize the machine. In order to stabilize router tables, the framework or body should be as large as possible. If you are making a router table out of plywood, adding drawers near the floor (and filling them with tools) will enhance stability. Tim Hewitt at HTC (makers of metal mobile bases) has sold many bases for both shapers and router tables. His product stabilizes these machines because the mobile base has three wheels externally located on a welded metal frame. The location of the wheels is important because being outside of the machine and frame increases the footprint size of the machine. HTC has had no complaints or problems relating to shaper or router table stability.

Both machines have three active sides — the infeed, the outfeed and an open side. All three require that the adjacent areas be clear of obstructions. The fourth side, the side behind the fence, is usually positioned near a wall. Shaper and router table space requirements are determined by the length of workpieces. If, for example, frame-and-panel cabinet doors are the only thing made, the clear area should be no less than 4' on the three active sides. However, if you are shaping or routing entry door pieces or floor-to-ceiling cabinet sides, the clear area for the infeed and outfeed directions should be at least 10'.

Using a Joinery Machine

The compact joinery machine is relatively new to the woodworking world, but because of its usefulness, it's being found in more and more woodshops. This machine has a router mounted horizontally and permits cutting action along X, Y and Z axes. That is, the horizontal router can be moved up and down, and the table holding the workpiece moves in and out and side to side. These machines allow for the efficient cutting of mortises and tenons, dovetails, finger joints and such.

Because this machine is used for

Here is the Multi-Router joinery machine with a custom-made dust hookup.

joinery, the workpieces are shorter and smaller, thus not requiring large open areas around the machine. I use a Multi-Router joinery machine mounted on a mobile base, and when I need it, I move it from a storage area to a suitable work area. In use, a joinery machine probably is easier to manage when it's near the workbench. For example, if you are making a set of six ladderback chairs, that translates into 102 pieces, 156 mortises and 156 tenons. That's quite a few pieces to keep tidy. The workbench is ideal for sorting, organizing and keeping track of all the pieces and their joinery situations. The only drawback to this machine is that the horizontally mounted router flings

dust and chips over a wide area, like a geyser of dust.

If you plan on using this machine near clean areas, I would suggest that you construct some sort of dust collection device. Factor the location of a joinery machine into your layout and provide for a 4" or 5" flexible dust collection hose to dangle directly over the router bit area. That way, the discharged debris will be caught while it's airborne. Normally, dust collector ductwork is attached to specific machines and is rarely dangled near the workbench. If you do place a dangling collection hose near the workbench, be certain to add a open/close gate or a large plug at the end of the hose: There is no reason

Here are simple workstands for a planer and a drill press.

to have an open hose anywhere in the woodshop, especially near the workbench.

MOVING AROUND THE SHOP

Once the sawing, planing and joinery are finished, all that is left are the final stages of woodworking: assembly, gluing, sanding and finishing. These stages all require space — both for your movement while working and calm space while the workpiece is glued, clamped and finished.

Open Up Space With Mobile Tools

Most small woodshops are tightly organized, with walkways, and little open space. Yet, assembly and finishing require open space. Generally, the solution is to move equipment out of the way to open up space; moving equipment can be facilitated if machines are mounted on mobile bases. However, heavy machines without mobile bases probably shouldn't be moved. Dragging a machine across the woodshop will most likely injure you and damage the machine and floor. Commercially made mobile bases are available for just

about any machine. HTC has a catalog offering a comprehensive supply of well-made bases for any type and brand of tool. They also will make customized bases for older or unique machines.

If you decide to make a mobile base, don't make it so that the machine is easily tipped or the wheels are too large. It's very easy to make custom stands, just make the wood frame as low to the floor as possible, use lockable caster wheels, and design it so the wheels are off the floor and out of the way when the machine is used.

Harry Charowsky has a modest-size woodshop and all his machines, tables and workbench are on mobile bases of his own design. He uses an outdoor covered area adjacent to the woodshop to move the machines into when he's not using them. Harry installed a removable threshold to make it easier to move heavy machines through the door. The threshold is a wide board with an attached standard-size threshold. It simply rests on the concrete and tightly seals the room from outside air when

the door is closed. When he needs to move things, he just lifts it out and then there is no bump to impede moving things in and out.

Focus on the Workbench to Save Space

Another common assembly solution is to use the workbench for the final woodworking steps. The problem with using the workbench for assembly, gluing and finishing is that workbenches aren't necessarily wide enough for some furniture and cabinet constructions. And the workpiece is usually too high for comfortable work. A workbench height of 12" to 24" is ideal for assembling furniture; however, a bench at this height is useless for many other projects. A simple solution is to have low sawhorses to temporarily support a sheet of plywood, particleboard or MDF. Assembly and clamping require a perfectly flat surface, so the sheet material should rest as flat as possible on the sawhorses. I've seen many woodshops that have the sheet material attached with screws to a simple frame, which is nothing more than four edge pieces and several cross-frame pieces. When it's not in use, the flat-surfaced assembly is leaned against a wall or used as a catchall for general woodshop use. Once the sheet material is worn out (chipped, gouged, dried glue spots, etc.), simply flip it over and use the other side until it too is hopeless, and then replace it with a fresh sheet.

Plan for Glue-Up and Assembly Space

I have bruised myself more during the slow time that occurs while a workpiece is clamped than during the entire construction process. Why? I think it's because I've lowered my guard. While sawing, planing and so on, I am very focused on what I'm doing. But after the workpiece is clamped up and just sitting there, I'm usually cleaning up, putting tools away and not paying much attention to that clamp handle protruding out into the walkway. Therefore, leg and hip bruises. The moral of this tale is that clamped workpieces require an out-of-the-way place because of their disruption of normally open spaces. Or, you could simply leave the room while the glue dries.

Don't Forget About Ceiling Height

So far, woodshop layout has mainly focused on floor area. The other dimension that should be factored into layout plans is floor-to-ceiling height. While it may be impossible to increase the height within an existing woodshop, there are several things that you can do to maximize floor-to-ceiling height.

The most troublesome feature of woodshop height is the difficulty involved in moving long boards. Even if you are primarily lathe turning, carving or doing other small-scale projects, there will be times when lifting lumber is required. Lifting and transporting lumber is further complicated by the location and height of machines, workbenches, hanging objects and storage units. Furthermore, light fixtures are often lower than the ceiling. Moving an 8' board can make you feel as if you are jousting with the dark knight or battering down the castle wall!

Obviously, if you are designing a new woodshop, the simplest thing to do is to increase the floor-to-ceiling height. Ceiling heights of up to 12' will make almost any woodworking easier. When a new house is being built over a basement of concrete blocks, inquire about having one or two additional rows added to the basement walls so that there will be more overhead room. (I'm sure the additional construction expense will be negated when you use the basement woodshop, plus the additional height will probably increase the value of your house.)

Dealing With Low Ceilings

If you are setting up your woodshop in an existing garage or basement, there are several methods of dealing with standard room height.

1. Recess all light fixtures flush to the ceiling.
2. If fluorescent lights are suspended below the ceiling, install the fluorescent lights in commercially available clear safety tubes (if the light is broken, the glass shards remain in the plastic tube).
3. Remove or minimize all objects that hang from the ceiling (unnecessary light cord and so on).
4. Position machines and storage units next to a wall when moving long items. Having an open center area in the woodshop will facilitate moving long lumber.
5. Rough cut long lumber outside the woodshop.
6. If there's a window, use it for negotiating long lumber into the woodshop.
7. If the ceiling is paneled or finished, consider removing the ceiling material so that the rafters are exposed. The open area between rafters, especially above the workbench area is useful for maneuvering boards. The exposed rafters also permit additional storage and places to hang items. Dust collector ducts, air lines and wiring can be routed above rafters.
8. Work within your limits. If you do have a small and cramped woodshop, be realistic and build things that fit in the room. It is dangerous and frustrating attempting to build large items when the room size is more suited to small, handheld-size items.

Planning for Dust Collection

No matter how the final woodworking stages are done, it is a process that effects the entire woodshop — and sometimes the nearby living quarters. The most obvious by-product of this stage is sanding dust and finishing product fumes. Additionally, the woodshop may even be more cramped while a finish is drying. These factors affect woodshop layout in the following manner: Since dust and fumes can be controlled by proper collection and ventilation, it makes sense to arrange the woodshop accordingly. Set up the dust collector and sanding and finishing areas away from doors and windows — there is no need having air currents spreading dust over a wider area. Design the layout so that dust doesn't travel more than 1' to 2' from the work area. If possible, have the dust collector hidden behind a partition or screen. Even the ceiling-mounted air filtration units can circulate fine dust, and it may be necessary to reposition it until a minimum circulation of dust is determined. By minimizing dust, there is less work when applying finishes. Cleaning the entire woodshop is a tedious chore complicated by waiting for airborne dust to settle before being able to apply a finish. In fact, oil finishes are probably popular simply because they don't need a dust-free woodshop. Varnishes and, to some degree, lacquers, don't take kindly to fine dust. If you do have a dust contamination problem associated with varnish applications, there are many finishing books with instructions on how to rub out rough varnish finishes.

chapter *six*

Customizing Your Woodshop

THERE ISN'T A FORMULA FOR the ideal woodshop. There is you, your requirements, your budget and your expertise. Don't get sidetracked by the unnecessary.

Sam Maloof, a great American woodworker, tells the story about being approached many years ago by several very earnest engineers. They had slide rules (definitely pre-calculator), protractors, tape measures and clipboards filled with charts. Their quest was to determine the proper heights, widths, lengths and shapes to construct the ideal chair. They wanted to interview Sam about his chairs, because Sam made the most comfortable wood chairs around. (In my opinion, they are even more comfortable than upholstered and pillowed chairs.) These bright and well-meaning engineers were looking for a formula, a template, or a system of shapes and angles for building something that would apply to everyone. Sam was amused by their questions, because he didn't have a formula or a chart for building his chairs. He told them that he built a chair by feel: He sat in it, and if he was comfortable then the

chair's owner would also be comfortable. The young engineers left, scratching their heads and pondering this natural approach to chair design.

NO TWO SHOPS ARE ALIKE

This story relates to designing woodworking shops because I've never met two woodworkers that have woodshops of the same shape or size.

Nor have I met two woodworkers that have the same tools, machines, lumber pile or specific woodworking style. And these differences exist even though woodworkers tend to read the same books and magazines. There are simply too many personal features, budgets, locations and room configurations for there to be significant similarities between woodshops

Luthier Robert Girdis had used a small room for many years to make beautiful guitars.

Let's say you just purchased a house with an extra building, such as the one shown in the three photos on this page. How would you design both the ground-level and loft spaces into a woodshop?

This is the ground-level view of your imaginary new building.

— or for me to say there is a uniform woodshop design. I know a lathe turner who specializes in turning miniature objects, and yet her woodshop is large enough to park an airplane in it. I also know woodworkers who have full shops in single-car, low-ceiling garages and are building plywood cases and cabinets. To illustrate one very simple problem in generalizing woodshop design, suppose that two woodworkers have bought exactly the same tools and plan on setting up a woodshop in order to build exactly the same wood projects. The only difference is their woodshop configuration: One is a 12' × 30' rectangle with two doors and windows on three walls; the other is a 19' × 19' square with no windows and one door. Even though both woodshops have approximately 360 square feet, it doesn't take much to visualize that wall storage, machine placement and overhead lighting will be very different for the two woodshops. Windows and a second door create such limitations that only creatively designed storage units are effective.

What is appropriate for designing a woodshop is considering a standard set of variables that more or less apply to every woodshop. Sort of the "food, clothes and shelter" basics of the woodshop. For woodshops these elements would be: woodshop location, interest, finances, machinery, tools and storage.

Study existing woodshops. In spite of the inevitable differences with your future woodshop, existing woodshops do offer ideas and potential problem-solving solutions. Study machine locations, especially their relationship to other machines and open space (work areas). Note the locations of workbenches and storage areas for frequently used tools. Other principal concerns are lumber storage, finishing supply storage, finishing areas, clamp storage, electrical outlets, dust collection ducts and openings. Ask "Why did you do that?" and take note of the response.

START WITH PEOPLE YOU KNOW

To find woodshops, first talk with friends and neighbors who do woodworking. Because they are friends and neighbors, you probably can trust their advice. Joining local woodworking clubs and guilds is also a great source of information. Generally, woodworkers join these clubs to share information. And you will find that, because most of them have gone through the struggle of designing woodshops, they aren't shy about sharing their solutions.

This is the loft of your space.

Look at Schools and Pro Shops

Schools and professional woodworking shops, although they are tempting as sources of information, aren't necessarily useful for home-woodshop applications. That's because schools and professionals don't have the same purposes, room sizes, machines and tools, budgets and interests as the home woodworker. A school might be a repository of machinery valued by teachers with specific points of view; the professional woodshop might rely on expensive processing machines with no hand tool applications whatsoever. Having said that, if the opportunity arises for you to visit these woodshops, do it, and then use the information as a benchmark of a different woodworking evolution.

Additional Shops to Check Out

Other woodshops that might offer some value, if for no other reason than studying storage solutions, air filtration and workbenches, are those used by artists, jewelers, painters and auto mechanics. These woodshops will have single-purpose applications, yet each offers unique problem-solving solutions. As you study these shops, remember that your woodshop will be generalized in nature, but how a sculptor or mechanic stores tools can be invaluable information.

MAKE YOUR MASTER PLAN

All designs evolve from somewhere. There are historical and personal factors in how we perceive environmental needs. The woodshop is not some haphazard, all-of-a-sudden wild card sent to you from Mars. Typically, home woodshop design is developed from:

- what others have done
- what magazine and book editors think is important
- movies and TV
- how schools design classroom woodshops
- how commercial businesses set up for efficiency
- having a space and randomly setting up shop

Because woodworking seems like a "practical" craft, the woodshop is often set up and arranged as if it were an antiseptic, nonpersonalized

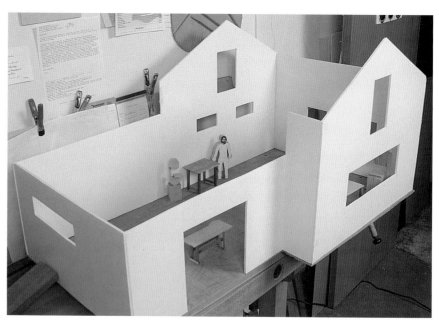

Before construction ever began, Robert Girdis built a mock-up of his ideal woodshop.

Here's the Girdis woodshop under construction. The woodshop is located on the house property.

room. Consider this: How many woodshops have you ever seen that have an individualistic flare? And, I don't mean handmade benches, cabinets and such. How often are there pictures of family, a bulletin board with drawings or even a potted plant? How different is the layout or how creative is the use of space?

I have visited many woodshops and have come to divide woodshops into two camps: the utilitarian and the artistic. The particular woodworking emphasis is not important in this observation. Carvers, turners and furniture makers are all subject to the same two divisions. What is important is the attitude and personality of the woodworker.

The utilitarian woodshop relies on a no-nonsense approach to work. Machines and cabinets are rigidly

You see here the corner and the workbench in the finished Girdis woodshop.

This is the completed Rob Girdis woodshop. The main building measures 24' × 24', and the attached secondary room measures 20' × 20'. The side walls are 13' high, and it is 21' to the roof peak.

arranged, there is a formality to tool location and the woodworker has to adapt to the limitations of the room. These woodshops seem to be extensions of the machines and the work materials and less of the owner. Well-crafted cabinets, workbenches or other man-made shop aids, while usually lending an air of the owner's skill, aren't the issue. I'm referring to the overall nature of the woodshop. Stuff is organized, and there is a sense that anyone visiting for the first time could quite easily use the woodshop. The emphasis is on production or, arguably, on conformity. That is, "Everyone else has a woodshop that looks like this, so I will do the same."

I feel that the "practical" and "production" part of woodworking is greatly overdone. While it is true that there is a need for organization and step-by-step construction methods, unless you are in a 40 to 60 hours per week woodworking business, you are building things for other reasons than production. Yet, woodworking is steeped in the lore of thousands of years of woodworking with the interpretation that objects were made for

Dave Buck's in-the-forest woodshop measures 24' × 32' with a 6' roof overhang for working outside — and staying dry.

practical reasons. Everything we know and use has some historic connection to wood. There is little doubt regarding the usefulness (practicality) of most historic wooden objects and the tools used to make them. But we are now in a different time, with very different values than people had in 1940, 1840 or 1240! As a result of today's large population there certainly are quite a few woodworkers. However, in terms of the actual percent of careers, there are few people earning a livelihood at plane-and-saw woodworking. There is a large contingent of hobby woodworkers and more artist woodworkers than ever before. Leisure and hobby are now integral facets of woodworking.

Few machines and tools are really as cost effective as would be necessary in a competitive business. Certainly, the nostalgia for a "traditional" woodshop is appealing, but it should not be the sole element for designing a woodshop. For the most part, we make things with wood because we like to make things with wood. But we still attempt to design our woodshops from two different styles. The first interpretation is that the woodshop should look somewhat like an early American or Arts-and-Crafts-era woodshop. The second design notion is that the woodshop should look like an Early American or Arts-and-Crafts-style woodshop, but it should also include the ability to turn out thousands of widgets a day!

The artistic woodshop is more of an interpretation of the owner's viewpoint and lifestyle. There is use of paint, other than white, and the use of decoration. These woodshops are rare, but they are delightful. It's amazing what a few drawings, pictures or small objects can do for a room. Not all woodshop time is devoted to pushing wood through a machine, and the artistic woodshop offers objects for reflection or visitor curiosity. There is a definite sense of the woodworker in these woodshops.

My sense is that these rooms have evolved from conceptualizing the work spaces of fine art painters, sculptors or interior designers. Often, there is less reliance on having excessive tools. Instead, there are enough tools and machinery for the purpose of the owner. What I have seen and heard from this type of woodworker convinces me that they have very specific intentions for using their woodshop, while at the same time, they have the woodshop reflect their ideas and sensibilities. And they aren't distracted by the newest gizmo and accessory — unless it fits a need. In fact, some actually have an indifference to tools because they prefer to concentrate on the things they make. The emphasis is on making ob-

John MacKenzie rescued an old chicken coop and brought it to his home property. After rebuilding it, he landscaped and decorated the woodshop exterior so that it became part of a pleasant backyard.

Doug Matthews built a barn-shaped woodshop to visually fit the rural setting where he lives; note his home is located near the woodshop. Doug restores and repairs antique furniture and has just set up a showroom in the woodshop's second floor area to display and sell antique furniture.

This is the exterior of Steve Balter's shop.

Steve Balter has a display room in the front of his workshop.

jects and less about having "one of everything." Functionally there is often more open space and better lighting. Since there is less stockpiling of tools, there is less premium on storage.

The utilitarian, no-nonsense design is like a navy submarine. That is, there is the sense that once submerged in work, the sub/woodshop is isolated and requires total self-sufficiency. This woodshop, like the submarine, requires incredible nook-and-cranny storage for all the things that might be needed. The artistic woodshop, while having the necessary tools plus a bit of the frivolous, is more like a backpacker's pack in its simplicity: You might choose to leave some essentials behind, while making room in your pack for a favorite book.

After you have conceptualized your woodshop design, it's time to make a master plan. The master plan is a general plan of room size, potential features and tools. These are, in turn, filtered through your woodworking discipline and style. Create this plan with as much intensity and enthusiasm as possible. Plan as if designing a kitchen or master bedroom. Obviously, the master plan can be changed as you proceed with developing the woodshop. However, the master plan is the ideal starting point. It will be the first visualization of your future woodshop.

Choose Your Tooling and Storage

Make a list of all the machines, the tools and the storage areas that you ultimately will want.

FURNITURE OR CABINETRY SHOP If you want to build furniture, consider:
- workbench
- drill press
- table saw
- disc/belt sander
- band saw
- joinery machine
- router table or shaper
- dust collector
- jointer
- scroll saw
- planer
- air compressor

Also consider storage cabinets and shelves for:
- routers
- biscuit joiner
- drills
- clamps
- sanders
- hand tools
- spray equipment
- finishing supplies
- air tools
- lumber and plywood

WOODCARVING SHOP
- workbench
- dust collector
- band saw
- scroll saw
- grinder (powered sharpening device)
- drill press
- disc/belt sander

And storage cabinets and shelves for:
- rotary carving tools
- clamps
- sanders
- drills
- burrs and bits for rotary tool
- finishing supplies
- assorted hand tools (carving chisels and mallets)
- lumber and small pieces of wood

WOODTURNING SHOP
- lathe
- drill press
- workbench
- dust collector
- band saw
- grinder (or a powered sharpening device)

And storage cabinets and shelves for:
- lathe tools
- lathe accessories
- drills
- hand tools
- sanders
- finishing supplies
- sanding supplies and sandpaper
- lumber, blocks, logs and small pieces of wood

MISCELLANEOUS NEEDS List all other important features that are useful for any woodshop:

- electrical service panel
- electrical outlets (110V and 220V)
- plumbing (sinks, toilets and so on)
- secondary lighting (spotlights)
- windows
- doors
- containers for scrap wood

Design the Woodshop on Paper

Use ¼" grid paper and use a scale of ¼" = 1'. First, draw the shape of the woodshop. Include all permanent elements of the room, such as support beams, steps, water heaters. On another sheet of paper, draw representational shapes of all machines, shelves and storage units and cut them out with scissors (or copy the images on page 283 and use those). Now, try the cutouts in different locations on the floor-plan drawing. Note the way that open space or machine positions differ from your preconceptions of an idealized layout. It may seem that particular machines, which should be easy to place, become difficult to locate because of windows or doors. Storage units may have to be modified from original designs because of machine placement or electrical outlets.

Designing With a Paper Grid and Paper Tools

Obviously, it's easier to move pieces of paper than machines and cabinets, and the benefits of this technique are far-reaching. Generally, the problem with home woodshops is too little space, not too much space. Placing items becomes a struggle toward efficiency. When arranging the paper cutouts, it might become apparent that the floor plan and machinery don't match. There may not be enough space for your needs. It may be impossible to have a comfortable blend of machines, cabinets, safe areas around machines and open work areas. The paper cutouts will aid in this discovery, which is part of the reason that you should include every possible item on the master plan list. Don't leave out machines and shop furniture that will be acquired in the future. Even if the purchase of something is several years off, include it in the master plan. All too often the owner of a cramped woodshop will spend too much time attempting to overcome the problem of space limitations. Storage becomes convoluted, machines are too close together and, instead of working on projects, time is spent either moving things around or finding, or hiding, objects. Be prepared for future acquisitions.

Planning for the Future

Here's an issue that's complicated and somewhat vexing: How do you know how to start out compared to where you will end up? Perhaps you've seen beautiful handmade furniture, bowls and carvings at a craft fair, and this has inspired you to take up woodworking. But you've had no woodworking lessons or experiences with other woodworkers. What do you do to get started? Let's assume that you read woodworking books and magazines, watch do-it-yourself videos and visit tool stores. All of these are very inspirationally produced by experts. But do these sources really help you to find a starting place? The question is, will you make furniture, turn bowls or carve? What if you set up a woodshop for carving and later find that lathe-turned bowls are your real interest?

Relax. When you create the master plan, realize that most machines are for general-purpose applications. Table saws and band saws aren't designed for single-purpose use. However, carving chisels and lathe tools are single-purpose tools. Fortunately, you can start out with a half dozen of these tools and not spend a large sum of money. And if you decide that carving isn't for you, it's easy to sell them. If you aren't certain of the type of woodworking you want to pursue, initially stay as general as possible, realizing that some tools are worth purchasing, if for no other reason than for experimentation.

BUDGETING FOR SHOP SETUP

If you are setting up a woodshop for the first time and have never purchased machinery, tools and supplies, don't get discouraged. I have talked with hundreds of beginning woodworkers and heard many very similar questions. Usually beginning woodworkers have specific budget amounts and space limitations as their first priorities. These conditions are quickly followed by questions about what type of machinery and hand tools should be purchased. After these issues, questions follow about specific brands, where to purchase machinery and tools, what books and magazines are recommended and where one can find how-to and hands-on instruction. The response to these questions is like the solution to a complicated mathematics problem: Start at the beginning, do your step-by-step work on paper, and progress through every step until the solution is found.

Translating that type of formula into designing a woodshop is straightforward. Suppose that your budget is $3,000 for machinery and tools, the potential woodshop area has 200 square feet, and you are planning on generalized woodworking for yourself and your family. First, what will $3,000 purchase? Make a list of possible selections. Also factor into this list whether you are planning to purchase locally or through mail-order catalogs and whether you prefer machines made in the U.S.A. or those made in foreign countries.

Prioritize Your Purchases

Obviously both lists are over budget, and neither list includes hand tools,

Potential Machines and Costs

LIST A		LIST B	
Cabinetmaker's table saw	$1,600	Contractor's table saw	$800
15" stationary planer	1,000	12" portable planer	400
6" stationary jointer	1,300	6" portable jointer	300
12" band saw	900	10" band saw	350
Heavy-duty lathe	2,000	Benchtop lathe	450
16½" floor drill press	400	Benchtop drill press	100
Scroll saw	500	Scroll saw	200
Cyclone dust collector with duct	1,000	2-bag dust collector on rollers	400
3-hp plunge router	280	1½-hp standard router	200
Router table w/additional router	400	Router table only	100
Plate jointer	200	Plate jointer	200
14V cordless drill	210	12V cordless drill	185
Finish sander	80	Finish sander	80
4" x 24" belt sander	225	3" x 21" belt sander	170
Total	**$10,095**	**Total**	**$3,935**

sharpening supplies, sandpaper and so on. The next step is to prioritize the tool list and purchase the most important items first. For general-purpose woodworking, the scroll saw and lathe may not be necessary. However, design the woodshop location as if all the listed machines and tool items were available. It's much easier to create the layout requirements in the planning stage than to retrodesign a woodshop when space is unavailable or wasn't factored into construction plans.

If you plan on cutting large amounts of plywood and can't decide between a cabinetmaker's table saw (e.g., Delta's Unisaw), because you think it would be more advantageous for this procedure, and a contractor's table saw, because it better fits your space, consider the following alternative. Size plywood into smaller sections with a circular saw or jigsaw by cutting approximately ⅛" wider than the measured layout lines and cleaning the rough-cut plywood edges using a router, a straight bit and a clamped straightedge. Or construct auxiliary tables on both sides and outfeed areas of the table saw so that the plywood is manageable during cutting.

When I started woodworking, I had only a vague concept of what tools to purchase. At that time, there were no magazines devoted to woodworking and the hardware stores were primarily devoted to the trade (i.e., contractors and builders). And 20-some years ago, the main articles in the mechanic-type magazines were either "Table Saws Versus Radial-Arm Saws" or "How To Build a Plywood Dingy." It was difficult to find information or sources for antique tools, specialty tools, foreign-made tools or high-quality tools. Over the years, I have purchased a variety of table saws, routers, drills and assorted gadgets. Most of my earlier purchases have been replaced with upgraded versions, and the original tools were sold through the newspaper classified section. The point is, your skills, pocketbook and interests change with time. If you know what you want now, that's great. But don't worry if you aren't sure — you will know in time. So if you can't afford a particu-

lar machine at the moment, purchase something that is affordable and upgrade later on. If you want to try something different, go ahead and try it. If it isn't right for you, it's easy to resell most tools; there's always eBay.

PLANNING STORAGE

The storage in most woodshops that have evolved over years of use is generally haphazard. It's common to see cabinets built in odd locations because the space was unused or was too awkward for other uses. When a woodshop is properly planned and designed, cabinets and shelves fit the room and present an orderliness that makes work easier. If possible, construct storage cabinets in modular units. A set of smaller cabinets is easier to build and easier to move within the room. For example, a 9'-long wall is available for cabinets. It's conceivable that one 9' cabinet could be installed. However, it's difficult to build something that large and then install it. It would be much better to build a set of three cabinets, each 3' long. In fact, build one as a start, and then build the others as the need for more storage arises.

Make paper cutouts of generic rectangular shapes to represent potential storage units. If the storage is wall-mounted above another unit or apparatus, color the elements different colors so that they are visually separated.

Storage Options:

- floor to ceiling
- wall-mounted above machines or benches
- under stairs
- under machines
- flush fit between wall studs
- overhead in rafters

PLANNING MACHINE LOCATION

Two general rules apply to the locations of the major machines — table saw, radial-arm saw, jointer, planer and band saw, in the shop. First, cer-

Tom Dailey's woodshop is located in a ground-level basement. Plywood is brought in through the back door, then cut with a panel saw.

tain machines, like the jointer and radial arm saw, are only used from one side. Second, there has to be enough room around other machines, such as the table saw and planer, for wood to enter and exit the machine. When using the paper cutouts, a logical starting point is to place the one-side-only machines against walls. Optionally, certain machines can be grouped together, such as placing the jointer and planer side by side. But make sure to allow enough space for long boards to safely clear a machine without bumping into other woodshop items. For example, if a heavy board 2" × 8" × 80" is processed on a jointer, the operator not only has to maintain the board on the machine, but he also has to be able to take the board from the outfeed table and not ram it against other woodshop items. In other words, the entry and exit areas around certain machines must be clear: This space is as important as the space the machine occupies.

Table Saw

If full sheets of plywood are routinely cut, place the saw centrally in the woodshop and build secondary support tables. Keep the pathway to and from the table saw unobstructed so that the plywood can be safely handled and moved. For small woodshops, panel saws are an alternative to the table saw. These are wall-mounted units that support the plywood, with a track-mounted circular saw for making the cuts.

Radial-Arm Saw

If long boards are routinely cut with a radial saw, the saw should be placed against a wall, with long secondary support tables on either side. Many woodworkers with basement woodshops set up a radial-arm saw in the garage and perform rough cuts there, and then move the shorter pieces to the woodshop. Note: If the radial-arm saw is in the garage and away from the main woodshop, it should be equipped with a lock for the on/off switch. This prevents children or other curious types from turning on the saw when the owner isn't present.

Band Saw

If the band saw is used primarily for ripping and resawing long boards, it too can be located against a wall. The work is moved parallel to the wall, providing a clear pathway for board entry and exit from the blade. However, if the band saw is used to make curved cuts, the board is moved in a radial manner, much like a clock hand, with the blade at the center point. For this type of use, the band saw should be more centered in the woodshop, away from walls.

Dust Collector

The dust collector, although very useful, has to be one of the most difficult machines to place in the woodshop. It has an awkward shape, and certain models radiate fine dust and noise. Ductwork, gates and connectors are also potential complications. If you don't want multiple ducts or hoses, there are portable collectors with short lengths of hose, that can be placed near a machine. This method only works if you're doing limited work with the floor free of obstructions. The best method is placing the dust collector somewhere away from the work area and using ducts to the machines.

To control the dust that settles around a collector, and to reduce the noise level, the dust collector can be located in a closet-type of room. If you choose to do this, be certain that there is air flow into the room. Cut a square hole in the door and cover it with a furnace filter. The filter keeps dust from exiting the room, and the hole will reduce air pressure within the room. I've seen a dust collector room that, when the collector was running, created so much air pressure that the door couldn't be opened. That isn't wise.

Miscellaneous Tools and Machines

A number of machines are used to primarily process shorter lengths of wood. This allows for some freedom in floor plan use. The drill press, router table, shaper, scroll saw and joinery machines can be located in less open areas. Occasionally, the router table or shaper is used for longer pieces; the machines can then be moved for these specific operations.

PLAN FOR ELECTRICAL AND PLUMBING NEEDS

When a new building is under construction, there is a sequence to the order of events. That is, electricians and plumbers complete their work before drywallers and painters. While this sequence should apply when converting a basement or garage into a woodshop, the electrical wiring and plumbing are often undervalued. It is not uncommon to see that the one or two existing outlets in the garage or basement are overused with extension cords and extension bars. If there is a laundry sink or toilet already in the garage or basement, it is usually left as is. Wouldn't it seem to be much smarter to upgrade both the electrical systems and plumbing while designing the woodshop?

Wiring the Shop

The importance of having a proper electrical service cannot be overstated. First, I advise against using very long extension cords. Not only do they create more floor clutter, but long extension cords can lead to unnecessary electrical motor wear. A representative from an air compressor company once told me that the majority of compressors returned for motor repairs were those that were used with extension cords. Apparently, owners forgot that longer air hoses were a better way to work at a distance from the compressor. I have one retractable ceiling-mounted extension cord in my woodshop. It's 30'-long 14/3 SJT wire and rated at 13A, 125V, 1,625 watts. I only use it with hand drills, finish sanders and similar tools. I would never use it for band saws and other stationary machines.

The placement of machines relative to the proper outlet is fundamental. If you want to use the table saw at a particular location, then having an isolated 110V or 220V outlet at that location is mandatory. Since this section is about guidelines for designing the woodshop, the key factors are: wiring from an existing service panel (interior or exterior to the wall), installing a subpanel, outlet locations and location of lights.

Interior wiring is difficult when the wall studs and ceiling rafters are already covered. The standard technique is to cut holes in the wall or ceiling and "fish" the new wires in place using a fish tape tool. New wiring that is not within walls should be run through metal conduits that are firmly attached to the walls. If the room framework is still exposed, it's straightforward to run wiring through the studs, around windows and door frames to the service. Subpanels are a very good choice when upgrading the woodshop. They are easily mounted near the main service panel, and conduit can then be routed anywhere in the woodshop.

The design of the outlets should accommodate both the placement of machines and the use of electrical tools at various locations. There should be outlets near both ends and at the center of the workbench, as well as outlets near the open areas in the woodshop that can be used for assembly and detail work. For example, you have constructed a 3'-wide by 7'-high bookcase and want to use a router for detail work on its sides. If the bookcase is set on the workbench, it may be too high for safe and easy work. If the bookcase is on the floor in an assembly area, the work height is correct. An overhead outlet or outlet about three feet from the floor will facilitate the router's use.

Shop Plumbing Concerns

The same generalities apply to plumbing. Is plumbing necessary in a woodshop? From a design viewpoint, if form and function are considered, the question is, "What value does plumbing serve?" What I value in a woodshop sink, besides washing my hands, is that it permits me to maintain waterstones for sharpening, mix dyes and water-soluble finishes, clean the HVLP spray gun and nozzle, clean restoration projects and use the new polyurethane glues. All of which are necessities. Warning: If there is a sink in the woodshop, don't use it to dispose of toxic solvents, flammable liquids and other hazardous wastes. Water, soap, dirt and grime are the only things that should go down the drain.

Garage and basement woodshops are often near laundry rooms. This proximity permits the addition of new water pipes to the woodshop area. Copper and PVC pipes are fairly easy to work with and it shouldn't be too complicated to route pipes several feet to the woodshop. If you aren't sure about cutting into water pipes, call a plumbing contractor for assistance. Undoubtedly, he can do the work faster than a woodworker!

Once the electrical system and plumbing needs have been determined, add these elements to the master plan and draw them onto the planning grid. Hopefully, the proposed design will accommodate all of these elements.

A SUMMARY OF THE WOOD-SHOP DESIGN PROCESS

1. Create a master plan of all the key woodshop elements: machines, tools, workbench, open areas, lumber racks, storage, electrical and plumbing.
2. Be realistic, as much as possible, and know your own personal interests.
3. Be somewhat hypothetical in choosing the woodshop elements.
   At this point you haven't spent any money.
4. Make paper mock-ups of different woodshop layouts.
5. Be reasonable. Understand that a woodshop takes time and money to create and that you can proceed at your own pace of acquisition.
6. Always consider alternatives. Buy inexpensive, resell and buy more expensive. Consider multipurpose machines. Consider hand tools instead of power tools.

Hiring a Contractor

Some tasks may be too complicated or require specific expertise. There are many advantages to hiring a contractor or other specialist when remodeling or building a new woodshop. The problem is how do you know who to hire?

Never underestimate the complexities of building or remodeling a woodshop. Just as with a house, the fundamentals of framing, electrical, plumbing, concrete, trenching and all the other construction techniques are required.

While there are many who are skilled enough or have enough time to do their own work, often it is better and faster to have someone else do the work.

If you've done your design work and choose to hire a contractor, you must be comfortable with your choice. After all, this person is going to turn your drawings into your ideal woodshop.

Selecting a contractor isn't that simple. The building process is complex and expensive so you must be certain that it will go according to your stated objectives and budgetary limits.

- If you don't know of a reliable contractor, ask friends and colleagues for their recommendations.
- Watch for any remodeling work being done in your own area. Pay attention to any signage on trucks or yard signs. Ask the homeowner if they are satisfied with the work being done.
- Inquire at local lumber yards, building supply centers and hardware stores for recommendations.
- Check with local builders or trade associations.
- Ask all potential contractors for references and photographs of their work. Note: It's easy to have photos of any attractive project. Check photos for images of the contractor, the company's sign, some sort of indication the work was actually done by the person showing the photos.
- Once you have selected a contractor, talk with him concerning recommendations for subcontractors.
- Indirect recommendations often occur after several unrelated sources recommend the same person.
- A personal note: I don't like contractors' advertisements with only a telephone number listed. I want to see a street address or at least a city name.

chapter *seven*

Examining Real Woodshops

IT'S IMPOSSIBLE TO FIND REPRE- sentative woodshops that reveal all the mysteries of setting up a wood- shop. Each of the shops that I have visited is unique and represents the owner's personality and woodworking style. The quest for the perfect woodshop really begins and ends with each person's own effort. And while it's enjoyable to peek into an- other woodshop, often the only trans- ferable items are bits and pieces of problem-solving. We seem to have a collective desire to construct "model cities," "dream houses" and "ideal workshops," but the reality is that these places are curiosities. Anyone remember the futuristic cities of the 1939 New York World's Fair, Disney- land's House of the Future or General Electric's 1960s All-Electric House? The point is, while we idealize a per- fect woodshop, your perfect wood- shop is right in front of you — it's in the garage, the basement, the extra room, the attic or a closet. All you need to do is get started.

The following perspective is from Alan Boardman, a highly regarded, very talented woodworker and au- thentic expert on tools, joinery and wood. I attended his lectures on join- ery and tuning up hand tools about 20 years ago and he showed me the fantastic adventure of woodworking. I now prize the small (marble-size) wooden puzzles he makes.

"Regarding the ideal woodshop, if one exists, I'll bet it is owned by someone who does no woodworking whatsoever," says Boardman. "My shop is a total disgrace and I love it. Every minute I spend wondering how to make it closer to ideal is a minute I am not enjoying working in it. My wife calls it my hellhole. It is a jumble of offcuts and boxes that I have long ago stopped wondering what's in them. I can hardly move about in the place or swing a board or find a pre-cious piece of rare wood I have been saving for decades for that worthy project, yet I am always happy there and never think of food or aging pains. If others think like I do, maybe the ideal shop is better described in human terms than where every ma- chine should be placed and how to store odd nuts and bolts. Incidentally, I haven't always felt this way. I used to dream of a perfect shop. But now that I am retired and theoretically have the time to redo it, I find that I don't want to. I like it the way it is."

The woodshops shown in this chapter can be classified into three types: the garage and basement woodshop, the separate-building woodshop on the home property and the rental-space woodshop. These example woodshops have been in ex- istence for some time, and each of them definitely reflects the personali- ty and style of the owner.

54 GARAGE AND BASEMENT WOODSHOP #1
MARK KULSETH'S WOODSHOP

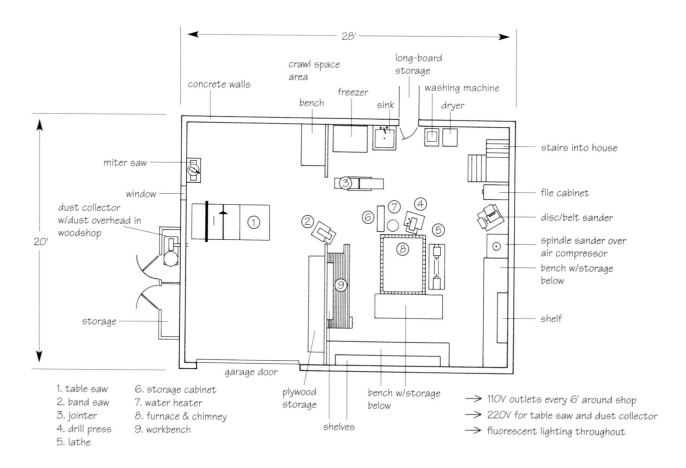

28'

concrete walls

crawl space area

long-board storage

washing machine

bench

freezer

sink

dryer

stairs into house

miter saw

window

file cabinet

dust collector w/dust overhead in woodshop

disc/belt sander

20'

spindle sander over air compressor

bench w/storage below

storage

shelf

garage door

plywood storage

bench w/storage below

shelves

1. table saw
2. band saw
3. jointer
4. drill press
5. lathe

6. storage cabinet
7. water heater
8. furnace & chimney
9. workbench

→ 110V outlets every 6' around shop
→ 220V for table saw and dust collector
→ fluorescent lighting throughout

MARK KULSETH HAS BEEN USING his woodshop for about five years. His woodshop is in a single-car garage and the adjacent laundry and storage areas in a 64-year-old house. His woodshop measures 20' × 28' (560 square feet). It is wired from the main house electrical service for both 110V and 220V use. Additionally, some areas of the woodshop have a floor-to-ceiling height of 6' 5". Mark is a part-time professional whose main woodworking interests are making custom furniture and some repairs and restorations. He also collects antique tools.

While there is little free space in Mark's woodshop, he

Mark Kulseth has an older home with a single-car garage attached to the laundry room and storage area. The table saw is located near the back wall of garage.

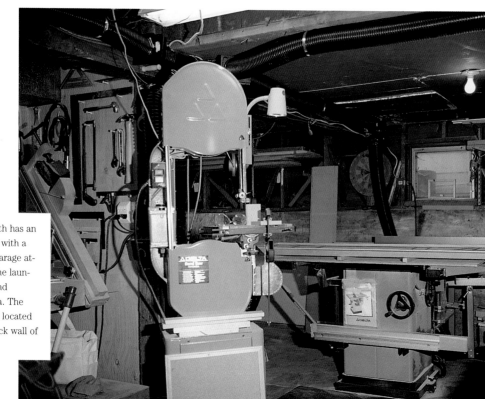

has maximized the existing floor and wall areas so well that he can build standard-size cabinets and furniture.

His principal machinery (in order of importance) includes:

- 10" Delta Unisaw with 52" fence and outfeed table
- 14" Delta band saw with riser block
- 20" Jet drill press
- Delta 6" × 48" belt sander
- 12"-disc sanding machine
- Jet 1200 CFM dust collector
- Walker-Turner lathe
- traditionally designed workbench

If Mark had more floor space he would add a wide-belt sanding machine, a downdraft sanding table and a 5' square work surface that is accessible from all four sides.

There are several nifty features to Mark's woodshop: He has grouped benches and tools around the furnace and chimney, has displayed plumb bobs from under the stairs, has a hidden storage area for lumber and has combined built-in bench tops/cabinet storage and shelves for antique tools. When I first visited his woodshop I was taken with how Mark has stored tools and stuff in every conceivable location — between rafters, behind walls and suspended in corners. My thought was that if he ever moved to another woodshop, he would need significant cabinet storage to handle all of the tucked-away items hidden in his woodshop. He should also use a metal detector to be certain that nothing is left behind!

Safety is important in Mark's work. He says that he has learned from the mistakes of others and he always wears eye and hearing protection. There is a first aid box and three fire extinguishers in the woodshop. Also, flammable and combustible materials are kept in a metal locker. Rags are rinsed in water, air-dried and then placed in a small metal garbage can

Kulseth's woodshop with countertop area and shelf storage. Mark plans to install cabinet doors in the near future. Note that the spindle sander sits on the box that houses the air compressor.

Kulseth's woodshop and more countertop and shelving for antique tools.

inside the woodshop.

I believe that woodworkers who work in confined areas, as Mark does, often develop a keen sense of what situations are best for ideal working conditions. Mark said that if he could design his ideal woodshop, he would have "a woodshop with ample space, wood floors, tall ceilings and maybe a separate finishing room and office, free of dust. But more than anything, I would love a shop built in a natural setting, away from the city, with mountain views, trees, a river and so on. To do this, I must have the business demands for my products."

Mark sees a relationship between himself, his woodshop and his woodworking skills: "I try to make my shop reflect my personality and skills as a craftsman. If I'm making a tool rack, I make it with care and pride to show my skills. It makes it much more enjoyable to view my tools. I also collect antique tools and many are displayed in my work area. I often reflect on the craftsmen of old while trying to solve my building problems. This reflection seems to inspire a higher quality in my craft."

Mark Kulseth uses the underside of his staircase to display his plumb bob collection.

Mark Kulseth stores his antique plane collection above his workbench. An angled hold-down device is in the foreground.

A crawl space (hidden behind the chart in the photograph) is actually a large area for storing lumber.

2 GARAGE AND BASEMENT WOODSHOP #2

DAVID BEYL'S WOODSHOP

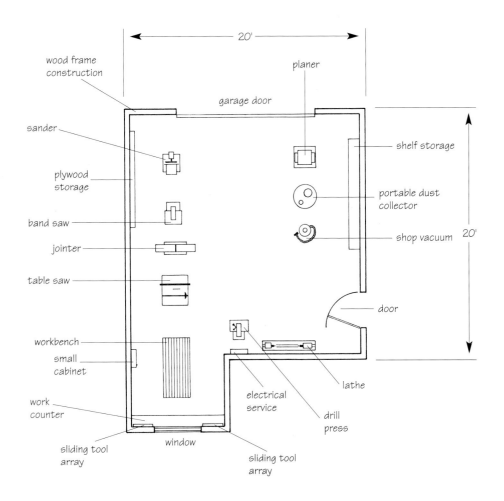

20'

wood frame construction

planer

garage door

sander

shelf storage

plywood storage

portable dust collector

band saw

shop vacuum

jointer

20'

table saw

door

workbench

small cabinet

work counter

lathe

electrical service

drill press

sliding tool array

window

sliding tool array

DAVID BEYL'S WOODSHOP WAS A two-car garage. The house is 27 years old and David has had the woodshop for 13 years. It measures 20' × 20', with an 8' ceiling. It has a subpanel with both 110V and 220V wiring. David is a part-time professional who specializes in building furniture, repairing antiques and teaching woodworking. He spends about 20 hours a week in the woodshop. His principal machinery (in order of importance) includes:

- 10" Delta cabinetmaker's saw
- 6" Jet jointer

David Beyl has a two-car garage woodshop. To maximize space, there are numerous sliding panels mounted in front of the windows.

- 14" Delta band saw
- 12" disc, 6" × 48" belt sander
- 16" Delta radial drill press
- 12" Shopsmith planer
- Shopsmith dust collector
- 14" Delta scroll saw
- Campbell-Hausfeld air compressor
- 12" Delta lathe

David's woodshop is 20' × 20' feet, that is, a square floor pattern with almost no nooks or crannies. Interestingly, David's concept of woodworking seems to match the straightforward woodshop layout. He's somewhat of a minimalist and only has tools and machines that he uses. Nothing more, nothing less. The simplicity of the woodshop also lends itself to teaching woodworking. Students aren't working in clutter, and they are learning to use the basic machinery in a clean and straightforward woodshop environment.

Just because David has identified his woodworking style and woodshop arrangement doesn't mean that he wouldn't improve his woodshop. If he remodeled the woodshop he would include a built-in dust collection system, recessed lighting (fluorescent and incandescent), a sink with hot water, a gas heating system, a separate office area, convenient storage and a modern-design workbench.

A feature I particularly admired was David's use of sliding tool storage partitions. These partitions are four panels that slide like sliding closet doors, except the units are wall-mounted and slide back and forth in front of a window. Slender tools such as chisels, screwdrivers, pliers and files are stored on the racks.

David Beyl's workbench, shown here, features many small drawers.

David Beyl has small cabinets which have page-like sections for holding small tools.

The David Beyl woodshop has a wood storage unit that is hinged at one end and then rolls out at the other end. This storage unit is used primarily for plywood and cut-off pieces of plywood.

3 GARAGE AND BASEMENT WOODSHOP #3
GEORGE LEVIN'S WOODSHOP

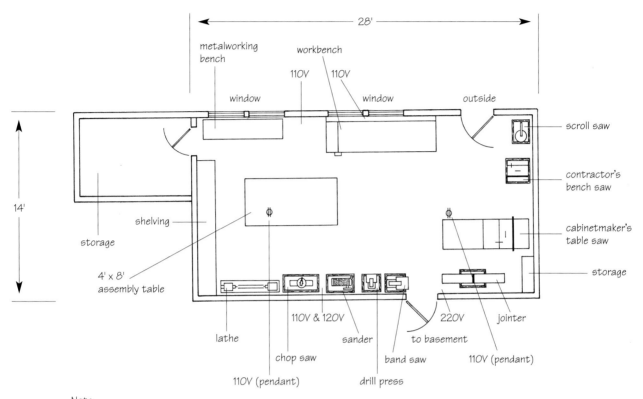

28'

metalworking bench

workbench

110V   110V

window   window   outside

scroll saw

contractor's bench saw

14'

shelving   cabinetmaker's table saw

storage

storage

4' x 8' assembly table

110V & 120V   220V   jointer

lathe   sander   to basement

chop saw   band saw   110V (pendant)

110V (pendant)   drill press

Note:
All stationary machines
(except lathe) are on casters.

THE GEORGE LEVIN WOODSHOP is located at basement level with a window view and door access to the outside. The woodshop is approximately 14' × 29', it has standard-height ceiling and is equipped with 110V and 220V electrical wiring. The house is 71 years old, and George has been using the woodshop for 22 years. He considers himself to be a part-time professional and builds Federal and Deco style furniture and other built-ins. He spends about 20 hours a week in the wood-shop.

His principal ma-chinery (in order of importance) includes

George Levin's woodshop is about the size of a one-car garage. He has a beautifully designed workbench mounted against a wall.

George Levin's table saw is mounted on a shop-made mobile base.

A heavy belt sander is mounted on a shop-made mobile base. Note the customized sander fence.

- 10" Delta Unisaw
- 10" Inca Model 510 jointer/planer
- 8" Grizzly jointer
- 14" Powermatic band saw
- 10" disc, 6" Delta belt sander
- 24" Delta scroll saw
- 6" × 32" Delta (Homecraft) lathe

If there was space in the woodshop, George would have a panel saw. Also, if he could design an ideal woodshop, he would include a spray booth, large doors, plenty of windows, level access to the outside, wood flooring, sink, toilet, dust collection system, room for wood and sheet goods storage.

George Levin's workbench and window view.

George's woodshop is an elongated rectangle, and he has optimized working conditions within the space by making mobile bases for the machines. These bases are made of wood, have locking wheels, and they are both sturdy and easy to use. It is easy to roll the table saw into a more open position, use it and then return it. Another principal feature is a 4' × 8' assembly table. This table is about 24" high, and the top is a sheet of ¾" melamine particleboard. The table is

used for stacking rough-cut pieces, for assembly and gluing of workpieces and for finishing work. When the top surface is no longer workable, it is flipped over to access the other side. And when both sides are worn out, a new piece is installed and the old top is disposed of.

George has a spectacular workbench. Its wonderfully unique construction is a fine example of craftsmanship and represents an im-

pressive comprehension of design. The workbench measures about 3' × 12' and it is mounted against a wall. Looking at the front, the right-side half is composed of two rows of drawers that have customized pockets for hand tools; the left side is an open area, usually filled with large sleeping dogs. There is only one metal vise, mounted on the left-front edge and it has an adjustable companion holder (workpiece support) that can be located on any of the four vertical bench supports. Instead of the typical bench dogs, the bench top has a metal track perpendicular to the vise. An adjustable stop slides in the track so that various width boards can be easily secured. Other details include a narrow tool tray located along the entire back edge, and the top surface material is hardboard. When the hardboard wears out, it is unscrewed, removed and then replaced with new hardboard.

George has a sense of humor and his woodshop reflects his personal view of things. In a way, his woodshop is a collage of bits and pieces of personal history, world events, successes of children and just fun stuff. A plain storage cabinet is totally covered with tiny pictures of dogs, and although the cabinet contains nuts and bolts, it's referred to as the "dog cabinet." George once was an avid aviator, and so it stands to reason that the ceiling is covered with pictures of airplanes and an upside-down remote control airplane! Where most of us have machines with the manufacturer's name prominently displayed, George has covered his band saw with vacation pictures, quotes and other less commercial concepts. There are numerous calendars from the 1960s, posters of long-ago lectures, old clocks and assorted keepsakes — enough interesting things to keep a smile on anyone's face. Judging by the woodshop, George Levin is a happy man. His comments about his woodshop: "This room is an extension of myself, so it contains pictures and memorabilia reflecting some of my other interests so that I really feel 'at home' when I am working there."

George Levin designed his workbench holding system which features a slot perpendicular to the vise. The slot contains a movable and lockable bench dog.

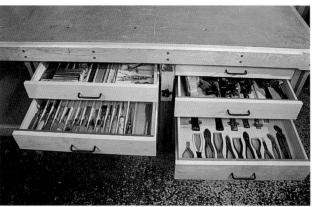

The Levin bench has drawers with custom locations for all tools.

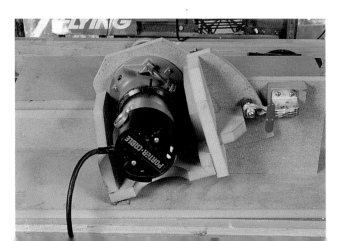

Because the Levin woodshop is small, George has many jigs and fixtures that he uses at his workbench. Shown is his mortising jig.

SEPARATE-BUILDING OR SEPARATE-ROOM WOODSHOPS #1
THE CHARLES CASWELL WOODSHOP

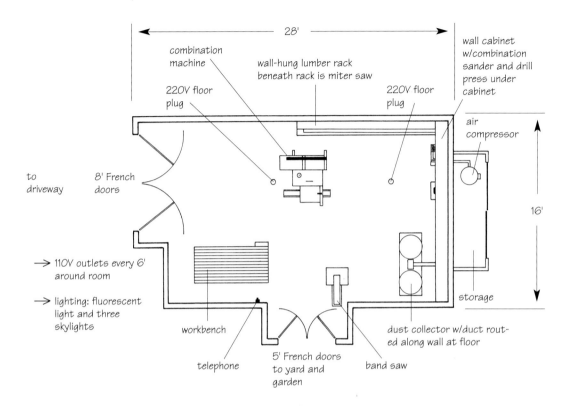

combination machine

wall-hung lumber rack
beneath rack is miter saw

wall cabinet w/combination sander and drill press under cabinet

220V floor plug

220V floor plug

28'

to driveway

8' French doors

air compressor

16'

110V outlets every 6' around room

lighting: fluorescent light and three skylights

workbench

telephone

5' French doors to yard and garden

band saw

dust collector w/duct routed along wall at floor

storage

AFTER YEARS OF WORKING IN other people's woodshops, Charles decided to build his ideal woodshop. His goal was to design a woodshop that would be on his own property and separate from the house. His house property's shape is that of a typical city lot, that is, a long and narrow rectangle. The house is an older style with the garage as a separate structure set back from the house and next to the property line. Charles removed the old garage and then designed the woodshop to look like a new garage. The exterior is reminiscent of the bungalow style, with door overhangs and clapboard siding. The major exterior feature that reveals something of the nature of the building is that Charles installed French doors instead of a garage

Here's the exterior of Caswell's shop. Note that double French doors are located where a garage door would be located.

door. Charles also built the walls with sound insulation so that the neighbors wouldn't be hearing machinery noise. From my own experiences visiting the woodshop, I had to be fairly close to it to hear the muffled sounds of a dust collector and planer being used. His soundproofing consisted of standard wall insulation between wall studs and then covering that with ½" sound board. Drywall board was installed in the normal fashion and the wall was finished and painted.

Charles is a full-time professional woodworker and spends over 50 hours a week in the woodshop building furniture. His woodshop is 2 years old and has 450 square feet, 110V and 220V wiring. There are electrical outlets at convenient wall locations and 220V floor plugs near the table saw. His principal machinery (in order of importance) includes:

- 10" Robland X31 table saw with sliding table
- Robland X31 jointer/planer combination machine
- 18" Laguna band saw
- Ryobi miter saw
- AMC radial-head drill press
- Robland X31 shaper
- Robland X31 horizontal mortiser
- Grizzly belt/disc combination sander

Charles had a four-bag dust collector in the woodshop but he felt that the hookup at the machines was inadequate; that is, the factory-constructed fittings were ineffective at the source of dust. He also wanted a larger, more power unit, including a chip separator located in a separate space. After the first photographs of his woodshop were taken, he replaced the upper filter bags with filter bags that trap dust to the 5-micron level. This considerably reduced dust blow-back into the work area, but he still wasn't satisfied. Subsequently, he sold the four bag dust collector and all the 4" ductwork and installed a cyclone collector with 5" ductwork and a Delta ceiling hung air filtration unit. The cyclone was an immediate improvement; it is much quieter and there is now minimal dust in the shop.

Charles also has a 6-hp, 80-gallon air compressor located in a shed behind the back wall. He doesn't consider it to be a principal tool because he uses it mostly for cleanup work. He

Charles Caswell built a two-car-garage-size woodshop at the end of his driveway on a typical city lot. This interior view shows the open ceiling, skylights, lighting, main storage cabinets and machinery. Not seen, to the right side, is a traditional workbench. This woodshop is noteworthy for its straightforward layout and comfortable and uncluttered work conditions.

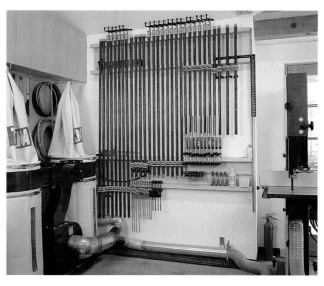

You can see here how clamps are stored in Caswell's woodshop.

bought the large compressor partly because of value and partly because it's quieter than the smaller "oil-less" compressors. Under normal usage it cycles on a few times a week.

The woodshop features a very comfortable bright and airy working area with an open ceiling, skylights and one 5'-wide and one 8'-wide French door. For storage, Charles built a single row of cabinets across the back wall. These cabinets are located at approximately head height and are the main storage in the woodshop. There is also a wall section with pegboard, used for oversize tools and accessories. There is lumber storage, positioned above the miter saw area, which is used for planed boards and material being prepared for the next work project.

When he first set up his wood-

shop, Charles made a beautiful, traditionally designed workbench. At the time, the workbench seemed like a good idea. Now that he is busy making furniture, the workbench is not used and is taking up floor space — space that he needs for other purposes. Currently, the workbench is supporting a vacuum press, and he is debating on what to do with the workbench — to sell it or put it in storage.

The woodshop reflects Charles's attitude about woodworking: It is thoughtful, organized and well crafted. He has enough tools and machinery for any work, and the room is clean and open so there's no inefficiency due to clutter and congestion. He is very content with his woodshop and would only add a warehouse area for curing and storing lumber.

2 SEPARATE-BUILDING OR SEPARATE-ROOM WOODSHOPS #2
TED BARTHOLOMEW'S WOODSHOP

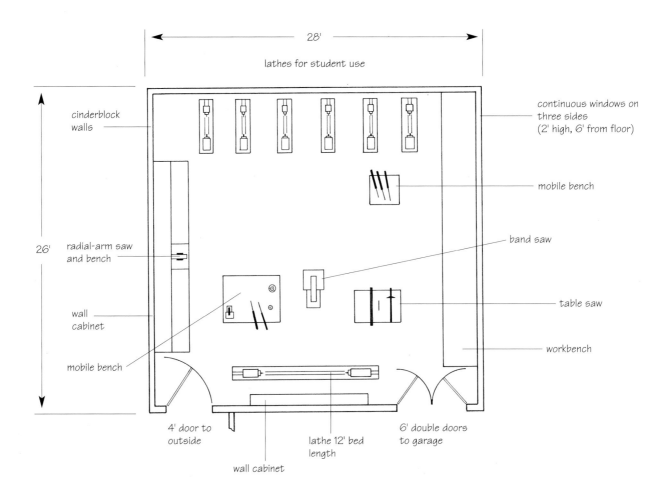

28'

lathes for student use

cinderblock walls

continuous windows on three sides (2' high, 6' from floor)

mobile bench

band saw

26'

radial-arm saw and bench

table saw

wall cabinet

workbench

mobile bench

4' door to outside

lathe 12' bed length

6' double doors to garage

wall cabinet

THE TED BARTHOLOMEW WOOD-shop is one of the most unusual woodshops that I've visited. Ted's woodshop measures 26' × 28' (728 square feet) with a 9' ceiling. There is both 110V and 220V wiring. The room, built as a wood-shop 20 years ago, is located next to a garage. The most no-ticeable feature of the room is that there are windows located 6' from the floor, continuous on three walls. These windows are 2' high, and the lighting is similar to that of sky-lighting. What makes the woodshop unique is that Ted is a "serious ama-

Ted Bartholomew's woodshop is attached to a two-car garage. Windows are contin-uous on three sides of the shop.

Ted Bartholomew's custom lathe is designed for working on either side of the machine. The portable tool storage cart is easily moved throughout the woodshop.

teur" who specializes in woodturning: He manufactured his own wood lathe and likes turning large bowls. He also teaches woodturning.

There are large and small movable tables and carts for storing lathe tools and accessories. His lathe features a pneumatic forward and reversing system so turning work can be done on either side of the lathe. In order to make it easy to access lathe tools, the tools are simply laid on a cart and the cart is moved to the area of work. These movable tables and carts also make it easier to work when there are several students working at the lathes. Ted is very

happy with his woodshop but he would like to install a dust collecting system.

His principal machinery (in order of importance) includes:
- several Bartholomew lathes (the number varies)
- antique lathe — 4 hp, capacity of 22" overbed, 7' outboard, 12' overall
- various lathes for student work
- Walker-Turner 16" band saw
- Craftsman 10" radial-arm saw
- 10" Delta Unisaw
- drill press
- 1" belt sander

RENTAL-SPACE WOODSHOPS #1
DEAN BERSHAW'S WOODSHOP

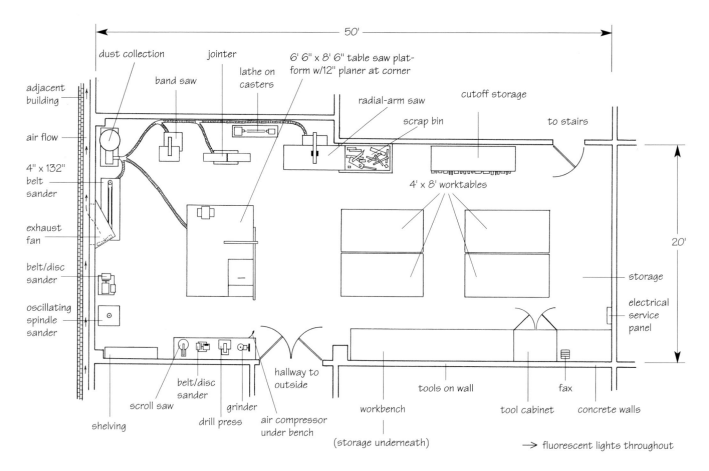

DEAN BERSHAW IS A FULL-TIME professional woodworker specializing in contemporary furniture. He has been in his current woodshop 3½ years and spends 30 to 50 hours a week there. He rents part of the basement in a commercial building that was built in the 1950s. His woodshop measures 50' × 20' (1000 square feet) with a ceiling height of 7' 8" under ceiling beams and 9' between beams. There is both 110V and 220V wiring. His principal machinery (in order of importance):

- 10" Jet 3-hp table saw
- 6" Grizzly jointer
- 12" Delta planer
- 10" Delta radial-arm saw

Dean Bershaw's woodshop is located in the basement of a commercial building. This area is used for smaller work projects and tool storage.

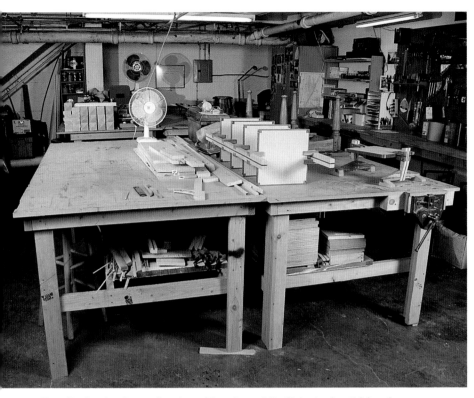

Dean Bershaw has four workstations with surfaces of 4' × 8' sheets of particleboard.

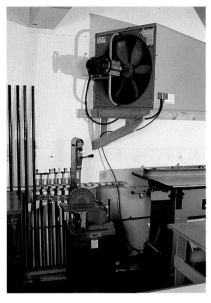

Air circulation and ventilation are critical in Dean Bershaw's basement woodshop. The only direct access to the outside is an opening to a 5" space between building walls. He built a diagonally mounted fan housing so that air could be exhausted into the narrow space between buildings.

- 9" Grizzly disc sander
- Mark 1 drill press
- Grizzly 2-hp dust collector
- router table with Porter-Cable router, Incra jig fence
- 24" Windmaster fan
- Campbell-Hausfeld 6-hp, 30-gallon air compressor
- 4" × 132" Delta belt sander
- 12" Delta lathe
- Star oscillating spindle sander
- Delta sharpening center

Having a commercial operation in a concrete basement offers several challenges worth noting. Basements in industrial/commercial areas aren't necessarily the easiest locations to find. Both vendors and customers require clear instructions in order to find Dean's woodshop. Although Dean doesn't expect walk-in business, he does invite designers and buyers to visit him while projects are under construction. Other basement complications include no direct access to the outside, risk of water damage (broken/leaking pipes) and ventilation.

Dean's woodshop is in the back section of the building's basement; consequently there are no windows, doors or other vents to the outside. However, at one time there was an opening in a wall which was later bricked in when another building was built next to that wall. Dean removed the bricks and discovered that there is a 5"-wide space between the buildings. He built an angled exhaust fan housing and installed it in front of the opening. This clever arrangement exhausts stale woodshop air into the 5" space. This fan, although it does remove residual dust particles, is not meant to be a dust collector — it is used to refresh and circulate air in the woodshop. And there are no windows on either of the walls at higher locations (i.e., no one will be bothered by exhausted woodshop air).

Although water leakage is always a worry, it has yet to happen. Preparing for such a problem, Dean has made all storage units, tables and workstations as modular units so that they are easy to move.

If Dean remodeled his woodshop, he would add a spray booth, office space and living quarters. He would include space for multiuse capabilities, such as automotive work and metalwork, and he would also add windows, higher ceilings and openings at opposite ends of the woodshop for through-circulation.

The principal factor that makes this location attractive is the rental rate. The rent is affordable, allowing him to keep his operating costs low. He is willing to compromise with ceiling height and no windows in order to be competitive. Dean realizes that time is of the essence when doing custom work. Any woodshop improvements have to serve a purpose and must not require significant amounts of time to accomplish. Dean also states: "I have bought tools for a specific job but they all have subsequent value for general-usage applications. In my view, the less specific the application, the better."

ANOTHER APPROACH
JAMES LEARY'S WORKPLACE

JAMES LEARY, A SUCCESSFUL PRO-fessional woodworker, does mostly house remodeling and refurbishing — without a woodshop building. Instead, he takes his woodshop with him to the job site. His large van holds all that he needs; he simply drives up and begins to work. He says that he made a design choice: He could have built custom storage within the van but decided not to. Instead, he decided to use tool cases that are specific for each power tool. His reasoning was that fixed storage is somewhat limiting. For example, if a job requires drills and reciprocating saws, but not routers and power washers, he can leave the unnecessary equipment at home. Also, the tool cases all have shapes and sizes that are easily identified for quick selection while working. And modern tool cases are easy to carry, are reasonably dustproof and water resistant and hold extra bits, blades and accessories. There is one other bonus: Customers enjoy and appreciate his readiness and thoroughness.

James Leary doesn't have the typical woodshop — his woodshop is his van. He does remodeling and general woodworking and drives his woodshop to the worksite.

Here is almost everything out of James' van.

APPLY TO YOUR OWN WOODSHOP
I have visited dozens of woodshops and they all have the basic assortment of tools, storage and such. Does having a particular brand of tools make the woodshop better? No. Does having a large space make woodworking better? Perhaps. Does personal problem-solving help make an ideal woodshop? Yes.

Although a woodcarver or someone working on small-scale projects doesn't necessarily require large areas for work, the general-purpose woodworker does benefit from having adequate space. Unfortunately, if you have 100 square feet of woodshop, you can't simply wish up another 50 square feet to make the room better. What you can do is:
- Wisely plan out the space.
- Buy appropriately sized machines.
- Have only the machines and tools that you need.
- Build storage units to fit space.
- Be happy and build things.

From Those That Have Built Woodshops

"If I had only known ..." is often the start of conversations with those that have built their own woodshops. While there is universal satisfaction with the completed shops, everyone has tales of how complex or expensive the project was. I have listened to stories about wearing out too many tools, underestimating the volume of building materials and the hardships of doing heavy work without assistance. Some wished that they had planned for larger woodshops and others wished they had been less elaborate. And just like those that have woodshops in home garages or basements, these woodworkers also have wish lists — after the woodshop has been completed. "I need more space, I want to add a room for wood storage, I wish I had a sink and toilet, I should have added skylights, I didn't have enough money to ... ."

Even if you have more space than necessary (which hardly ever occurs), the same basic steps apply. Each of the woodshops I have featured is a consequence of these basic steps. All of the woodworkers have adapted to the room configuration, organized the machinery and storage around their needs, and then proceeded to make furniture, turn bowls, repair antiques, collect old tools, remodel houses and lose themselves in the enjoyment, wonder and mystery of woodworking.

chapter *eight*

Powering and Lighting the Shop Effectively

THERE'S NO DENYING THE FACT that electricity is the fundamental necessity of the modern woodshop.

WARNINGS ABOUT ELECTRICITY

Before you begin to do anything with electrical wiring there are a few cautions. Never attempt any electrical work if you have doubts about the wiring layout or the consequences of your effort. The two agencies you should be aware of are your local building departments (usually city and county) and the utility company. The building department has electrical inspectors who can explain local codes and requirements concerning permits for the work and any necessary inspections. Requirements, regulations and amended versions of the National Electrical Code (NEC) vary from area to area. It is very important to follow the codes and guidelines established for your area. The utility agencies can assist in the location of underground cables and will recommend the correct approach to any electrical service upgrades. Often, it's less time-consuming, more economical and safer to hire a licensed electrical contractor to install new wiring,

electrical service panels or other custom work. Electrical work is similar to woodworking: Both require specialized tools and supplies. If you don't have the correct tools, be prepared to rent, buy or borrow them. A visit to an electrical supply store is enough to make you realize that there are scores of supplies, many of which have to meet your local electrical codes.

EVALUATE YOUR ELECTRICAL NEEDS

There are several starting points in the evaluation of electrical requirements for a woodshop. The first, and most obvious, is that if the existing room has a single overhead light with a pull chain and only one or two outlets, the room is underpowered for woodworking machinery. Check the electrical service panel for the circuit breaker to the potential shop location; if there is only one 15- or 20-amp circuit, the service will need upgrading. If you start up a table saw and the lights dim, perhaps you should stop woodworking and upgrade the electrical service.

How you upgrade or install ade-

quate electrical service for a woodshop location is dependent on whether you're remodeling or building a new room. It's certainly more straightforward installing wiring and outlets in a new construction. Routing cables through open framework is much simpler than when walls, doors and ceilings are in place.

Electricity Essentials

There are many comprehensive books on basic wiring that detail all of the various electrical requirements and upgrades for a house. Many of these books are written for do-it-yourselfers, so they're easy to read and follow. What I want to address are the specific electrical essentials of the woodshop. These essentials are:
- safety
- adequate electrical supply
- 110V and 220V service
- sufficient outlets
- proper lighting

SAFETY RULES

There are two main safety considerations: the type required when actually upgrading a system and the safety of having the correct amperes, cables, outlets, etc., once the upgrading is done. While these may seem similar, they're distinctly different.

Proper upgrading generally consists of knowledge, information, common sense, proper tools and supplies. To safely complete an electrical upgrade requires knowing the machinery and tool electrical requirements, code-compliant installation of outlets, use of the proper types and sizes of cables, outlets, etc. If you have any reservations about any of these points, it might be best to call in an electrical contractor. After all, electrical current is invisible until there is electrical shock or electrical fire.

Never work on a live circuit. Always disconnect the circuit at the service panel. That means switching the circuit breaker to an 'off' position or removing a screw-in fuse. Remember that the electrical power will still be live to the service panel from the power utility lines (either below or above ground). So even if you switch the main power off, the power will still be live to the service. It's sort of like closing a dam's spillway: Water may not be leaving the dam, but there is water on the other side of the dam.

Be certain that the circuit is off by first turning on a light that's plugged into that circuit. If it goes out when the circuit is switched off, then you may proceed with the next step.

It's always a good idea to tell others that you are disconnecting a circuit. This is especially important when working at some distance from the service panel. You might even tape a note to the service panel warning others that you are working on the service.

Never work on any electrical fixtures, the service panel, the wiring or anything else electrical when there are wet spots, moist conditions or standing water. Dry the area as much as possible. Open windows and doors to aid in drying damp basements. If there is moisture on the floor, construct a platform of dry boards over the wet areas.

USE THE CORRECT TOOLS

Common tools that you probably have in the woodshop that are useful for electrical work:

- mat knife — for cutting wallboard and, with the blade barely exposed, cutting sheathed cable
- hammer — the obvious
- screwdrivers — also obvious
- Allen wrenches — fittings and terminals often are secured with hex screw heads
- square-drive screwdrivers — many electricians now use screws with square holes instead of slot or Phillips heads. Square-drive screws are fast and easy to use.
- tape measure — the obvious
- keyhole saw — for sawing holes in walls and hard-to-reach locations prior to installing boxes or cables
- hacksaw — for sawing conduit to length
- cordless drill with drill bits — the perfect drill when the power is off

Specialized Tools

- engineer's or lineman's pliers — used to twist bare wires together and then cut the last ⅛" off so that the twisted wires fit into a wirenut; large serrated jaws can bend flat metal
- diagonal cutting pliers — for cutting wire; fits in confined locations
- needle-nosed or snipe-nosed pliers — for picking up and holding small parts in confined locations
- wire strippers — adjustable to different wire gauges for removing insulation
- multipurpose electrician's wire strippers/tool — several features: wire stripper, wire cutter, crimper and bolt cutter

- insulated screwdrivers — entire screwdriver, except blade tip, is coated with insulation
- conduit bender — long-handled device for bending metal conduit to various angles
- fish tape — thin metal line for pulling cable through enclosed areas; i.e., walls and ceilings
- cable ripper — a cutting device for slitting the sheathing on cable
- electronic metal and voltage detector — a device similar to stud finder that locates any metal object and detects AC voltage within a wall
- continuity Tester — used to determine whether an electrical path is complete. Simple to use when checking fuses, switches and plugs. It has a battery and indicator light and is only used when the power is off! Handy to have, even if not an electrician.
- voltage Tester — used to determine if power is present. The probes are touched to a hot line and the ground thus causing the indicator to light. It is used with the power on. Useful for checking DC/AC voltage, outlets, motors, appliances and fuses. Useful if you have some experience working with electricity.
- volt-ohmmeter, or multitester — used for testing a variety of conditions, including voltage, low-voltage current, resistance to ohms and continuity. Useful for checking outlets, fuses, wires, plugs, motors and electronic circuits. Useful if you have some experience working with electricity.
- circuit analyzers — look like an oversize electrical plug. The simplest version can determine if there is power to a receptacle, whether it is properly grounded and whether the wiring is correct. There are more sophisticated circuit analyzers that can check

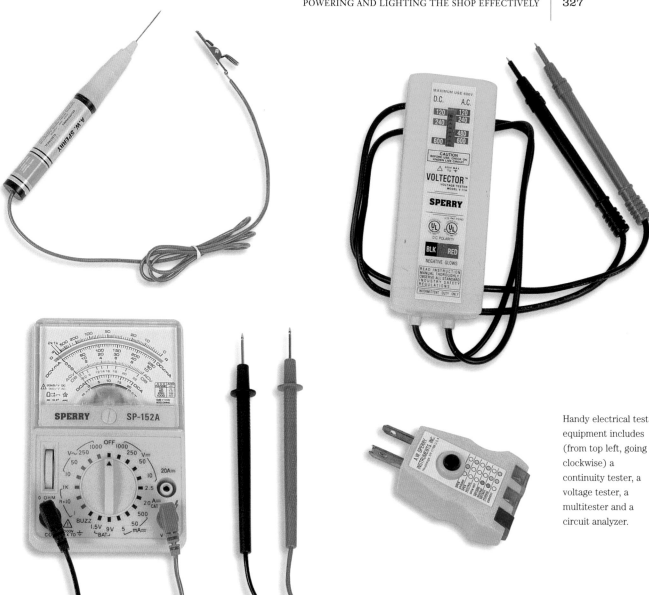

Handy electrical test equipment includes (from top left, going clockwise) a continuity tester, a voltage tester, a multitester and a circuit analyzer.

tip

It's a good idea to have insulated handles on pliers and other metal tools. Don't rely on insulated tools as the only safety precaution, always turn circuits off before working on them.

from the receptacle back to the service panel for voltage drops or for current leaks. Handy to have, even if not an electrician.

ELECTRICAL SUPPLIES
Be certain that the electrical supplies you select are approved or meet local building codes. If you aren't sure

about this, then it would be best to consult certified experts. There are too many choices — guessing which part or wire size to use is the wrong approach.

Wire is a single strand of conductive metal enclosed with insulation. Cord is stranded wires protected by insulation. It can consist of two or three stranded wires within the insulation and is used for appliances, lamps, etc. Cable has two or more color-coded insulated wires that are protected by sheathing.

In the United States, the colors of the individual wire are agreed upon: Black or red is the power or hot wire, white or gray is the neutral,

and green or green with a yellow stripe is the ground wire. Sometimes ground is a single uninsulated copper wire.

Wire Type and Size
It's very important to use the correct wire size and type when upgrading an electrical system. Local codes will specify what sorts of cable and cable conduits are permitted in your area.

Wire Types
TYPE NM has a thermoplastic insulation and is capable of withstanding a wide range of temperatures. It's used for most household circuits.

Number of Wires in a Conduit*

WIRE SIZE	½" CONDUIT	¾" CONDUIT	1" CONDUIT	1¼" CONDUIT
14	4	6	9	9
12	3	5	8	9
10	1	4	7	9
8	1	3	4	7
6	1	1	3	4

*Actual number is also governed by local codes

TYPE UF (underground feed cable) is waterproof and is used for damp and outdoor locations.

TYPE USE (underground service entrance) is used for underground or overhead service entrance and direct burial to garages and woodshops.

TYPE THW is used for outdoor hanging or indoor conduit as service entrance cables and for conduit to a subpanel.

Nonmetallic (NM) cable is the most common plastic-sheathed cable. It's often referred to as Romex, which is a trade name. The sheath is usually moisture resistant and flame retardant. Normally, there are insulated power wires and a bare ground wire inside of the sheath.

Armored cable, referred to by the trade name BX cable, has an outer armored layer, usually flexible galvanized steel, that often contains two or three wires wrapped in paper.

Conduit is usually galvanized steel or plastic pipe. It's generally available in ½", ¾", 1" and 1¼" diameters. The correct size to use depends on the diameter and number of wires inside the conduit.

Wire Size

Wire size, basically the diameter of the wire excluding insulation, is extremely important when upgrading an electrical system. There are standard reference numbers, usually printed on the outside of wire insulation, that are based upon the American Wire Gauge (AWG) system.

Common Copper Household Wire (By Gauge) & Its Ampere Rating:

GAUGE	AMPERE RATING
No. 18	7 amperes
No. 16	10 amperes
No. 14	15 amperes
No. 12	20 amperes
No. 10	30 amperes
No. 8	40 amperes
No. 6	55 amperes

Gauge numbers are inverse to their size; that is, the smaller the number, the larger the wire diameter. The maximum current that a wire can safely manage is stated in amperes (amps). Wire diameter and the amount of amperes are directly related. Smaller diameter wires have greater resistance to electrical current flow; consequently, as the current flow increases so do friction and heat. To avoid melting wires and electrical fires, use larger-diameter wires for heavier electrical needs.

CALCULATING ELECTRICAL USAGE IN THE WOODSHOP

No matter what electrical circuits or subpanels are added to the house's electrical service, the total house load must not exceed the service rating. Generally, older homes having no electrical modernization have 100-amp services. Newer homes generally have 200-amp services. If you are not certain about the service, look at the main circuit breaker in the service panel — it should be labeled. If you have 100-amp service, consult with both the utility company and a licensed electrician about upgrading to a 200-amp service.

The woodshop is probably going to have machines and power tools, unless, of course, you're taken with the joy of only working with hand tools. Generally, woodshops will have one woodworker using no more than two machines at one time (table saw and dust collector, drill press and vacuum). The advantage of this is that the electrical system isn't going to need to support the simultaneous operation of all the woodshop's machinery. As you plan the electrical layout, make a best guess as to the frequency of use of tools and machines. Not only will this aid in determining circuit requirements, but it will also aid in planning the placement of outlets. The reality of upgrading woodshop electrical systems is that it's often easier to install separate outlets on separate circuits than to have one circuit with multiple outlets. For example, in my woodshop I have three machines requiring 220V service: the table saw, jointer/planer and band saw. Rarely, if ever, are two machines running at the same time. So it's possible for the three machines to have their outlets wired to the same circuit. However, these machines are located in different areas of the woodshop and it was much easier to install outlets at each of the machine locations and route wires through one or more conduits. Since there was adequate space in the subpanel, it was a straightforward addition of circuit breakers and wire. The exception to this is the dust collector, which is also 220V. Because it's operated simultaneously with each of the stationary machines, there was no choice — it

Typical Machine & Tool Ampere Ratings

Note: Machines and tools are 110V-120V with exceptions noted.

MACHINE/TOOL	AMPERAGE
10" Table saw	8.3 @ 230V
10" Contractor's table saw	12.8
14" Band saw (½ hp)	9
10" Radial-arm saw	11/5.5 @ 120/240V
12" Miter saw	13
6" Jointer	9.5
12" Planer	15
Drill press	6
6" X 48" Sander	8.4 @ 240V
2-hp Shaper	16/8 @ 110/220V
12" Lathe (¾ hp)	11.4
Scroll saw	1.3
Dust collector (2 bag)	16/8 @ 115/230V
Dust collector (4 bag)	17 @ 230V
20-gallon Shop vacuum	10.5
3½-hp air compressor	15
Router, 1 hp	6.8
Router, 3 hp	15
Belt sander, 4" X 24"	10.5
Plate jointer	6.5
Finish sander	1.7
Spindle sander	3.5
⅜" Hand drill	4
Bench grinder	6
Strip sander, 1" X 30"	2.6
Jig saw	4.8
Circular saw	13
Heat gun	14
Benchtop mortiser	6
HVLP spray gun turbine	11.5

Above is a typical subpanel installed above the main circuit breaker panel. Below the main panel is a Gen/Tran unit — used for connecting a portable generator to the main panel in the event of a power outage. At left, you see the subpanel cover removed for a better look at the breaker switches and wiring.

required its own circuit.

The National Electrical Code sets minimum capacities for circuits regarding use and amperage:

- Small appliances — 20 amperes
- General lighting — 15 or 20 amperes
- Stationary tools — multiply the machine's amperage by 125%. The 125% factors the electrical surge that occurs when a machine is first switched on. For example, a 12" planer rated at 15 amps ($1.25 \times 15 = 18.75$) will require a 20-amp circuit.

OUTLETS, SWITCHES AND PLUGS

Until the day comes that we can use tools powered by wireless telemetry, woodshops will need outlets and switches. When designing a new electrical layout, placement of outlets and switches requires planning, guesswork and a bit of luck. The reality of woodshops is that work projects, new machines, relocation of cabinets, stacks of lumber and other fluctuating events will block existing outlets and switches from access. Often, well-thought-out locations aren't that handy once the woodshop is used. The ideal situation is never having to use extension cords because you have outlets wherever you work. This can be accomplished simply by locating outlets three to five feet apart throughout the woodshop, including the ceiling. This may seem excessive, but it's not. There are too many work conditions that occur away from the workbench area: Using a vacuum, sander, plate joiner, rotary carving tool or heat gun are but a few of the applications possible.

Two scenarios for installing outlets: If the woodshop area is a new construction, wires should be installed within the wall framework. If wall coverings are already in place, outlets can be installed on the outside of the wall surface if metal conduit and metal outlet boxes are used. Always check your local electrical codes concerning this type of installation. External conduit adds flexibility to designing and locating outlets, simply because conduit can be routed just about anywhere. Metal conduit pipe is easily bent to a variety of shapes and angles with a conduit bender. One option for the 90° bend at corners is to use short prebent right-angle conduit pieces. These are attached to the straight conduit with sleeve connectors. Conduit pipe can be cut wherever necessary and outlets installed.

Steven Gray has an unusual (for the home woodshop, that is) electrical system. His woodshop features overhead electrical rails. These feed rails are connected to the main power panel. What is unique is that trolleys slide within the rails, and lights or AC switches can be attached to the trolleys. The feed rail is both 110V and 220V. Both voltages are usable depending upon how the contact trolley wheels are aligned within the feed rail. It's a very neat system, with movable electrical items all in one track, both 110V and 220V outlets and different types of lighting.

Acceptable Outlets

- Grounded three-prong, 120V, 15 amp
- Grounded three-prong, 120V, 20 amp
- Ground fault circuit interrupter, 120V, 15 amp and 20 amp
- Grounded three-prong 220/240V

Note: Ungrounded two-prong 120V receptacles are unacceptable for shop use.

Use grounded three-prong 20-amp outlets in the woodshop. This will accommodate most woodworking tools (see the tool amperage chart on page 77). If an existing woodshop has ungrounded two-prong outlets, turn off the main power and replace the old outlets with grounded outlets. If there isn't a ground wire to the outlet, attach one from the outlet to the receptacle box or the nearest cold

Overhead electrical feed rail system in Steven Gray's woodshop.

Close-up view of the electrical feed rail. Each rail is on its own separate 30-amp circuit. The rail accepts any combination of outlets and lights. Both 110V and 220V can be used simultaneously.

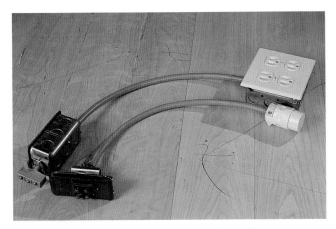

Switches and plugs are installed on the electrical feed rail system.

Various lights are installed on the electrical feed rail system.

water pipe. Check that the ground is functional by using a ground tester.

Ground fault circuit interrupter outlets (GFI) are designed to protect you from shock. GFI outlets monitor current; if the incoming and outgoing currents aren't within 0.005 amps, the GFI instantly cuts off the electricity (in ¼₀ second). GFI outlets are found in newer houses, generally in bathrooms and outdoor locations where someone may have wet hands and feet. If you are installing outlets in damp basements or around sinks, you should install GFI units. As with all electrical installations, check local codes or hire a licensed electrician if you have any questions regarding the installation.

Switches

Switches are rated according to amperage and voltage, so it's important to choose the correct switch for compatibility with circuits, wire and outlets.

There are four basic types of switches:

- Single-pole switches have two terminals, one for the incoming hot wire and one for the outgoing hot wire. The switch toggle is imprinted with ON/OFF.
- Double-pole switches have four terminals and are used primarily for 240V circuits. The switch toggle is imprinted with ON/OFF.
- Three-way switches have three terminals. One terminal is labeled COM (common), and the hot wire is connected to this terminal; the other two terminals are switch leads. Two three-way switches are used to control a circuit from two different locations. The toggle has no ON/OFF imprint.
- Four-way switches have four terminals and are used with two three-way switches to control a circuit from more than two locations. The toggle has no ON/OFF imprint.

Plugs

Despite the proliferation of battery-powered tools, there are still many tools and machines that have AC plugs. Usually these plugs receive quite a lot of use and wear, often because of the neglectful act of pulling the cord and bending the prongs. When plugs need replacing, replace them with dead-front plugs. This type of plug has no exposed wires or screws and the prongs are surrounded by smooth plastic. If there are screws on the plate surrounding the prongs, they are recessed and are only for securing the plug body together.

If you are attaching wires to a 125V plug with three prongs, connect the black wire to the brass terminal, the white wire to the silver terminal and the green wire to the green or gray terminal.

Polarized plugs are identified by having one brass prong (hot) and one silver prong with a wider tip. The plug is designed to fit into an outlet in only one direction. This plug is commonly installed on smaller appliances and woodworking tools.

LIGHTING THE WOODSHOP

There are two distinct types of lighting in most woodshops: fluorescent lighting and minimal use of all other types of lighting. Fluorescent lighting fixtures are probably used the most because they are inexpensive and commonly available. Other lighting types are thought to be useful as house lighting and not for woodshop lighting. While there is some truth to the generalization that fluorescent lights are useful in the woodshop, perhaps their limitations are overlooked.

Woodshop lighting is woefully neglected in today's woodworking. There's a cornucopia of aftermarket improvements to almost everything electric within the woodshop except lighting. Lighting stores and hardware stores usually have jumbled lighting displays, making it nearly impossible to view and judge lighting fixtures one at a time. The one exception I've found is a GE display of different fluorescent lamps. This display is a set of identical photographs, individually set in a series of recessed boxes, each lit by a different fluorescent lamp. This display nicely reveals the color-rendering differences of fluorescent lamps.

Unfortunately, few light fixtures seem to be designed specifically for woodshops. Those that are tend to be either sterile-looking white metal devices or cheap-looking clip-on reflector hoods. This simply means that it's up to the woodworker to solve shop lighting questions through both personal experience and research. Trial and error may seem like a difficult path to follow, but it does allow you to customize your woodshop.

When evaluating lights and fixtures, consider that there are several key elements to using light: color, shadow, contrast and reflection. These are the products of lighting that we see in both dynamic and subtle ways. They give usefulness, meaning and emotional connection to woodworking. Many artists refer to the process of their work as "painting with light." Woodworkers should also control and use light for both acceptable room lighting as well as artistic and aesthetic reasons.

Color is perhaps the most subjective and difficult aspect of light. A simple request proves this point: Define "red." We may generally agree upon the notion that tomatoes and apples are red, but it's extremely difficult to describe a particular color and have agreement on it: Color perception is in the eye of the beholder. Furthermore, location, situation and light source will change color. For example, if a person is holding an apple and standing in the glow of a sunset, the apple will look different (warmer) than when it's sitting on a workbench situated under fluorescent lights (cooler). If the apple is placed under a green light, it will change color again — it will appear grayish. Imagine the effect that lighting will have if a dark cherry workpiece is subjected to warm or cool lights. Will that "golden oak" stain look yellowish or greenish?

Elements That Offer Some Control Over Color

The problem isn't just that color perception is subjective, it's often that a woodworker and client can't see the same color. Suppose that you restore a Stickley chair using only fluorescent lights and the client places the chair so that it's lit by an incandescent lamp. Color for a Stickley piece is very important. In fact, collectors pay such close attention to the color that it and value are connected. The chair will appear different under those various lights — and the client probably won't be happy. This difference of color is a function of wavelength variations. Different lighting will have warmer or cooler colors with many different combinations of spectral differences.

Warmer light is often thought of as the daylight at sunset or the light from an incandescent bulb. Cooler light is the light of noon, an overcast sky or fluorescent light.

One commonly used term that describes the differences in light is temperature, expressed in degrees Kelvin (K). This scale is invaluable for selecting light to match your needs. Generally, lower degrees Kelvin represents a warmer appearance and higher degrees Kelvin represents a cooler look.

Note: The Kelvin reference, while useful, is somewhat of a "ballpark" number. The visual color of an object will be influenced by such things as the age and darkening of a bulb or by the fact that two different lights (natural and warm) may have the same Kelvin value but different color renderings.

If your work demands color-balanced conditions so that the workpiece color is true, the woodshop lighting system must be designed accordingly. The most obvious solution is to have windows and skylights so that natural light floods the work area. If that's impossible (in basements, garages and interior rooms), a mixture of different fluorescent and incandescent lights might be the solution.

Shadow, Reflection, Contrast

One of the most vexing lighting assignments I had in art school was to place an egg on a white surface that also had a white background and, using a single photoflood lamp, light the egg so that there was complete definition of the egg and no bleeding of white from the egg to the surface or background. After more than a few hours, I thought that I had a workable scene. The problem was one of

tip

The amount of light required by a person to perform a task is directly related to age. At the age of 40, the requirement is three times greater than that for a 10-year-old. At the age of 60, the need is 15 times that for a 10-year-old.

Degrees Kelvin Ratings

LIGHT SOURCE	DEGREES KELVIN
Daylight at sunrise	1,800 K
Incandescent lamp (tungsten)	2,600 K
Halogen lamp	3,200 K
Warm white fluorescent lamp	3,000 K
Cool white fluorescent lamp	4,200 K
Daylight at noon	5,000 K
Photoflood lamp (tungsten)	3,200 to 3,400 K
Photoflood lamp (daylight)	4,800 to 5,400 K
Photo strobe (electric flash)	5,200 to 5,400 K
Daylight-balanced film	5,000 to 5,400 K
"Sunshine" fluorescent lamp	5,000 K
"Daylight" fluorescent lamp	6,500 K

Degrees Kelvin is also useful if you are photographing your woodworking. The type of lights or strobes and film used will warm or cool the subject.

degree, too much or too little shadow, too much or not enough reflection and too much or too little contrast. Lighting focused straight on from the camera produced flat light; lighting from the side produced strong shadows; and diffuse lighting softened the image but at times produced no tonal separation. And all of these lighting setups were further changed if the light was close to or far from the subject.

In the woodshop, the location, type and intensity of lights will produce a continuum of unacceptable and acceptable lighting conditions. Work area illumination requires careful light placement so that the area is shadow-free. Obviously it's possible to cover every square inch of ceiling with lights, but that's very inefficient. A better method is using the correct lights at their correct location. Flat lighting can be beneficial to a cabinetmaker wanting to see dovetail layout lines clearly. However, flat lighting isn't very useful for woodcarving. Lighting that is 45° to 90° to the carving will create better and more useful shadows that enhance the carving process. The texture and incisions from carving tools are very visible and the carver can use the shadows to enliven details.

If a carver knows the location and lighting conditions of the site a large carving will finally reside in, lights can be temporarily placed in the woodshop to duplicate that lighting. This preparation can spare the carver future problems. For example, a large statue of a Greek warrior will be permanently lit by two overhead spotlights. Knowing this, the carver can dramatize specific features, such as the helmet against the skin or the shape of a flowing cape. The carver can also shape facial features, such as the nose and eyebrows so that the face isn't ruined by ugly shadows.

Generally, it's best to locate light fixtures so that light falls directly over a work area. If there are numerous fluorescent lights throughout a work area, the diffuse light should limit shadowing. If, for example, there's a fluorescent light positioned above and behind someone at a workbench (or table saw), there will be shadows in the work area. This will occur even with the diffuse lighting of numerous fluorescent lights. To avoid this problem at the workbench, I have placed one double 8' fluorescent light fixture above the workbench and I have three double 8' fluorescent light fixtures positioned perpendicular to the workbench and slightly behind and above the work side of the bench. These fixtures are approximately 5' apart and the ceiling height is 9'. The result is that I have diffuse, shadow-free lighting at the workbench. When I need more light intensity at the workbench, I clamp an incandescent Luxo articulated lamp on the corner of the workbench. This gives a spotlight effect, ideal for carving and seeing very fine drawing lines.

Ceiling height, or the distance from the light to the work area, is also important. The general rule is that for any type of light (direct or diffuse, incandescent or fluorescent), the closer to the work area the stronger the shadows. The opposite is also true: The more distance between light and work area, the weaker the shadows.

Types of Lamps

There are three main types of lights for use in the woodshop: tungsten-filament lamps, halogen lamps and fluorescent lighting.

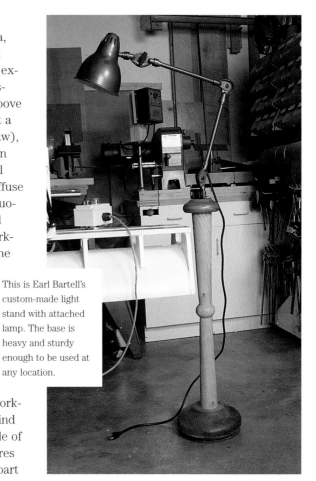

This is Earl Bartell's custom-made light stand with attached lamp. The base is heavy and sturdy enough to be used at any location.

TUNGSTEN-FILAMENT BULBS Tungsten-filament bulbs are the most common bulbs found in homes. These are made of clear, frosted or tinted glass. Tungsten lamps are the most common lamps because their light is similar to the warm tone of natural light and because they have history on their side — this is the bulb that Edison invented. Tungsten bulbs are everywhere, and it's easy to change lighting conditions by simply replacing one bulb with another type of tungsten bulb. Clear bulbs produce a bright and more contrasting type of lighting. Frosted bulbs produce a diffused lighting; tinted bulbs can add a diffused warmth to the environment. Spotlights and floodlights are also tungsten bulbs. These have body shapes and front lenses that either focus or diffuse the light. Generally, the beam angle is 15° to 25° for spotlights and 30° to 75° for floodlights.

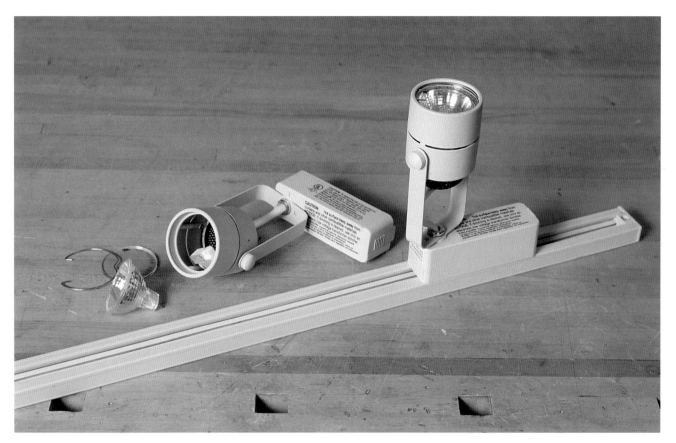

In those locations that need more direct and less diffused light, I have replaced fluorescent lights with this type of halogen track lighting. This type of light gives a brilliant white light, lasts about three times longer and uses about 65% less energy than a standard incandescent light. This particular halogen light requires a 50-watt reflector bulb that is equivalent to the light of a standard 150-watt reflector bulb. It has a built-in transformer which converts 120V to 12V.

HALOGEN LAMPS What we refer to as halogen lamps are actually tungsten-halogen lamps. There are two basic halogen lamp types: low voltage and standard line voltage. Low-voltage halogen lamps require a transformer and operate at both lower voltage and lower wattage than standard line-voltage halogen lamps. They are usually designed as reflectors, allowing them to be directed at specific work areas. Low-voltage halogen lamps are relatively small and lend themselves to use in recessed fixtures. Generally, the beam angle from the reflector is 5° to 30°.

Standard line-voltage halogen lamps are more efficient than standard incandescent tungsten lamps, but they have the disadvantages of expense and high temperatures. Light fixtures must be capable of dis-

sipating heat, and line-voltage halogen lamps should be kept away from any flammable materials — not a simple task in the woodshop. Recently, there have been safety notices regarding fires being started from certain styles of line-voltage halogen lamps, and screens have been made available for retrofitting on the lamp housing to keep cloth, paper and other flammable materials from touching the bulb. Furthermore, avoid touching the bulb with your bare hands because skin oil will affect the bulb and shorten its lifespan.

FLUORESCENT LAMPS There is a distinct division between home and commercial lighting: That is, most homes have tungsten lighting and most businesses use fluorescent lighting. The reasons for this difference are both

Choose Your Lighting Carefully

It's expensive to illuminate a woodshop, so carefully choose the best for yours.

- Use long-life, reduced-wattage bulbs whenever possible.
- If color is important, use bulbs that approximate daylight.
- Have zone lighting so that areas not in use can be unlit.
- Paint walls, ceiling and other surfaces such as pegboards, light colors.
- Use light colors for the maximum light reflection.
- Use incandescent spot lamps at drill press or band saw.
- Use droplights over workbench if you need more of a spotlight effect and less diffused light.

historical and economical. Simplistically, houses have always been built and designed with incandescent lights as the principal lighting. What we can learn from commercial use is that fluorescent lighting is a source of low-cost, efficient, diffused lighting. As a dramatic comparison, tungsten bulbs have an average life of 750 to 1,250 hours; fluorescent lights have an average life of 20,000 hours.

Fluorescent lamps are available in a variety of lengths, shapes and colors for any woodshop requirement. There are different color sensitivities, ranging from cool to warm white. Before purchasing the different varieties of fluorescent lights, make sure that the lamp and the fixture are compatible by checking the lamp's wattage with that of the ballast.

Poor-quality fluorescent lights have created a bad reputation for better quality fluorescent lights. Typical problems associated with low-quality fluorescent lights are leaking ballasts, humming or vibration noise and pulsing light. These are generally not problems in better made units, at least not until they've been in service for very long periods.

One problem that occurs in woodshops is that of long boards reaching fluorescent lights. Lights above workbenches and table saws are often hit, showering the woodworker with glass particles. Avoid this by using clear plastic sleeves or tubes which fit fluorescent lamps. If the lamp is hit and breaks, the glass shards remain in the plastic sleeve.

TYPES OF FLUORESCENT LAMPS When shopping for fluorescent lamps, find a hardware or electrical supply store that stocks a full array of lamp types. There are at least eight different types of fluorescent lights. Store displays and product packaging should furnish lamp designations, including references to color rendering, degrees Kelvin, watts and lumens. Product names, such as "cool white"

Typical Fluorescent Lights (48" tubes, GE products)

BULB NAME	°KELVIN	LUMENS*	WATTS	CRI**
Sunshine	5,000 K	2,250	40	90
Daylight Delux	6,500 K	2,250	40	84
SP-35, moderate white	3,500 K	3,200	40	73
Kitchen & Bath	3,000 K	3,200	40	70
Residential/Shoplight	4,100 K	3,150	40	72
SP-41, cool white	4,150 K	3,200	40	42

*Lumens is a unit of measurement that expresses the total quantity of light given off by a light source. For practical purposes, if comparing incandescent and fluorescent light, fluorescent lights use much less energy than incandescent bulbs and still produce similar or better light levels.

- 100-watt incandescent bulb is 1,710 lumens
- 75-watt incandescent bulb is 1,190 lumens
- 20-watt fluorescent light is 1,200 lumens
- 32-watt fluorescent light is 2,850 lumens
- 40-watt fluorescent light is 3,050 lumens

**Color rendering index (CRI) is a measurement of color shift when an object is illuminated by a light. CRI ranges from 1 to 100, with natural daylight and incandescent light equal to 100. Therefore, lights with a higher CRI produce more natural colors.

Note: Foot-candles is a measure of lumens per square foot, as measured on a working surface or floor area. For an office, the general working range is 15 to 70 foot-candles. If you are doing precise work, such as woodworking or drafting, 100 to 200 foot-candles is usually recommended. And if you think that is bright, on a cloudless sunny day, the sun gives off 1,000 foot-candles!

or "warm white," are older designations. To comply with newer U.S. government standards regarding fluorescent lights, companies have had to redesign lights. Since the newer versions of "cool white" are different from the older products, newer product names were necessary. Hence, "Sunshine or SP-41."

HIGH-INTENSITY-DISCHARGE LAMPS This lamp wasn't mentioned earlier because they are a fairly new type of lamp and are not commonly used. High-intensity-discharge (HID) lamps include metal halide lamps, mercury lamps and high-pressure sodium lamps. These have primarily been used for industrial purposes but are slowly being accepted for other uses (mostly for architectural and security purposes). There are disadvantages to using HID lamps: They require warming up and cooling down peri-

ods when they are turned on and off, and they produce a bluish light that gives an unfamiliar coloring to most things, including woodworking projects. Currently, the metal halide lamps are the only HID lamps that approach normal colorization. HID lamps, even though they are energy efficient, aren't useful for the woodshop because of their color rendering and fixture configuration.

chapter *nine*

Implementing Your Dust Collection System

If you are using machines and sanding materials for woodworking, then you are making a mixture of waste products: chunks of debris that fall in a large radius area and airborne particles which permeate the entire woodshop.

If you work exclusively with hand tools — hand saws, hand planes, chisels and scrapers — the principal waste will mostly be solid chunks deposited on the floor where you stand.

MANAGING SHOP WASTE
1. Remove floor debris with a broom or shop vacuum.
2. Capture machine-made dust and chips at the source with a dust collector.
3. Filter airborne particles with an air filtration system — or wear a filter mask.
4. Work in a wind tunnel so that all debris is blown out the door and into the neighbor's yard.
5. Ignore the problem and work in piles of chips and clouds of dust.

I have seen few totally chip-and dust-free woodshops. Most woodworkers make some effort to remove most of the debris. Although many woodshops have some sort of dust collection system, very few have air filtration systems. And even with operational dust collectors, there is dust in most woodshops. Surprisingly, few woodworkers use filter masks, and I've even found several woodshops that rely on air flow from open doors and windows to minimize air-suspended particle dust.

There are many sizes and types of dust collectors and air filtration systems. There are readily available dust collectors powerful enough to have three separate 25'-long ductworks and to simultaneously remove debris from three separate machines. Additionally, there are many magazine articles detailing how to build everything from collector ductwork systems to air filtration systems. Over the past 10-plus years there has been considerable interest in the process of ductwork collection and air filtration.

Why are Woodshops Still Dusty?
The curious reasons why there are so many dusty woodshops:
- There are those who still don't care about the hazardous or unsafe nature of dust. It's a strange mind-set, based on a perception that since woodworking tools and machines make chips and dust, the woodworker should just let the stuff fall where it may. This false perception equates productivity with the amount of dust and chips on the floor (and everywhere else). The myth that a busy woodshop is a dusty woodshop still exists.
- Another erroneous notion about dust collection is that home woodshops don't have the same volumes of productivity as professional woodshops, hence there is less dust. The Occupational Safety and Health Administration (OSHA) has rules and standards for dust levels in commercial woodshops, and they have standards about air quality, safety equipment, proper installation of dust collectors and many other issues relating to the

hazardous nature of dust because dust is unsafe. It is wrong to think that since the home woodshop is not regulated by OSHA, the need for proper dust management equipment isn't necessary.

- Collectors and filtration systems are not purchased because they aren't primary machines such as table saws or routers. Dust collectors don't directly help cut better edges or make better dovetails. It is also easy to think of dust collectors as something that we own but aren't overly enthusiastic about. Most woodworkers don't wake up in the morning thinking, "I can't wait to go to the woodshop and turn on the dust collector!"
- Dust collection systems aren't cheap. A basic dust collector costs from $300 to $1,000. 4"-diameter ductwork costs approximately $2 to $4 per foot. Fittings, such as elbows, reducers, shutoff gates and Y and T fittings cost $10 to $20 each, and replacement filter bags cost $25 to $75.
- Cost is often the only factor considered when purchasing a dust collector. There are numerous low-priced collectors that are popular simply because they are inexpensive. To be fair, some of these units probably are adequate if they only have 6' of hose and are hooked to a single machine. In order for manufacturers to make low-cost collectors they often simplify the collector's frame size, use low-quality impellers, include small-capacity filter bag sizes (and also use low-quality filter material), and install inexpensive (and lower hp) motors.
- Dust collection and air filtration systems are frequently either installed incorrectly or are inadequate for the volume of debris produced. Very often the technical specifications of dust collec-

tors aren't well understood. It's critical to understand certain technical information when purchasing a dust collector.

DUST COLLECTION BASICS

There are a few noteworthy technical considerations specific to dust collection:

- SP (static pressure) is resistance to air in a ductwork and is measured in inches of water. Resistance is often referred to as friction.
- CFM (cubic feet per minute) is air volume.
- FPM (feet per minute) is air velocity.

The question is: How do you know if a dust collector is right for your woodshop, if it is installed correctly and if it can efficiently remove debris? Several important variables affect the performance of any collector:

- technical specifications (hp and CFM)
- distance from the collector to a given machine (ductwork run)
- number of fittings
- smoothness within the ductwork system
- diameter of ductwork
- number of machines

Dust System Considerations

Dust collectors and air filtration systems need to be integrated into the entire woodshop. In fact, a case could be made that the dust collection system should be one of the first installations within a woodshop, and all machines and other features should be installed subsequently. Consider that when a new house is being constructed and the framing is finished, plumbing and electrical components are installed. Ideally, that is how dust collectors should be viewed. However, most woodworkers usually purchase a dust collector after they start generating mounds of debris from their machines. Then the dust collec-

In order to collect dust at the sanding machine, I built a plywood housing that encompasses both disc and belt sanding ports. The housing also encloses the belt beneath the table. Plastic fitting for the dust hose is available at most hardware stores.

Here is a close-up of the sanding machine's dust hose housing.

The drill press table in my woodshop features different table inserts for different-diameter sanding drums. The fence has a holder for a vacuum hose.

Here's the sanding drum lowered into the table; the vacuum hose is mounted on top of the table.

Here's the sanding drum lowered into the table and the vacuum hose mounted to the lower box.

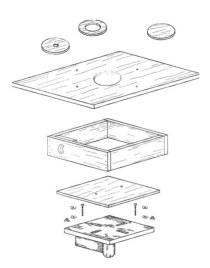

This is an exploded view of the drill press table above: The frame has a hole for the vacuum hose. The top surface has a center hole with a rabbeted edge for the holding discs. The discs have different-size cutouts to accommodate sanding drums.

tor is retrofitted to the woodshop.

Very few machines are adequately designed for dust control. To make a dust collection system functional, it must be fitted to machines so that all dust and chips are collected. This is a fundamental weakness of any woodshop collection system. Few factory machine hookups are efficient. It seems that manufacturers, in general, view dust collection as an afterthought. Consider the power tools that produce dispersed dust: planers, routers, all sanders, scroll saws, plate jointers and table saws. How many of these machines are designed with high-quality connections for dust collecting? For example, an efficient table saw dust collection should have two collection areas: The area below the table should have a collection enclosure close to the saw blade, and there should also be collection above the saw blade, preferably integrated with the blade guard. Unfortunately, these features mostly exist on the more expensive table saws.

Most experienced woodworkers eventually construct collection hookups for their machines. Well-established woodshops often have all sorts of shop-made fittings and specialized hookups on machines. These are usually made of plywood or particleboard, and sometimes acrylic-type plastics, and they are characterized by form-fitting the machine's cutting area, dust chute or wood ejection area.

Locating the Dust Collection and Air Filtration Systems

As an analogy, most woodworkers locate dust collectors much like the antiquated houses that were built before indoor plumbing and electricity. When these new conveniences were first installed in houses, they were attached to the outside of walls. (Antique tool collectors now prize the hand planes used to make channels in moulding for the exterior attachment of electrical wires.) A modern person would never consider having electrical wires exposed and running around the outside of doors and moulding, nor having water pipes visible in a kitchen or bath. Yet, that same modern person will generally not think that retrofitted and exposed dust collection ductwork is inappropriate. I realize that there are many reasons for exposed ductwork systems:

- basement woodshops with concrete walls
- using portable collectors with short hoses
- ease in suspending ductwork from rafters (joists, etc.)
- exposed ductwork is less expensive to install

New woodshops are being constructed that integrate ductwork systems into walls and under flooring. This approach requires the same mind-set that's used to install water pipes and electrical wiring. That is, there must be precise design planning of the system. Like an electrical circuit box or water heater, the dust collector must have a fixed location. This location should be somewhat removed from the general work area of the woodshop, and it should be accessible for cleaning. Furthermore, the number and location of machines should be determined prior to building the system.

I suppose it's reasonable to ask, "What's the gain of having a ductwork system built into walls and flooring?" The answer is that an internal ductwork system is out of the way, and consequently, wall and floor space is freed up and made available for other

John MacKenzie has underfloor dust collection ductwork.

uses. Most woodshops are small, and every visible surface is used for some sort of storage. Long expanses of 4"-diameter, horizontally mounted cylinders complicate the placement of cabinets, lumber storage, lighting and everything else required in the woodshop. Second, machines that are located in the central woodshop area and away from any wall create a complication regarding ductworks. For example, a table saw in an open area that is hooked up to an exposed ductwork system will have a ductwork or hose resting on the floor. This not only makes maneuvering large or heavy objects difficult, but walking over exposed ductwork is one hazardous step away from tripping.

Furthermore, the ductwork itself will eventually be damaged by being stepped on or by heavy objects falling on it. In fact, having ductwork or hose located below floor level for a table saw is enough of a justification for such a system. Of all the principal woodshop machinery, the table saw probably has the most awkward ductwork or hose arrangement. This is due to the fact that table saws have dust fittings at floor level, and the saws are generally situated in open areas, away from walls. When machines are located near walls, machines then have a back (unused) side, making it easier to install ductwork that is out of the way. It's also difficult to have ductworks and hose connections that drop from ceiling areas to the centrally located table saw. These perpendicular hoses will be in the way of lumber, and they create safety problems (the material being cut can bump into the ductwork and back toward the blade and the operator).

Requirements for An Internal Dust Collection Ductwork System

- Existing woodshops may be impossible to retrofit with an internal dust system unless there is extensive remodeling or there is a sufficiently large underfloor crawl space. Ductwork is usually from 4" to 10" in diameter and this means that systems destined for walls, ceilings and floors require sufficient open areas to accommodate these dimensions.
- If walls are not to be remodeled, wood enclosures can be made so that ductworks are enclosed within. This wood box can be located either at the wall/ceiling interface or the wall/floor interface. At either location, the ductwork is enclosed and safe from bumps and damage. Furthermore, these wood enclosures can be easily integrated with cabinets and other storage units.
- Ductwork systems that include drop-downs from the ceiling area are somewhat easier to install if there is sufficient room above joists or there is attic space. Install metal ductwork systems similar to central heating and air conditioning ductworks. However, ductwork drop-downs in the middle of a room should always be considered a nuisance; that is, drop-downs probably will be in the way of other woodshop functions (moving lumber, etc.).
- In-the-floor ductwork has the most to offer in both usefulness and in the degree of difficulty in installation. If there is sufficient floor-to-ceiling height in the woodshop, the most straightforward solution is to construct a subfloor; that is, build a new floor above the existing floor so that there is space for the ductwork system. The new subfloor should be stoutly constructed to support the heavy loads of machines and lumber. The real bonus is that ductworks can be brought up through the floor next to a machine, or even within a machine's cavity. This minimizes tripping over and/or bumping ducts and hoses.

If a new woodshop is being constructed with concrete floors, there are several considerations for ductwork below the floor. The basic room design must include adequate floor thickness and floor-to-ceiling height. Ductwork channels must be created with forms and poured cement. Instead of a single continuous floor surface, it will be necessary to carefully pour cement in different areas between forms and to ensure those areas are flat and true to each other. Once the concrete is hard, ductwork is placed in these channels and the open channel is then covered with wood, brick or concrete blocks.

The very nature of woodshop design is constant change and the incorporation of new ideas, products and evolution. Although the marketplace is now filled with a variety of similar dust collectors, the use and setup of those dust collectors is changing. It wasn't that long ago that few woodshops had any dust collection whatsoever. Now we are using dust collection systems and are attempting to customize them to our individual woodshops. Presently, it may be adequate to use dust collectors in the familiar way, using metal ductwork attached to walls and ceilings with a short length of flexible hose attached to a machine. In the near future, more and more woodshops will be set up with more efficient ductwork systems hidden in walls, ceilings and floors. Just as there was no interest in air filtration systems 20 years ago, the integrated ductwork system will undoubtedly be part of future woodshops.

SETTING UP DUST COLLECTION AND AIR FILTRATION SYSTEMS
Gather Information

Use magazine advertisements as the first source of information, and request technical information from the manufacturers and retailers that supply the collection and filtration systems. Request information about dust collectors, filtration systems, ductwork, flexible hose, remote on/off devices, high-efficiency filter bags and grounding kits. Once you have gathered your information, make comparison charts that include:

- model
- motor hp
- motor repair service location
- amperes
- voltage
- CFM (maximum)
- static pressure
- dBA at 5 ft. (dBA is a unit of measurement that expresses the relative intensity of sound. The least-perceptible sound to pain-level sound ranges from 0 to about 130 dBA.)
- hose-diameter hookup at collector
- number of hose outlets on collector
- bag capacity
- type of bag material (traps what micron size of dust particles?)

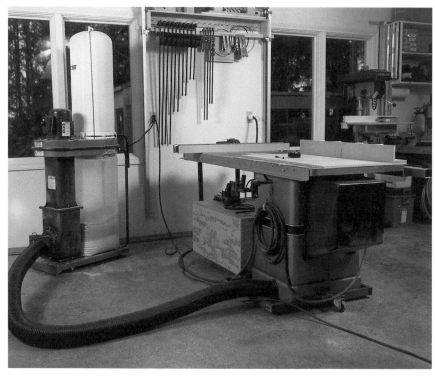

This table saw has a portable dust-collector hookup. Jon Magill plans on replacing this stiff hose with a more flexible type. He works with one machine at a time and he isn't bothered by moving the dust collector to another machine when changing operations.

- drum size
- cost of basic unit
- cost of add-on accessories

Choose a Type

There are three basic types of dust collectors: single-stage, two-stage and cyclone. Each type will collect dust. Aside from design differences, the main considerations for choosing which type to use are the number of machines and amount of dust and debris created, length of ductwork, ease of removing captured waste from bags or barrels, noise level and cost.

SINGLE-STAGE DUST COLLECTORS Single-stage collectors are visually characterized by having two or four filter bags. The bottom bags collect larger debris, and the top bags filter the finer dust and return air back into the woodshop. This type is usually the most portable and affordable in the marketplace. There are two common drawbacks to the single-stage collector, both of which are easily

remedied. It is often stated that, because the debris travels directly through the impeller housing, there is unnecessary wear on parts. Manufacturers of better-quality units often make heavy-duty impellers or design the impeller so that a bent fin can be easily replaced. Optionally, an in-line separator can be installed before the collector in order to separate out larger debris. These inexpensive units are installed between the woodworking machine and the dust collector. They simply replace the lid on a garbage can. Chips are then deflected via baffles into the garbage can and only very small debris and dust continues through to the main dust collector.

I have used this style with four bags for over 15 years and have never had mechanical problems. However, I strongly recommend that no large wood fragments or cutoff pieces be vacuumed into the impeller — that would probably cause damage. I don't have a floor sweep, a floor-level de-

Doug Matthews keeps his dust collector tucked behind an unfinished interior wall. The planer and jointer are easily hooked up to the collector when they are used. Note how he has also used this area for clamp storage.

bris pickup attachment, connected to the system because I don't want large, heavy objects zooming through the ductwork and slamming into the spinning impeller. The second serious drawback of the single-stage collector is the blowing of fine dust through the filter bags and back into the woodshop. The filter bags that come with most collectors are porous enough to allow fine dust through the bag weave. As a consequence, larger debris is caught in the bags and fine dust migrates throughout the woodshop, creating unpleasant and unnecessary air pollution. Replacement filter bags that filter down to 1 micron particle size are recommended.

TWO-STAGE DUST COLLECTORS Two-stage collectors are characterized by a blower motor on top of a collector drum (35 or 55 gallons) with a side-mounted filter bag. Generally this type is mounted on wheels. These are designed so that larger debris settles into the drum, and fine dust is captured in the filter bag. The significant drawback is that the motor housing is heavy and it has to be lifted off in order to empty the collector drum (which is also heavy when it's full). This is a tiresome process, especially if you need to frequently empty the drum. Those that use this type often use ropes and pulleys to raise the housing off the drum.

CYCLONE DUST COLLECTORS Cyclone collectors appear to be industrial; it's a tall steel cylinder with a funneled midsection and a 35- or 55-gallon collector drum. Debris enters the upper chamber and is cyclonically separated. Larger debris spirals downward into the collection drum, and the fine dust is caught in filters located within or near the cyclone unit. The exterior filters, called shaker bags, are a series of tall, thin bags, that effectively trap dust particles and filter the exiting air. Most of the cyclone units are fairly quiet when operating. This is due in part to having a muffler for quieting the exiting air. Interestingly, there are two types of cyclone systems: commercially made units and do-it-yourself units (*WOOD Magazine*, Issue 100, November 1997).

Stay Within Code

Check local building codes concerning the placement of collectors. Certain types of collectors may need to be located outside of the main woodshop.

Lay Out Your System

Draw a layout for your woodshop. Locate the collector so that it's out of the way without requiring unnecessary ductwork lengths. As a reference, consider the vein pattern in a leaf. Determine the length of the ductwork, the number of fittings (elbows, etc.) and the diameter of the ductwork.

The Oneida cyclone dust collector, shown above in Charles Caswell's shop, has the air filter within the cyclone. It also features a muffler (protruding horizontally just below the motor), 5" ductwork, 35-gallon fiber barrel and a remote on/off switch located on the combination machine.

For this cyclone dust collector, the filter bags are suspended in a closet. The cyclone unit is located outside of the woodshop, behind the closed door, visible through the window.

Typical Air Flow Requirements for Various Machines

MACHINE	CFM
Table saw	300-350
Band saw	400-700
Disc sander	300-350
Jointer	350-440
Planer	400-785
Shaper	300-1,400
Lathe	350-500

CFM Requirements for Duct Diameters

DUCT DIAMETER	CFM@3500 FPM
3"	170
4"	300
5"	475

Static Pressure by Duct Diameter

DUCT DIAMETER	INCHES OF STATIC PRESSURE*
3"	7.5
4"	5.5
5"	4.2
6"	3.5

*3,500 FPM per 100' of duct

Note that the length of ductwork and its internal smoothness, as well as the shape and number of fittings, all increase frictional resistance to air flow. Any internal friction and/or air turbulence decreases collection efficiency.

Ducts and fittings that have gradual directional changes will help make a system more efficient. Avoid ductwork runs having abrupt angles or turns. If possible, avoid using 90° T fittings; instead, use 45° to minimize turbulence. If different diameters are required, use tapered connectors for smoother transitions between the ductworks.

Companies such as Air Handling Systems by Manufacturers Service Co., Delta Machinery Corp. and Oneida Air Systems, Inc., all provide excellent information regarding how to determine CFM for the system, ductwork air velocity, system resistance, and the proper size of ductworks and fittings. If you send Oneida Air Systems a blueprint of your woodshop, they will design the correct ductwork for your woodshop — free.

Consider Your Needs

The diameter of the ductwork will affect air flow. Wood dust requires a minimum velocity of 3,500 FPM within the main ductwork or debris can settle out of the airstream, leading to blockage problems. The two variables that relate to ductwork diameter are velocity and static pressure. Larger-diameter ductwork increases static pressure and reduces air velocity; as ductwork diameter decreases, static pressure decreases and air velocity increases. The main consideration is to minimize static pressure loss. To accomplish this you must measure each ductwork run; that is, the length from the machine to the collector. Also, each fitting causes a reduction in air velocity, so fittings must also be factored into the length measurement. The common practice is to assign an equivalent length for a fitting. For example, a 90° elbow is equivalent to 6' of duct, or a 45° elbow is equivalent to 3' of duct. Therefore, a ductwork run that consists of 20' of straight 4" ductwork, three 90° elbows and one 45° elbow is equivalent to 41' of ductwork.

To use this value, there is another step to calculate the actual static pressure for the ductwork run. Static pressure is usually based upon 100' of ductwork. 4"- and 5"-diameter ductwork are the most commonly used sizes.

For the example of 41', multiply 0.41 (41' of 100') by 5.5, equaling 2.55" of static pressure ("inches of water"). If the filter bags are dirty, an additional static pressure loss should also be added to the value. As a generalization, add a value of 1, thus equaling 3.55". Note: This is for one ductwork run without any branch runs. If several machines are hooked up to the collector but are operated one at a time, the ductwork diameter will be dependent on the machine with the greatest CFM requirement.

If you are creating a complicated network of ductwork and fittings, careful calculations of ductwork length and all fittings is required. Determine the static pressure value for the entire system and compare that value with those of the various dust collectors in the marketplace. This value isn't absolute: there are a number of factors that influence the actual rating. Air leaks, ductwork crimps and rivets, ductwork interior smoothness, corrugated flex hose, dirty filter bags and machine hookup attachments are only a few of the variables influencing dust collector efficiency.

Metal Ductwork

Metal ductwork is slightly more difficult to install than plastic (PVC) pipe, but it is easier to ground against static electricity. Oneida Air Systems recommends using 26- to 24-gauge, or heavier, galvanized straight pipe for small custom woodshops. Heating and ventilation ductwork (usually 30 gauge) is too thin for dust collection because it can be easily dented. This causes disruption in the air flow; also the thin walls can collapse under dust collector fan pressure.

Flex hose should be used for connecting metal ductwork to a machine. Keep the lengths to a minimum because of the increased air resistance within the uneven hose.

Plastic Pipe

The common method for grounding plastic pipe is to run a ground wire inside the entire length of the pipe and then attach it at either end to the machine and the earth ground. The disadvantage of this method is that wood debris can break the internal wire unbeknownst to the operator. Debris can also lodge around the wire and eventually cause a blockage. I won't use plastic pipe because static electrical charges build up as dust travels rapidly through it — and airborne dust has the potential to be highly combustible. I talked with one woodworker who thought he had done all the correct hookups and grounding for using plastic pipe. Yet, late one night, when no one was using the woodshop, there was a static discharge within the pipe which sparked into residual dust and his woodshop was lost to fire. Another person told me his story of attempting to add more PVC pipe to an existing system. The PVC pipe was grounded and the system was off. When he hand sawed into the pipe, there was a static discharge powerful enough that it knocked him across the room.

AIR FILTRATION

Air filtration is perhaps one of the most important features that relate to a woodworker's health. Fine dust particles will stay in air suspension for hours. These particles are so small that they are almost invisible. However, a person in the woodshop will breathe these particles into the nasal and throat passages and lungs. There is much evidence as to the health risks of breathing dust, so the ideal woodshop should have a

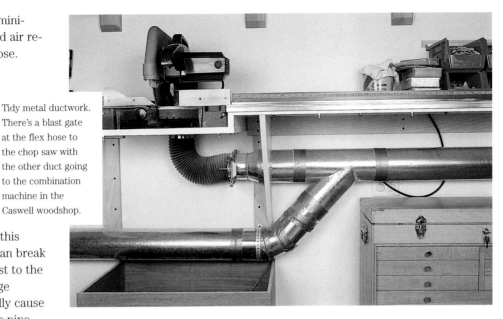

Tidy metal ductwork. There's a blast gate at the flex hose to the chop saw with the other duct going to the combination machine in the Caswell woodshop.

method of removing these particles. As a doctor woodworking friend once said, "You don't breathe the large chips that settle out on the floor, you breathe the tiny airborne particles that you can't see."

I had numerous woodworkers tell me they think that their woodshops got dustier after they installed dust collectors. So, the first thing to do before using a new dust collector is to make the dust collection system free of dust leakage. Leakage can occur at the machine and the filter bags. Well-fit hookups at the machine are mandatory. If the machine's factory-made hookup seems inadequate, make your own. Second, most dust collection bags are susceptible to dust migrating through the fibrous weavings. Most standard-issue bags capture dust sizes of 10 to 50 microns; smaller sizes escape back into the woodshop environment. The best solution is to check with the dust collector manufacturer about replacing the bags with high-efficiency filter bags, which will filter particles down to 1 micron in size.

Air filtration units are also becoming popular. These units are hung from the ceiling in the room's air circulation pattern and filter the air. By using a continuous-duty fan and a se-

Plastic Pipe Guidelines

If you are determined to use plastic pipe for dust collection because "Old George at your woodworkers' club uses it," you should at least do the following:

1. Ground the pipe by installing a taut ground wire inside of it.
2. Also ground the plastic pipe by wrapping a ground wire spirally around the outside of it. Both types of grounding should be done to all pipes in the system, and the wires should be properly attached at either end to machines and a proper ground location.
3. Assemble the plastic pipes so that they can be unassembled for cleaning out chip blockages (use pipe connectors and ductwork tape).
4. Occasionally check for any internal blockage and for continuity in the internal ground wire (look for chip buildup around the wire and for wire abrasion).

ries of filters, very fine airborne dust (1 to 5 microns) is trapped and clean air is circulated back into the woodshop. The air filtration unit is not meant to be a dust collector. Rather, its purpose is solely to filter the finest dust from the air. Commercially made units cost approximately $250 to $700. However, it's fairly easy to make your own air filtration unit by building a plywood box (approximate size would be 12" × 24" × 36") and installing a furnace-type fan (¼ hp) with several high-quality slide-in furnace type filters. Carbon filters can be added to the air filtration unit so that fumes and odors are also filtered out of the woodshop.

The ideal solution for dust collection, especially if your woodshop is attached to your house, is to have an efficient unit that is both quiet and powerful enough to use with several machines operating. For most woodshops, suspend metal ductwork from the ceiling and make certain that the ducts are properly sealed, free of leaks and properly grounded against static electricity buildup. The hookup fittings should be well made and fit tightly on the machines. The dust collector should have high-efficiency filter bags and a manageable system for removing the drums or bags when they are filled. Finally, an air filtration unit should be hung from the ceiling so that fine dust is also captured. If that doesn't make a dust-free woodshop, open a window and the door.

Accessories

I suppose that anything purchased separately from the basic dust collector is considered an accessory. But several noteworthy items will definitely improve dust collectors. Check for availability — or adaptability — with specific models of dust collectors. Accessories include:

- high-quality filtration bags — look at the specifications of these bags and be certain they offer at least a 99% efficiency in

Here is a Delta air cleaner suspended from a ceiling.

filtering 1-micron particles
- in-line separator — this item is installed between a machine and dust collector and looks like a garbage can lid; it has no moving parts and simply sits on a standard garbage can; an inexpensive improvement for most dust collection systems
- positionable vacuum hose — Lockwood Products makes the Loc-Line vacuum hose, a nifty articulated self-supporting (up to 3') ball-and-socket type of hose that is ideal for dust pickup at the drill press or the router table; a 2½" vacuum hose — the typical shop vacuum; the Loc-Line system has many different fittings, including both a round and a rectangular nozzle, slide valve (blast-gate), 3" PVC adapter and shop vacuum adapter
- automatic blast-gates — Ecogate manufactures a system of computerized blast-gates that automatically open or close when a machine is either turned on or off; control box allows you to set the sensitivity of the sensors, and can be programmed to keep one or more gates open; this system reduces the time of manually working blast-gates, saves electrical energy and actually assists in woodshop cleanliness; plus, not a complicated installation

A small blower fan is used to vent the shop of very fine airborne dust.

A TYPICAL DUST COLLECTION SYSTEM

The most confusing aspect of setting up a dust collection system is understanding the relationships of air volume or CFM (air measured in cubic feet per minute) and static pressure (the resistance to air at rest in a ductwork) to the length and diameter of ductwork and the number of machines in the woodshop.

Let's assume that your woodshop is in either a garage or basement and you are the only person operating machinery. Your plan is to connect the dust collection system to a table saw, band saw, jointer, planer, disc/belt sander, lathe and drill press:

1. After you have reviewed the specifications of all potential dust collectors, select the one that has the greatest horsepower (at least 1½ to 3 hp) and is rated greater than 700 CFM at 5" to 6" of static pressure. For example:
   - Grizzly model G1029, 2 hp, 1,182 CFM at 5.00" of static pressure
   - Oneida air blower, 2 hp, 900 CFM at 8.00" of static pressure
   - Delta model 50-181, 2 hp, 1,100 CFM at 8.50" of static pressure
   - Bridgewood BW-003, 3 hp, 1,950 CFM at 5.80" of static pressure
   - Oneida air blower, 3 hp, 1,350 CFM at 8.00" of static pressure

2. Determine the filter bag area. Typical bag sizes range from 10 to 40 square feet. As a guide, have at least 1 square foot of filter bag area for every 10 CFM. For example, a 10 square foot filter bag is useful for a 1,000 CFM collector. If the filter bag area is less than the rated CFM, install larger bags.

3. Install metal 6" and 5" main ductwork going out from the collector. Generally, 6"-diameter ductwork is used nearest the collector and then it's reduced to a

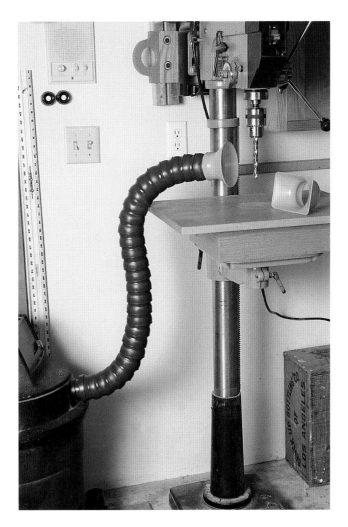

The Loc-Line flexible vacuum line (2½" I.D.) is self-supporting — to approximately 36" — and with an adapter fits the 2¼" connector hose hole of a shop vacuum. This is a long overdue solution for collecting dust at the drill press or other machines that don't have built-in collector capabilities. Shown are 36" of Loc-Line, the 4½" round nozzle and the 6" × 3½" rectangular nozzle. Various other accessories are available, including a 3" sheet-metal duct adapter.

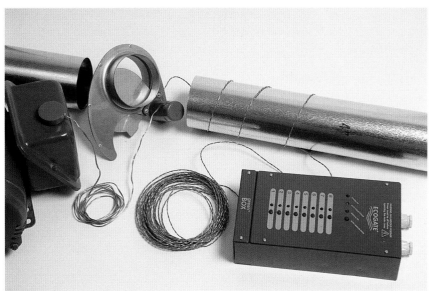

The Ecogate electronic blast-gate has sensors to detect which gate to automatically open or close when debris is moving within the ductwork, thus saving the operator time, and lowering electrical operation costs. I have laid out the basic configuration (from left to right): a woodworking machine motor, sensor pad with wiring to the Ecogate, ductwork with the spirally wrapped connector wire from the gate to the electronic control box.

5"-diameter ductwork further from the collector.

4. Please don't use plastic pipes. Plastic pipes can be dangerous because of the significant static electricity charges that are generated when air, wood dust and chips travel through the pipes.

5. Securely assemble the ductwork system with pop rivets, sheet-metal screws or ductwork tape. Seal all ductwork with silicone sealer, and be sure there are no small openings or cracks, which cause air loss.

6. Minimize the use of elbows and turns. Use large-radius elbows when branching off of the main ductwork to the individual machines; don't use 90° T fittings. Also, use 45° Y fittings for any turns off of the main ductwork line. If it's necessary to use smaller diameter hose, use reducer fittings on the machine side of the elbows. Use metal ductworks up to within approximately 3' of the machine. Then, use flexible hose as the 3' connector to the machine. Properly ground the flexible hose by wrapping the ground wire around the hose and attaching one end to the metal ductwork and the other to ground.

7. Use gates (blast-gates) at all machines to control air to each machine. Place the gate between the metal ductwork and the flexible hose.

   • When using the dust collection system, keep blast-gates closed at unused machines.

   • If the dust collector is in an out-of-the-way location, install a remote control device for wireless on/off operation. These units are available from most sellers of dust collectors.

Wood Toxicity Safety Guidelines

• Always wear some form of face mask or respirator. Disposable masks are often form-fit around the nose and mouth; reusable respirators have replaceable filter cartridges. If these are inadequate for your needs, there are space-age-looking air purifying respirators. These have a hard hat with a clear plastic face shield. The shield form-fits the entire face, and at the back of the hard hat is a fan unit that blows filtered air over the top of the head and down across the face. Note that you are breathing filtered air — and not breathing through a filter. While these units are expensive, they offer features not found in standard filter masks, such as full-face protection from flying debris (they are popular with lathe turners) and comfort for woodworkers with beards or eyeglasses (standard filter masks and respirators don't fit well on beards and under eyeglasses).

• Wear long-sleeved shirts to keep dust off your arms. Don't wear loose or unbuttoned shirts because loose clothes and machinery are a disaster waiting to happen. Long-sleeved T-shirts are a better choice.

• If you are sanding, create air circulation away from the work area. Place a portable fan at one end of the workbench and sand at the other end. The fan should blow dust away from you.

CONSIDER WOOD TOXICITY

Perhaps after the discussion of machines and collectors, there is another topic that needs to be mentioned — toxic woods. While dust collectors will remove the majority of dust and chips, it is inevitable that some dust is going to fall on your skin and be breathed into your lungs.

Sometimes I think that working with wood is like having a tiger for a pet — it looks great, but it can bite your hand off. While everyone has different sensitivity levels, wood is known to cause skin and eye allergies as well as respiratory and cardiac problems. Some woods are classified as primary irritants because they are highly toxic (West Indian satinwood, for example). Other woods are classified as sensitizers because they may cause physical reactions after repeated exposures (such as cocobolo).

One of the toxic conditions that is often difficult, if not impossible, for consumers to know about is wood contaminated with pesticides and preservatives. Treated lumber in the United States is labeled as such, and the manufacturers post handling guidelines for their products. Unfortunately, while there are many chemicals banned from use in the United States, those chemicals are often used by foreign companies with no posted notices or guidelines.

If you have questions about wood toxicity, consult your own physician, the Occupational Safety and Health Administration (OSHA), your local city health department, and/or textbooks on poisonous plants.

A Partial Listing of Woods and Their Potential Hazards

WOOD	REACTION LOCATION*
Arbor Vitae	respiratory
Bald Cypress	respiratory
Balsam Fir	skin, eyes
Beech	respiratory, skin, eyes
Birch	respiratory
Black Locust	skin, eyes
Blackwood	skin, eyes
Boxwood	respiratory, skin, eyes
Cashew	skin, eyes
Cedar, Western Red	respiratory, skin, eyes
Cocobolo	respiratory, skin, eyes
Ebony	respiratory, skin, eyes
Elm	skin, eyes
Goncalo Alves	skin, eyes
Greenheart	respiratory, skin, eyes
Hemlock	respiratory
Mahogany, African	respiratory, skin, eyes
Mahogany, American	skin, eyes
Mansonia	respiratory, skin, eyes
Maple, spalted	respiratory
Myrtle	respiratory
Oak	skin, eyes
Obeche	respiratory, skin, eyes
Oleander	respiratory, skin, eyes
Olivewood	respiratory, skin, eyes
Padauk	respiratory, skin, eyes
Pau Ferro	skin, eyes
Purpleheart	nausea, malaise
Redwood, Sequoia	respiratory, skin, eyes
Rosewood, Brazilian	respiratory, skin, eyes
Rosewood, East Indian	respiratory, skin, eyes
Satinwood	respiratory, skin, eyes
Sassafras	nausea, malaise
Snakewood	respiratory
Spruce	respiratory
Teak	respiratory, skin, eyes
Walnut, black	skin, eyes
Wenge	respiratory, skin, eyes
Willow	respiratory, nausea, malaise
Yew	nausea, malaise, cardiac
Zebrawood	skin, eyes

*This does not represent the order in which any ailments or problems occur.

This information on wood toxicity is from "Health Hazards in Woodworking" by Stanley N. Wellborn, *Fine Woodworking*, Winter 1977, *American Woodturner*, June 1990.

chapter *ten*

Creating Useful Storage Space

WHY STORE STUFF AT ALL? I'VE never been certain about the concept behind the need for storage. Do we store things for organizational reasons, for clutter control, for easy access or simply because we have too much stuff? Ideally, any part, accessory or tool should be within reach during the work process. Realistically, however, everyone has shelves, cabinets, drawers, walls, hangers, rafters, bins, boxes, barrels, racks and trunks full of the useful, rare, odd and ordinary. We usually have favorite tools stored individually at arm's length, and everything else is put away. Diet books and storage books have something in common — sheer numbers. There are hundreds of books, magazines and videos offering every conceivable solution to taming the flotsam and jetsam — or the delicate and valuable objects — of our lives. And one more point: Woodworkers make objects. We either make artistic objects or we make cabinets, shelves, drawers or boxes for storing and displaying everything and anything.

Woodworkers are collectors. We collect everything that seems useful, and we justify our collecting with the rationale that we need it — or will need it someday. It always sounds reasonable to say, "I need a complete set of brad-point drill bits, including $\frac{9}{64}$" and $\frac{7}{32}$". Realistically, you may only need $\frac{1}{4}$", $\frac{3}{8}$" and $\frac{1}{2}$" brad-point bits, but there's always the uncertainty that leads you to believe that a set of 12 bits is necessary. Besides, the tool catalogs enthusiastically declare that having a set of 12 bits is invaluable.

In addition to collecting extras of any given object, woodworkers also collect interesting tools, wood, information (books, magazines and plans), accessories, gadgets and finishing products. We generally obtain these items as if space and storage aren't of any concern. We don't just have one of anything; we like sets and collections so much that we go on quests to complete a particular set. We specialize in our tools and things so much that we become experts on the rare and unusual. We join clubs devoted to antique tools or wood samples. We track down obscure and out-of-the-way dealers in order to possess hard-to-find Stanley Bedrock planes or pieces of Pink Ivory. No one should doubt that woodworkers are

Here's a view of clamp storage in my woodshop. The upper 4" × 4" beam has an angled face so that clamps are suspended at an angle. Shorter bar clamps are suspended from $\frac{1}{2}$" metal dowels inserted into a secured 2" × 4" board.

Types of Woodshop Storage

- Floor-level and wall-hung cabinets
- Modular, freestanding cabinets
- Portable units
- Shelving
- Pegboard
- Lumber storage

at the center of the storage issue as both creators and users.

ORGANIZE SHOP STORAGE

After you have established the locations of machines and the workbench within the woodshop space, it's time to organize storage. If the room is built and the machines are in place, start by standing near each machine and imagining what work will be like and what tools and accessories might be needed while working. Determine the needs for all machines and then make a master list for the entire woodshop. An example list might include:

Table Saw
- three saw blades
- tenon jig
- push sticks
- miter guide
- featherboard
- angle fence
- dado set

Band Saw
- five blades
- circle cutter
- miter guide
- fence

Planer
- dial indicator
- spare knives
- table wax

Drill Press
- drill index
- multispur bits
- sanding drum set
- extra-length bits

Three types of storage are shown in the above photo: cabinet storage for the drill press, pegboard storage for infrequently used accessories and workbench shelf storage for frequently used tools.

Consider Your Options

Once the list is completed, consider storage options: shelves, open wall hangers, open cabinets, closed cabinets, drawers and so on. Then ask yourself, is one or more storage units necessary? Is there a need for one local storage center, or does each machine need its own storage? Note those tools, such as a dial indicator, that should be kept dust-free and those tools unaffected by dust (band saw blades). Also, drill bits are easily lost in clutter; they are best kept in orderly sets.

DESIGN STORAGE SPACE

The next planning step is extremely critical to the overall shop plan. Basically, two very different designs can be selected, and each will fundamentally affect the woodshop. The choice is that of having randomly designed storage or having unified storage.

Random Storage

Random storage is characterized by what is generally done: a hodgepodge of shelves, pegboard, hooks, hangers,

Here's an inside view of the drill press cabinet shown in the top photo.

Harry Charowsky swears he knows where everything is in his random tool storage system.

Simple dividers keep small hand planes from rubbing and bumping.

A thin board ($\frac{1}{8}$") with attached dividers separates chisels and isolates the cutting edges.

Use a thin drawer to store all the screws, collets, plates and other small items used with routers. By lining the tray with fuzzy felt, the numerous small items don't migrate in the tray.

cans and cabinets. Unified storage is exemplified by cabinets similar to those found in kitchens, baths and design books. Most woodshops have random storage because new things are added over long periods of time. Interestingly, hodgepodge storage doesn't mean that things can't be found. After a while, most woodworkers know where they stored the No. 8 brass roundhead screws. It all becomes second nature. Unfortunately, despite the fact that they are inefficient, waste space and are usually covered with thick layers of dust — shelves are still the most common storage arrangement.

Unified Storage

Unified woodshop storage should, at its essence, maximize the available space or area allotted for storage. This can be accomplished by designing storage units so that there are no dead areas. For example, instead of making a 5'-high cabinet, make it floor-to-ceiling and use the upper shelves for infrequently used items. Or construct European-style cabinets because they have less wasted internal space. Design a mixture of storage types so that they complement each other. Have a cabinet, for example, for storing hand planes. And next to the cabinet use pegboard for hanging hammers and yardsticks.

MATERIALS AND STORAGE DESIGN

The design of storage units will be influenced by the type of materials used. Solid-wood construction procedures will be different than those needed for working man-made materials.

Solid-Wood Construction

If solid-wood constructions are desired, a number of woodworking tools

and skills are required. For example, suppose you want to build a Shaker-style wall cabinet. The following are the generalized steps needed to duplicate or simulate this early-1800s construction:

1. Purchase rough lumber approximately 1" to 1½" in thickness. Allow for waste, and order 20% to 30% more than the project requires. Typical woods are pine,

cherry and oak.

2. Plane lumber to different thicknesses, varying from ⅜" to 1".
3. Use a hand plane or joiner to square and straighten edges.
4. Glue boards edge to edge to make wider pieces.
5. Construct the basic cabinet box using joinery: traditional dovetails or modern joints, such as box joints, plate joinery, dowels or screws.
6. Construct internal framework consisting of different sizes of wood. Use hand tools or a router to make rabbets and sliding dovetail-type joints.
7. Construct frame and panel doors consisting of tongue-and-groove and mortise-and-tenon joinery. Use chisels, saw, hand planes, router table or shaper.
8. Construct drawers with dovetail joints. Use hand tools, a router and a dovetail jig.
9. Fit doors and drawers to cabinet so that seasonal weather changes won't cause them to stick, bind or be too loose fitting.

Using Man-Made Materials

In contrast, the construction of a modern cabinet using man-made materials follows a different set of steps.

1. Purchase ½"- and ¾"-thick materials. Itemize cutting list and purchase necessary amount of materials. Typical materials are particleboard and medium-density fiberboard (MDF).
2. Cut materials to size.
3. Assemble materials with butt or rabbet joints. Use a router, plate joinery, screws and nails.
4. Cover exposed edges with veneer-type tape or strips of solid wood.
5. Use either face-frame or the frameless European cabinet construction for the front of the cabinet.
6. Construct drawers with dadoes and grooves. Use a router, screws or nails.

CABINET CONSTRUCTION

Most modern cabinet constructions use a blend of man-made materials and solid wood. It's common to see cabinets that have plywood sides, top, bottom and shelves, and solid-wood doors, door frame and drawer fronts.

Face-Frame Cabinets

Typically, the face-frame cabinet has a 2"-wide frame covering the front edge of the cabinet. The frame thus reduces the size of the cabinet opening, with doors and drawers smaller than the cabinet width. Doors are typically attached to the frame with exposed hinges; drawer fronts usually overlap onto the frame. The toe space at the cabinet's base is made by cutting notches into the side pieces.

European-Style Cabinets

The frameless or European cabinet has no face frame. Instead, the front edges are covered to the same width as the cabinet box material thickness. Doors and drawers are usually flush to the cabinet edges and each other. That means more usable interior space. European cabinets are sometimes referred to as "the 32 millimeter system" because of the standardization of using 32 millimeters as the space between hinge fittings, shelf-support holes and cabinet joints. Frameless cabinets are generally made as a box and then attached to a separate base frame. This allows for the toe space as well as different height bases.

DO IT YOURSELF OR NOT?

It's an old saying that woodworkers should build their own woodshop cabinets and benches in order to understand, practice and refine their various woodworking skills. While there is nothing wrong with this viewpoint, I would like to offer an update on this old saying by breaking it down into various elements,

somewhat like a logic puzzle. Ponder the following thoughts and questions.

1. Is building storage cabinets for the woodshop really a preparation for using the woodshop?
2. If you are an amateur or hobby woodworker, how much time do you have to devote to woodworking?
3. Is cost-effectiveness an issue?
4. What machines and tools are available for building storage?
5. How will you transport materials?
6. Is the location for storage unusual, unique or average (i.e., the need for special or standard-size storage)?
7. What will you learn about woodworking by cutting plywood, particleboard and drilling holes?
8. Can you make it the same as, or better than, commercial storage units?
9. Is the woodworking process (including making storage units) one of self-expression, personal enrichment and an element of quality of life?
10. Do you have the space for working with sheet goods?
11. Do you have the physical strength for handling full-size sheets of ¾"-thick plywood?
12. Is making everything in the woodshop a rite of passage?

Consider Time and Money

It's not easy to answer each of these questions with a simple response. However, a few parts are very real; that is, time and money. Very often it takes considerable time to design, purchase materials, build and install cabinets and other storage units. We may watch someone on TV build a cabinet during a 30-minute program, but I can assure you that real life woodworking takes significantly longer. Ask yourself, "How much is my free time worth?"

Don't Dismiss Purchasing Storage Units

I appreciate the love affair with working wood. The magic of taking a raw material and turning it into personal and useful objects is something I never tire of. At the same time, I realize home improvement centers sell cabinets and storage units at very affordable prices. In fact, it is often less expensive to purchase these units than it is to build them. For example, I recently looked at a 36"-wide by 12"-deep by 72"-tall cabinet that had two doors and adjustable shelving. The cost was under $100. That's a persuasive argument for not "doing-it-yourself"!

Of course, there are very real, legitimate reasons to buy and use off-the-shelf storage units. An incredible variety of these units are sold at home improvement centers, including wire shelves and bins, airtight plastic containers, tall cabinets with shelves and doors, and drawer units. They are designed for bedrooms, dens, laundry rooms, kitchens and garages, and most are adaptable for woodshop applications. These units usually come in flat boxes, and you assemble the units at home. I'm impressed with bedroom closet storage units because they often are composed of smaller drawers and many small cubicles and are designed to cover entire walls. These are the features that would adapt to a woodshop (glue bottles would fit nicely into a shirt cubicle and tie racks could hold sanding belts or extension cords). Besides being affordable, ready-made storage offers a simplicity that's valuable, especially if you're just starting out in woodworking and are not equipped to work with large sheets of particleboard and plywood.

BUILDING SHOP STORAGE

Basic storage units are shelves, wall hooks and hangers, bookcase-style

Built-in workbench with open storage area. Plastic containers are used for holding odds and ends.

open cabinets, racks and cabinets with shelves, drawers and doors. Wall-hung devices and shelves are inexpensive and easily installed; cabinets require more materials, construction skills and machinery. Very often simple shelving, hooks and hangers are used because of installation simplicity. Pegboard wall coverings offer real storage value, and open shelving has serious limitations. The disadvantage of open shelving is that shelves unattached to wall hangers are easily unbalanced and subject to tipping when heavy tools are stored on them. Open shelving units are useless for storing items that you want dust free; items should be sealed away in boxes when dust-free storage is required. And if there are several boxes on a shelf, detailed labeling is required; otherwise, it's difficult to locate items. Perhaps it's best to think of shelving as a bag of candy: It's OK to to have one or two pieces (a few shelves), but don't have a diet of it (not everywhere in your woodshop).

Ideally, woodshop storage should be based upon cabinets and/or pegboard. Within these two storage types

are worlds of possibilities. Furthermore, pegboard offers simple storage solutions and cabinets offer creative storage possibilities.

Building European-Style Cabinets

European frameless cabinet design has definite benefits. The design is somewhat simplified because there is no framework attached to the front of the cabinet. That is, doors are attached to the cabinet sides and not the frame which encircles the front of standard face-frame cabinets. The lack of a frame means better access to the entire inside area of a cabinet — there are no hidden spots as there are behind face-frame constructions. And, while it is true that there are improvements in face-frame hinges, the heart of the European-style cabinet is sophisticated hinges. They come in models that have adjustable tension settings that open to different degrees and that will softly close with a touch. Finally, European-style cabinets require no hardwood — since there is no face frame — and they are usually made from particleboard with a veneer tape on the edges.

CHOOSING MATERIALS

Georgia-Pacific is one of the larger manufacturers of man-made materials, and they broadly classify the common materials into "engineered board and structural panels." Particleboard, medium-density fiberboard (MDF) and hardboard are termed engineered board, and plywood and oriented-strand board (OSB) are structural panels. Structural panels are used primarily for house construction. Quality grades of particleboard, MDF and hardboard make ideal cabinet materials if they are used properly. They are readily available, cost less than solid wood or plywood and have dimensional stability, flatness and no voids.

EVALUATING MAN-MADE MATERIALS The disadvantages of particleboard must also be considered. First, particleboard is made with urea-formaldehyde glue, and there are health concerns regarding formaldehyde. To minimize the vapors escaping from particleboard, all particle surfaces and edges should be sealed.

Particleboard can be purchased with a coated surface, or a variety of materials can be glued onto it. Surface materials are usually plastic laminates, melamine or wood veneer. Plastic laminates and melamine are smooth surface materials, available in different colors. Laminates include brand-name materials such as Formica and Wilsonart, and they are generally more expensive than melamine. However, even novice woodworkers can glue laminates to particleboard; melamine is bonded to the surface at the factory. Melamine is the most common and affordable surface material; it is a tough plastic-type material that seals the particleboard or MDF and resists wear, chemicals and stains.

Almost any wood is available as wood veneer. Businesses that specialize in veneers generally stock rarewood veneers, such as Brazilian Rosewood, or more common woods

Here, a tall cabinet holds accessories near the workbench. The cabinet features an angled shelf for easy access to hand planes.

Pegboard storage.

such as walnut and oak. These veneers are available in sheets and rolls, and they are often sequentially numbered, like pages in a book. This permits matching of grain and color patterns for striking finished appearances. Wood veneer is attached to particleboard or MDF with wood veneer glue, or it's available as factory-attached surfaces.

Other disadvantages of particleboard are that it doesn't hold screws well, it's not moisture resistant and its edges are subject to crumbling if roughly handled. Coated particleboard must be cut with good equipment. Commercial cabinet shops use very large-surface table saws with sliding tables. These saws often have two saw blades, a scoring blade and a sawing blade, that then produce a chip-free cut. Smaller, contractor-type table saws might be too small to handle the size and weight of a full sheet of particleboard or MDF. Remember that MDF is heavier than particleboard.

If your table saw is large enough to handle particleboard sheets, you

Open cabinet for frequently used power tools.

should use a high-quality tungsten-carbide saw blade designed for manmade materials. The generally recommended saw blade has a triple-chip grind; that is, every other tooth has three cutting edges. I use a Forrest Manufacturing Company saw blade that produces chip-free, clean, sharp edges in melamine-coated particleboard and it isn't the typical triple-chip design. This blade has a high alternate top-bevel profile (model Duraline HI A/T). The average alternative top-bevel saw blades have 15° to 25° angles, the Forrest blade has a positive rake with a 40° angle so that, as the blade spins down into the bottom melamine surface, it cleanly pierces the material and makes a clean exit cut.

EVALUATING OTHER MATERIALS Although the list of disadvantages of particleboard may seem overwhelming, a similar list

can be made for solid wood. Durability, toxicity, weight, cutting ability, finishes, cost and availability are all applicable concerns related to solid wood. The relevant issue is to know the advantages and disadvantages before working with any material.

USING PEGBOARD

If cabinets aren't the type of storage that works best in your woodshop, consider covering all wall areas with pegboard. Use tempered hardboard pegboard because it's more durable than the nontempered type. It holds up well under repeated attachment of the metal hangers. Attach ¾" by 2" by necessary length strips to the wall, attach the pegboard to the strips and then paint the pegboard with a light, nonreflective paint. As you work in a particular area, you will begin to hang tools and accessories relevant to the nearest machine or work area. Peg-

board, unlike cabinets and custom storage units, allows for easy woodshop rearrangement. Simply remove all tools, accessories and hangers and reposition them in new areas. Additionally, if you move away and remove everything but the pegboard from the woodshop, the new owner will have a presentable room covered entirely with an attractive wall covering.

Pegboard Storage Tower

A useful storage option for smaller woodshops is a movable storage tower, which looks like a gadget-loaded telephone booth on wheels. The sides can be constructed of solid sheeting, pegboard, recessed shelves or drawers. This unit can be rolled to work areas and then stored in a less used area when it's not needed. Because it's a tower, don't store heavy objects in the upper half — keep weighty objects near the base so that

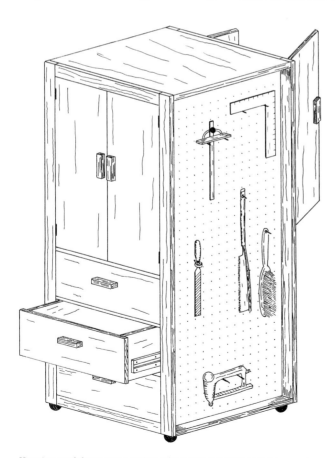

Here is a modular storage station, which includes pegboard side panels.

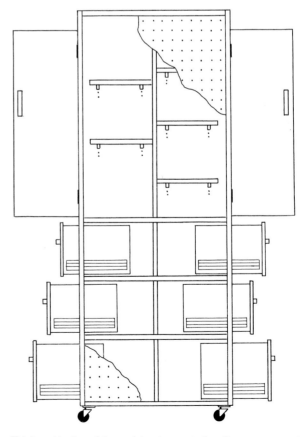

This is a side view of the modular storage station. Shown are opened doors and adjustable shelves. As shown, the station has six drawers.

Tom Dailey built storage drawers in the heavy-duty frame supporting a metal lathe.

Here is a storage tower with a large assortment of tools and supplies. It includes drawers, pegboard, magnetic holders, bins and shelves. Earl Bartell has a small woodshop so the storage tower is kept in a central location.

it doesn't tip over. Locking wheels are optional, but are worth considering. If the tower is to be left in one place for a prolonged period, it would be safer to lock the wheels.

USING "WASTED" SPACE

Many stationary machines, including the table saw, jointer, planer and band saw, sit on dead space; that is, their stands are open-structured tables or sheet-metal boxes that are mostly empty. I suggest that it's a better use of woodshop space if the metal-legged stands are replaced with shop-made storage units. An under-machine cabinet can accommodate general storage, or it can serve as specialized storage for a particular machine. Any design, simple or complex, can be adapted so that an enclosed table-like cabinet with drawers and doors is both safe and functional. Lockable wheels are optional, although it's often very useful to be able to move a machine for

either unusual applications or storage.

Movable Storage Modules

Large wall-storage cabinets are cumbersome to make and they usually don't relocate well to new locations — within the woodshop or in new location woodshops. Making smaller storage modules has many advantages: They are easier to make and use, and they are much easier to relocate within the woodshop.

Roll-around modules with locking wheels make ideal companions to workbenches and stationary machines. A variation of these rolling modules are sets of movable (but no wheels) storage modules — each having the same shape, height, width and depth. They can be set on different-height bases or stacked on each other. Build these units to be the same height as your workbench, table saw or other surfaces so that there is same-height support of oversized materials. The width and depth should be selected to fit your wood-

Jon Magill has a mobile base under his table saw. Magill also installed drawer storage for his frequently used table saw and his router table accessories.

shop configuration. Using 18" as an example width, setting a series of 18"-wide storage units side by side produces 3'- and 6'-wide structures. A simple top can be set on the structure, making a very usable work surface. Or another set of units can be set on top of the lower set producing a wall of storage. I recommend that all storage units be attached to walls

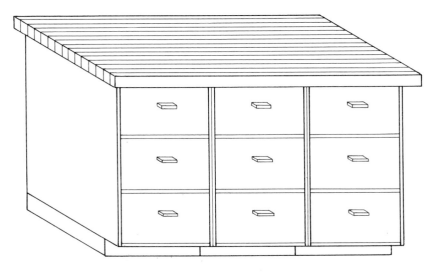

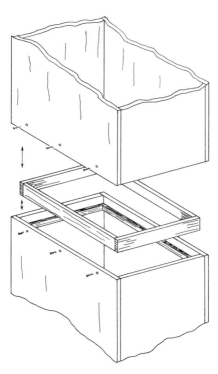

Three modules with a laminated workbench top.

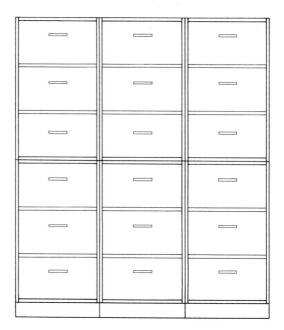

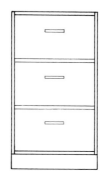

The basic module is shown below. This unit is approximately bench height and consists of three drawers. The drawing on the left consists of six basic modules — all the same size.

When stacking, secure the modules together using a retaining ring and screws.

n't resist, or I've gotten telephone calls concerning the sale of someone's private stock of wood. Inevitably, these various quantities of lumber need storage areas in my woodshop. And, the constant question is "How much permanent storage should be devoted to lumber that will soon be made into furniture?" Since lumber is transitory, storage should be designed with simplicity, easy access and accommodation of unusual types and sizes of lumber in mind.

once they are positioned. Use long drywall screws with fender washers through the storage unit's back and into wall studs. The bonus of this design is that it's possible to reconfigure storage areas as necessary. Adding new units, repositioning units or taking them with you if you move are all easily accomplished.

LUMBER STORAGE

Lumber storage is the opposite of tool storage. Tools are used and then returned to storage; lumber is in a constant cycle of replenishment, storage and use. Lumber only returns to storage as smaller pieces.

Furthermore, lumber sizes and quantities are also in flux depending on the projects at hand. There's particleboard and plywood for cabinet constructions, solid wood for furniture, and random sizes for carvings and lathe turnings. Wood also is brought into the woodshop simply because woodworkers enjoy wood. Many times I have stumbled on beautiful pieces of wood that I just could-

Wall-Hung Rack

For safety and durability, make wall hangers a suitable thickness. If the total weight of stored lumber is slight (moulding strips, long dowels and thin slats), 2"-thick hangers are adequate. If you plan on storing heavier loads, use 4×4s for the hangers. Use sections of 1" × 16" heavy metal pipe for the supports. Drill the support holes through the 4×4 at a slight angle (approximately 4°). Attach the hangers to wall studs with lag bolts and washers. Attach as many hangers as seem reasonable for the load (wall studs are every 16").

Storage Rack

The ideal lumber storage rack should allow access to all four sides. By being able to walk around a storage rack, you can find and easily remove lumber without having to move an entire stack to get to a board in the back. It's a tiring, time-consuming process to constantly sort through lumber to find the right wood for a project, and boards at the back or bottom of a stack are often overlooked. If you can see the lumber from all sides of the rack, removing it will be simpler. Realistically, most woodshops do not have the space for a walk-around rack; lumber is stored against a wall. If space is limited, build a lumber rack with access at its narrower end. That way long boards can be slid in and out with minimum effort.

Make your lumber racks according to the amount of lumber you usually store. It doesn't make sense to build an automobile-size structure if you only store 100 board feet of lumber. However, if you have stacks of lumber to store, build a rack. The frame-work can be made of 2×4s with ½"-thick particleboard shelves. The rack's size depends upon room size and the length of stored lumber. For a small-size woodshop consider a 4'-wide by 10'-long rack. Don't make the rack too tall because it's unsafe to store heavy lumber at elevation, and besides, it's difficult to look at lumber that's above shoulder height.

VERTICAL STORAGE RACKS Another version of lumber storage is a series of vertical stalls. The framework is attached to the floor, ceiling joists and wall studs. The stalls can be any reasonably sized openings so that wood and man-made materials are stored on their ends and are easily accessed.

Here you can see the storage of long, thin wood strips and the miter saw work area in Caswell's shop.

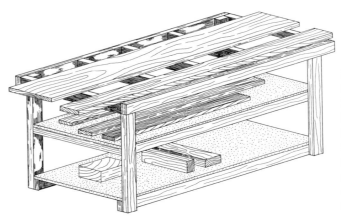

Here is a lumber storage rack. The frame is made of 2×4s and particleboard. It can be made in almost any size. Don't make it so tall that it becomes top-heavy and dangerous.

Here are three wood storage "walls" mounted perpendicular to the woodshop wall. Secure these to the wall studs and ceiling joists and anchor them to the floor with steel angle pieces.

Storing Sheet Materials

First, a warning regarding sheet materials such as plywood, particleboard, MDF, hardboard or any other material that is 4' × 8' in size. If your woodshop is small, if your table saw has a small surface area, or if you feel that the material is difficult to handle, don't attempt to cut the full-size sheet on the table saw. Instead, place the sheet on the workbench or saw horses and cut the sheet to a more manageable size using a circular saw or jigsaw.

This recycled fish market crate is used for storing turning blanks.

If you have a lumber rack, a simple storage solution for sheet materials is to move the rack 6" to 12" from the wall and then use this "back pocket" for the sheets. Secure a strip of plywood to the floor to facilitate sliding the sheets in and out. Sheet materials would then rest against the wall and be contained against the side of the lumber rack.

Storing Scrap Wood

Actually, scrap isn't the correct word. Odds and ends might be a better term. These seemingly useless left-overs are actually a valuable resource. After setting aside the odds and ends, the little that's left is waste, the stuff to throw out or burn. Odds and ends are useful for:

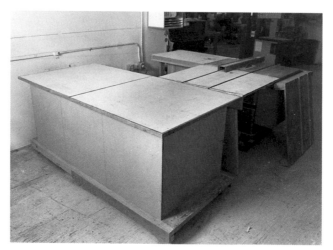

The auxiliary support table for this table saw is also used for storing small pieces of wood, as seen in these two photos.

- testing machine setup
- determining the looks of various finishing products
- cutting dowel-type plugs to contrast with or complement project wood
- repair work, matching grain and color for antique restoration
- making drawer and door pulls
- making wedges for tenons
- small-size scroll saw pieces
- small-size carvings
- small spindle turnings
- toy constructions
- game pieces
- tool or knife handles
- pieces for woodshop jigs and fixtures

Storing odds and ends, cutoff pieces and other irregular-size pieces is perhaps one of the most difficult storage problems in the woodshop. The typical solution is being over-whelmed and then storing the odds and ends haphazardly in bins and boxes. That means that every time a small piece of wood is needed, the entire box has to be emptied. Since there is no rational order regarding the size and shape of smaller pieces, it is difficult to sort and store them by that method. My generalized storage of smaller pieces is by length, color and, depending upon quantity, type of wood. In the end, I have shelves and shallow bins with group-ings of dark and light woods, or groupings of walnut, cherry, oak and maple lengths.

For storing very small pieces (2" to 8" in length), I use clear plastic storage boxes — the kind available in most home centers. Currently, I have about 12 of these and I keep them no more than half full.

One clever storage system uses various-diameter cardboard tubes to store longer pieces. Tubes are gener-ally available in 3" to 12" diameters. Cut plywood (or particleboard) disks to fit one tube end and nail in place. The tubes are then placed horizontal-ly on shelves, and pieces easily slide into them. Large-diameter tubes can be found at better hardware stores or at concrete supply houses. These tubes are used as molds for pouring concrete foundations (they are some-times referred to as sonotubes). Tubes are generally available in 6' lengths and can easily be sawn into 2' or 3' sections.

Here is a typical cubbyhole storage of small pieces of wood usually found in a carver's woodshop.

chapter *eleven*

The Workbench

THE WORKBENCH IS A TOOL. IT'S OK to make it attractive, but also make it useful — and don't be nervous about nicks.

THE UNIVERSAL TOOL

The workbench is the universal tool found in any type of woodshop. It's difficult to imagine any type of woodwork being done without some sort of elevated flat work area. Even if we divide woodworking into power tool users and non-power tool users, there is still agreement that the workbench is a necessity. However, the type of workbench used is very much open to discussion. After all, workbenches have been used for thousands of years which makes for more than a few workbench designs to consider. The workbench may be nothing more than a bench top supported against a garage wall, or it may be a reproduction of a classic Shaker workbench. Quite possibly because of the historical nature of woodworking, the workbench is one of those tools that is evaluated or designed with a reference to the concept of traditional.

Because of the popularity of, and the availability of information concerning woodworking, almost every historical workbench has been built; that is, ancient Roman, Japanese, Chinese, medieval English, French, German and Early American, to name a few.

Having said that the supply of information is rather extensive, I would like to focus on the workbench that might function best in today's woodshop. In some ways, the traditional workbench, complete with maple top, front and shoulder vises, is an

Close-up of antique workbench in Tom Dailey's woodshop.

This is a modern version of the old-fashioned tool chest. Approximate measurements: 16" × 24" × 36".

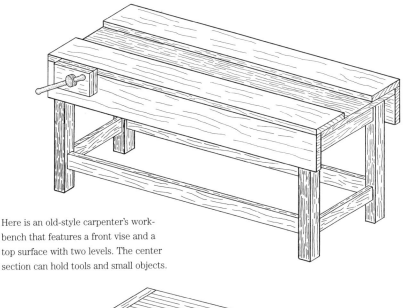

Here is an old-style carpenter's workbench that features a front vise and a top surface with two levels. The center section can hold tools and small objects.

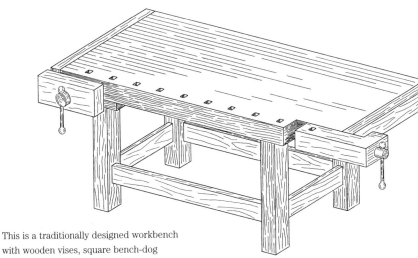

This is a traditionally designed workbench with wooden vises, square bench-dog holes and an open understructure.

anachronism — a throwback to another time and place. Perhaps workbenches are analogous to automobiles. The traditional workbench is like an antique classic car — a thing of beauty, a showcase item fussed over by a meticulous owner. By comparison, the workbench made with MDF and designed for use with routers and table saws is like a new pickup truck — a utilitarian object made for heavy use.

What confuses the issue of workbench design is the very enrichment that makes the workbench desirable. Just what is the ideal workbench, or does such a thing actually exist? Are we blessed or cursed by the historical workbench? Does the modern woodworker actually have access to modern workbench theories and designs? Are the advocates of traditional woodworking ignoring the obvious, and are the power tool users missing the beauty and function of a traditional workbench?

Bench Basics

The stereotypical workbench is about 3' wide and 6' long and has side- and front-mounted vises and a reasonably flat work surface. This workbench probably has some sort of storage either below the bench top or in a tool tray or rack behind the top's back edge. The stereotype workbench is well made and has a thick hardwood laminated top, stout legs and is very heavy. Some workbenches are so heavy that it takes four people to lift and move them. If this workbench is traditionally designed, it has a row of holes accompanying the end vise. These holes are there to secure bench stops (short pieces of wood or steel) so that a board can be held fast between the vise and the bench stops. Generally, this type of workbench was designed and built for use with hand tools, principally bench planes, hand saws and chisels. The other major physical feature is bench height. This is a function of the relationship between the woodworker's height and the height of a board to be worked, both on the surface and on the edge. If a bench is either too high or too low, the woodworker can't maximize body comfort and strength, and the work process will be compromised. If the bench is too lightweight, the planing action will cause the bench to rack diagonally or skip around the floor.

If one studies the workbenches of the time just before the proliferation of electric tools in the United States, it's very noticeable that workbenches were rather utilitarian looking. They had large surfaces, a tail vise and front vise and some sort of device for supporting long boards. Many of the benches appear to be constructed of thick, wide boards with an open-leg housing. Of course, there were exceptions to the open leg design, and there were benches with storage areas. However, tools were generally stored in tool chests kept near the workbench.

Few of us now store tools in large tool chests that look like steamer trunks. Today's woodworker prefers to build large wall cabinets, or multiple wall cabinets, for storage. We now design workbenches so that there is some storage under the bench top. Having smaller woodshops does require the full utilization of all spaces; the additional bench structure and weight of the stored tools helps to make a strong and heavy workbench, thus reducing vibrations and bench movement when it's used.

DESIGNING A WORKBENCH

The real question about workbench design is: How will the workbench be used? Nostalgia aside, that revered turn-of-the century workbench was used for long hours of work and commerce. Someone stood at that bench for many hours a day and made things with hand tools. That tool chest was filled with assorted hand planes, moulding planes, braces,

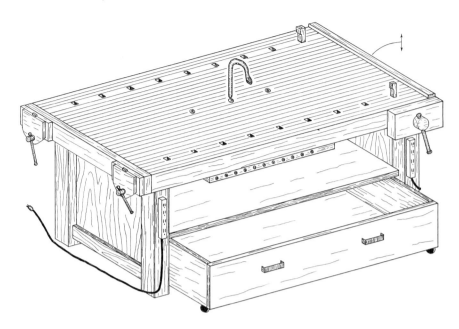

This concept workbench features two rows of bench-stop holes, two end vises, one front vise, a storage shelf, a rollout storage container, electrical boxes on its front legs, an adjustable edge stop, a hinged support leg and a bench hook in the center of the worktop.

auger bits and so forth. These chests were frequently so filled with tools that one description of them might be crammed orderliness. Often, hundreds of tools were nestled within a maze of special boxes, drawers, containers and holders. Also, the lumber used was large and heavy, and rough boards were often hand planed and hand sawed. This was state-of-the art equipment, as well as the work style for that time. Is that how the modern woodworker now works? If so, then there are many historical texts available that will help to recreate that type of workbench. If, however, you are using electric tools and working with plywood, perhaps a different workbench design is in order.

This isn't about not using hand tools or bashing traditional tools. Instead, it's important to design the workbench so that its function matches today's needs. Although it's very possible to own and drive an antique car, it doesn't make sense to use that car for stop-and-go rush-hour driving. The same applies for the workbench. If we use the traditional workbench for modern work,

perhaps we are creating an unnecessary struggle. Generally, hand tools are now the secondary processing tools and are mostly used for detail work, such as trimming, cutting joints or planing an edge. The primary processing tools are the table saw, compound miter saw, radial arm saw, band saw, jointer and planer. Furthermore, the principal tools that aid in refining boards into objects are routers, drills, sanders, scroll saws and biscuit joiners. And the old fellows of the past didn't have plywood, particleboard, MDF and other 4x8 sheet goods to work. Plywood and other related man-made materials, besides being heavy and awkward to move, aren't made to be cut, shaped or prepared with hand tools.

The issue is that we now use an assortment of hand and power tools and materials requiring workbench performance far different than that of 1849 or 1905. If you're building a workbench for the first time, this might be the time to reassess the typical workbench design and build one from a fresh perspective.

Design Considerations

- workbench height
- material used for bench top
- surface area required for accommodating materials
- size and shape of workbench relative to the type of work and tools
- movable or not
- freestanding or against wall
- holding system(s) for routing, drilling, belt sanding, finish sanding, carving, hand tool use (planes and saws)
- use of clamps on the workbench
- tool storage
- electrical hookup
- vises: front, side, specialty
- make single, special or multipurpose benches

Workbench Height

Bench height is one of the most important dimensional features to consider. The proper height will allow the user to work comfortably and to efficiently use tools. Improper bench height leads to stooping over, sore back and neck muscles and awkward arm movements. I once was instructing a class on using hand planes and a student showed me a board edge that he had just finished. I sighted down the 5'-long board and was very impressed. There wasn't one place on the edge that was square to the board's surface. In fact, the board was reminiscent of a Mobius strip. Not wanting to hurt his feelings, I asked him to demonstrate his planing technique to me. What became obvious was that the work surface was too high and the strange edge was a result of his unnatural reach to the board and the change of his body position as he moved down the board's edge.

There are several popular heights for general-purpose workbenches. Most commercially made workbenches are 33" to 36" in height. Of course, it would be impossible for manufacturers to offer an infinite variety of bench heights. Therefore, if you want this type of workbench, it would be best to purchase either the correct height bench or one slightly lower. It's much easier to place blocks under the legs to raise the bench than it is to cut the legs and make the bench shorter. I'm 6' 1" and my workbench is 35" in height. I'm not sure that's an ideal height for others, but for me it's comfortable.

To determine the height for a workbench, you must first determine the height from the floor to the top of the work you are doing. For example, a 1" by 10"-wide board is to be edge planed. If the board is clamped in a position so that the edge is up, the edge height is then approximately 43" from the floor. This was computed by assuming a 35"-high work-bench, and the board has 2" of width in a front vise. If that same board needs surface work, the floor-to-work surface height is 36". If you are comfortable working within the 36" to 43" range, 35" is a good bench height.

First, prioritize the tools that you will use most at the workbench. Make a list of the tools that you will use, from most to least. For a hypothetical example, the most-used to least-used workbench tools might be a router, belt sander, chisels, hand planes and hand saws. Now, make a best guess as to the height above the bench top that these tools would be used. Generally, the router, belt sander and chisels will be used on flat stock (¼" to 4" in height), and hand planes will be used mostly on edges (¼" to 24" in height). You may want to make mock-ups of various heights and pantomime the motions involved in using belt sanders, routers and hand planes.

Since there is no perfect height, pick a height that seems to average out the various work heights from this pantomime effort. Have someone else watch you doing the pantomime to find out if you unconsciously stoop over while working. Surprisingly, this is common, and you may find that at certain heights you keep a straight back and are also comfortable in this position. You might find that the generic 33" to 36" heights are fine, or

 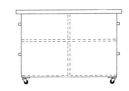

This low, mobile workstation features drawers on both sides of the unit and wheels. Lockable wheels are recommended. The unit is approximately 16" to 24" in height.

you may find that 30" or 38" is more comfortable for your needs. Woodworkers don't come in one size, and there is no reason to assume that workbenches should either.

There is one other situation in which bench height is critical. There are a number of jigs and fixtures that are useful for specialized work, including such things as the Leigh Dovetail Jig or a shop-made tenoning jig. If the jig is clamped to the workbench, the workpieces must be shorter than the distance to the floor. There are two solutions: Dig a hole in the floor for the longer boards, or raise the jig above the workbench. Since the hole option isn't reasonable, many woodworkers have built higher benches for this function. Do not operate a router at a raised bench in a way that your face is in-line with the cutting action: This is very dangerous. Nor should you use a movable step stool or ladder to reach the jig. The best method is to build a box that's 3" to 10" in height, attach the jig to it and then clamp the entire assembly to the workbench.

If I had the space, I would have two workbenches. One bench would be at a standard height and would be used for joinery, clamping and general purpose use. The other bench would be approximately 18" to 28" in height, and it would be used for placing chairs, chests and other furniture pieces on for assembly, detail work and finishing. When detailing or finishing a piece that is either sitting on the floor or up on the standard bench, it always seems to have a wrong visual perspective, or the piece is in an awkward, hard to reach position. A lower bench makes it easier to see and move the piece.

Benchtop Materials

Is a laminated maple bench top better than one of 2×4s and MDF? The

Low workstations are perfect for work projects that are too tall for a standard workbench.

maple top certainly looks better, but does it add to the functionality of the bench? Traditional workbenches are usually made of hardwoods such as maple, beech, or oak, but these benches were developed when natural wood was the only material choice. Much can be said about the natural beauty of wood benches, a beauty enhanced by the patina of age and use. When you are making fine woodworking pieces, it seems almost natural to visually connect a beautiful bench with the workpiece. There is the old adage that you should use your best tools when attempting your best work. Perhaps the luster and charm of a seasoned hardwood bench do help motivate a woodworker toward a higher level of work. A hardwood bench that has dovetail and mortise-and-tenon joints is a constant reminder of the best of woodworking and craftsmanship. The hardwood bench top does have features beyond beauty. A 2"- or 3"-thick benchtop is ideal for work that requires the pounding of a mallet or hammer. The

top's thickness and density offer a solidity that minimizes tool recoil, bounce-back and workpiece stability. The sheer weight of a solid-wood bench top also provides stability and stiffness which means that heavy materials and projects won't distort the top. Hardwood tops are easy to maintain; as the top wears or even distorts, it can be reflattened with hand planes or belt sanders.

But there are other considerations regarding laminated workbench tops. The principal drawbacks to a laminated top are that they are expensive, difficult to make and heavy to move. There is approximately 54 board feet of wood in a 3" × 36" × 72" benchtop. Add on an additional 20% for waste and that's about 65 board feet to purchase. Call a local lumberyard and get a quote for the current price of maple, cherry and oak.

When preparing wood for a bench top, each lamination surface must be planed very flat. Then the entire lamination assembly must be carefully aligned when it is glued so that it will remain very flat during and after gluing. Any twists that occur during glue-up will result in a piece requiring difficult work to make it flat. Other factors to consider: A laminated top is heavy and awkward to move, and when it's being glued up, heavy-duty bar clamps spaced about 6" apart on either side of the workpiece are also required. Someone once said that you need a workbench in order to build a workbench. That's very true when dealing with the gluing-up process. A workbench is flat and therefore the ideal surface on which to rest the clamped-up workpiece. If you plan on using a garage floor as a resting surface for the glued assembly, can you be certain that the floor is flat? If it isn't, the uneven floor will introduce twists to the clamped workpiece.

I've noticed that many more woodworkers are now building bench tops with man-made materials. Part of the reason for this is that it's easier to construct the top with sheet materials. A frame is built first and then one or more layers are added. Often the top layer is attached with screws so that it can be replaced when it's worn. The principal materials used are MDF, tempered hardboard and particleboard. Solid-wood edges are attached to the top so that the sheet materials are contained and don't break or crumble.

It's much easier to build a 3' × 8' top from these materials than it is to build one of hardwoods. There is enough material in two 4×8 sheets to construct a 2¼" × 32" × 96" top (two 32" and two 16" strips). The compromise necessary when using man-made materials is that the top isn't as dense or resilient as hardwoods. However, flatness is easier to attain, and the top can be replaced or repaired easily. I've also noticed that some woodworkers pencil-sketch directly onto particleboard tops. Some actually draw, with T-square and triangles, full-size drawings of their

Doug Matthews likes having a variety of portable workstations for his antique restoration business. This workstation is used much like a typical workbench.

This portable workstation is used to support a router table.

current projects. When that project is completed, the drawings are erased and the surface is ready for the next one.

SURFACE AREA REQUIRED FOR MATERIALS It may seem obvious that a workbench holds stuff on the top surface, but when one is working on a project with stacks of wood and there are odds and ends of wood, assorted tools, power cords, glue bottles and so on, the top of the bench gets cluttered rapidly and the bench seems small. I suppose the cliche, whatever size you have will always fill up, applies. So the solution is to build the largest bench possible. A large bench isn't just for building large projects. Actually, the workbench is the only

open flat area in a woodshop that isn't flooring or doesn't have a blade projecting out of it. The bench then becomes the focal point and command center for everything from stirring paints to sorting screws. Rarely is my workbench empty. And when I use it for sorting wood for a project or to stack furniture parts, some part of the bench is still filled with assorted tools and notebooks.

When I read books about the Shakers and their woodshops, what I see are beautiful, clean and empty workbenches — and I wonder what those large surface benches looked like when they were being used. I imagine stacks of wood, assorted tools, boxes of hardware and cans of finishes everywhere on that bench. I appreciate that the Shakers placed great value in neatness and cleanliness, but I do believe that during work, those large workbenches were covered with stuff.

Freestanding or Against a Wall

Workbench location is simple: Place it against a wall or let it stand in the woodshop so that you can walk completely around it. If space is at a premium, place the bench against a wall. This reduces some uses, such as placing long boards and clamps across the bench and using all four edges. However, the workbench will be more stable when it's attached to a wall, and the wall above the workbench usually becomes a storage area for commonly used tools.

Freestanding workbenches can be left at one location or moved as necessary. I appreciate the freestanding workbench because I can position long bar clamps across the bench when gluing, and because I can work completely around an object on the bench. Not having to move an object is especially useful when repairing antiques or applying finishes. Tool storage is further away with this type of bench, but it's not that much of a distance and generally isn't a problem.

Shape of Workbench

Another stereotype of workbench design is the rectangular bench — 22" × 72", 24" × 78", 30" × 66", etc. Generally, this shape is comfortable for most hand tool work; however, when coupled with the traditional two vises, this shape doesn't always lend itself to power tool use. End vise and bench stops were designed to secure a board when using hand planes and chisels. The vise stop and benchtop stop usually are about ¾" wide, and the board is pinched between the two. When you study most traditional workbenches,

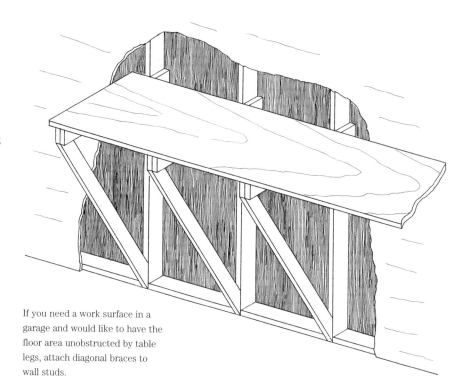

If you need a work surface in a garage and would like to have the floor area unobstructed by table legs, attach diagonal braces to wall studs.

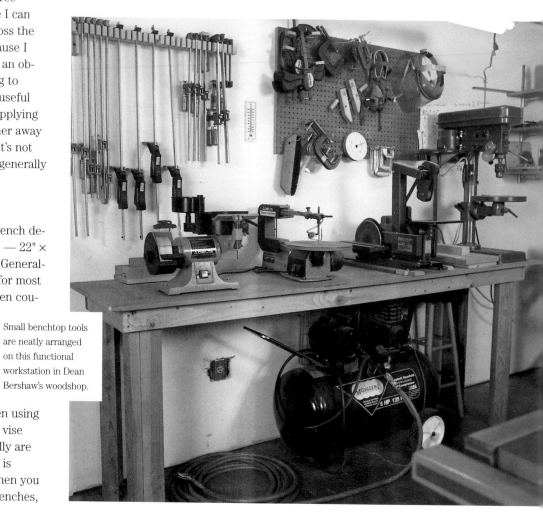

Small benchtop tools are neatly arranged on this functional workstation in Dean Bershaw's woodshop.

Derrick Burke's woodshop is a converted carport with limited space (single-car size). So he attached a space-saving simple workbench to a wall. The bench features a replaceable particleboard surface with round dog holes and a Record vise with stop.

Harry Charowsky's workbench, made from 2" × 6" fir boards measures 29½"-wide by 114½"-long by 36¾"-high. It features drawer storage, movable workpiece support, shop-made hardware for vises, and it has a shop-made mobility system (underneath the bench) that makes it easy for one person to move the workbench.

Dave Buck has more than enough space in his woodshop for this oversize workbench; 144"-long by 39"-wide by 33¾"-high, it weighs approximately 1,500 pounds.

it becomes clear that the design emphasis is the bench-stop system, and these benches were designed to secure more or less narrow boards. Traditional workbenches are definitely pre-electric and pre-plywood.

A description of a working-condition scenario is in order to picture limitations. Suppose a 24" square of plywood requires a rabbet on all four edges. If the bench stops are used, the router with fence and bit can only cut one edge at a time, and therefore the board will have to be unclamped and re-clamped three more times because you cannot continuously cut all four edges in one pass. Most likely the router fence won't clear the bench top and the two bench stops are also obstructions. Of course this four-edge rabbet can be cut on the router table, but there are times when the workbench offers easier setup, except for the bench stops. Another common problem with the bench stop and end vise occurs when belt sanding. The nature of a belt sander is that the belt turns so that when it's running, the belt pulls the workpiece toward its back end and the operator. Since the workpiece is pulled in one direction, it's a common practice to place the workpiece against a bench stop and sand. This works reasonably well, except when the workpiece is wider than a few inches. When the belt sander is aligned to the bench stop, it pulls squarely against the stop. If the sander is at one side or the other of the board, it will cause the board to pivot against the stop, making sanding nearly impossible. The traditional solution to this is to use both bench stops to secure the workpiece. If, however, there are numerous workpieces of assorted lengths, the operator will constantly be moving bench stops to different bench holes and tightening, loosening and retightening the vise. This makes for slow work, especially when using a fast and powerful power tool like the belt

sander. Another solution is to clamp a long strip of wood in the end vise so that the entire width of the workpiece is touching it. This reduces the pivoting motion and makes sanding much easier and quicker, but many of the traditional end vises aren't designed for this type of clamping. And some traditional workbenches that have rear-mounted tool trays also have narrow flat areas, and these two features make it difficult to secure wider workpieces. If the workbench is against a wall, wider workpieces may not have sufficient space for safe and easy work.

Knowing the type of work destined for the workbench is critical to its design. With that information you can configure the workbench accordingly. There are definite work conditions relative to the type of material being used for projects. A stack of plywood pieces could actually tip over a lightweight bench. Or the workbench shape might make it difficult for certain constructions. The general shape of the workbench will affect more than woodshop area square footage. If will affect the ease of positioning work projects, tool use, tool storage and operator maneuvering. I'm not a fan of the traditional Scandinavian bench, which has an L-shaped wing projecting from the edge. Part of this dislike is because I'm left-handed — and the benches I've used aren't. But more importantly, I really don't like that front projection. I realize this traditional design was a cornerstone of hand tool usage and many hand tool advocates still like this design, but for me, it's awkward to use and easy to bump into when walking by the bench. I see no reason to have this type of clamping/holding projection for hand tool use.

Movable or Not?

Smaller woodshops often require machine mobility. More machines are being mounted on mobile bases than ever before. Mobile bases permit the

woodworker to move very heavy machines from storage to an area of use and then return the machine to storage. Mobile-base frames have locking wheels so that the machine can be used safely. Generally, workbenches aren't considered mobile objects, but a few years ago, table saws and jointers were thought of only as stationary machines. I would suggest that if a workbench is made mobile, a retractable mechanism should be used for the locked position. This allows the workbench to be moved, but when it's in position the bench legs would be in direct contact with the floor. If the workbench is in some sort of carriage that has locking wheels, the legs aren't directly touching the floor. Aside from mobility, it's necessary to avoid micromovement in the bench once it's in position. If the floor's uneven, shims are easily tapped under the legs. Workbenches that are in carriages will have micromovements that are annoying and bothersome when you are trying to do fine detail work. Solid contact with the floor is best. One possible solution is to make a hinged wheel system for each leg set that can be flipped up out of the way once the bench is in position.

Movable workstations work well when the woodshop shares space in a garage. Folding sawhorses (handmade or store-bought) are set in position, the work surface is secured, and tools are then attached to the workstation.

Holding Systems

Is there anything in the woodshop that's a single-function object universal enough to encompass all woodworking needs? Can you do work with only one drill bit size, one chisel or one grit of sandpaper? If you can manage this feat, I'm impressed. The very nature of woodworking is one of increments and subtle adjustments. Rough-sawing a piece is the opposite of fine-tuning. The very nature of a

This is Jon Magill's portable workstation for a horizontal router table and a planer. The commercial sawhorses have a retaining track on their top surface, and they retain cleats that are mounted on the underside of the work surface.

holding system should be easy to use; it should grip and tightly hold the workpiece, and it should store away quickly and efficiently. Complicated holding systems consisting of many parts should be viewed with skepticism. Infrequently used parts and accessories are easily lost, abandoned or forgotten.

Without overdoing the diversity concept, there are a few basic woodworking functions that require specialized workbench holding systems:

- routing
- drilling
- belt sanding
- finish sanding
- carving
- hand tool use (planes and saws)

Ideally, any workpiece should be secured so that clamps or stops don't interfere with tool use. For example, it's very easy to secure a workpiece to the workbench with a C-clamp, except that it's nearly impossible to continuously use the router because the clamp blocks access. The same problem applies to carving. If the workpiece is secured with C-clamps, the carver has to be careful not to push the chisel into the clamp, or the clamp has to be constantly moved to reveal carving area.

To avoid this problem when routing and sanding, there are two commercial systems: a foam pad, similar to the padding found under wall-to-wall carpeting, and vacuum vises. Vacuum vises offer incredible holding strength, but they require an air pump motor and an air line, and they are expensive. Vacuum vises might be better suited to commercial woodworking because their efficiency is related to all-day usage and time savings. The foam pads are inexpensive, easily used, easily stored away and replaceable.

The end of the workbench is easily modified to hold different types of board stops. These simple devices are useful for capturing workpieces,

woodshop is the variety of tools and machines that are used between these two extremes.

Assuming this point is accurate, why should we assume that a workbench should have only one or two methods of securing workpieces? Does the traditional bench-vise and bench-stop system perform adequate work for cabinetmakers, lathe turners, carvers, antique restorers, picture frame makers and miniaturists? Or should function be the measure of bench design? I know that I've modified my workbench to accommodate router and belt sander use and the periodic woodcarving that I do. That's the heart of this issue: Define your most performed tasks and develop specialized holding systems for those tasks. Standard-issue holding systems might get you close to the best way of holding something, but efficiency necessitates fine-tuning the holding systems.

The principal purpose of any holding system is to secure the workpiece while work is being done. The

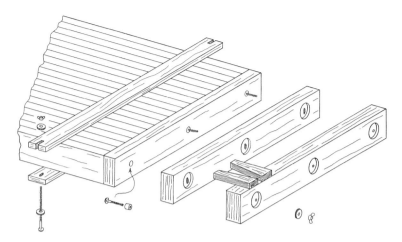

Different edge pieces that can be attached to the end of the workbench are shown at left. The workbench edge has a cap piece that includes three exposed bolt threads. These bolts are attached through glued dowel sections. The board in the center features three recessed locations with elongated slots. The bolt threads are through these slots, and the edge board is secured with wing nuts. The edge board can be raised as a catch board at the end of the workbench. This is useful for belt sanding workpieces. The edge board with two attached wedge-shaped pieces at the right side of the drawing is also secured with wing nuts to the three bolt threads. This edge board is useful for securing workpieces when edge planing with hand planes.

Note: There are a number of other edge board designs possible that can be incorporated onto the end of the workbench.

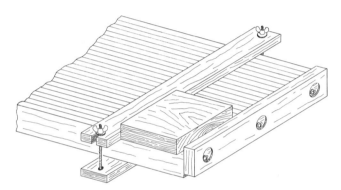

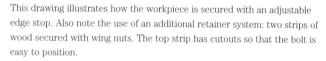

This drawing illustrates how the workpiece is secured with an adjustable edge stop. Also note the use of an additional retainer system: two strips of wood secured with wing nuts. The top strip has cutouts so that the bolt is easy to position.

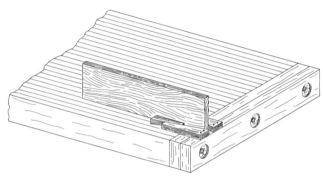

This drawing illustrates how a workpiece is secured with the use of additional wedges.

and work well for belt sanding or relief carving.

This bench accessory can be further enhanced by the addition of a thin strip located at the other end of the workpiece. This secures the workpiece so that sanding, some routing and other surface work can be done. These strips can be clamped or made to fit bench-dog holes. They also can be shaped to match odd-shaped workpieces.

The router is such a useful tool (it's really nothing more than a high-speed motor with handles!) that a separate workbench dedicated to router use is worth constructing. This workbench should be built higher than a standard bench, approximately 40". This height is determined by

holding a router with your elbows bent at 90° and measuring the distance from the floor to the bottom of the router. The bench should be somewhat narrow, approximately 12", and 48" to 60" in length. The narrow width permits router access to either side of a workpiece that is off the benchtop. Also, construction projects, such as boxes or drawers without tops or bottoms, can be slid onto the bench top for work. Attach an end vise with a 12" stop and drill rows of holes along both edges. If you drill round bench-stop holes, bolts with square heads make excellent stops. They will pivot when either a straight or curved workpiece is aligned against them. The base must be constructed so that the router

bench won't tip over. Heavy pedestals with broad feet are recommended.

Another useful workbench accessory is the sanding platform. Make the platform box approximately 3" to 6" in height and whatever length and width you choose. It is clamped to the workbench, and it has a port for attaching a vacuum hose. The top surface is perforated with either slots or holes so that when the vacuum is used, dust is drawn down into the box.

There is so much diversity in woodcarving that there isn't a single holding system for all applications. For some carvers, a heavy-duty leather glove is adequate. They simply hold a small piece of wood in the gloved hand and carve with the other.

Other carvers might be using large die grinders to shape a tree stump. This sort of workpiece is heavy and probably requires minimal clamping. Typically, carvers use some sort of screw or lag bolt mounted point up through the workbench top and secured into the base of the workpiece. Another option is power arms. These have movable head plates that are attached to the base of the workpiece. By lever action, the head can be moved so that the workpiece can be worked on at an infinite variety of angles. Generally, power arms are not meant for very heavy workpieces.

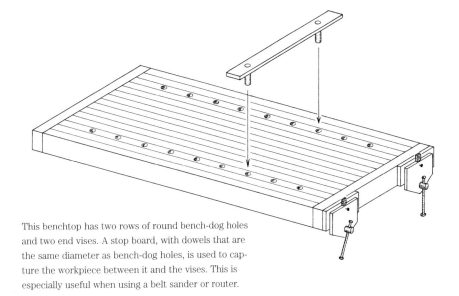

This benchtop has two rows of round bench-dog holes and two end vises. A stop board, with dowels that are the same diameter as bench-dog holes, is used to capture the workpiece between it and the vises. This is especially useful when using a belt sander or router.

Clamps on the Workbench

In most woodshops, floor space is a luxury and the workbench serves multiple purposes. The workbench is the flattest work surface in the woodshop, and if it's wide enough, it can be used for clamps when gluing. I use my workbench to support bar clamps up to 4' long for gluing. Since my bench is 7' long, I can glue up substantial workpieces. The I-beam-style bar clamps are shaped to rest on their clamp fittings, making it easy to set them almost anywhere on the benchtop.

Another useful clamping situation is being able to secure workpieces anywhere on the workbench with adjustable, deep-throat clamps. If the workbench has drawers, tool trays and other irregular-shaped constructions under the benchtop, this usually reduces clamping in that area.

I chose to have the benchtop edges free of any obstructions so that I could use clamps on all four edges. This permits me, for example, to clamp a workpiece on the back edge and then continue working at the front edge.

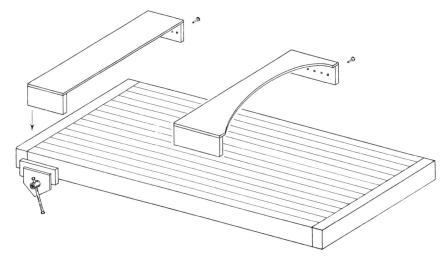

This benchtop has only a front vise. Stop boards, with both straight and curved edges, can be held in the vise and secured on the opposite edge with screws. These stops are very useful when using the belt sander. The operator stands at the left end of the vise and the workpiece is butted against the stop board. When power sanding, the workpiece is drawn against the stop and secured. If a sander is used from the right side, the board will no longer be secured and an additional stop or clamp is then required.

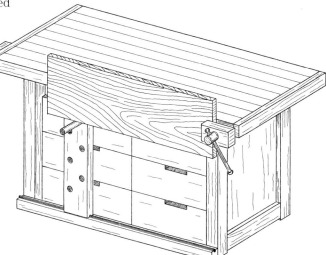

Here's a workbench with drawers. A heavy workpiece is held with the vise and movable support. The support has holes at different heights.

Workbench Tool Storage

The ideal tool storage would be that all tools used at the bench are stored within arm's length. Since most woodshops are compact, storage is reasonably close. However, there are tools that are used so frequently that some storage at the work-bench is necessary. Once again, prioritize your tools and decide on the most important. The typical storage area is at the wall behind the workbench, the workbench itself and shelves and cabinets somewhere within the shop.

Many workbenches incorporate a tool well or tool tray that is located either on the back edge or the end of the workbench. The world seems to be divided into two groups: lovers and haters of tool trays. I'm not fond of them because they always seem to be filled with debris and hand tools that are hidden under other tools. My biggest gripe is that tool trays minimize workbench clamping area, and they create extra benchtop width but no extra top area for supporting wide workpieces such as chair legs. To overcome these shortcomings, instead of a permanently installed tool tray, make a tray that is movable and has a top lid. The tray can then be secured at any location or can be removed altogether. The lid will help keep unwanted debris at bay and will add additional surface area.

First consider several of the limitations of storage near the workbench. Wall storage behind a bench means that storage is useful only if you can reach it. Tools stored 6' from the floor probably can't be reached if you are standing in front of the bench. Storage underneath a bench top is always subject to being blocked by clamps, workpieces and anything else positioned in front of the bench. The workbench area is space-limited, and there is no need to store tools

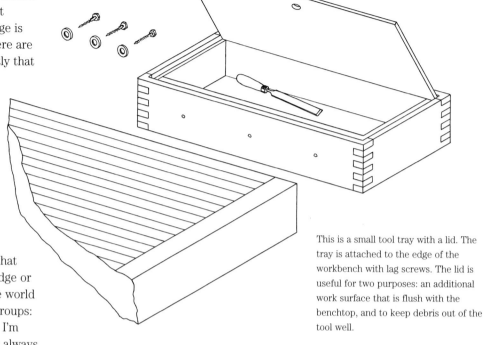

This is a small tool tray with a lid. The tray is attached to the edge of the workbench with lag screws. The lid is useful for two purposes: an additional work surface that is flush with the benchtop, and to keep debris out of the tool well.

here that are infrequently used. I store a few power tools on a shelf in the workbench, and the majority of items, such as power tools, measuring tools, chisels and block planes, are two or three steps away in drawers and open cabinets. My personal choice of power tools stored at the workbench is based on frequency of use and the notion that some tools just seem to belong at the workbench. I have a cordless drill, a 4" × 24" belt sander, several finish sanders and a plate joiner all at arm's length. I also store several plastic containers on this shelf. In them, I keep an assortment of nails, small screws and washers. Routers and other power tools are about 6' away, and most of the hand tools are about 4' away. The importance of these distances becomes obvious when work is underway. The closer the tools are to the work project the less frustrating it is. In fact, traveling 6' during some constructions seems like 20'. Someone once said that, given time, anyone can cut dovetails, but to cut good dovetails quickly requires a master

craftsman. If the time factor related to finding and selecting tools can be reduced, we take one more step toward better craftsmanship.

Electrical Hookups

We have entered the 21st century, so feel free to add electrical outlets to the workbench. I suggest electrical strips attached to the legs as the principal outlets for the workbench, with additional wall outlets at either end of the workbench area. Electrical outlets behind the benchtop create the problem of electrical cords running directly over the workbench. This adds to the confusion and clutter which intensifies during project construction. Additionally, it's dangerous to have electrical cords draped over the work area simply because these cords are too easily cut by sharp cutting tools or operating power tools. Electrical cords that dangle freely to the floor are much safer. Electrical outlets mounted on the front edge or underside are awkward and inconvenient to use, and are often in the way of clamping work.

Outlet strips are really fancy extension cords. For most electrical tools, extension cords of a reasonable length are OK. However, as the amperage increases in the more powerful tools, it's best to carefully read the section of the owner's manual related to extension cords. Some electrical tools come with long power cords, and the additional length of an extension cord can lead to electrical problems. My belt sander is rated at 10.5 amps, 1,220 watts and has a 15' power cord, and it doesn't like extension cords. When I have used an extension cord, the circuit breaker switches off after a few minutes of use.

It's always difficult, and maybe pointless, to state that one tool is more important or more useful than another. However, after working at the workbench for several hours, I always seem to end up with a tangle of power cords attached to various sanders, drills, plate joiners, heat

guns and such. Then I use the battery-powered cordless drill. It's probably the most taken for granted, yet wonderful, power tool in the woodshop. The drills are available in a large variety of sizes, shapes, powers and colors. They are powerful enough to drive numerous drywall screws, and the battery can be recharged in less than 30 minutes. With a keyless chuck, it's quick and easy to change bits and drivers. The cordless drill could be the perfect tool for the woodworker, especially when at the workbench.

Choosing a Vise

Once again, tradition dictates a particular element of workbench design, namely that workbenches have at least two vises. Typically, the front vise is mounted on the left front, and the shoulder vise is mounted on the

left edge. If you are left-handed (like me), reverse that pattern for the proper left-handed orientation.

I believe it's important to pose these questions: Could vises be located at other workbench locations? Why not on the back corners or even the front center? Does a bench need a typical vise for the majority of woodworking functions? Are there manufactured and shop-made holding systems that could replace the standard vise? The answers are probably yes and no. First, it's very difficult to dismiss hundreds of years of workbench design. The modern vise is the evolutionary end product of thousands upon thousands of hours spent at a workbench. The result of this research and development is that Man is a clever creature, and innovations are always just a blink of the eye away. Look in any tool catalog, current or historic, and there are hundreds of clamping and holding devices. Quite possibly, a few might work better for your applications than a standard vise.

What you do want is the ability to firmly secure workpieces with a holding device that is quick and easy

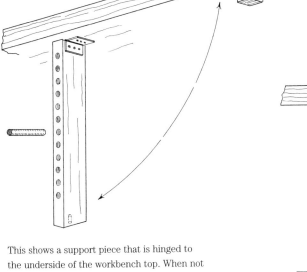

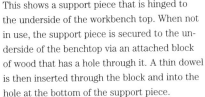

This shows a support piece that is hinged to the underside of the workbench top. When not in use, the support piece is secured to the underside of the benchtop via an attached block of wood that has a hole through it. A thin dowel is then inserted through the block and into the hole at the bottom of the support piece.

This drawing shows the details of the movable support. The support top has a tenon and slides in a groove on the underside of the benchtop. The support bottom has a half-round groove (cove cut) and slides on a metal rod that is attached to the frame piece. Use metal dowels in support pieces because wooden dowels can be broken by heavy workpieces.

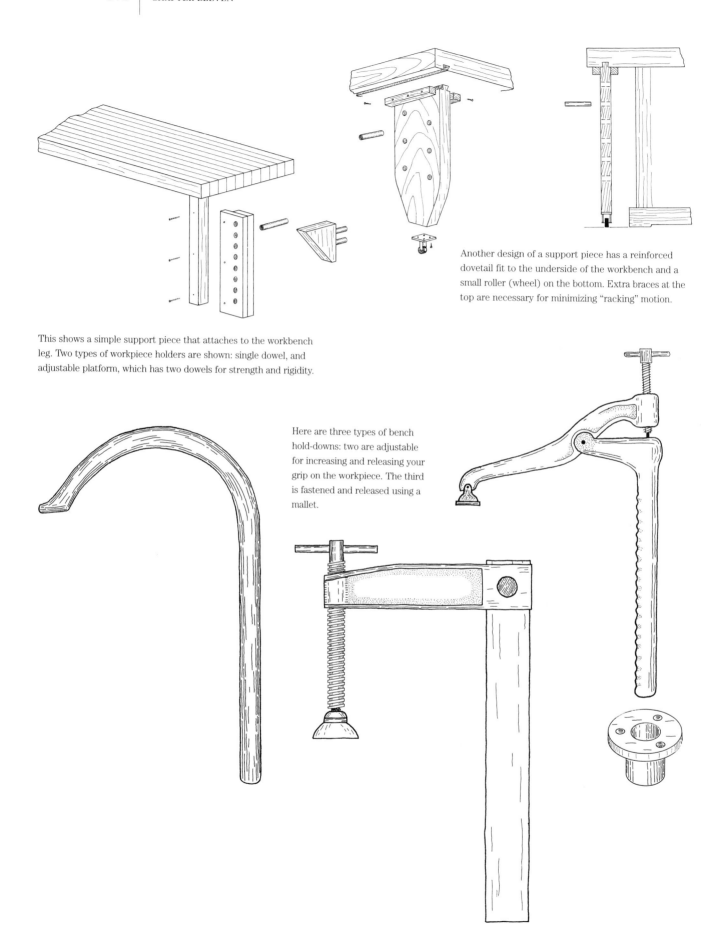

Another design of a support piece has a reinforced dovetail fit to the underside of the workbench and a small roller (wheel) on the bottom. Extra braces at the top are necessary for minimizing "racking" motion.

This shows a simple support piece that attaches to the workbench leg. Two types of workpiece holders are shown: single dowel, and adjustable platform, which has two dowels for strength and rigidity.

Here are three types of bench hold-downs: two are adjustable for increasing and releasing your grip on the workpiece. The third is fastened and released using a mallet.

to operate. For example, the traditional vise with a long metal screw, approximately 1" diameter by 12", requires time and effort to turn the handle to open or close the vise. The option is a manufactured vise with a quick-release trigger. If the vise is open to its widest (approximately 14") and you need to close it, simply squeeze the trigger and slide the vise face to the closed position. This requires minimum effort and much less time than a traditional vise. If you feel that this comparison is unfair, I would suggest that you time yourself opening and closing both vise types ten times and see which you prefer.

If you choose to use metal vises, be sure to attach wooden faces to the jaws. Often these vises don't close together perfectly, and so it's necessary to adjust the wooden faces with shims until the jaws are parallel when closed. Maintain vises by periodically tightening the mounting bolts, keeping the screw mechanism clean and free of debris, and once in a while adding a dab of grease to the mechanism.

Another useful accessory is created by attaching a hinged leg to the underside of the bench. This leg (1" by 3" by distance to floor) should have through-holes several inches apart into which a ½" metal rod is positioned. The rod then acts as a support for long boards clamped in the front vise. When not in use, the leg is returned to the underside of the bench and secured with a pin.

Other vise-type options worth considering for the workbench include:
- leg vises
- patternmaker's vise
- machinist's vise
- miter vises
- wedges
- bench holdfasts
- bench hooks
- toggle clamps
- band clamps
- rope

The movable support piece on the Charowsky workbench.

resources

This list is not meant to be encyclopedic. Rather than list every possible woodworking resource, I'm listing those that I have read, used, enjoyed, and feel comfortable recommending.

Magazines

Fine Woodworking
Taunton Press
63 S. Main St., P.O. Box 5506
Newtown, CT 06470-5506
800-283-7252
www.taunton.com/fw
fw@Taunton.com

Popular Woodworking Magazine
F&W Publications, Inc.
1507 Dana Ave.
Cincinnati, OH 45207
515-280-1721
www.popularwoodworking.com
popwood@fwpubs.com

WOOD Magazine
Better Homes and Gardens
P.O. Box 37471
Boone, IA 50037-4471
800-374-9663
www.woodmagazine.com
woodmail@woodmagazine.com

Woodshop News
35 Pratt St.
Essex, CT 06426
860-767-8227
www.woodshopnews.com
woodshopnews@worldnet.att.net

Woodsmith Magazine
2200 Grand Ave.
Des Moines, IA 50312
515-282-7000
www.woodsmith.com
woodsmith@woodsmith.com

Books
HOW-TO AND TECHNICAL INFORMATION
Build Your Own Mobile Power Tool Centers, John McPherson, Betterway Books 1995

Dictionary of Woodworking Tools, R.A. Salaman, Astragal Press 1997

Make Your Own Jigs & Workshop Furniture, Jeff Greef, Popular Woodworking Books 1994

Tage Frid Teaches Woodworking 1 & 2: A Step-By-Step Guidebook to Essential Woodworking Technique, Tage Frid, Taunton Press 1994

Setting Up Your Own Woodworking Shop, Bill Stankus, Sterling Publications 1993

Tune Up Your Tools, Sal Maccarone, Popular Woodworking Books 1996

Understanding Wood: A Craftsman's Guide to Wood Technology, R. Bruce Hoadley, Taunton Press 2000

Understanding Wood Finishing: How to Select and Apply the Right Finish, Bob Flexner, Reader's Digest Press 1999

Wood Joiner's Handbook, Sam Allen, Sterling Publications 1990

Woodworking with the Router: Professional Router Techniques and Jigs Any Woodworker Can Use, Bill Hylton and Fred Matlack, Reader's Digest Press 1999

INSPIRATIONAL AND DESIGN
Japanese Woodworking Tools: Their Tradition, Spirit and Use, Toshio Odate, Linden Publishing 1998

The Fine Art of Cabinetmaking, James Krenov, Sterling Publications 1992

The Furniture of Gustav Stickley: History, Techniques and Projects, Joseph J. Bavaro, Thomas L. Mossman, Linden Publishing 1997

The Nature and Aesthetics of Design, David Pye, Van Nostrand Reinhold 1978

Sam Maloof Woodworker, Sam Maloof, reprint edition, Kodansha International Ltd. 1989

Books by Eric Sloane (Ballantine Publishing) — these are hard to find, mostly out of print, but worth searching for:
ABC Book of Early Americana
A Museum of Early American Tools
A Reverence for Wood
An Age of Barns
Diary of an Early American Boy
Eric Sloane's America

Tool and Supplies
Air Handling Systems, Manufacturer's Service Co., Inc.
(dust collector ductwork and fittings)
5 Lunar Drive
Woodbridge, CT 06525-2320
800-367-3828
www.airhand.com
sales@airhand.com

Ecogate, Inc.
1821 Tyburn St.
Glendale, CA 91204
888-ECOGATE
www.ecogate.com
info@ecogate.com

Forrest Manufacturing Co., Inc.
(tungsten-carbide saw blades)
461 River Road,
Clifton, NJ 07014
800-733-7111
www.stores.yahoo.com/forrestman

Garrett Wade Co.
(general hand tools, supplies, power tools)
161 Avenue of the Americas
New York, New York 10013
800-221-2942
www.garrettwade.com
mail@garrettwade.com

HTC Products, Inc.
(mobile bases)
332 E. Lincoln Ave.
Royal Oak, MI 48068
800-624-2027

The Japan Woodworker
(traditional Japanese hand tools)
1731 Clement Ave.
Alameda, CA 94501
800-537-7820
www.japanwoodworker.com
support@thejapanwoodworker.com

Klingspor's Sanding Catalogue
P.O. Box 3737
Hickory, NC 28603-3737
800-228-0000
www.sandingcatalog.com
sales@woodworkingshop.com

Lockwood Products, Inc. (Loc-Line)
5615 SW Willow Lane
Lake Oswego, OR 97035
800-423-1625
www.loc-line.com
info@loc-line.com

Oneida Air Systems, Inc.
(cyclone dust collectors, fittings, filter bags)
1001 W. Fayette St.
Syracuse, New York 13204
800-732-4065
www.oneida-air.com
oasinc@dreamscape.com

Packard Woodworks, Inc.
(lathe turning supplies)
P.O. Box 718, 101 Miller Rd.
Tryon, NC 28782
800-683-8876
www.packardwoodworks.com
packard@alltel.net

Tool Crib of the North
(discount mail order, mostly power tools)
P.O. Box 14040
Grand Forks, ND 58208-4040
800-358-3096
www.toolcribofthenorth.com

Wilke Machinery Co.
(machinery for home or commercial shops)
3230 Susquehanna Trail
York, PA 17402-9716
800-235-2100
www.wilkemach.com
contactwilke@wilkemachinery.com

The Woodturner's Catalog
(lathe turning supplies)
1287 E. 1120 S.
Provo, UT 84606
1-800-551-8876
www.woodturnerscatalog.com/index.html

Wood Carvers Supply, Inc.
(carving tools and supplies)
P.O. Box 7500
Englewood, FL 34295-7500
800-284-6229
www.woodcarverssupply.com

Rockler Woodworking and Hardware
(formerly The Woodworkers' Store)
(general supplies, some tools)
4365 Willow Drive
Medina, MN 55340
800-279-4441
www.rockler.com
support@rockler.com

Woodworker's Supply
(power tools, machinery, accessories, general supplies)
1108 North Glenn Road
Casper, Wyoming 82601
800-645-9292
www.woodworker.com

Woodcraft
(general hand tools, supplies, power tools)
210 Wood County Industrial Park
P.O. Box 1686
Parkersburg, WV 26102
800-225-1153
www.woodcraft.com

Organizations

American Association of Woodturners (AAW)
3499 Lexington Ave. N., Suite 103
Shoreview, MN 55126
651-484-9094
www.woodturner.org
aaw@mail.citilink.com

Early American Industries Association
167 Bakerville Rd.
South Dartmonth, MA 02748-4198
www.eaiainfo.org

The Furniture Society
P.O. Box 18
Free Union, VA 22940
804-973-1488
www.furnituresociety.org
mail@furnituresociety.org

Guild of American Luthiers
8222 South Park Ave.
Tacoma, WA 98408
www.luth.org

Hardwood Manufacturer's Association
400 Penn Center Blvd., Suite 530
Pittsburgh, PA 15235
800-373-WOOD
www.hardwood.org

International Wood Collector's Society (IWCS)
2300 W. Range Line Road
Greencastle, IN 46135
www.woodcollectors.org

Mid-West Tool Collector's Association (M-WTCA)
Rte. 2, Box 152
Wartrace, TN 37183-9802
www.mwtca.org

National Woodcarver's Association
P.O. Box 43218
Cincinnati, OH 45243
www.chipchats.org

One final reference: Use the Internet. Almost every company that makes tools and supplies has a Web site.

BEST OF THE BEST...

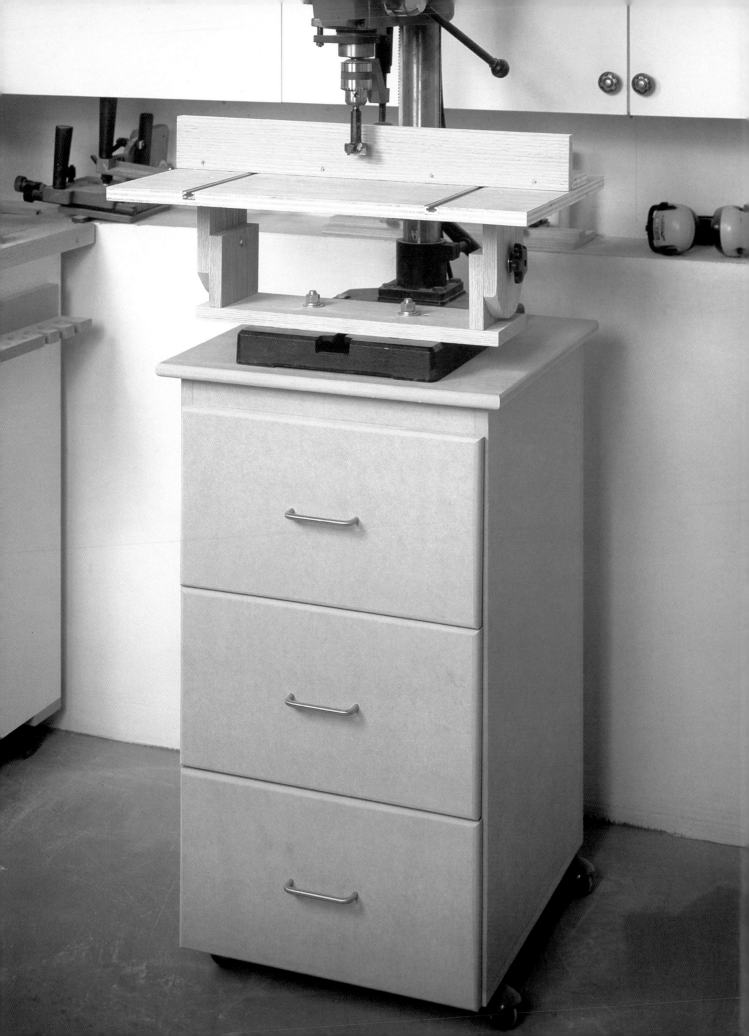

The material in this compilation appeared in the following previously published Popular Woodworking Books, and appears here by permission of the authors. (The initial page numbers given refer to pages in the original work; page numbers in parentheses refer to pages in this book.)

Proulx, Danny	Building Woodshop Workstations © 2003	Pages 1, 4-127 (5-129, 378-380)
Stack, Jim	Building the Perfect Tool Chest © 2003	Pages 1-3, 6–126 (130-254, 381-383)
Stankus, Bill	How to Design and Build Your Ideal Woodshop, revised edition © 2001	Pages 1, 4–63, (255-377)

 Published by Popular Woodworking Books, an imprint of F+W Publications, Inc., 4700 East Galbraith Road, Cincinnati, Ohio 45236. (800) 289-0963. First edition.

Other Popular Woodworking books are available from your local bookstore, hardware store or direct from the publisher.

09 08 07 06 05 5 4 3 2 1

Woodworking Projects for Your Shop / edited by Popular Woodworking Books–1st ed.
p. cm.
ISBN 1-55870-754-9 (hc.: alk. paper)

Cover designer: Brian Roeth
Production Editor: Jennifer Ziegler
Production Coordinator: Kristen Heller